Advances in African Economic, Social and Political Development

Africa is emerging as a rapidly growing region, still facing major challenges, but with a potential for significant progress—a transformation that necessitates vigorous efforts in research and policy thinking. This book series focuses on three intricately related key aspects of modern-day Africa: economic, social and political development. Making use of recent theoretical and empirical advances, the series aims to provide fresh answers to Africa's development challenges. All the socio-political dimensions of today's Africa are incorporated as they unfold and new policy options are presented. The series aims to provide a broad and interactive forum of science at work for policymaking and to bring together African and international researchers and experts. The series welcomes monographs and contributed volumes for an academic and professional audience, as well as tightly edited conference proceedings. Relevant topics include, but are not limited to, economic policy and trade, regional integration, labor market policies, demographic development, social issues, political economy and political systems, and environmental and energy issues.

More information about this series at http://www.springer.com/series/11885

Willem H. Boshoff
Editor

Business Cycles and Structural Change in South Africa

An Integrated View

Springer

Editor
Willem H. Boshoff
Department of Economics
Stellenbosch University
Stellenbosch, South Africa

ISSN 2198-7262 ISSN 2198-7270 (electronic)
Advances in African Economic, Social and Political Development
ISBN 978-3-030-35753-5 ISBN 978-3-030-35754-2 (eBook)
https://doi.org/10.1007/978-3-030-35754-2

This Springer imprint is published by the registered company Springer Nature Switzerland AG.
The registered company address is: Gewerbestrasse 11, 6330 Cham, Switzerland

This book is inspired by the pioneering work of Prof C.G.W. Schumann at Stellenbosch University and dedicated to past, present and future students of the South African business cycle.

Preface

In 1938, Prof C.G.W. Schumann—one of the leading South African economists of his time—published *Structural changes and business cycles in South Africa: 1806–1936*. In that monograph, Schumann embarked on the first comprehensive overview of the South African economy, with special emphasis on the business cycle and its interaction with long-run growth drivers. The subsequent growth in the macroeconomics literature on South Africa and the myriad of social, political and economic changes in the country over the past 25 years suggest that it is timely to aggregate our existing knowledge and expand our understanding of the cycle in a new era. Indeed, understanding changes in the business cycle is a pressing policy issue: while the South African economy has seen significant structural changes and fluctuations since the 1990s and strong economic activity in years prior to the crisis, a post-crisis lethargy—not unrelated to political developments—has characterised economic outcomes over the past 10 years. Structural constraints, and the inability of policymakers to address these constraints, played a key role in the weak post-crisis upswing and the subsequent (and ongoing) recession. These developments suggest that a synthesis and reassessment of our knowledge of the South African business cycle and its relation to long-run growth is timely.

My interest in this book project is also driven by at least two other considerations. Progress in economic research in South Africa—and arguably other emerging market contexts—requires periodic and systematic efforts to connect the insights from a small pool of geographically dispersed and often under-funded economists studying the South African economy. Despite the advances of a globalised world, and the excellent support from organisations such as Economic Research Southern Africa and the National Research Foundation, connecting and focusing research efforts remain a deep challenge. My hope is that this volume will provide some focus for macroeconomics research—at least in relation to the business cycle—for the coming years.

Another motivation for this book is the 2020 centenary of the Department of Economics at Stellenbosch University. This department, of which I have been a faculty member since 2006, has a distinguished history as a policy-relevant research institution. One of the earliest attempts at promoting policy- and practice-oriented research at the department involved the creation of the Bureau for Economic Research (BER). Originally envisioned by Prof Schumann, and today a leading source of economic data and business cycle analysis in South Africa, the BER is an example of how academic knowledge can be brought to bear on difficult policy questions in South Africa. This volume attempts to continue in this tradition, aiming to support policymakers in identifying and predicting the business cycle.

Apart from maintaining a tradition of policy-relevant research, the department has also emphasised the advantages of diversity in research method, which is also reflected in the diversity of methods employed in this volume. I believe that the combination of sophisticated econometric methods with descriptive analysis—whether in narrative or in descriptive quantitative form—produces a richer picture of both systematic regularities and important idiosyncrasies across cycles. Consequently, the contributions in this volume feature methodologies ranging from dynamic stochastic general equilibrium (DSGE) models to agnostic statistical approaches to narrative analysis.

Since originally envisaging this project in 2014, I have received excellent support from Prof Andrie Schoombee, chairperson of the Department of Economics, including granting me a 6-month sabbatical to complete this and other research projects. I also wish to acknowledge the extensive discussions with Prof Stan du Plessis, chief executive officer of Stellenbosch University and a fellow economist, that have contributed greatly to my thinking about business cycles.

Stellenbosch, South Africa
May 2019

Willem H. Boshoff

Contents

Introduction

W. H. Boshoff

Modern macroeconomics is concerned with understanding short-term fluctuations in aggregate economic activity, because of its welfare implications. The 'Great Moderation', preceding the global financial crisis, convinced many in the profession that the business cycle has been conquered and that scholarly attention should be turned to understanding long-run growth puzzles. The global financial crisis brought the Great Recession and lacklustre economic growth, encouraging a renewed interest in understanding cycles and their long-run effects. While the South African economy escaped the worst of the Great Recession, economic performance since 2008 has been equally disappointing, raising questions about how structural problems are manifesting in the behaviour of the South African business cycle. This volume engages with this academic—and accompanying policy—challenge.

As explained in the following chapter, the volume commences with two chapters in Part I that look back, both to the accumulated body of literature on the South African cycle and to newly uncovered sources providing historic data. Two subsequent chapters in Part II then relate to South African economic recovery following the crisis, comparing recovery behaviour in the South African business cycle with cycles elsewhere, and highlighting the complex role of South African policies and institutions in shaping the post-crisis recovery. This is followed in Part III by an intensive analysis of key drivers of the South African cycles, first based on a narrative history of individual cycles since the 1970s and then using modern DSGE models to unpack key relationships. The final two chapters in Part IV focus on methods for better predicting the cycle, firstly studying the role of sentiment and secondly evaluating the multistage, multivariable leading-indicator forecasting approach used by the Reserve Bank. A concluding chapter ties together the various

W. H. Boshoff (✉)
Department of Economics, Stellenbosch University, Stellenbosch, South Africa
e-mail: wimpie2@sun.ac.za

W. H. Boshoff (ed.), *Business Cycles and Structural Change in South Africa*, Advances in African Economic, Social and Political Development,
https://doi.org/10.1007/978-3-030-35754-2_1

insights, linking these insights to popular narratives dominating policy discourse in South Africa.

The following sections provide an overview of the aims and some of the findings of each of the chapters.

1 Part I: Looking Back

A study of the South African business cycle should arguably commence with an assessment of the state of the scholarly literature. In the chapter 'What Do We Know About the South African Business Cycle?', Boshoff and Du Plessis (2020) present a review of the literature related to South African cycles along three dimensions: measurement, prediction and connection to macroeconomic stabilization policy. This thematic assessment covers, predominantly, the post-1960 cycles in South Africa. This should be supplemented by pre-1960 data, to provide a better understanding of the interaction between the cycle and long-run structural forces in the South African economy. In the chapter 'The South African Economy in the Twentieth Century', building on recent advances in historic data, Boshoff and Fourie (2020) therefore present new GDP data for South Africa, which covers the entire twentieth century and provides useful quantitative evidence on the structural evolution of the South African economy since unification and about its impact on the business cycle.

2 Part II: The Financial Crisis and Its Impact on the Cycle

One of the key messages from Part I relates to the impact of the global financial crisis on the South African business cycle. Boshoff and Fourie (2020) provide quantitative evidence on how the structural transformation towards a tertiary sector-based economy amplified the correlation between the aggregate cycle and cycles in the services sector, including those in finance. In addition, Boshoff and Du Plessis document the weak post-crisis expansion in South Africa. This remains an international policy concern 10 years after the financial crisis, with observers remarking that post-crisis business cycle behaviour is different—especially when considering US cycles. It is therefore important to understand, firstly, to what extent business cycles are similar internationally and how they have changed since the cycle. In chapter "Business Cycle Recoveries: A Comparative View", Boshoff and Becker (2020) focus on the so-called 'recovery' stage of business cycles, which refers to the first part of an expansion. Their analysis shows that the South African economy, like many other economies, have never experienced the 'bounce-back' post-recession growth that is characteristic of US cycles. Boshoff and Becker also provide supplementary evidence on recovery behaviour in various components of South African output. Their findings also suggest that there are deeper structural problems, beyond the financial crisis, that give rise to unique—and concerning—business cycle features in South Africa.

Boshoff and Du Plessis (2020) identify the relative dearth of research on the business cycle stance of South African stabilization policy since the global financial crisis. Therefore, in the chapter 'The Role of Institutional Structure in Mediating the Impact of the Financial Crisis on the South African Business Cycle', Freytag (2020) describes how a myriad of institutional factors in the South African economy jointly served to moderate the impact of the crisis and to enable recovery. Freytag subsequently argues that structural weaknesses—including the institutional decay of the past decade—has significantly increased the probability that future financial crises will translate into recession in South Africa. The focus on one set of structural weaknesses also provides an appropriate entry for Part III, which will explore core drivers of South African business cycles and the impact of structural change.

3 Part III: Key Drivers of the South African Business Cycle

The analyses in both Part I and II suggest a close interaction between the South African business cycle and the structural evolution of the economy. While the long-run analysis by Boshoff and Fourie (2020) highlights this interaction, all previous chapters point to weak recoveries and, more broadly, weak expansions from the 1970s onwards, with the exception of the pre-crisis boom. Freytag (2020) also points out the success of the entire institutional structure in managing the Great Recession, though raise serious questions about the weakening of this institutional structure during the Zuma presidency and persistent structural constraints. Part III therefore seeks to unpack the core drivers of the South African business cycle, with an emphasis on long-run changes in the social, political and economic structure of the economy.

In doing so, Part III consists of two substantial chapters, each with a unique methodological approach. The chapter 'A History of South Africa's Modern Business Cycle', by Laubscher (2020), offers an extensive narrative as well as a descriptive quantitative analysis of each individual cycle since the mid-1970s. The analysis proceeds by identifying four structural epochs:

- The period 1974–1993 of structural economic deterioration, characterized by weaker global growth and the implosion of the apartheid regime
- The 1993–2007 period of post-apartheid economic revival; and
- The post-global financial crisis period (including the Great Recession).

Laubscher analyses the drivers and the unfolding of each cycle within these structural epochs, identifying both idiosyncratic and common features. Three interesting insights emerge, which are explored in greater detail in subsequent chapters of this volume. Firstly, Laubscher details the clear role of monetary and fiscal policy in shaping the evolution of South African cycles. While the literature has often studied the average effects of policy over a specific sample period (refer to the chapter by Boshoff and Du Plessis (2020) for a review of that literature), the cycle-specific analysis in this chapter provides a more nuanced picture of policy effects. Secondly, Laubscher emphasises the remarkable stability of the cyclical relationship with G7 industrial production. Thirdly, Laubscher details the resilience of the economy in the face of various political and economic shocks.

The second chapter of Part III, chapter 'On the Estimation and Application of Structural Decompositions of the South African Business Cycle', by Hollander and Van Lill (2020), analyses South African business cycle dynamics using dynamic stochastic general equilibrium (DSGE) modelling. These models, which dominate contemporary empirical macroeconomics, are useful in studying the underlying microeconomic foundations of cycle dynamics, shedding light on some of these structural questions.

In their chapter, Hollander and Van Lill compare the insights from several alternative DSGE models of the South African economy, including models that incorporate financial frictions as well as open-economy models. This variation is useful in understanding, inter alia, the role of various demand shocks in propagating the cycle. While stressing the variety of conclusions offered by alternative DSGE specifications, the authors highlight the important role of labour market rigidities and credible monetary policy in shaping how demand shocks have affected output and other macroeconomic variables in South Africa over the past 20 years. They find especially the rigidity in the labour market to be persistent and a common feature of all models, including those incorporating financial sector features. Hollander and Van Lill find the risk premium and exogenous spending to be key drivers of output fluctuations in South Africa in the short and medium run, while the risk premium seems to have longer term effects as well. Monetary policy, at the face value, seems to play a smaller role in output fluctuations in some of the models, though the underlying credibility of policy appears to have much to do with this: models that include financial shocks assign a significant role to equity price shocks.

In a historical variance decomposition for the sample period 1995–2017, Hollander and Van Lill compare the main sources of various cycles over this period. Consistent with Laubscher's narrative interpretation, persistent supply-side factors contributed to the early parts of the 2002–2007 expansion, with credit demand from 2006 driving the final stages of the expansion. Furthermore, while demand factors seem to be key to both the weak recession of 2001 and the Great Recession, credit demand conditions appear to have been much more salient. Their model specifications also generally ascribe the most recent recession (to date not concluded) to weak domestic demand, with accommodative monetary policy more than offset by large and persistent shocks to the risk premium and inflation.

While Hollander and Van Lill caution against simplistic causal interpretations, it would appear important to further study the role that the risk premium—also as reflected in business uncertainty and confidence—plays in South African business cycle dynamics. We turn to the predictive content of confidence for cyclical turning points in Part IV.

4 Part IV: Predicting the South African Business Cycle

One of the key business cycle variables highlighted in Part III is that of business and consumer sentiment in South Africa. Indeed, Laubscher (2020) argues that changes in business sentiment have played an important role in the unfolding of successive business cycles since the 1970s. Even if one disagrees with assigning a causal force to sentiment, sentiment-based indicators do appear to hold predictive power. Consequently, Binge (2020), in chapter 'Business Confidence and the Business Cycle in South Africa', investigates recent advances in the literature on measuring sentiment to construct business confidence indicators for South Africa. Binge's approach relies on micro survey data, from the Bureau for Economic Research at Stellenbosch University, and therefore departs from recent alternative attempts at measuring confidence using aggregate macroeconomic or, alternatively, financial data. Binge finds evidence that confidence offers unique predictive information, findings that align with the earlier chapters.

The final chapter of the book, chapter 'Assessing the 2013 and 2017 Business Cycle Turning Points Signalled by the SARB's Composite Leading Business Cycle Indicator', by Venter (2020), continues to explore forecasting tools for the South African business cycle. In particular, it involves a description and assessment of the South African Reserve Bank's forecasting strategy, as embodied in composite leading indicators.

5 Conclusions

The findings in this volume provide insights into narratives that frequently feature in South African policy discourse, often linking particular structural features of the economy to observed short-run (i.e. business cycle) outcomes. Popular themes include arguments related to irrationally negative business sentiment (and its impact), the resilience of the South African economy, the impact of 'financialization' and the role of international demand in shaping our cycle. Chapter 'Conclusions' deals with these various arguments. It also presents a summary of the insights in this volume based on the taxonomy provided by Boshoff and Du Plessis (2020) in the next chapter. That taxonomy classifies the state of knowledge on the business cycle into three broad groups: literature dealing with the identification and properties of the cycle, literature on the forecasting of the cycle and literature on the role of macroeconomic stabilisation policy. In this way, chapter 'Conclusions' situates the research in this volume both in the existing body of scholarly research and in policy discourse on the South African business cycle.

References

Binge, L. H. (2020). Business confidence and the business cycle in South Africa. In W. Boshoff (Ed.), *Business cycles and structural change in South Africa*. Heidelberg: Springer.

Boshoff, W. H., & Becker, L. H. (2020). Business cycle recoveries: A comparative view. In W. Boshoff (Ed.), *Business cycles and structural change in South Africa*. Heidelberg: Springer.

Boshoff, W. H., & du Plessis, S. A. (2020). What do we know about the South African business cycle? In W. Boshoff (Ed.), *Business cycles and structural change in South Africa*. Heidelberg: Springer.

Boshoff, W. H., & Fourie, J. (2020). The South African economy in the twentieth century. In W. Boshoff (Ed.), *Business cycles and structural change in South Africa*. Heidelberg: Springer.

Freytag, A. (2020). The role of institutional structure in mediating the impact of the financial crisis on the South African business cycle. In W. Boshoff (Ed.), *Business cycles and structural change in South Africa*. Heidelberg: Springer.

Hollander, H., & van Lill, D. (2020). On the estimation and application of structural decompositions of the South African business cycle. In W. Boshoff (Ed.), *Business cycles and structural change in South Africa*. Heidelberg: Springer.

Laubscher, P. (2020). A history of South Africa's modern business cycle. In W. Boshoff (Ed.), *Business cycles and structural change in South Africa*. Heidelberg: Springer.

Venter, J. C. (2020). Assessing the 2013 and 2017 business cycle turning points signalled by the SARB's composite leading business cycle indicator. In W. Boshoff (Ed.), *Business cycles and structural change in South Africa*. Heidelberg: Springer.

Part I
Looking Back

What Do We Know About the South African Business Cycle?

W. H. Boshoff and S. A. du Plessis

A significant amount of macroeconomic research on the South African business cycle has appeared since the late 1990s, mostly with the turning point cycles identified by the South African Reserve Bank (SARB) as an empirical starting point. The main objectives of this literature are, firstly, to improve business cycle identification, secondly, to study the predictability of South African cycles and, thirdly, to evaluate the impact of macroeconomic policy on the business cycle. Over the past ten years, since the global financial crisis, the business cycle—or, as some would see, the absence of a cycle—has generated much theoretical and policy interest. As we seek to better understand these business cycle dynamics, and ultimately their interplay with political and international developments, it is important to review the existing body of knowledge and to identify pressing gaps in that knowledge.

An overview of the South African business cycle research requires at least a cursory overview of developments in the broader international literature. A comprehensive overview of the international literature is not attempted here and the focus is on describing important contributions to the South African literature, situating these in the international literature. We start with an overview of the concept and measurement of the business cycle. Our overview will focus on turning point cycles, in keeping with the approach followed by the SARB, which we describe briefly below. This overview provides the conceptual basis for our survey of South African work across three themes in the business cycle literature: (1) the

Cornel Bekker and Louis Becker provided excellent research assistance.

W. H. Boshoff (✉) · S. A. du Plessis
Department of Economics, Stellenbosch University, Stellenbosch, South Africa
e-mail: wimpie2@sun.ac.za; stan@sun.ac.za

W. H. Boshoff (ed.), *Business Cycles and Structural Change in South Africa*, Advances in African Economic, Social and Political Development,
https://doi.org/10.1007/978-3-030-35754-2_2

properties of the South African cycle, (2) forecasting the South African cycle, and (3) stabilization policy in South Africa.

1 The Concept and Measurement of the Business Cycle

Systematic macroeconomics, as established by the *General Theory* (Keynes 1936), developed in order to explain fluctuations in economic activity (especially intermittent crises), with emphasis on the first decades of the twentieth century. Yet the study of economic fluctuations reaches further back, to the work of the classical economists. The early economists, including Adam Smith, Jean-Baptiste Say, David Ricardo, Thomas Malthus and John Stuart Mill attempted to understand the functioning of economies where agriculture played a significant role.

Like business cycles in modern economies, fluctuations in preindustrial economies were commonplace, even if they sprang from alternative sources. Fluctuations in predominantly agricultural economies are often related to the recurrence of weather patterns, which give rise to alternating periods of relatively greater and relatively weaker yields. Accordingly, economists sought to link economic fluctuations to cycles in sunspot activity (Jevons 1884) or even the alignment of planets (Moore 1914), both considered to have an impact on agriculture via their impact on weather patterns. Drawing from advances in the physical sciences of the time, these natural phenomena were thought to exhibit periodicity amenable to mathematical study, which later gave rise to sinusoidal models of "business cycles," as economic fluctuations began to be called.

Toward the end of the nineteenth century, the rise of industrialization and deeper capital markets introduced economic disruption much larger than those associated with agricultural fluctuations. This volatility was of an apparently unpredictable nature and undermined the view of economic fluctuations as periodic phenomena. Instead, the public was confronted with "alternate periods of activity and sluggishness" (Mitchell 1923) in the economic system. This endogenous "rhythm of business activity" (Mitchell 1923) spawned a rich early literature[1] as economists sought to understand its sources (see Mills 1867; Pigou 1927). This recurrent rhythm in aggregate economic activity, without periodicity, incentivized economists to develop a clearer definition of the "business cycle."

Mitchell (1927) was the first to offer such an explicit definition, arguing that the business cycle is "*. . . a type of fluctuation found in the aggregate economic activity of nations that organize their work mainly in business enterprises: a cycle consists of expansions occurring at about the same time in many economic activities, followed by similarly general recessions, contractions, and revivals that merge into the expansion phase of the next cycle; this sequence of changes in recurrent but not periodic; in duration business cycles vary from more than one year to ten or twelve*

[1]See Achuthan and Banerji (2004) for a nontechnical history of cyclical measurement.

years; they are not divisible into shorter cycles of similar character with amplitudes approximating their own."

In conceptualizing the business cycle, then, Mitchell highlighted three aspects. Firstly, business cycle phases are characterised by alternating periods of prosperity and depression in aggregate economic activity. Secondly, business cycles meet certain duration requirements. In particular, business cycle refers to those short-term fluctuations of a particular frequency. Thirdly, business cycles are pervasive—they permeate the economic system and are visible across a variety of sectors and markets in a modern economy.

Prior to the 1930s, empirical analysis of business cycles was limited to mostly the qualitative assessment of the historical record. This was due to a lack of comprehensive macroeconomic data that would allow the scientific study of business cycles, that is, the identification of recurring patterns. The limited empirical analysis also reflected underdeveloped macroeconomic theory, which had not yet advanced much beyond the quantity theory of money (Wicksell 1898; Fisher 1906, 1907 are notable exceptions). An important part of Mitchell's contribution was to gather a multitude of data series on economic activity and to develop an empirical framework, based on this data, for identifying and studying modern business cycles (Burns and Mitchell 1946). This data was key to the development of Mitchell's business cycle identification method.

With coworker Arthur Burns, Mitchell developed a method for identifying business cycles based on a frequency concept: they understood business cycles as a type of economic fluctuation that covers a particular period and should be distinguished from shorter term noise or long-term changes in growth trends. To operationalize this frequency concept, Burns and Mitchell introduced the turning point in economic activity as a tool for identifying business cycles: business cycles were to be identified by reference to upper and lower turning points (peaks and troughs) shared widely across economic activity. That is, Burns and Mitchell understood the task of business cycle analysis as one of identifying peaks and troughs in a variety of economic series in order to infer the presence of a common business cycle.

The Burns and Mitchell approach gained significant popularity among policy-makers in subsequent years and the approach is commonly followed by committees responsible for business cycle dating, including at the NBER in the USA (see Artis et al. 2004).

At the time, one of the practical challenges in studying business cycles, in the manner suggested by Burns and Mitchell, was data. In the absence of national accounts data, Burns and Mitchell were forced to study hundreds of economic time series to identify potential turning points. Subsequently, Bry and Boschan (1971) developed a nonparametric algorithm to identify a set of local peaks and troughs in data series. In keeping with Burns and Mitchell's focus on frequency, a key step in the Bry–Boschan (BB) procedure involves the application of a set of censoring rules, which reduce an initially large set of potential turning points by imposing a minimum phase and cycle duration. As will be discussed later, Harding and Pagan (2003a) showed that the BB algorithm, applied to aggregate output only, yielded business cycles similar to those produced by an application to a large number of disaggregated economic series.

While the Burns and Mitchell's approach became widespread among policymakers, it gained less acceptance in academic research. The increased availability of national accounts data and advances in statistical methods (led by contributions from Koopmans, Marshak, Frisch, and Tinbergen) encouraged the steady rise of formal econometric modeling (Pagan 2003). Indeed, Tjalling Koopmans attacked the Burns and Mitchell work as "measurement without theory" (Koopmans 1947). These scholars who moved away from the Burns and Mitchell framework were motivated by the argument that turning point cycles do not have well-defined statistical properties, rendering them less amenable to econometric analysis. During the early 2000s, the work of Harding and Pagan (2001, 2003a, b, 2006) sought to address the statistical underpinning of turning point analysis. We return to this issue later in the chapter.

Business cycle methods employed by policymakers therefore diverged from those employed by academia. This divergence led Harding and Pagan (2006) to identify two[2] classes of business cycle identification method: methods that identify cycles by reference to turning points as discussed, and methods that view cycles as "serially-correlated deviations of output from trend" (Blinder and Fischer 1981: 227). The latter class of methods have dominated the academic literature from the 1960s. While this book allows for a variety of business cycle views, the turning point cycle is its preferred definition, as it accords with the approach taken by policymakers and is consistent with the public's intuitive understanding of the business cycle.

The decision about the approach to identifying and describing the cycle is one of two critical decisions required in business cycle analysis. A second decision involves the transformation of the economic time series in which cycles are to be identified, that is, the decision whether to remove trends from time series prior to identifying turning points. Separating the two themes—the method of business cycle analysis (in our case, turning point identification) and the transformation of the data provide for greater clarity when comparing business cycle techniques.

Harding and Pagan (2003a) distinguish between three types of cycle: classical cycles, deviation cycles, and growth rate cycles. Classical cycles are cycles defined in the level of an economic time series. These cycles do not require data transformation (by removing trends, for example), which may reduce the transparency and replicability of cycle analysis. Classical cycles also correspond with an intuitive understanding of cycle phases as alternating periods of prosperity and decline in aggregate economic activity.

Classical cycles—and classical contractions, in particular—are rare, given that contractions would require absolute declines in real output. The absence of classical cycles needs not imply the absence of the business cycle. In keeping with the original understanding of Burns and Mitchell, business cycles refer to fluctuations

[2]A third, though rarely used, class of methods assume sinusoidal periodicity.

within a particular frequency range (between 1.5 and 8 years, at least based on the original work of Burns and Mitchell[3]). In time series with pronounced trends, the low-frequency information may dominate higher frequency information related to the business cycle. Consequently, some analysts prefer to remove low-frequency information, by subtracting a so-called permanent component from the raw data series. Cycles based on the resultant "deviation" series are called deviation cycles (or "growth cycles"). As discussed later, this permanent component, often identified by time-series filtering (or, in simpler application, approximated by a deterministic time trend), is not unique. An alternative approach, which also removes low-frequency information but does not depend on time-series filtering, would be to study "growth rate" cycles, calculated on the growth rates of the underlying time series. Even so, growth rate cycles remain deviation cycles: in the case of growth rates, the value of the original series in a previous period is taken as the permanent component.

In light of these theoretical considerations, we now consider the South African business cycle, using the turning point methodology applied on both level and detrended data. Indeed, as discussed in this chapter and the rest of this volume, it is important to clarify the cycle concept associated with particular stylized facts of the South African business cycle. As will be shown, our understanding of the properties of the South African business cycle, its predictability, and its relation to macroeconomic policy often depend on the method and data used for the identification of the cycle. Before proceeding to the broader literature, we commence with a brief review of the official business cycle dating in South Africa.

2 The South African Business Cycle

The early history of business cycle analysis in South Africa is closely linked to the Burns and Mitchell approach. The first rigorous attempt at identifying turning points in the South African business cycle was at Stellenbosch University in the middle of the previous century, with Du Plessis (1950) dating business cycles from unification in 1910 to 1949.[4] The SARB commenced the publication of turning points in 1970, based on the work of Smit and Van der Walt (1970), for the period after 1946. Van der Walt (1982, 1983), Pretorius (e.g. Venter and Pretorius 2004a, b), and Venter (2005) subsequently continued this methodological tradition at the SARB.

From a methodological perspective, the SARB identifies business cycles based on an integrated assessment of the turning points suggested by three different methods (Venter 2018). The first method entails the study of the composite coincident

[3]The upper end of the frequency range (8 years) is somewhat lower than the 10 to 12 years range identified earlier by Mitchell (1927).

[4]Refer to Boshoff and Fourie (2020) in this volume, which revisits data and business cycle turning points in South Africa for the entire twentieth century.

business cycle indicator, which the SARB constructs from a small set of economic time series related to aggregate production, sales, income, and employment (Venter 2018). Deviation cycles from this composite coincident indicator provide the first set of potential reference turning points. The SARB also publishes composite leading and lagging indicators, to which we return later in this chapter. The second method entails the construction of a historical diffusion index based on an inspection of more than 200 economic time series: the SARB first determines deviation cycles for each individual series and then, for each period, calculates the proportion of series classified as expanding and contracting. The second set of potential reference turning points is defined for those periods when the diffusion index moves beyond or below 50%. The third set of potential reference turning points is obtained, in a similar fashion, from a "current" diffusion index, based on the percentage changes of the individual series underlying the historical diffusion index. In a qualitative assessment based on judgment, the SARB identifies the final references points from these three sets of potential reference points. The SARB dates are reported in Table 1. Figures 1 and 2 plot the various turning points against the monthly measure of aggregate economic activity in South Africa (using the SARB composite coincident indicator).

The SARB reference turning points are often used as a benchmark in academic work and the broader public traditionally relies on these official turning points to assess the state of the South African economy and the likelihood of recession. Even so, the media has recently (August 2018) emphasized the onset of recession, even though the last peak identified by the SARB is in November 2013 (Business Day 2018). In this case, the long lag associated with the SARB's identification process may well yield a post-2013 trough and, later, a 2018 peak. Even so, this mismatch suggests that it is important to assess the extent to which alternative views of the South African business cycle depend on the identification method and data. In particular, the following sections explore three sets of questions related to the South African business cycle. Firstly, how sensitive is the turning point chronology, presented in Table 1, to the choice of method and data? Specifically, how do the properties of the perceived business cycle differ when relying on classical as opposed to deviation cycles methodologies and how do they differ when relying on multiple data series rather than GDP only? These properties include the properties of the aggregate business cycle (in terms of duration and amplitude), the properties of cycles in particular components of output, and the properties of co-movement (that is, the alignment of turning points across different economies). Secondly, given the welfare consequences of especially recessions, how successful are economists at predicting South African turning points, whether determined for classical cycles or deviation cycles? Thirdly, how successful have monetary and fiscal policies in South Africa been in stabilizing business cycles in South Africa?

Table 1 Official chronology of the South African business cycle, as determined by the South African Reserve Bank, 1945–2019

Upward phase start month	Upward phase end month	Duration of upward phase (months)	Downward phase start month	Downward phase end month	Duration of downward phase months)
Post-war	July 1946	7	August 1946	April 1947	9
May 1947	November 1948	19	December 1948	February 1950	15
March 1950	December 1951	22	January 1952	March 1953	15
April 1953	April 1955	25	May 1955	September 1956	17
October 1956	January 1958	16	February 1956	March 1959	14
April 1959	April 1960	13	May 1960	August 1961	16
September 1961	April 1965	44	May 1965	December 1965	8
January 1966	May 1967	17	June 1967	December 1967	7
January 1968	December 1970	36	January 1971	August 1972	20
September 1972	August 1974	24	September 1974	December 1977	40
January 1978	August 1981	44	September 1981	March 1983	19
April 1983	June 1984	15	July 1984	March 1986	21
April 1986	February 1989	35	March 1989	May 1993	51
June 1993	November 1996	42	December 1996	August 1999	33
September 1999	November 2007	99	December 2007	August 2009	21
September 2009	November 2013	51	December 2013	–	

Source: South African Reserve Bank Quarterly Bulletin S-157 (March 2019)

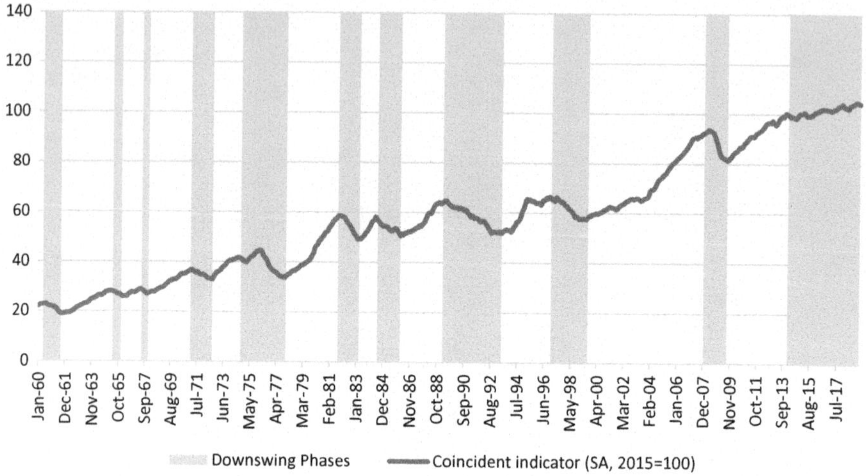

Fig. 1 Measure of monthly South African economic activity (the SARB coincident composite indicator) with SARB recession phases superimposed. Source: South African Reserve Bank

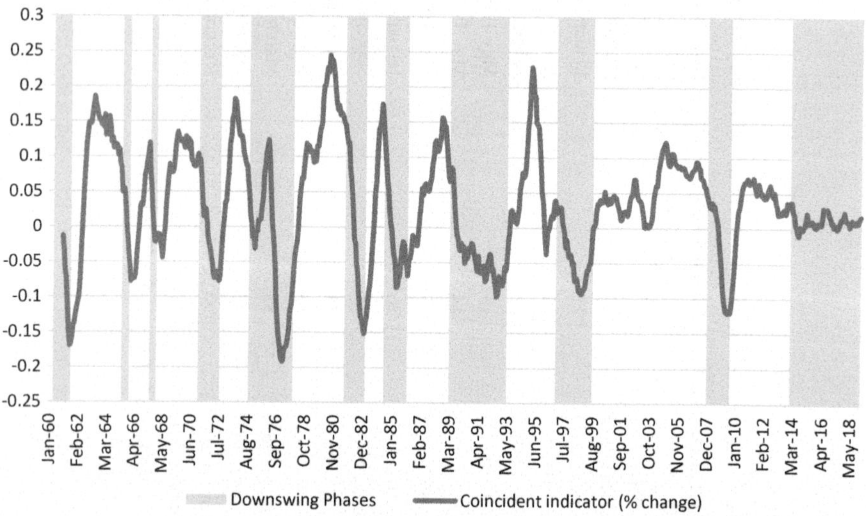

Fig. 2 Measure of monthly growth in South African economic activity (the SARB coincident composite indicator) with SARB recession phases superimposed. Source: South African Reserve Bank

3 Properties of the South African Business Cycle and Their Relation to Various Identification Methods

We start by considering the sensitivity of business cycle turning points, identified by the SARB, to the choice of methodology and data. As explained below, our assessment distinguishes between parametric and nonparametric methodologies for identifying turning points and between data-rich methods and methods reliant on GDP only.

The SARB methodology for identifying turning points adopts a nonparametric approach, as per Harding and Pagan's (2003a) classification of business cycle identification methods.[5] A parametric approach is one in which the data is assumed to be drawn from a population described by a parametric distribution function (such as the normal distribution). A parametric approach to the identification of turning points therefore entails first fitting a particular distribution to the data, such as GDP or a multivariate dataset, and then relying on that model to identify turning points.

Parametric approaches are popular in the scholarly literature and were championed on the basis of their statistical superiority: to many scholars, parametric approaches are systematic and rigorous as opposed to nonparametric approaches, whose algorithms and decision rules may appear arbitrary. Nonparametric approaches also do not allow for easy inference, given that nonparametric tests are often of lower power. South African work applying parametric approaches include Moolman (2004), which identifies turning points in growth rate cycles, and Bismans and Le Roux (2013), which identifies turning points in classical cycles.

In contrast with the scholarly assumption about nonparametric methods, Harding and Pagan (2003a) showed that nonparametric approaches to turning point identification have well-defined statistical properties. Given that both methods admit statistical analysis it is possible to compare the turning point chronologies suggested by various parametric and nonparametric approaches.

It is also important to assess the impact of the SARB's multivariate analysis, as opposed to a turning point analysis of GDP data alone. The multivariate approach employed by the SARB—consistent with that of the NBER and various central banks who identify turning points—was originally motivated by the lack of reliable aggregate measures of economic activity in South Africa. This data problem has been ameliorated, potentially strengthening the case for identifying South African business cycles from GDP alone (Du Plessis 2006). Even so, on pragmatic grounds, multivariate approaches may be preferable, given that GDP is only available at quarterly frequency and is often revised (Van Walbeek 2006).

---

[5] Harding and Pagan revitalised the literature on nonparametric business cycle identification in the early 2000s with a set of publications—see the debate between Harding and Pagan (2003a, b) and Hamilton (2003).

3.1 Comparing Turning Point Cycle Methodologies for South African Cycles

For the purposes of comparing the various methodologies and approaches to data, a piecewise review of the literature would be less informative, not least because various research papers rely on data covering different sample periods. However, Bosch and Ruch (2013) compare turning points produced by various parametric and nonparametric approaches, for both multivariate data and GDP only. In what follows, we set out their analysis.

Bosch and Ruch (2013) compare results for three data approaches: (1) approaches relying on GDP only, (2) approaches relying on multivariate data that are similar to the multivariate analysis of the SARB, and (3) the SARB's approach. For each of these data approaches, Bosch and Ruch compare various parametric and nonparametric techniques.

The authors first study both parametric and nonparametric methodologies based on GDP data. The parametric method is based on the Markov-switching (MS) model, which fits a statistical model of GDP growth, assuming alternative states or regimes for the data-generating process. Typically, two states are assumed, with one state representing recession and another state expansion. For each time period, the model suggests a probability of being in a particular state, which is then used to calculate when there is a change in state (either from recession to expansion or vice versa). This change in state is interpreted as a business cycle turning point.

Bosch and Ruch compare this parametric method applied to GDP with two nonparametric methods, based on the BB methodology discussed earlier. They apply the method to monthly GDP growth (linearly interpolated) and to detrended[6] quarterly GDP (to compare with the earlier results of Du Plessis (2006)). It is therefore important to note that the Bosch and Ruch evaluation of GDP turning point cycle methodologies relies on deviation cycles, including growth rate cycles.

Secondly, the authors proceed to "diffusion" models, which rely on an expanded dataset, beyond GDP, from which turning points are derived. Their monthly dataset consists of various aggregate measures of economic activity and is consistent with the dataset used in the construction of the SARB's composite business cycle indicator. Bosch and Ruch extract business cycle turning points from this larger dataset using a two-stage process. In the first stage, they apply principal component analysis, which seeks to identify common (or "principal") components shared across the various time series. These common components are taken to represent the business cycle, given that the cycle is a composite concept that is diffused throughout various sectors and economic variables. Bosch and Ruch consider two versions of their diffusion model, one in which only the first principal component is

[6]Note that this involves subtracting a deterministic (linear) time trend (Du Plessis 2006). Harding and Pagan (2001) suggest that this form of detrending is most appropriate, as it does not result in a significant loss of information about the turning points.

Table 2 Comparison of identified cycles from 1981 to 2011 (expansion and contraction phases separate) identified using parametric (P) and nonparametric (NP) methodologies, as reported in Bosch and Ruch (2013)

Method	Number of cycle phases	Phase duration	Phase amplitude (%)	Phase steepness (%)
Expansions				
SARB	4	16	16.2	1.0
GDP				
GDP (P)	6	13	11.6	0.9
GDP growth rate (NP)	8	6	6.3	1.0
GDP detrended (NP)	7	8	9.2	1.2
Diffusion models				
Diffusion 1 (P)	10	6	6.4	1.0
Diffusion 1 (NP)	9	6	5.6	0.9
Diffusion 2 (P)	7	7	7.9	1.1
Contractions				
SARB	4	10	3.9	0.4
GDP				
GDP (P)	7	6	2.2	0.3
GDP growth rate (NP)	9	7	3.2	0.5
GDP detrended (NP)	6	7	1.7	0.2
Diffusion models				
Diffusion 1 (P)	10	7	2.5	0.4
Diffusion 1 (NP)	9	7	3.7	0.6
Diffusion 2 (P)	8	10	3.1	0.3

Source: Own calculations on SARB GDP data using Bosch and Ruch (2013) turning points

analysed for turning points[7] and another version in which the first seven principal components are considered. In the second stage, they apply both parametric and nonparametric approaches to identify turning points in these components. For the parametric methods, they rely on MS methods.[8] They also apply the nonparametric BB method to the common component identified by the first diffusion model.

Finally, Bosch and Ruch report the SARB turning points, in order to compare the turning point chronologies suggested by the GDP-based and diffusion-based analyses.

Table 2 reports the number of cycles and the phase duration, output amplitude and output steepness for contractions and expansions for each of the methods.

[7]Statistically, the first principal component carries most information, that is, it captures the largest portion of variance in the data.

[8]The converse has not been attempted in the South African literature, where turning points are identified for every individual series and then aggregated to a common set of turning points (Harding and Pagan (2006) suggests such a clustering approach).

A comparison of the turning points suggested by the various methodologies reveals considerable diversity. Firstly, the SARB methodology identifies fewer turning points than any of the other methodologies. None of the alternatives come close to mimicking the SARB's official chronology. The average number of cycles suggested by alternative methods (whether parametric or nonparametric) is 8—twice as many as the number identified by the SARB's official method. Even those methodologies (parametric and nonparametric) that rely exclusively on GDP data identify at least 6 cycles (specifically, including turning points in 2001 and 2003), whereas the other methodologies also identify additional cycles in the 1990s. One may conclude that the SARB's methodology favors identifies cycles with a lower frequency cutoff compared with other methods. That is, the SARB's identification strategy excludes some higher frequency fluctuations, which other methods would label as business cycles.

Secondly, parametric and nonparametric methods produce different cycles. If one compares the parametric and nonparametric methods based on GDP growth, one could either conclude that there are 6 or 8 expansions and 7 or 9 recessions. This is consistent with Harding and Pagan's conclusion that parametric methods do not approximate nonparametric methods, even those nonparametric methods that rely exclusively on GDP data.

Parametric methods for turning point identification rely on a data-generating process that neatly separates into two regimes (an expansion and a contraction regime between which the system switches). In contrast, the results for both GDP and for the first diffusion model favor three, rather than two, regimes. Bosch and Ruch highlight the difficulty of matching this third regime with either of the other two conventional regimes. In the case of the GDP model, the third regime is characterised by large positive growth rates, leading Bosch and Ruch to combine it with the conventional expansion regime to date expansions. In the case of the first diffusion model, the third regime is characterised by large negative growth rates, representing extreme recessions in South Africa (early 1980s and 2007). In this case, they combine the regime with the conventional contraction regime. While the second diffusion model does not produce such a regime, it will be important to investigate these "transition" regimes further. Some initial work by Boshoff and Becker (2020), in this volume, considers the recovery stage of expansion phases in South Africa, investigating whether these represent a separate phase of the business cycle.

Thirdly, the richness of the data used may appear to influence the determination of turning points, but the method for extracting turning points from a rich data set may well be more important. Diffusion-based models suggest more turning points (and hence more cycles) than models based exclusively on GDP. This difference may be due—at least in part—to the method used in extracting cycles from the data rather than the fact that the rich data set presents different information from that contained in GDP. The cycles produced by diffusion-based models are deviation cycles: these models rely on principal component analysis to extract a cyclical component from an underlying series. The deviation cycles produced by diffusion-based models are however different from the deviation cycles identified by detrending GDP, further highlighting the challenges of detrending. Even so, the rich dataset underlying diffusion-based models may well suggest additional or alternative turning points, given that these models require cyclical behavior to be present across a great many time series.

Apart from the differences in the number of turning points suggested by the various methodologies, their results also differ in terms of phase characteristics. The amplitude and duration (though not the steepness) of SARB cycles are much higher than those of any of the other cycles—a direct consequence of the differences in the number of cycles. More important, the ratios of the average expansion duration to contraction duration, and of the average expansion amplitude to contraction amplitude, differ for diffusion models and other approaches. The SARB methodology and GDP-based methods identify expansions that are longer and of higher amplitude on average than contractions. In contrast, the diffusion-based models identify expansions that are shorter on average than contractions. The amplitude of expansions identified by diffusion-based models is higher but significantly less so than for other methods. This is in part a reflection of the larger number of cycles identified by the diffusion-based models.

These differences in phase characteristics are important to economists interested in structural growth patterns in South Africa. The average duration of the four SARB cycles is biased upwards by the prolonged upswing from 1999 to 2007, which creates a picture of long expansions and shallow recessions. An analysis sensitive to diffused growth would identify a greater number of expansions that are, on average, much weaker and shorter than suggested by the SARB's methodology.

The diversity suggested by our comparative analysis suggests that the South African business cycle analysts, as elsewhere, must specify the issues they are interested in with the particular research and choose a business cycle method to match. Where the emphasis is on identifying cycles that accord with the broader public's understanding, Harding and Pagan have argued that a classical cycle view is potentially closest to how the public perceives of recession. The most recent South African experience, in relation to an upper turning point identified by the SARB for November 2013, corroborates their argument (Boshoff 2018). The SARB's identification of an upper turning point drew relatively little attention in the media, mostly as output growth was sharply decelerating, but the output was still expanding. It was only in 2018, when output finally started contracting, that a significant public debate about the recession—erroneously connected to the government's fiscal challenges—was initiated. In fact, the way in which the debate evolved, would have it that the recession had only commenced in 2018.[9]

As noted earlier, the long lag characteristic of the SARB's approach may have delayed the identification of a subsequent trough and the more recent peak discussed

[9]This cycle concept underlying this debate is a classical cycle version of the so-called "technical" recession, according to which a recession is identified if output contracts for two consecutive quarters. This clearly differs from the longer time horizon of the BB algorithm. It is therefore clear that the South African public still very much holds a classical cycle view.

in the media. At last one reason for the SARB's preference for a long lag can be traced to the significant revisions to national accounts data in South Africa (Van Walbeek 2006). For example, Hall and McDermott (2016) show that a reliance on a larger dataset may somewhat reduce the impact of subsequent data revisions, which may result in significant differences between "technical recession" approaches and the standard BB method employed at central banks.

3.2 Stylised Facts About the Properties of Cycles in Components of South African Output

The comparative assessment of cycle methodologies can be expanded to include fluctuations in *components* of aggregate economic output, given that such cycles may differ markedly from the aggregate business cycle. In particular, we consider briefly the literature dealing with cycles in components of aggregate expenditure in South Africa as well as the literature on provincial and/or local business cycles.

Burger (2010) studies the cyclical behavior of consumption, investment, net exports, and other components of aggregate expenditure up to 2006. Burger's cycle concept is that of "serially correlated deviations from trend," rather than turning point cycles. South African scholarly work in this tradition is somewhat limited, with the notable exception of Burger (2008). By definition, this cycle concept is applied to deviation cycles: it involves the detrending of macroeconomic variables, followed by a study of cross-correlations (see, for example, initial work by Kydland and Prescott (1990), Romer (1999), Stock and Watson (2003)).

Before considering the results, it is worth noting that Burger does derive turning points in the deviation cycle of GDP—obtained from an application of the Hodrick and Prescott (1997) filter (Hodrick–Prescott filter, hereafter)—and argues that these compare well to the SARB's official turning points. This is an important observation in itself, as it departs from the results of Bosch and Ruch, implying a closer relation between turning points in detrended GDP and those identified by the SARB. It underlines the variety of results possible for detrended data, as discussed above.

The larger part of Burger (2010) focuses on covariance analysis among the various deviation cycles of components of output on the one hand and that of aggregate output on the other hand. One of the advantages of avoiding a turning point approach to cycles is that it allows a study of changes in covariances over time. Burger compares variances and covariances over the periods 1960–1976, 1976–1994, and 1994–2006, finding output volatility in South Africa to have declined significantly in the second and third periods. The decline in the volatility of aggregate output is reflected in a decline in the volatility of consumption and various components of investment. In the third period, Burger finds that cycles in consumption—especially durable consumption—strongly lead the business cycle, with some evidence that investment in manufacturing and investment in nonresidential buildings also lead output cycles. Burger finds no strong relationship between export cycles and output cycles. The strong links with consumption suggest that the lower output cycle volatility in the third period is due to the consumption cycle, which has also seen its volatility decline.

Burger's findings are broadly consistent with the results from a turning point analysis by Du Plessis (2006), mentioned earlier. In addition to turning points in aggregate output, Du Plessis identifies turning points in a number of components of output. The analysis suggests high concordance[10] between consumption and output turning point cycles, and also some weaker evidence of concordance between investment (gross fixed capital formation) and output cycles. Also consistent with Burger, Du Plessis finds weak evidence of concordance between export and aggregate output cycles.

Burger and Du Plessis arrive at similar conclusions about cycles in components of output, despite significant differences in methodology. This contrasts with the sensitivity to cycle methodology discussed in the previous section. Of course, both the Burger and the Du Plessis analyses are bivariate in nature. One may also wish to study the relative contributions of investment and consumption over various cycles—in particular, to understand the extent to which investment has fallen behind in recent years, especially since the results from both Burger and Du Plessis suggest that investment has not been a primary driver of South African cycles. The narrative analysis presented by Laubscher (2020), in this volume, is one step in this direction.

Apart from disaggregation in terms of expenditure, disaggregation in terms of geography may also reveal important cyclical features. Much of the literature focuses on determining business cycle turning points in the national economy. To the extent that the structural composition—and hence drivers of growth—of regional economies differ from that of the national economy, understanding regional cycles may yield further policy insights (Krugell 2017).

Laubscher (2017) studies the business cycle recovery of the Western Cape economy, and its six constituent regions, following the 2009 recession. As the data is annual, the analysis does not entail region-specific turning points—taking the SARB's turning points from the national economy as indicative of turning points in the various regions. Even so, the data does allow a disaggregated picture across ten industries, which allows Laubscher to calculate the extent to which various regions and industries reacted to the national recession and their subsequent recovery. Further work, which depends on the future availability of higher frequency data, could include identifying the properties of turning point cycles in different provinces and studying recessions and recoveries over a longer sample period, in order to understand structural change.

[10]The degree of synchronisation between two series relates to the probability that the two economic series are in the same business cycle phase. The sample equivalent of this probability is the concordance index. It is calculated as the proportion of the sample period during which the two series share the same business cycle phase (Harding and Pagan 2006).

3.3 Stylised Facts About the Co-movement of Cycles in South Africa and Other Countries

Given a more complete understanding of how methodology interacts with our understanding of turning point (and other) cycles and their properties, we turn to a final set of properties concerning business cycle co-movement. Research on international business cycle co-movement has its origin with Backus et al. (1992) and Canova and Dellas (1993), who sought to understand the implications of trade and financial integration on domestic economic fluctuations. A large empirical literature subsequently emerged, with important contributions by Kose, Otrok, and Whiteman (2003) and, post-crisis, Kose, Otrok, and Prasad (2012). The South African literature mimics the developments in the international literature. It is useful to briefly survey this literature, in order to identify the salient stylized facts and again consider the methodological basis and data sources used in identifying business cycles.

In the period 2000–2010, business cycle co-movement studies in South Africa were primarily motivated by the need to understand how globalization—and the country's reintegration into the world economy following the democratic transition—impacted the South African business cycle. Of course, the impact of international trade and finance on the South African economy was already evident in the late nineteenth century. Boshoff and Fourie (2017) find trade integration to have had a significant impact on cycles in the Cape Colony. Furthermore, the current account was a binding constraint on the domestic economy during the second half of the 1980s (Edwards and Lawrence, 2008), as further discussed by Laubscher (2020) later in this volume.

The pre-2010 literature on business cycle co-movement is dominated by contributions by Alain Kabundi, Elsabe Loots, and various co-authors. Kabundi (2009) finds significant co-movement between business cycles in South Africa and the USA, over the sample period 1985–2003. Similarly, Kabundi and Loots (2010) find co-movement—albeit quite weak—between German and South African cycles over the period 1985–2006. To extend the analysis beyond developed economies, Kabundi and Loots (2007) employ a dynamic factor model to study the relationship between the South African business cycle and those of eleven Southern African countries, over the sample period 1980–2002. The Kabundi and Loots methodology allows a distinction of country-specific cycles, region-specific cycles, and a worldwide cycle. The authors find strong support for cyclical co-movement with Swaziland, Lesotho, Botswana, Zimbabwe, Angola, and the DRC, as well as mild support for Namibia, Mauritius, and Mozambique, with no support for Malawi and Zambia. Their main conclusion, namely that South African cycles are highly synchronized with those of other Southern African nations, is perhaps less surprising. More surprising is that regional cycles nevertheless explain very little of South African growth or growth in many other Southern African nations: in other words, country-specific features, on the one hand or global developments on the other hand are more important than regional developments in understanding the evolution of business cycles in Southern Africa.

Botha (2010) studies cyclical co-movement between a range of developing and developed countries (including South Africa), using principal component analysis on output, investment, and consumption data to extract common factors for every country and for G7 and world output globally. Botha finds little correlation between South African cycles and those in other G7 countries for the sample period 1961Q1 to 2008Q3. In the post-1980s period, the author finds a greater correlation with the G7 for the 1991 and 1997 recessions but none for the 1982 and 1985 recessions. Over the entire sample period, the author finds South African cycles to be generally uncorrelated with the cycles of other countries or groupings of countries.

In the period after 2010, business cycle co-movement studies turned its attention to understanding the relations between South African cycles and those in BRICS (following South Africa's inclusion in the BRICS political grouping in 2010), as well as other African countries. Çakir and Kabundi (2013) find strong co-movement between deviation cycles in South Africa and those in Brazil, India, and China but none in Russia. Furthermore, they find that common regional cycles explain a large part of fluctuations in the BRICS countries, which suggest stronger integration among these economies. The origin of these common cycles is not exactly clear, although previous research suggests increasing trade and financial integration among these countries. Furthermore, they find stronger lead relationships between cycles in China, Brazil, and Russia relative to South Africa, as compared to India. The sources of these differences are not explored. Claassen et al. (2017) study a panel of African and advanced economies for the period 1980–2011. Again employing a dynamic factor model, the authors find that business cycles among middle-income African countries (which include South Africa and Nigeria) have become more synchronized since the 1980s—both due to stronger trade and financial linkages—and that these cycles have become more synchronized with similar cycles in advanced economies.

While Claassen et al. (2017) allude to the so-called decoupling of business cycles in African countries from those in advanced economies, they do not test explicitly for a change in the relationship (Botha 2017), perhaps also due to the relatively short sample period covering the post-crisis period (2009–2011).

Consistent with the preceding discussions, it is striking that co-movement research in South Africa, and indeed the larger literature, is based almost exclusively on deviation cycle concepts. Given the nonuniqueness of deviation cycles these results are not conclusive and leave open the question of how sensitive the results are to the choice of time-series filter (Boshoff and McLean 2018). There is also no extensive work employing the nonparametric approach to study the correspondence between turning points in the South African business cycle and those in other cycles.

A second—and perhaps more important—concern is that much of the co-movement research in South Africa focuses on reduced-form, bivariate correlation analysis. There is no attempt at understanding the drivers underlying supposed co-movement or synchronization of cycles. This volume contributes toward this debate, with Hollander and Van Lill (2020) employing a DSGE model to study, inter alia, the role of international factors in driving South African business cycles. Elsewhere in this volume, as noted earlier, the narrative analysis of past cycles by Laubscher

(2020), should also assist in elucidating some of the drivers of particular cycles, including international economic and political developments.

4 Forecasting the South African Cycle

Given the state of our knowledge about the properties of the South African business cycle—and specifically its turning points—one may consider the extent to which such turning points can be predicted *ex ante*. The history of business cycle analysis is closely intertwined with the history of forecasting. Indeed, the need to avoid the welfare costs of the recession was a key motivation for Burns and Mitchell's original work.

Our arguments thus far have highlighted the conditional nature of stylized facts of the South African business, in the light of the variety of methodologies and data on which business cycle analyses are based. Similarly, one may argue that an assessment of business cycle forecasting must therefore also account for cycle concept, methodology, and data. The importance of clarifying the cycle concept and methodology is perhaps best understood by briefly considering the history of turning point forecasting in the Burns and Mitchell tradition.

In Burns and Mitchell's original analysis, the business cycle is a dispersed phenomenon: present in a range of economic sectors, business cycles show up in sequences of turning points, with some variables' turning points occurring earlier (or later) than other variables thought to coincide with the business cycle. It is this sequence, and in particular, the consistency with which some variables turn prior to the business cycle, that enabled Burns and Mitchell to take the first steps toward business cycle forecasting. Burns and Mitchell (1938: 1) labeled these variables "leading indicators," defining a leading indicator as "a fairly consistent indicator of cyclical movements in general business," referring to the extent to which an indicator's turning points lead business cycle turning points with a fairly stable lead interval (Granger 1989: 173). Subsequent work by Geoffrey Moore followed this definition, attempting to identify economic variables that meet this criterion (Moore 1950; Achuthan and Banerji 2004).

This approach to business cycle forecasting is decidedly non-parametric. It contrasts sharply with the range of econometric models employed in forecasting, which developed subsequently. Earlier models in this tradition often did not recognize that economic relations among economic variables may shift at turning points, resulting in relatively poor forecast performance (Diebold and Rudebusch 1999). Subsequent developments, attempting to incorporate nonlinear relationships, have improved forecast ability (see Clements and Hendry (1999) for an earlier assessment). Even so, one strand of the forecasting literature has turned attention back to predicting turning points explicitly, driven by the acceptance that the prediction of sign changes in a variable is easier than the prediction of the future sizes of that variable. In our overview of parametric forecasting of the business cycle, we focus on this particular set of models in the South African forecasting literature.

Much research effort has been devoted over the past forty years to developing tools for forecasting South African turning points. As discussed, a sizable part of this effort was borne by the SARB, with scholarly contributions gaining traction from the late 1990s. Therefore, our overview of business cycle prediction is split into three parts: an overview of the SARB's approach, an overview of individual financial variables as leading indicators, and an overview of alternative multivariate approaches.

4.1 Composite Leading Indicators at the SARB

In keeping with the work of Moore, Burns, and Mitchell, the SARB started publishing composite leading, coincident, and lagging indicators in 1983. This effort, spearheaded by JEM van Coller, derived from his own academic work in the late 1970s[11] (Van Coller 1980; Venter 2018). The composite leading indicator forms the basis for business cycle forecasting at the SARB (Venter 2017). The identification and forecasting stages of business cycle analysis rely on the same cycle concept, the same nonparametric methodology and a similar data. Below we review the elements and the evolution of the composite leading indicator and then proceed to survey research concerning its forecasting performance. As noted, an assessment of the performance of the indicator requires a clear understanding of the larger forecasting strategy of the SARB, which is often at odds with standard forecasting approaches, which may treat the composite indicator merely as another input variable for a macro-econometric forecasting model.

The SARB compiles composite business cycle indicators from a larger set of economic variables. For each composite indicator, the relevant variables are selected based on the correspondence between the turning points of the variables and those of the South African business cycle. In particular, the composite leading indicator is composed of variables that systematically lead the SARB's business cycle turning points by an average of three months or more.

In addition to practical requirements such as timely availability, appropriate frequency, and sample period, the selection criteria for inclusion in the composite leading indicator include the economic significance of the variable and its correspondence with the business cycle. The last criterion receives the most attention from the SARB (Venter and Pretorius 2004a, b).

The SARB periodically revises the various composite indicators, including the leading indicator. The history of revisions, as described by Venter (2018), suggests that the composition of the leading indicator has changed markedly since the 1980s. The SARB backdates the revised leading indicator, linking it with the previous version of the leading indicator such that the suggested turning points are unchanged

[11] Refer to Venter (2018) for a comprehensive historical overview of the development of composite indicators in South Africa.

Table 3 Component time series of the composite leading business cycle indicator

	Leading Indicator Series
BER opinion surveys	Volume of orders received by domestic manufacturers
	Average hours worked per factory worker in manufacturing
	Business confidence index: Manufacturing, construction, and trade
International indicators	Composite leading business cycle indicator of South Africa's major trading-partner countries (% change over 12 months)
	Commodity price index (US$) for South Africa's main export commodities (6-month smoothed growth rate)
Financial indicators	Real M1 money supply (6-month smoothed growth rate)
	Interest rate spread: 10-year government bonds minus 91-day Treasury bills
	Index of prices of all classes of shares traded on the JSE (6-month smoothed growth rate)
	Gross operating surplus as a % of GDP
Capacity indicators	Number of new passenger vehicles sold (% change over 12 months)
	Number of building plans approved: Flats, townhouses & houses larger than $80m^2$
	Job advertisements: The Sunday Times (% change over 12 months)

Source: Venter (2018)

between the two versions, even if there may be changes in the trends of the two versions (SARB, 2015: 14–17).

Currently, the composite leading indicator consists of 11 variables (Venter 2018), as reported in Table 3:

Figure 3 illustrates the South African composite leading indicator in levels, where the shaded periods indicate contractionary periods according to the official SARB turning points. Figure 4 is a similar graph, for the year-on-year growth rates in the leading indicator. As shown graphically, turning points in the indicator generally precede turning points in the South African business cycle.

While the rudimentary graphical analysis in Figs. 3 and 4 seems promising, the construction of the composite leading indicator, and the forecasting approach at the SARB relying on composite indicators have not been subject to much scholarly assessment, with the exception of earlier work by Cook and Smit (2001).

Cook and Smit (2001) describe the turning point forecasting procedure at the SARB. While earlier work by Van der Walt (1983) set the scene for the development of leading indicators at the SARB, the subsequent implementation of a leading indicator approach to forecasting was not analysed outside of the Bank prior to Cook and Smit (2001). Cook and Smit (2001) systematically investigate the ability of the (then) constituent elements of the SARB composite leading indicator to accurately predict turning points. This systematic investigation entails the first application of a parametric approach to turning point forecasting in South Africa.

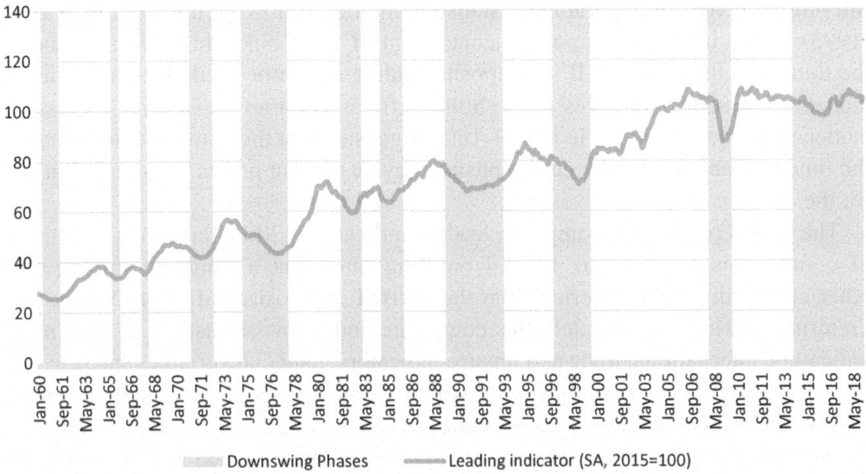

Fig. 3 Composite leading indicator compared to downswing phases. Source: South African Reserve Bank

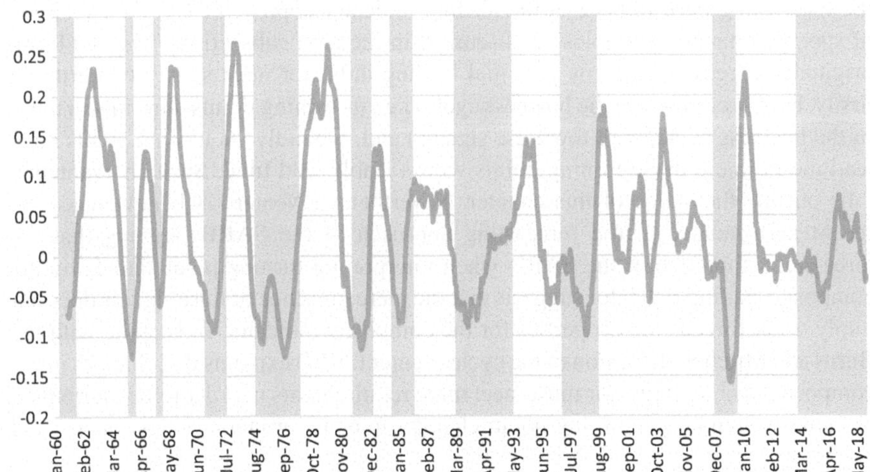

Fig. 4 Growth rates of composite leading indicator compared to downswing phases. Source: South African Reserve Bank

Cook and Smit (2001) understood the SARB's multistage approach to turning point forecasting. Described by Venter (2018) and discussed further below, the SARB's approach can be likened to a filtering procedure intended to eliminate false signals. For example, the SARB relies on the diffusion index, which measures the proportion of constituent series of the composite leading indicator, to confirm a signal from the composite leading indicator. Cook and Smit (2001) formalized this filtering procedure in a parametric statistical model, following the work of Nazmi (1993) in the USA. An important conclusion of the Cook and Smit analysis, at the time, was that the SARB's composite leading indicator needed revision, in the context of structural changes in the South African economy: extensive regression evidence for the sample period 1970–1999 suggested that the composite indicator at the time was able to predict earlier business cycle turning points accurately but not for the 1990s.

The SARB revised the composite leading indicator in 2004, reducing the number of components from 21 to 13 and omitting inter alia a range of mining and other commodity-related series from the revised composite indicator (Venter and Pretorius 2004a, b). This left the composite indicator consisting of sentiment indicators, international trade and finance indicators, financial variables and selected capacity measures—a composition in which secondary sector indicators are more evenly balanced with tertiary sector indicators, reflecting the changing structure of the South African economy. Further changes were implemented in 2015, with the omission of the share price index and an updating of other indicators (SARB 2015).

While the SARB has therefore revised the composite leading indicator since the early 2000s, there has been a little attempt in the academic literature to evaluate the forecasting performance of the leading indicator approach (with the exception of specific financial variables, as discussed in the next subsection). Moore (1950) originally suggested that any potential leading indicator must satisfy two criteria: firstly, it must conform to the business cycle (i.e., its turning points must match those of the business cycle, with few false signals) and, secondly, its turning points must lead the business cycle turning points with a stable lead time. Such an evaluation falls outside the scope of this chapter. Nevertheless, Venter (2017) evaluates the recent performance of the forecasting approach of the SARB, arguing that the three-stage approach of the SARB when interpreting turning point signals by the composite leading indicator suggests that the mere presence of false signals does not imply weak forecasting properties for the composite indicator. In keeping with the Burns and Mitchell definition of the cycle, Venter (2017) explains that changes in the composite leading indicator must meet three requirements in order to be interpreted as credibly signaling a turning point: changes must be pronounced, pervasive, and persistent.

A turning point in the composite indicator is interpreted as signaling a "pronounced" change, if the so-called six-month smoothed annualised growth rate in the composite indicator has turned and crossed the zero level for a period of longer than five months. Secondly, a so-called twelve-month smoothed diffusion index is calculated to identify the proportion of constituent series of the composite leading indicator that is higher than their average levels over the preceding twelve months. If this rate dips below 50 or rises above 50 for a sustained period, the change is considered "pervasive." Finally, a smoothed "average duration of run" is calculated to assess the average of "the durations over which the indicators have been higher than their respective average levels over the preceding twelve months." A change in this indicator for a sustained period is considered "persistent."

In other words, the SARB's approach relies both on the composite series as well as the underlying constituent series to verify the turning point signal. In this sense, any false turning point in the composite series or in any one of the series may be ultimately disqualified if it is not pervasive or persistent. Venter (2017) argues that an application of this approach suggests that the South African business cycle, as in November 2017, did not yet emerge from the recession—despite the signal of a potential trough from the composite indicator.

In a brief assessment of Venter's findings concerning the performance of the SARB approach, Keeton (2017) laments the lack of a comparative analysis of various forecasting approaches. In particular, it would be useful to compare the SARB's success in forecasting turning points with that of individual financial variables, which received significant attention in the South African literature since the 2000s. Such a consideration is of practical importance, given the delay in the publication of the composite indicators (see Boshoff and Binge 2018). There is a typical five-month lag between the reference period and its associated leading indicator. One could argue that the purpose of the composite indicator is not only in predicting turning points but in providing a general indication of future economic activity. Nevertheless, if the purpose is turning point forecasting in a timely fashion, it is preferable to consider alternatives to the SARB indicator.

There is also a limitation to Venter's assessment of the SARB approach, as both the predictor and predicted variables are constructed from the same data set: the SARB relies in part on the leading indicator when identifying turning points, so that an evaluation of the forecasting success of the leading indicator must necessarily yield generally benign conclusions. For this reason, it is also necessary to consider alternative approaches.

4.2 Financial Variables as Leading Indicators

As noted, an assessment of the history of business cycle forecasting in South Africa must pay heed to the implications of structural changes in the economy for the predictive ability of particular variables. The structural transformation of the South African economy over the last thirty years, from one dominated by primary and secondary sector activities to a services-based economy, implies an elevated role for finance. In a later chapter in this volume, Boshoff and Fourie (2020) finds a breakdown in correlation between aggregate economic growth and financial sector growth between 1960 and 2000, given the acceleration in the latter; during this period, finance doubles in size relative to aggregate output (from 10% of GDP to 20%).

The increased role of finance and other services industries in our economy is reflected in the large number of financial variables included in the composite leading indicator, even in the original 1983 version (see Venter (2018) for a comprehensive history of these revisions). These included a range of monetary, stock market, and bond market variables. The revisions of the indicator in 1994 and again in 2004 involved the removal of some of these variables, specifically those capturing similar information, and the addition of a credit measure. Subsequent revisions in 2015 reflected the impact of increased financial integration, which implies the weaker predictive ability of domestic conditions by some variables, especially those related to the stock market.

The increased interest of the SARB in the predictive content of financial variables is mirrored in academic research since the 1990s. Academic research has paid specific attention to the leading indicator properties of individual financial variables, often focusing on the yield curve. In an early study, Nel (1996) finds evidence of a cointegrating relationship between the yield curve (measuring the difference between long- and short-term South African bond yields) and economic growth. Subsequent work, often in the parametric tradition, then focused on determining the extent to which the yield curve can act as a leading indicator. Table 4 reports the various studies, with respective sample periods, methodology, and best-performing predictive horizon. The most recent work, by Aye et al. (2018), combines selected information from the yield curve with information about economic uncertainty (based on the Economic Policy Uncertainty index of Brogaard and Detzel (2015)), as well as information based on common factors extracted from a large dataset of South African macroeconomic variables.[12] Aye et al. decompose the term spread into an expectation component and a term premium and study the accuracy of a parametric forecasting model, which includes the expected term spread component as well as other information on economic uncertainty. Their model outperforms other models, specifically avoiding false recession predictions for the 2002–2003 period. They also find the strongest predictive ability at a horizon of four quarters ahead, as opposed to the six quarters identified in other work, as shown in Table 4. It is also clear from Table 4 that most research of the predictive ability of the yield curve is based on data from the 1980s, 1990s, and 2000s.

Apart from the yield curve, other financial variables are investigated for their leading indicator properties (see Moolman (2003) and Boshoff (2005, 2006) and Van Rensburg (1990)). Table 5 sets out the set of financial variables considered by Moolman and Boshoff—in Moolman's analysis the focus is only on year-on-year growth rates, whereas Boshoff focuses on both the levels and the year-on-year growth rates.

Using a parametric approach, based on probit models, Moolman (2003) investigates the forecasting ability of South African and international financial variables over a one to 18-month horizon, for the period 1978 to 2001 (see Table 5, first column). Moolman finds positive results for the yield curve and the short-term interest rate, finding that their forecasting performance improves over time. In a comparative analysis of these performances of these variables and that of the SARB's composite leading indicator, Moolman finds the individual indicators to

[12]See a subsequent chapter in this volume, by Binge (2019), on the predictive content of confidence, which is related to economic uncertainty.

Table 4 Turning point forecast performance of the South African yield curve

Studies	Sample period	Methodology	Best predictive horizon
Moolman (2004)	1979Q1–2001Q3	MS and logit	6 months
Boshoff (2005)	1986Q1–2004Q12	Turning point matching (nonparametric)	None (too many false signals to enable matching)
Khomo and Aziakpono (2007)	1980Q1–2004Q2	Standard and modified probit	6 months
Clay and Keeton (2011) and Botha and Keeton (2014)	1981Q1–2010Q4	Standard and modified probit	6 months
Aye et al. (2018)	1990Q1–2012Q1	Standard probit	4 quarters

Table 5 Financial variables investigated by Moolman (2003) and Boshoff (2005)

Variables	Moolman (2003)	Boshoff (2005)
Stock market prices	JSE all share index	JSE all share index
	JSE financial share index	JSE financial share index
	JSE mining share index	JSE mining share index
	Price-earnings ratio	Price-earnings ratio
		Dividend yield
Interest rates	Short-term real interest rate (3-month BA rate)	Short-term real interest rate
	Long-term nominal real interest rate (10-year government bond yield)	Long-term nominal real interest rate (10-year government bond yield)
	Yield spread (long-term minus short-term interest rate)	Yield spread (long-term minus short-term interest rate)
Monetary aggregates	M3 money supply	M3 money supply
	M2 money supply	
	M1 money supply	M1 money supply
International indicators	Nominal effective exchange rate	Nominal effective exchange rate
	Real effective exchange rate	Real effective exchange rate
	Rand-Dollar exchange rate	Rand-Dollar exchange rate
		S&P 500
		US federal funds rate
		US government bonds long-term yield (10 years)
		MCSI emerging market share index
		JP Morgan emerging market bond index

outperform the SARB indicator, based on the number of false signals and, more important, based on the publication lag of four to five months for the SARB.

Using a nonparametric approach, as described earlier, Boshoff (2005, 2006) investigates the leading indicator properties of a range of financial variables, over the period 1986 to 2004 (see Table 5, second column). In particular, Boshoff employs the approach by Moore (1950), discussed earlier: the leading indicator properties of financial variables are evaluated on the basis of two criteria: firstly, the extent to which they conform to the business cycle and, secondly, the stability of the time period between their turning points and those of the business cycle.

The first criterion ensures that only those variables are identified that do not transmit an excessive number of false turning point signals. For this purpose, concordance analysis—rather than correlation analysis—is required. As explained earlier, concordance measures the proportion of the sample period during which both the indicator (lagged) and the corresponding business cycle measure are both in the same phase (either both experiencing upswings or downswings). The second criterion then considers whether those variables that meet the concordance criterion have a relatively stable forecasting horizon. While the original evaluation by Moore involved a descriptive analysis of such lead time stability, it is possible to statistically evaluate such stability. Boshoff (2005) attempts such a statistical evaluation for potential financial variable leading indicators in South Africa, finding that no one financial variable satisfies the requirement. Therefore, while Boshoff finds considerable synchronization between business cycle and financial cycle phases (as reflected in other studies), an evaluation of the stability of the lead time interval suggests that no one financial variable is an individually suitable leading indicator of the South African business cycle.

It is also useful to consider some of Boshoff's findings and its implications for the SARB leading composite indicator. Regarding monetary aggregates, there is clear evidence that real M3 performs better as a leading indicator than real M1, which is used by the SARB as a leading indicator. Regarding the stock market, none of the growth rates in any of the local share price indices were significant, while only the classical cycles in the Resources Index and real economic activity exhibited significant co-movement. As noted, this aligns with the decision of the SARB to drop the share price variable from the composite leading indicator, in light of weaker correlation with real economic activity in recent years (Venter 2018). Furthermore, Boshoff's findings support the use of the yield curve as a leading indicator at a longer horizon, similar to the results discussed above. However, the nominal three-month Treasury bill yield, performed better over shorter leads, consistent with Moolman's findings. The results also suggested that the absence of any international financial variables from the composite leading indicator was a potential deficiency. The concordance statistics of classical cycles in US interest rates with South African business cycles were among the highest. Moreover, the growth rate in the JP Morgan Emerging Market Bond Index had significant concordance with growth rate cycles in South African GDP. The real effective rand exchange rate also exhibited significant co-movement with the GDP growth cycle.

In work that follows the deviation cycle concept, Auret and Golding (2012) and Sayed et al. (2017) study the leading indicator properties of South African stock prices. Auret and Golding (2012) study the extent to which deviation cycles in South African stock prices and real output (proxied by GDP and industrial production), both derived from a Hodrick–Prescott filter, are correlated over various lag orders, for the sample period 1969–2010. They uncover a significant general relationship for three subperiods 1969–1988, 1988–1997, and 1997–2010, though they do not consider turning points in particular—implicitly assigning equal weights to all data points. The strong findings for the last sample period are particularly surprising, given the contrasting findings from the SARB and Boshoff (2005, 2006). Similarly, Sayed et al. (2017) evaluate the sample period 1998 to 2016, find that aggregate stock market indices for different market segments (the All Share Index, the Industrial Index, the Resources Index, and the Financial Index) lead the South African growth rate cycle, again without focusing on turning points. In this sense, these analyses at best form part of an initial stage of assessment of leading indicator suitability and do not alter Boshoff's findings concerning the stability of lead interval.

4.3 *Multivariate Approaches*

While individual financial (or other) variables may hold predictive power for the cycle, the analysis suggests that multivariate approaches (such as the SARB's) may have benefits. At the same time, one would want to overcome the problem facing the SARB's analysis, namely that the identification of a cycle peak or trough requires the investigation of a multitude of economic variables and a considerable time lag. Leamer (2008) investigates the problem, in the context of US business cycle. He suggests an algorithm based on a limited number of variables—payroll employment, civilian employment, industrial production, and the unemployment rate—to date peaks in the US business cycle between 1973 and 2008. Leamer's algorithm consists of three stages: (1) identify probable recession periods based on predefined thresholds for declines in the first derivatives of industrial production, payroll employment, and unemployment, (2) identify peaks and troughs in the individual data series using a six-month second derivative rule, and (3) calculate the median of the peaks and troughs across the individual series to obtain the final turning point dates.

Inspired by the Leamer approach to relying on limited data to date the cycle, Laubscher (2014) also develops a limited-data algorithm for dating the South African business cycle over the period 1981Q3 to 2013Q4. We note that, while Laubscher's algorithm also entails a multistage evaluation, it is somewhat different from that of Leamer's: the latter's three stages entail alternative data transformation or analytical approaches applied to the same data, whereas Laubscher studies different data at different stages and employs analytical techniques different from Leamer's. In the first stage of Laubscher's suggested algorithm, a potential peak is identified if the probability of recession, based on a parametric logit model of the yield curve, exceeds 50%. The prominent role assigned to the yield curve is consistent with the literature, as discussed earlier, although the yield curve results do not have the final say in this algorithm. Laubscher finds that the yield curve, in contrast to other research, does not generally perform well in predicting recessions: in Laubscher's analysis, the recession probability for a logit model based on the yield curve never exceeds 40%.

In the second stage, Laubscher suggests investigating five series, namely a business confidence index (as measured by the BER), manufacturing production volumes, manufacturing production capacity utilization, manufacturing hours worked, and wholesale sales. In particular, Laubscher (2014: 19) derives the following five conditions for a recession:

(a) A decline in the (5-month centered moving average) RMB/BER business confidence index over 9 months at a rate of 24% or more.
(b) A decline in the (5-month centered moving average) manufacturing production volume index over 6 months at a rate of 1.2% or more.
(c) A decline in the manufacturing capacity utilization index over 6 months at a rate of 1.4% or more.
(d) A decline in the (5-month centered moving average) manufacturing hours worked index (BER survey) over 9 months at a rate of 6.7% or more.

(e) A decline in the (5-month centered moving average) wholesale sales volume index over 6 months by 2.3% or more.

Thereafter, in the third stage, Laubscher suggests determining which of the five series in stage two have reached a turning point, using a similar algorithm and censoring rules to those employed in the BB algorithm described earlier. Finally, in the fourth stage, Laubscher recommends reconciling the turning points from the individual series based on the median date (see Laubscher (2014) for full details).

Laubscher (2014) presents empirical evidence that the business cycle peaks suggested by the multistage algorithm would have successfully matched the 1981, 1984, 1989, 1996, and 2007 SARB peak dates. At the time, the recession of 2013 was not yet officially determined.

As discussed earlier, the SARB does not officially distinguish growth from classical recessions and the economic data presented earlier suggest that the current recession is of the former type. As noted, while the SARB has always employed some form of deviation cycle concept, past recessions have always been associated with output declines. Boshoff and Binge (2018) therefore consider the performance of the Laubscher algorithm in predicting a (strong) growth cycle downswing. Boshoff and Binge (2018) plot peak and troughs for each of the five variables, together with the official recession phases of the South African economy, including the current recession. It is clear that only three of the five series (the minimum number) predict the cycle peak that precedes the current recession (Fig. 5):

Table 6 further compares the performance of Laubscher's algorithm in predicting the most recent downturn and in predicting previous recessions.

Table 6 suggests that the lead time of the underlying indicators have not been as stable, although the multistage structure of the approach—similar to the SARB's approach—does ensure that at least some of the spurious signals are removed.

Laubscher's multivariate approach raises a number of interesting themes. Firstly, it is striking that the yield curve plays an important—but not determinative—role in Laubscher's algorithm and that no other financial variable adds further information. Secondly, it is clear that a multivariate approach is preferable to any individual leading indicator, which bodes well for the SARB approach. Thirdly, it is striking that the majority of series in Laubscher's algorithm are manufacturing-related series. In this sense, the Laubscher algorithm differs quite significantly from the SARB's composite indicator. What does this imply about the sources of cyclicality in the South African economy? Finally, the prominent role of sentiment in both the Laubscher and SARB approaches suggests that sentiment may be correlated with the causal mechanism of the business cycle and, hence, may have predictive power. In a later chapter in this volume, Binge (2020) further explores the relationship between South African business cycles and various measures of business confidence.

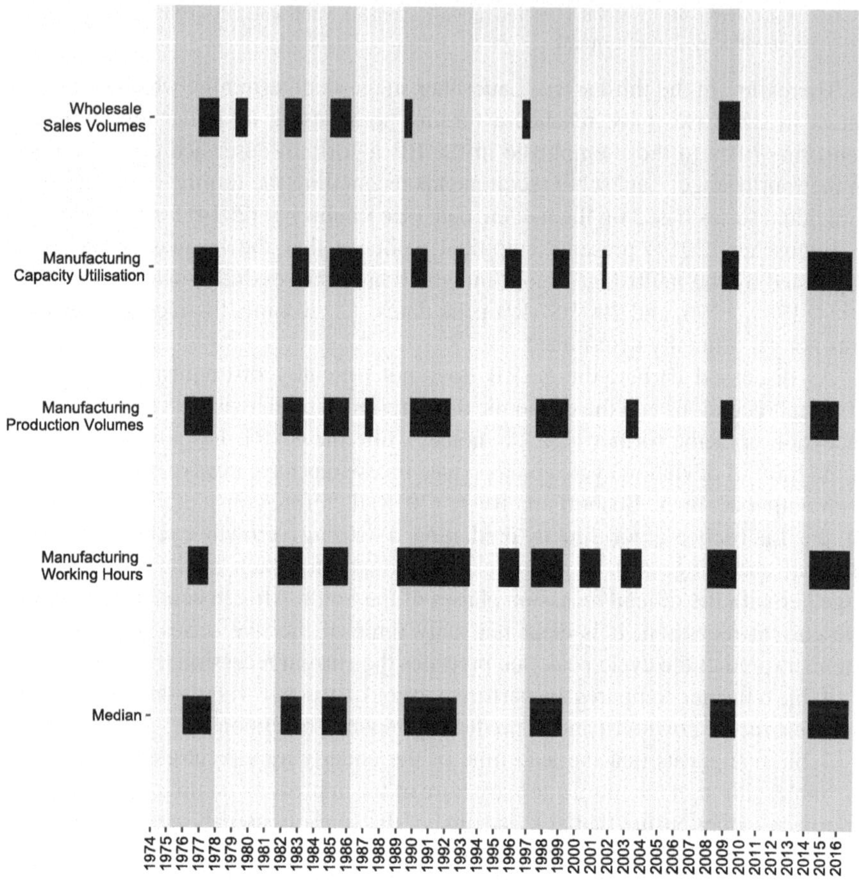

Fig. 5 Recessionary periods in the four indicators of Laubscher (2014) relative to official SARB recessions. Source: Boshoff and Binge (2018)

Table 6 Date of classical cycle peak in Laubscher (2014) variables and number of months lead (+) / lag (−) relative to November 2013 peak in SARB business cycle

	Yield spread	Business confidence	Manuf. volume	Manuf. working hours	Manuf. capacity utilization	Wholesale sales
November 2013	–	01/15 −14	02/14 −3	12/13 −1	12/13 −1	– –
November 2013 (using growth cycle definition)	–	04/13 +7				04/13 −7
Median lead or lag for 5 peaks before 2013	−1	+4	+4	−1	+7	+2

Note: Dates reported in mm/yy format

4.4 *Statistical Approaches*

An alternative approach to using leading indicators in order to predict turning points in the broader economy is to rely on a purely statistical approach, similar to the parametric approach of Moolman (2003), to dating the cycle discussed earlier. Such an approach does not rely on any independent leading indicator and, instead, sees past output data as the best leading indicator of output in the future. Botha et al. (2006) fit a set of nonlinear threshold autoregressive models on South African GDP for the sample period 1961Q1 to 2002Q1 and then forecast GDP for the period 2002Q2 to 2004Q1. Their nonlinear models implicitly provide a turning point forecast, as the models rely on identifying separate data-generating processes during recessions and expansions. The authors find accurate predictions of the 2003Q4 turning point in output growth.

5 Countercyclical Macroeconomic Policy in South Africa

Given a better understanding of the identification and forecasting of South African business cycles, we turn to an assessment of South African policy attempts at managing the welfare cost of these cycles. The driving force behind the seminal work of Burns and Mitchell in the 1930s and 40s was not only the urgent need to understand cyclical fluctuations in the wake of the Great Depression and to better predict future business cycles but also to assist policymakers in responding timeously to cycles. Since the end of the Second World War, monetary and fiscal policy have been used, in varying degrees, to stabilize economies by smoothing business cycles (Romer and Romer 1994). This subsection reviews evidence on the relationship between South African monetary and fiscal policy on the one hand and the business cycle on the other hand. Our focus is again on the conditional nature of the stylized facts; we are interested in establishing how the methodology for identifying cycles influences the assessment of countercyclicality.

Stabilization policy is an important topic in the South African literature prior to 2008, as economists sought to understand the "great moderation" of the South African economy—a period of comparatively low volatility in output growth and inflation and reflecting the experience in developed economies (Stock and Watson 2003). One dimension of this literature deals with the claim that macroeconomic policymaking is a driver of economic stability (Aron and Muellbauer 2005). Du Plessis et al. (2007) present a comprehensive overview of the precrisis literature on the cyclicality of South African fiscal and monetary policy. It is worth revisiting the broad findings of their review, complemented by research since the global financial crisis, to recapture the stylized facts and, as before, to understand their sensitivity to the particular cycle methodology.

5.1 *Fiscal Policy Pre-2008*

Du Plessis et al. (2007) survey the relatively large literature on the cyclicality of fiscal policy in South Africa (including Ajam and Aron (2007), Burger and Jimmy (2006), Du Plessis (2006), Du Plessis and Boshoff (2007), Horton (2005), Ortiz et al. (2007), Swanepoel (2007), Swanepoel and Schoeman (2003), Swanepoel (2004), and Thornton (2007)). The authors conclude that the cumulative evidence, until 2007, of the countercyclicality of South African fiscal policy is ambiguous and requires further empirical analysis. We argue below that this ambiguity is, at least partly, attributable to the variety of cyclical concepts that underlie the empirical approaches in the literature.

A popular approach in this literature is that of the structural budget balance, in which various components of government revenue and expenditure are adjusted for the business cycle and then compared to the cycle. This literature relies on a deviation cycle concept, typically derived using the Hodrick–Prescott filter and suggests somewhat contradictory conclusions. Swanepoel and Schoeman (2003), using annual data from 1970 to 2000, estimate output elasticities for various fiscal income series (direct taxes, indirect taxes, total revenue, and grants) and fiscal expenditure series (UI benefit payments, total expenditure, and net lending, budget balance). Using these elasticities, these authors calculate structural balances and compare these to the GDP deviation cycle, also derived from the Hodrick–Prescott filter. For the period 1986–2000, and especially for the period after 1994, Swanepoel and Schoeman find the discretionary fiscal policy in South Africa, measured by the structural budget balance, to have often exacerbated the business cycle (contracting during recessions and growing during expansions), rather than acting countercyclically. They also find weak evidence of the countercyclical movement of the automatic stabilizers.

Employing a similar approach, Du Plessis and Boshoff (2007) approach the problem with a different deviation cycle concept, based on the Blanchard and Quah (1989) methodology. This methodology allows the identification of a long-run component in GDP, based on long-run restrictions imposed on a structural VAR. The resultant deviation cycle, as well as a dataset of higher frequency, leads Du Plessis and Boshoff (2007) to different conclusions. They do not find compelling evidence of cyclicality in South African fiscal policy and identify various subperiods that yield evidence consistent with both pro- and countercyclicality. They also find evidence of well-functioning automatic fiscal stabilizers over the sample period. Ortiz et al. (2007), in cross-country work, find that South African structural balances were systematically reduced since the 1990s, implying a cyclical behavior.

Du Plessis and Boshoff (2007) also challenge results from another strand of the literature relying on fiscal impulse analysis, which considers the change in the fiscal stance due to changes in discretionary expenditure and taxes to assess policy cyclicality. This literature implicitly relies on the deviation cycle concept; using Hodrick–Prescott filters applied to annual data. The implications of the nonuniqueness of deviation cycles are in full display here: Horton (2005) finds countercyclicality from the mid-1990s to mid-2000s, while Ajam and Aron (2007) and Swanepoel (2007) find evidence to support pro-cyclicality.

Apart from the problem of identifying deviation cycles uniquely, much of the above research is in dominant business cycle tradition, which views business cycles as "serially correlated deviations from trend." As discussed earlier, we favor an alternative conceptualization of the cycle, which focuses on turning points. This is the cycle concept employed by Du Plessis (2006), in a direct study of the cyclicality of government expenditure—an alternative approach to assessing policy cyclicality (Fatás and Mihov 2003). Du Plessis (2006) finds evidence of the countercyclical discretionary fiscal policy. This contrasts with Burger and Jimmy (2006), who also study cyclicality directly, but employs a deviation cycle concept, finding evidence of pro-cyclicality for the period 1961 to 2004.

One of the striking conclusions from our reading of the pre-2008 literature is that the assessment of fiscal cyclicality depends critically on cycle methodology. While the results for research based on deviation cycles often favor concluding in favor of pro-cyclicality, it is clear that alternative measures of trend—including those based on structural methods—may well reverse such findings. Much of the research favoring pro-cyclicality is within the academic tradition of viewing cycles as "serially correlated deviations from trend." The results for turning point cycles are different and potentially support concluding in favor of countercyclicality.

5.2 Monetary Policy Pre-2008

In their overview of the countercyclicality of South African monetary policy since the 1980s, Du Plessis et al. (2007) identify two strands in the literature, one dealing with the contemporaneous relationship between the business cycle and another that accounts for the lags in monetary policy transmission. As far as the former is concerned, it is useful to note the three-pronged approach employed by Du Plessis and Smit (2007) in studying the countercyclicality in South African monetary policy for the sample period 1980–2006. First, they study how interest rates respond in the eight quarters following a turning point, calculating the cumulative change in interest rates. Second, they identify turning point cycles in interest rates and match these with business cycle turning points, calculating the extent of correspondence (using the concordance metric discussed earlier). Third, they utilize the macro-econometric model of the Bureau of Economic Research at Stellenbosch University to generate counterfactual output over each of the previous recessions, under the assumption that interest rates did not change. The authors find, firstly, that interest rates did not move countercyclically, secondly, that interest rates and business cycles co-move and, thirdly, that monetary policy had exacerbated output losses during recessions in the sample period. Even so, for sample periods that lean more heavily on post-1990s data and especially when relying on methods that make sufficient allowance for lags, stronger evidence of post-1990s pro-cyclicality emerges (see Du

Plessis (2006)). Interestingly, similar results emerge from a study based on deviation cycles (Swanepoel 2004).

Du Plessis et al. (2007) extend the evaluation of the cyclicality of monetary policy using a structural vector autoregression (SVAR) model for the period 1960 to 2006. Based on correlations between a cumulative demand shock (identified with monetary policy) and a cumulative supply shock, the authors find monetary policy mainly acting countercyclically after 1994, although the evidence is mixed for the period 2004–2006. Using a counterfactual analysis, the authors also conclude that monetary policy over the entire sample period has had a stabilizing effect on output, compared to the case where monetary policy shocks are eliminated from the model.

5.3 Policy After 2008

Perhaps the most important policy contribution of the early policy literature has not been in providing conclusive stylized facts, but in emphasizing the importance of systematic and rules-based policymaking in South Africa (Sachs and Stuart 2013). This is reflected, for example, in the medium-term budget framework and the structural budget rule adopted in 2011. The SARB also engages with the problem of estimating trend output extensively (see Botha et al. 2017).

Even so, there has been little new research—and certainly no peer-reviewed published work—on the stance of monetary or fiscal policy in South Africa after the global financial crisis. This despite the Treasury admitting that an important driver of the expansion of fiscal expenditure since 2008 has been to counteract slower economic growth. This assertion needs to be tested empirically. At the same time, monetary policy in South Africa would have had to operate in a new international environment, characterized by very low interest rates and the use of unconventional monetary policy tools, including quantitative easing.

A second important question is the countercyclical role of alternative macroeconomic policy tools, including macroprudential policies. Van Vuuren (2012) investigates the implications of the countercyclical bank capital requirements for South Africa, as set out in the Basel III rules. The author analyses how bank capital charges would have changed had the Basel III rules been in effect over the period 2000–2011. Related to our discussion of the centrality of the business cycle concept, Van Vuuren (2012) notes the implication of relying on the Hodrick–Prescott filter in determining cyclical activity in banking and the broader macroeconomy, finding that different variations of the filter may lead to perverse outcomes—for example, requiring banks to hold higher levels of capital for prolonged periods after a recession has subsided. Further investigation of the cyclicality of banking capital provisions, both current and foreseen, is therefore important.

A third important question—and central to the issues in this book—concerns how structural change affects the relationship between macroeconomic policy instruments and real economic outcomes. Klein (2011) finds aggregate markups in South Africa to move countercyclically and contributing to stickiness in South

African inflation. This, in turn, may constrain the room for monetary policy to react countercyclically: if inflation responds slowly to weaker economic outcomes, monetary policy may be slower to respond.

6 Conclusions

This chapter provides an overview of key South African literatures related to the business cycle, with specific emphasis on turning point cycles. Our overview of extant research proceeds along three lines: identification of the cycle, prediction of the cycle and the interaction of the cycle, and macroeconomic stabilization policy. Our focused assessment suggests a number of questions, some of which receive attention in the following chapters.

Our evaluation of various approaches to identifying the cycle followed several themes: firstly, turning point identification methodologies for South African turning points, secondly, cyclical properties of components of South African output, and, finally, studies of business cycle co-movement with other economies. Here our general conclusion, consistent with Harding and Pagan, is that the tendency to introduce increased parametric sophistication for purposes of studying South African cycles is not necessarily productive without a clear appreciation of the variety of business cycle concepts. This has implications, also for co-movement studies, all of which appear to rely on detrending techniques that do not produce unique cycles.

As far as forecasting of turning points is concerned, understanding the complementary role of financial and real-economy variables in forecasting turning points, for the purpose of unifying often mixed conclusions on the forecasting performance of financial variables. More generally, a more comprehensive assessment of the comparative performance of the SARB and other approaches to predicting peaks and troughs in South African cycles may be quite helpful.

As far as key business cycle questions related to stabilization policy are concerned, there is a pressing need for further work on the business cycle stance of South African monetary and fiscal policy, after the global financial crisis. This is related to the need to further understand the structural change in the South African economy and how it interacts with the cycle.

References

Achuthan, L., & Banerji, A. (2004). *Beating the business cycle: How to predict and profit from turning points in the economy*. New York: Currency Doubleday.

Ajam, T., & Aron, J. (2007). Fiscal renaissance in a democratic South Africa. *Journal of African Economies, 16*(5), 745–781.

Aron, J., & Muellbauer, J. (2005). Monetary policy, macro-stability and growth. *World Economics, 6*(4), 123–147.

Artis, M., Marcellino, M., & Proietti, T. (2004). Dating business cycles: A methodological contribution with an application to the euro area. *Oxford Bulletin of Economics and Statistics, 66*(4), 537–565.

Auret, C., & Golding, J. (2012). Stock prices as a leading indicator of economic activity in South Africa: Evidence from the JSE. *Investment Analysts Journal, 41*(76), 39–50.

Aye, G. C., Christou, C., Gil-Alana, L. A., & Gupta, R. (2018). Forecasting the probability of recessions in South Africa: The role of decomposed term spread and economic policy uncertainty. *Journal of International Development, 31*, 101–116.

Backus, D. K., Kehoe, P. J., & Kydland, F. E. (1992). International real business cycles. *Journal of Political Economy, 100*, 745–775.

Binge, L. H. (2020). Business confidence and the business cycle in South Africa. In W. Boshoff (Ed.), *Business cycles and structural change in South Africa*. Heidelberg: Springer.

Bismans, F., & Le Roux, P. (2013). Dating the business cycle in South Africa by using a Markov-switching model. *Studies in Economics and Econometrics, 37*(3), 25–39.

Blanchard, O., & Quah, D. (1989). The dynamic effects of aggregate demand and supply disturbances. *American Economic Review, 79*(4), 655–673.

Blinder, A. S., & Fischer, S. (1981). Inventories, rational expectations, and the business cycle. *Journal of Monetary Economics, 8*(3), 277–304.

Bosch, A., & Ruch, F. (2013). An alternative business cycle dating procedure for South Africa. *South African Journal of Economics, 81*(4), 491–516.

Boshoff, W. H. (2005). The properties of cycles in South African financial variables and their relation to the business cycle. *South African Journal of Economics, 73*(4), 796–804.

Boshoff, W. H. (2006). *The properties of cycles in South African financial variables and their relation to the business cycle* (Unpublished M.Com. thesis). Stellenbosch University, Stellenbosch.

Boshoff, W. H. (2018, September). *Policy uncertainty will keep SA firmly in recession territory.* Business Day.

Boshoff, W. H., & Becker, L. H. (2020). Business cycle recoveries: A comparative view. In W. Boshoff (Ed.), *Business cycles and structural change in South Africa*. Heidelberg: Springer.

Boshoff, W. H., & Binge, L. H. (2018). Alternative cycle indicators for the South African business cycle. In S. Smirnov, A. Ozyildirim, & P. Picchetti (Eds.), *Business cycles in BRICS*. New York: Springer.

Boshoff, W. H., & Fourie, J. (2017). When did South African markets integrate into the global economy? *Studies in Economics and Econometrics, 41*(1), 19–32.

Boshoff, W. H., & Fourie, J. (2020). The South African economy in the twentieth century. In W. Boshoff (Ed.), *Business cycles and structural change in South Africa*. Heidelberg: Springer.

Boshoff, W. H., & McLean, L. (2018). What do deviation cycles measure? An analysis of the informational content of filter-based business cycles. *South African Journal of Economic and Management Sciences, 21*(1), a1689.

Botha, I. (2010). A comparative analysis of the synchronisation of business cycles for developed and developing economies with the world business cycle. *South African Journal of Economics, 78*(2), 192–207.

Botha, I. (2017). Comment: Business cycle co-movement between Africa and advanced economies. *Studies in Economics and Econometrics, 41*(3), 113–115.

Botha, F., & Keeton, G. (2014). A note on the (continued) ability of the yield curve to forecast economic downturns in South Africa. *South African Journal of Economics, 82*(3), 468–473.

Botha, I., Greyling, L., & Marais, D. J. (2006). Modelling the business cycle in South Africa: A non-linear approach. *Studies in Economics and Econometrics, 30*(2), 103–126.

Botha, B., De Jager, S., Ruch, F., & Steinbach, R. (2017). *The quarterly projection model of the SARB* (*South African Reserve Bank Working Paper Series* WP/17/01).

Brogaard, J., & Detzel, A. (2015). The asset pricing implications of government economic policy uncertainty. *Management Science, 61*(1), 3–18.

Bry, G., & Boschan, C. (1971). *Cyclical analysis of economic time series: Selected procedures and computer programs* (NBER Technical Working Paper No 20).

Burger, P. (2008). The changing volatility of the South African economy. *South African Journal of Economics, 76*(3), 335–355.

Burger, P. (2010). The South African business cycle: What has changed? *South African Journal of Economic and Management Sciences, NS13*(1), 26–49.

Burger, P., & Jimmy, C. (2006). Should South Africa have a fiscal rule? *South African Journal of Economics, 74*(4), 642–669.

Burns, A. F., & Mitchell, W. C. (1938). *Statistical indicators of cyclical revivals*. New York: National Bureau of Economic Research.

Burns, A. F., & Mitchell, W. C. (1946). *Measuring business cycles*. National Bureau of Economic Research: Washington, DC.

Çakir, M. Y., & Kabundi, A. (2013). Business cycle co-movements between South Africa and the BRIC countries. *Applied Economics, 45*(33), 4698–4718.

Canova, F., & Dellas, H. (1993). Trade interdependence and the international business cycle. *Journal of International Economics, 34*(1–2), 23–47.

Claassen, C., Loots, E., Kabundi, A., & Viviers, W. (2017). Business cycle co-movement between Africa and advanced economies. *Studies in Economics and Econometrics, 41*(3), 93–112.

Clay, R., & Keeton, G. (2011). The South African yield curve as a predictor of economic downturns: An update. *African Review of Economics and Finance, 2*(2), 167–193.

Clements, M. P., & Hendry, D. F. (1999). *Forecasting non-stationary economic time series*. Cambridge, MA: MIT.

Cook, M. P., & Smit, E. V. d. M. (2001). Forecasting cyclical turning points by means of a probabilistic approach: Some South African evidence. *Studies in Economics and Econometrics, 25*(2), 75–104.

Diebold, F. X., & Rudebusch, G. D. (1999). *Business cycles: Durations, dynamics, and forecasting* (1st ed.). Princeton: Princeton University Press.

Du Plessis, J. C. (1950). *Economic fluctuations in South Africa* (pp. 1910–1949). Stellenbosch: Bureau for Economic Research, Stellenbosch University.

Du Plessis, S. A. (2006). Reconsidering the business cycle and stabilisation policies in South Africa. *Economic Modelling, 23*, 761–774.

Du Plessis, S. A., & Boshoff, W. H. (2007). *A fiscal rule to produce counter-cyclical fiscal policy in South Africa* (Stellenbosch Working Papers 13/2007).

Du Plessis, S. A., & Smit, B. W. (2007). Countercyclical monetary policy in South Africa. *Studies in Economics and Econometrics, 31*(1), 79–98.

Du Plessis, S. A., Smit, B. W., & Sturzenegger, F. (2007). The cyclicality of monetary and fiscal policy in South Africa since 1994. *South African Journal of Economics, 75*(3), 391–411.

Edwards, L., & Lawrence, R. (2008). South African trade policy matters: Trade performance and trade policy. *Economics of Transition, 16*(4), 583–797.

Fatás, A., & Mihov, I. (2003, November). The case for restricting fiscal policy discretion. *Quarterly Journal of Economics, 118*(4), 1419–1447.

Fisher, I. (1906). *The nature of capital and income*. New York: Macmillan.

Fisher, I. (1907). *The rate of interest*. New York: Macmillan.

Granger, C. W. J. (1989). *Forecasting in business and economics* (2nd ed.). London: Emerald.

Hall, V. B., & McDermott, C. J. (2016). Recessions and recoveries in New Zealand's post-Second World War business cycles. *New Zealand Economic Papers, 50*(3), 261–280.

Hamilton, J. D. (2003). Comment on 'A comparison of two business cycle dating methods'. *Journal of Economic Dynamics and Control, 27*, 1691–1693.

Harding, D., & Pagan, A. (2001). *Extracting, analysing and using cyclical information*. Melbourne: Melbourne Institute of Applied Economics and Research.

Harding, D., & Pagan, A. (2003a). A comparison of two business cycle dating methods. *Journal of Economic Dynamics and Control, 27*, 1681–1690.

Harding, D., & Pagan, A. (2003b). Rejoinder to James Hamilton. *Journal of Economic Dynamics and Control, 27*, 1695–1698.

Harding, D., & Pagan, A. (2006). Synchronization of cycles. *Journal of Econometrics, 132*(1), 59–79.

Hodrick, R. J., & Prescott, E. C. (1997). Postwar U.S. business cycles: An empirical investigation. *Journal of Money, Credit and Banking, 29*(1), 1–16.

Hollander, H., & van Lill, D. (2020). On the estimation and application of structural decompositions of the South African business cycle. In W. Boshoff (Ed.), Business cycles and structural change in South Africa. Heidelberg: Springer.

Horton, M. (2005). Role of fiscal policy in stabilization and poverty alleviation. In M. Nowak & L. Ricci (Eds.), *Post-apartheid South Africa: The first ten years*. Washington: IMF.

Jevons, H. S. (1884). Solar periods and the price of corns. In *Investigations in currency and finance*. London: Macmillan.

Kabundi, A. (2009). Synchronization between South Africa and the U.S.: A structural dynamic factor analysis. *South African Journal of Economics, 77*(1), 1–27.

Kabundi, A., & Loots, E. (2007). Co-movement between South Africa and the Southern African development community: An empirical analysis. *Economic Modelling, 24*, 737–748.

Kabundi, A., & Loots, E. (2010). Patterns of co-movement between South Africa and Germany: Evidence from the period 1985 to 2006. *South African Journal of Economics, 78*(4), 383–399.

Keeton, G. (2017). Comment: Obtaining clear and timely business cycle turning point signals with a composite leading business cycle indicator. *Studies in Economics and Econometrics, 41*(3), 61–64.

Keynes, J. M. (1936). *The general theory of employment, interest and money*. London: Macmillan.

Khomo, M. M., & Aziakpono, M. J. (2007). Forecasting recession in South Africa: A comparison of the yield curve and other economic indicators. *South African Journal of Economics, 75*(2), 194–212.

Klein, N. (2011). *South Africa: The cyclical behavior of the markups and its implications for monetary policy* (IMF Working Papers WP/11/204).

Koopmans, T. C. (1947). Measurement without theory. *Review of Economic Statistics, 29*(3), 161–172.

Kose, M. A., Otrok, C., & Whiteman, C. H. (2003). International business cycles: World, region, and country-specific factors. *American Economic Review, 93*(4), 1216–1239.

Kose, M. A., Otrok, C., & Prasad, E. (2012). Global business cycles: Convergence or decoupling? *International Economic Review, 53*(2), 511–538.

Krugell, W. (2017). Comment: The business cycle resilience of the Western Cape economy: A regional analysis of the 2009 recession and subsequent recovery. *Studies in Economics and Econometrics, 41*(3), 35–38.

Kydland, F. E., & Prescott, E. C. (1990). Business cycles: Real facts and a monetary myth. *Federal Reserve Bank of Minneapolis Quarterly Review, 14*(2), 3–18.

Laubscher, P. (2014). *A new recession-dating algorithm for South Africa* (Stellenbosch Economic Working Papers 06/14).

Laubscher, P. (2017). The business cycle resilience of the Western Cape economy: A regional analysis of the 2009 recession and subsequent recovery. *Studies in Economics and Econometrics, 41*(3), 1–33.

Laubscher, P. (2020). A history of South Africa's modern business cycle. In W. Boshoff (Ed.), *Business cycles and structural change in South Africa*. Heidelberg: Springer.

Leamer, E. E. (2008). *What's a recession anyway?* (National Bureau of Economic Research Working Paper 14221).

Mills, J. (1867). *Credit cycles and the origin of commercial panics*. Manchester: Transactions of the Manchester Society.

Mitchell, W. C. (1923). *Business cycles and unemployment*. New York: National Bureau of Economic Research.

Mitchell, W. C. (1927). *Business cycles: The problem and its setting*. New York: NBER.

Moolman, E. (2003). Predicting turning points in the South African economy. *South African Journal of Economic and Management Sciences NS, 6*(2), 289–303.

Moolman, E. (2004). A Markov switching regime model of the South African business cycle. *Economic Modelling, 21*, 631–646.

Moore, H. L. (1914). *Economic cycles: Their law and cause*. New York: Macmillan.

Moore, G. H. (1950). *Statistical indicators of cyclical revivals and recessions* (National Bureau of Economic Research Occasional Paper 31). New York: National Bureau of Economic Research.
Nazmi, N. (1993). Forecasting cyclical turning points with an index of leading indicators: A probabilistic approach. *Journal of Forecasting, 12*, 215–225.
Nel, H. (1996). The term structure of interest rates and economic activity in South Africa. *South African Journal of Economics, 64*(3), 162–175.
Ortiz, A., Sturzenegger, F., & Talvi, E. (2007). *Monetary and fiscal policies during a sudden stop: Is tighter brighter?* Boston, MA: Kennedy School of Government, Mimeograph.
Pagan, A.R. 2003. Reflections on some aspects of macro-econometric modelling. Lecture to the African Econometrics Conference, Stellenbosch 2003.
Pigou, A. C. (1927). *Industrial fluctuations*. London: Macmillan.
Romer, C. D. (1999). Changes in business cycles: Evidence and explanations. *The Journal of Economic Perspectives, 13*(2), 23–44.
Romer, C. D., & Romer, D. H. (1994). Monetary policy matters. *Journal of Monetary Economics, 34*(1), 75–88.
Sachs, M., & Stuart, I. (2013). *Structural balances, fiscal rules and medium-term objectives*. Paper presented at the 2013 Biennial Conference of the Economic Society of South Africa.
Sayed, A., Auret, C., & Page, D. (2017). Do share prices lead economic activity in emerging markets? Evidence from South Africa using Granger-causality tests. *Investment Analysts Journal, 46*(3), 200–212.
Smit, D. J., & Van der Walt, B. E. (1970, September). *Business cycles in South Africa during the post-war period, 1946 to 1968*. Quarterly Bulletin. Pretoria: South African Reserve Bank.
South African Reserve Bank. (2015). Revisions to the composite leading and coincident business cycle indicators. *South African Reserve Bank Quarterly Bulletin*, 13–17.
Stock, J. H., & Watson, M. W. (2003, August). Has the business cycle changed? Evidence and explanations. In *Proceedings from the Federal Reserve Bank of Kansas City Symposium "Monetary Policy and Uncertainty"*, Jackson Hole, Wyoming.
Swanepoel, J. A. (2004). The monetary and fiscal policy mix in South Africa. *South African Journal of Economics, 72*(4), 730–758.
Swanepoel, J. A. (2007). *Indicators of fiscal stance in South Africa: A re-examination* (South African Reserve Bank Discussion Paper DP/07/03), Pretoria.
Swanepoel, J. A., & Schoeman, N. J. (2003). Countercyclical fiscal policy in South Africa: Role and impact of automatic fiscal stabilizers. *South African Journal of Economic and Management Sciences, NS6*(4), 802–822.
Thornton, J. (2007). On the cyclicality of South African fiscal policy. *South African Journal of Economics, 75*(2), 258–264.
Van Coller, J. E. M. (1980). A system of composite leading and coinciding indices of the South African business cycle. *Studies in Economics and Econometrics, 8*, 41–73.
Van der Walt, B. E. (1982). *Die identifisering en waardebepaling van ekonomiese aanwysers vir 'n studie van die konjunktuur in Suid-Afrika*. (Unpublished D.Com. thesis), University of Pretoria, Pretoria.
Van der Walt, B. E. (1983, March). *Indicators of business cycle changes in South Africa* (pp. 53–63). Quarterly Bulletin, No 147. Pretoria: South African Reserve Bank
Van Rensburg, M. P. J. (1990). *A reference cycle and leading indicator for South African financial markets: Some results.*. Unpublished MBA dissertation. Stellenbosch: Graduate School of Business, University of Stellenbosch.
Van Vuuren, G. (2012). Basel III countercyclical capital rules: Implications for South Africa. *South African Journal of Economic and Management Sciences NS, 15*(3), 309–324.
Van Walbeek, C. (2006). Official revisions to South African national accounts data: Magnitudes and implications. *South African Journal of Economics, 74*(4), 745–765.
Venter, J. C. (2005). *A brief history of business cycle analysis in South Africa*. Presentation to the OECD Workshop on Composite Leading Indicators for Major OECD Non-Member Economies, 25–26 April 2005.
Venter, J. C. (2017). *A brief history of business cycle analysis in South Africa*. Mimeograph.

Venter, J. C. (2018). The SARB's composite business cycle indicators. In S. Smirnov, A. Ozyildirim, & P. Picchetti (Eds.), *Business cycles in BRICS*. New York: Springer.
Venter, J. C., & Pretorius, W. S. (2004a, March). *Note on the revision of composite leading and coincident business cycle indicators* (pp. 67–72). (Quarterly Bulletin, No 231). Pretoria: South African Reserve Bank.
Venter, J. C., & Pretorius, W. S. (2004b, March). Note on the revision of composite leading and coincident business cycle indicators. *South African Reserve Bank Quarterly Bulletin, 231*, 67–72.
Wicksell, K. (1898). *Geldzins und Güterpreise*. Jena: Fischer.

The South African Economy in the Twentieth Century

W. H. Boshoff and J. Fourie

Between 1911, a year after the unification of the two British colonies and two Boer republics into the Union of South Africa, and 2017, 23 years after the first democratic elections, the South African economy transformed remarkably. While primary sectors like agriculture and mining had formed the backbone of the economy during the early decades, financial services and other tertiary sector industries were the biggest contributors to production by the end of the period. These processes of industrialisation and modernisation would, by the end of the century, make South Africa one of the richest countries, on a per capita basis, on the African continent.

This chapter introduces a newly constructed series of gross domestic product—and its sectoral components. Using this data, the chapter reviews the evolution of the South African economy over the twentieth century and relates these structural changes to changes in the characteristics of the South African business cycle. We do not aim to rewrite twentieth-century South African economic history. Much is already known about the rise of the mining and manufacturing sectors, the discriminatory labour laws and policies that underpinned this, the concomitant rise of finance and other services that both flowed from and contributed to mining and manufacturing, and the various interventionist government policies that, for good or bad, aimed to stimulate economic activity. What we instead hope to do is provide, for the first time, a consistent, comparable series of gross domestic product over the entire twentieth century and into the twenty-first century. This complete series,

W. H. Boshoff
Department of Economics, Stellenbosch University, Stellenbosch, South Africa
e-mail: wimpie2@sun.ac.za

J. Fourie (✉)
LEAP, Department of Economics, Stellenbosch University, Stellenbosch, South Africa
e-mail: johanf@sun.ac.za

W. H. Boshoff (ed.), *Business Cycles and Structural Change in South Africa*, Advances in African Economic, Social and Political Development,
https://doi.org/10.1007/978-3-030-35754-2_3

spanning 106 years, allows us to identify key periods of structural change and their interrelation with aggregate and sectoral cyclical behaviour. The result is a more nuanced interpretation of South Africa's twentieth-century economic performance.

1 Before 1910

As long as humans have populated the southern tip of Africa—and there is a good reason to suspect that this is where economic specialization of humans evolved—they produced things, mostly for consumption but also sometimes as investments. Southern Africa has a long history of agricultural and pastoral farming. Archaeological evidence of precolonial communities suggests pockets of dense settlement. We know of an active Indian Ocean trade, in gold, ivory and slaves, as far back as the eleventh century. In the south-western region, where hunter-gatherer San and pastoral Khoi lived, the Mediterranean climate made permanent settlement attractive for European settlement. When the Dutch East India Company searched for a halfway house to replenish its voyages to the East, the bay below Table Mountain was identified as the most ideal location. For the next 140 years, European settlers and the East Indies migrants they brought with them as slaves would displace the indigenous Khoesan, building an agricultural community of mostly wheat and wine farmers in the west, and pastoral farming in the drier interior. Britain replaced the VOC as coloniser in 1795, and after a short break, again in 1806, and from here the Cape Colony would be under British rule. Favourable tariffs for Cape exports to Britain, notably Cape wine, initially boosted the Cape economy. But by the 1850s, the Colony had slumped and economic performance was depressed. It would remain that way until the discovery of diamonds in the interior of the country, then home to two fledgling Boer Republics that were established after frontier farmers in the 1830s had trekked beyond the boundaries of the colony. This trek was proceeded by a series of bloody wars amongst the Bantu-speaking tribes, known as the Mfecane or the 'Wars of Calamity', which had caused mass starvation and migration throughout Southern Africa.

The discovery of diamonds and, 20 years later, gold would catalyse the mostly agricultural economies of the four territories—the Cape Colony and the Natal colony, colonised by Britain in 1843, and the two Boer Republics, the Orange Free State (1854) and the Transvaal (1852)—into an era of industrialisation and modern economic growth. This is quite evident from a first if incomplete series of per capita gross domestic product for the eighteenth to twentieth centuries constructed by Fourie and Van Zanden (2013), and reproduced in Fig. 1. GDP per capita seems to take off immediately following the discovery of diamonds, although it is also true that it becomes incredibly volatile. High-economic growth rates are also calculated by Greyling and Verhoef (2015) for the Cape Colony. These were a consequence not only for the extraction of minerals but also the auxiliary industries that developed alongside the mines. Herranz-Loncan and Fourie (2018) estimate, for example, that railways, built with the express purpose of connecting the interior mines with the

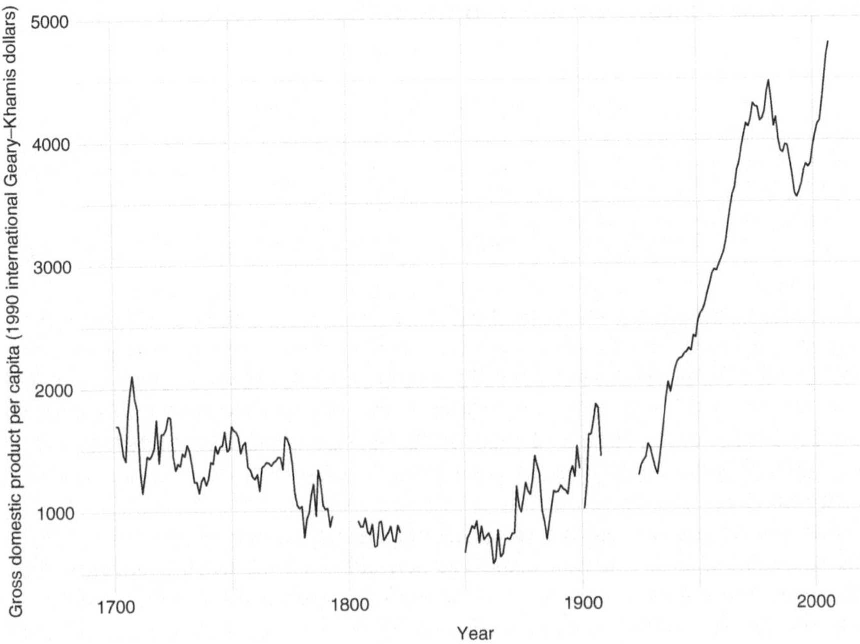

Fig. 1 Gross domestic product per capita (1990 international Geary–Khamis dollars). Source: Fourie and Van Zanden (2013)

coastal ports, accounted for at least 22% of the increase in the Cape Colony's labour productivity from 1873 to 1905. It may have been even more in the Boer Republics.

The Anglo-Boer War between 1899 and 1902, the most expensive colonial war in British history, devastated the South African interior. After the peace, many rural whites joined the large migration of black workers to the area around Johannesburg in search of employment, beginning a process of urbanization that would continue into the twenty-first century. Within two decades of its foundation, Johannesburg would be the largest urban centre in the country and its economic nexus.[1] The northward shift in economic power also affected the terms of unification; instead of a liberal system with a non-racial franchise, the new Union of South Africa had a limited franchise, favouring white, male voters. Such political power in the hands of a few would profoundly affect South African economic policies in the twentieth century.

[1] In the 1911 census, Johannesburg had a population of 237,100 people compared to Cape Town's 161,570.

2 Gross Domestic Product in the Twentieth Century

To assess South Africa's twentieth-century economic performance, we construct a measure of gross domestic product for 106 years, from 1911 to 2017. We do this by combining several sources. First, we transcribe a series of gross domestic product at factor cost from 1911 to 1968 (Botha 1968). We link this series to a series of gross domestic product at factor cost we obtain from the South African Reserve Bank (SARB 2018), available from 1946 to 2017. As a deflator, we use a GDP deflator that we calculate by dividing the gross domestic product at current prices (KBP6006J) over the gross domestic product at constant 2010 prices, from 1946 to 2016 (KBP6006Y). We then combine this with an index of consumer prices (1938 = 100) that we obtain from the Union Statistics (Bureau for Census and Statistics 1960: H23). Because these series do not link up perfectly, we adjust the 90 earlier years by the average difference for the 14 years (1946–1959) when the series do overlap. The full, final series of gross domestic product at factor cost is available in Appendix 1.

Figure 2 reports annual growth in aggregate output, between 1912 and 2017 and suggests important broad trends. The period from 1912 to 1945 appears to be characterized by high volatility—we find both the two-lowest growth years (1920 and 1931) as well as the two-highest growth years (1933 and 1935) in this era. There

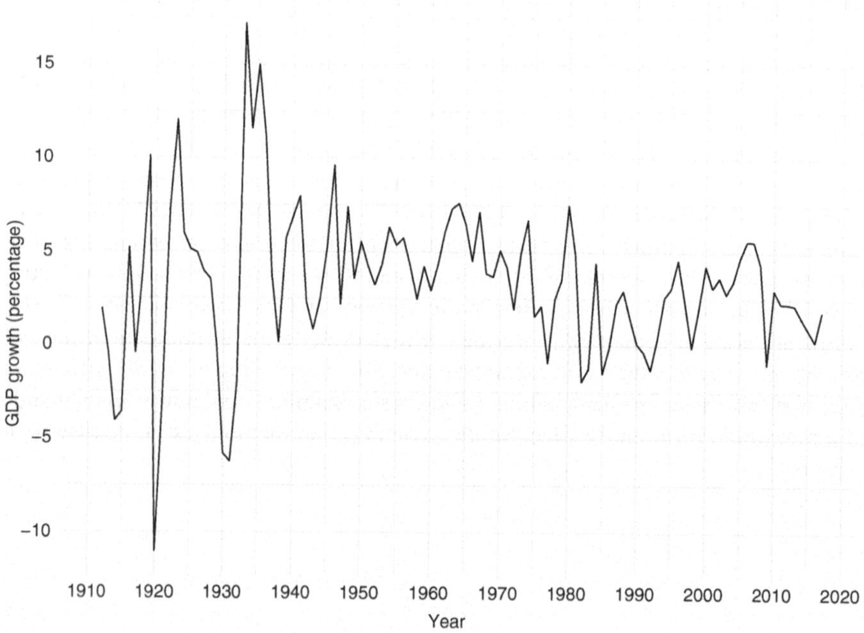

Fig. 2 Annual output growth in South Africa, 1912–2017. Source: See text

are several likely reasons for this, but two stand out: the period includes two major world wars as well as the largest depression of the twentieth century (Evidence of this can be seen in Appendix 2, which provides a breakdown of GDP growth by industry).

In the 43 years from 1933 to 1976, no negative economic growth is registered. Abolishing the gold standard, producing for the Second World War, and a global, postwar 'Golden Age' all contribute to these high growth rates. The late 1970s, 1980s and early 1990s, however, see a return to volatile—and decidedly weak—growth. The unravelling of the system of apartheid—a result of both internal and external pressures—contributes to the malaise. 1994 heralds a new era for South African politics and for its economy too. A period of stable growth is registered after 1994 (bar 1998, the consequence of an Asian financial crisis), with growth rates peaking beyond 5% in the late 2000s. The global financial crisis of 2007/2008 brings this era to an end. Growth falters and remains low until the end of the 2010s.

2.1 *Sectoral Breakdown*

Our series allow us to not only calculate gross domestic product but do so by sector. We use the standard taxonomy of sectors available in both our sources: agriculture, transport, mining, manufacturing, construction, utilities, wholesale and retail services, financial services, personal services, and government services. Figure 3 shows the composition of gross domestic product by sector from 1911 to 2016.

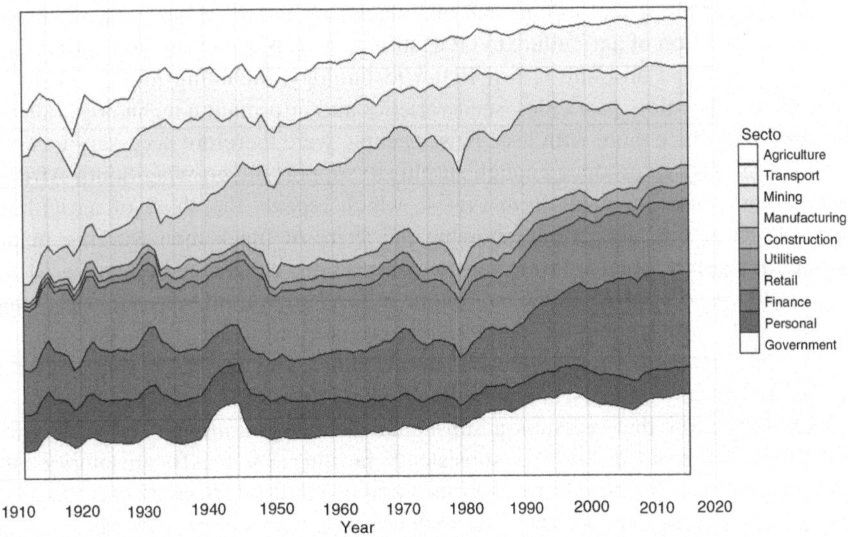

Fig. 3 Composition of gross domestic product by sector

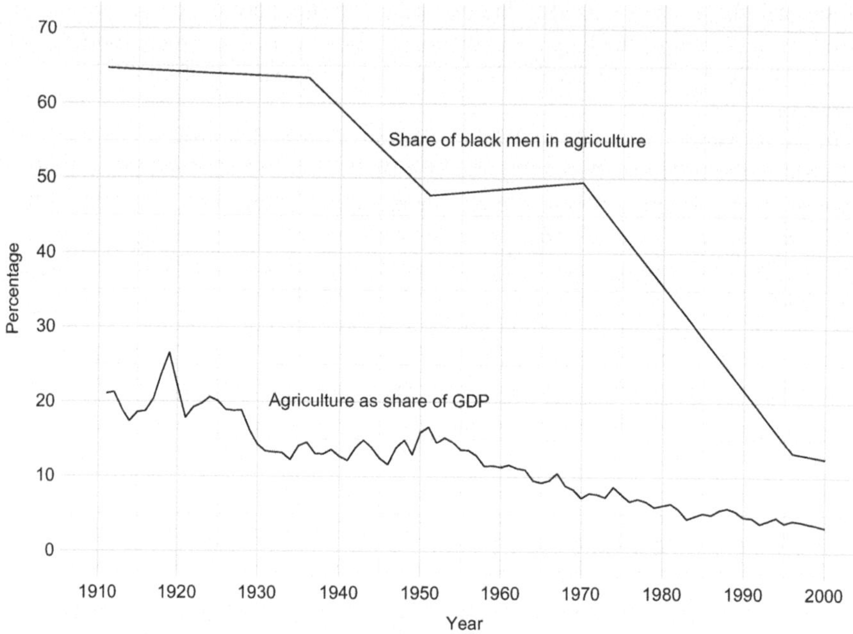

Fig. 4 The decline of agriculture as a share of GDP and employment of black men in agriculture according to census figures. Source: Ramela (2018); own calculations

As a share of gross domestic product, agriculture sees the largest decline over the period, from 21% of GDP in 1911 to 2.5% of GDP in 2016. This should come as no surprise; as the size of mining and manufacturing and, later, services, expanded, so the contribution of agriculture to GDP shrunk. This is not to say that agricultural output declined in absolute terms. Better technology, including improvements in equipment, irrigation, pesticides, seed varieties and information technology, allows farmers to produce more with less. Fewer people were therefore necessary to work the land in order to produce enough surplus to support the growing South African population. This is evident from Fig. 4, which repeats the share of agriculture in GDP series but adds a line showing the share of black men working in the agricultural sector (obtained from various censuses and calculated by Ramela 2018). While almost 65% of all black men work in the agricultural sector in 1911, that number falls to less than 13% in 2001. The much faster decline in the share of black men employed in agriculture than in agriculture's share of GDP suggests rapid productivity improvements, notably in the period after 1970.

Another sector that registers a substantial decline is mining. The sector that initially transformed the mostly subsistence-farming South African interior into an industrializing heartland, has seen its share of GDP fall from 27.6%, the most important sector in 1911, to 8.0%, the sixth largest (of the ten) in 2016. Much of this decline already happened during the first half of the century, when mining's share of GDP declined from 27.6% to 9.5% in 1948. This relative decline was mostly the consequence of a much faster increase in manufacturing, which in the 10 years between 1939 and 1949 more than doubled in output, increasing its share of GDP from 11.9% to 18.4%. Manufacturing's share of GDP would peak in 1981 at 24.2% and decline to only 13.6% in 2016.

Two sectors would be responsible for manufacturing's relative decline: financial services and government services. Between 1981 and 2016, finance would increase by ten percentage points, from 10.6% to 20.6% of GDP. At the same time, the government sector would increase from 11.3% to 17.7% of GDP, although much of this growth happened before 1994, when the government's share of the economy was 16.9%, higher than at any stage during the Second World War.

2.2 *Breakpoints*

Aside from the gradual shift in the structure of the economy from the primary sector to tertiary sector production, we can also identify breakpoints in the GDP series over time. In statistical terms, a structural break in a time series occurs when there is a permanent change in the mean or other moments of the data-generating process. We use the Bai and Perron (2003) methodology, which allows the identification of multiple structural breaks in a time series. A key benefit of the Bai–Perron approach over older structural break tests is that the number of breaks is determined endogenously. The method involves modelling the series of interest (in this case, GDP) as an autoregressive process, seeking to identify changes in the parameters of the process. The Bai–Perron test requires the specification of a trimming parameter, which determines the minimum distance between breaks. Our results are robust to the choice of trimming parameter values. The Bai–Perron test performs best where two potential dates for structural breaks are not closer to one another than the trimming parameter—a condition that is likely to be satisfied for a slow-changing series such as GDP.

We identify breakpoints over the course of 106 years using two goodness-of-fit measures, the residual sum-of-squares (RSS) and the Bayesian information criterion (BIC). The RSS suggests five breakpoints, while the BIC suggests four. Three of the four overlaps for both series: 1964, 1979 and 2001. Whereas the BIC suggests that the pre-1964 series has only one breakpoint, in 1947, the RSS suggests two, 1934 and 1949. The latter, we surmise, fits the historical record more accurately, and we therefore plot the breakpoints in Fig. 5.

The first period, from 1911 to 1934, is a period of volatility. Jones and Müller (1992), in their *The South African economy, 1910–1990*, says that the period between 1910 and 1933 was 'not a time of increasing economic prosperity'. Our results are somewhat different. Despite a deep but quick recession in 1920, we find positive if volatile economic growth for most of the post-World War 1 period until 1929. The Great Depression halted growth until South Africa left the gold standard in December 1932. The first break in our series—1934—is thus in the second year

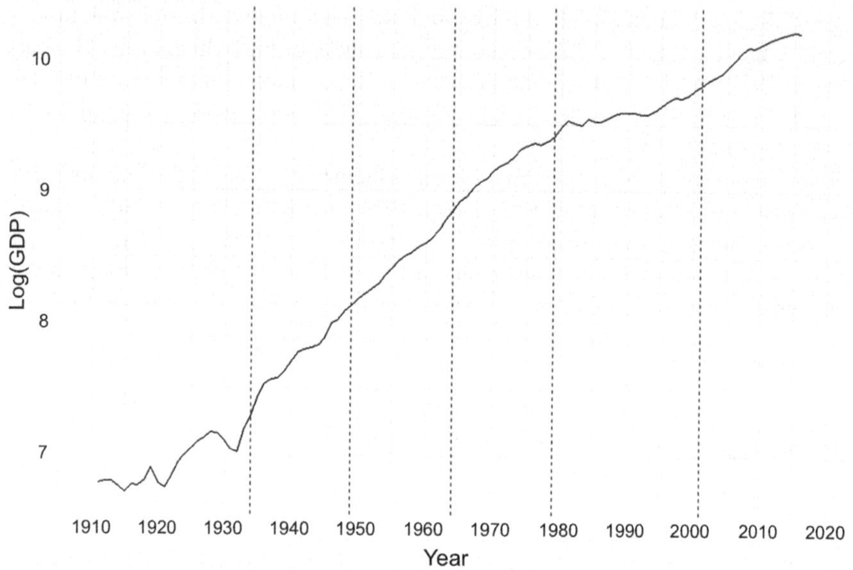

Fig. 5 Breakpoints in GDP series. Source: Own calculations

of the recovery, when gold mining in particular accelerated at unprecedented levels. The annual growth rates from 1933 to 1936 were above 11% per annum.

The second breakpoint follows the end of the Second World War (1945) and the election victory of the National Party (in 1948). It also coincides with the start of an era of stellar economic growth—an annual average of 5.1% between 1950 and 1967, notably through growth in manufacturing, peaking in 1964, the third breakpoint identified, with a growth rate of 7.6%.

Although the start of the 1970s marked the beginning of another era of volatility, growth was still largely positive. Here, though, the economic consequences of South Africa's apartheid policies become evident; in 1977, the year after the Soweto riots, South African output contracts. Global factors such as the decline of the Bretton Woods system, the international oil crisis of 1973 and weak growth rates and high indebtedness, notably elsewhere in Africa, contributed to the poor economic conditions.

After the fourth breakpoint, in the late 1970s, the South African economy enters a period of weak growth. Between 1982 and 1992, the South African economy grew, on average, only 0.44% per annum. As it is well documented elsewhere, the period is characterized by political turmoil, to maintain the safety and security of the apartheid apparatus, government expenditure increased significantly (Fig. 3). In August 1985, PW Botha was expected to announce further reforms for apartheid, but in what became known as his 'Rubicon' speech, he did the opposite, announcing substantially weaker reforms. This resulted in international financial sanctions; in September that year, South Africa introduced a dual exchange rate to discourage disinvestment. Levy (1999) warns that these sanctions probably did not have a large effect on an already stalling economy often ascribed to it; their effect, he suggests, was largely 'psychological'. Most of the damage had been done in the preceding decade. Indeed, as Fedderke and Simkins (2012) remark in a summary of the twentieth-century South African economy, internal 'political instability in South Africa became overt in the period 1976 and 1994', a period in which 'real per capita income dropped substantially'.

Democracy in South Africa not only brought political freedom but also economic growth. Between 1994 and 2001, the economy rebounded with an average of 2.7% per annum. Only 1998 recorded negative economic growth as a result of the Asian financial crisis spilling over to other developing countries. Even so, the true growth dividend of democracy would only materialise later. Apartheid reforms, and the relaxing of international sanctions, would have a positive if limited immediate impact on the economy.

The economy entered a higher growth phase after 2001, which represents the last breakpoint. While the end of 2001 was characterized by a sharp depreciation of the Rand, it is unlikely that this resulted in the break, although it would have contributed to the end of a growth recession in that period (Boshoff 2008 shows that South African business cycles are not tightly linked to exchange rate cycles). Between 2002 and 2008, the South African economy grew on average at 4.3% per annum. The improved performance is due both to improved total-factor productivity as well as accelerated capital accumulation (Fedderke 2002)—see Du Plessis and Smit (2007, 2009) for an overview of the literature on South Africa's post-democracy revival. This was supported by—and reflected in—a healthy fiscal position, with a total budget surplus in 2005 and 2006 and government debt reaching levels below 25% of GDP before the financial crisis.

In 2007–2008, and indeed prior to the global financial crisis, economists had predicted that the structure of demand driving growth (with implications for the current account) could not ensure sustainably higher growth in South Africa (Hausmann 2008). Our method does not allow the identification of breakpoints too close to the end of the sample period, though it is increasingly clear that 2008 was potentially a further breakpoint. Growth since 2009 has been very poor, averaging at less than 1.5% per annum. The global financial crisis, notably the decline in trade that followed, hurt the economy. But political factors mattered more: Jacob Zuma was elected president in 2009, and introduced a more populist fiscal regime, increasing expenditure on government employees notably (again, see Fig. 3). Whereas unemployment stood at less than 22% in 2008 (to be sure, still extraordinarily high), it had increased to above 27% by 2017.

2.3 *Living Standards*

Growth in the gross domestic product is one way to measure economic performance, but ultimately the aim of higher production and income is improved living standards.

Twentieth-century South Africa unfortunately lacks consistent and reliable series of living standards—wages, for example, or wealth indicators for all population groups over a century. Nattrass and Seekings (2011) provide an extensive discussion of the evolution and racial inequalities of social transfers and living standards over the twentieth century, although they, too, struggle to find a consistent series for the entire period. One way to overcome this is to rely on innovative records that measure, at the individual level, information that reflect biological standards of living. One such measure is height.

The height of an individual is the result of both genetic and environmental factors. Because genetics are slow to change, a change in the average height of a population should reflect changes in the environmental conditions, including access to nutrition and the disease environment. Access to proteins during the early years of life, for example, can substantially raise the adult height.

Mpeta et al. (2018) extract information from military attestation forms, cadaver records and more recent representative surveys to reconstruct the height of black men over the twentieth century. The results are reported in the upper plot of Fig. 6. Living standards as proxied by height—we use birth years even though the individuals are measured when adults—declined significantly during the first three decades, and only begin to turn around in the early 1930s.

We can compare this trend with GDP growth rates we calculate. The high volatility of growth, a consequence of war, disease, and the introduction of repressive and discriminatory land and labour policies, had adverse effects for black

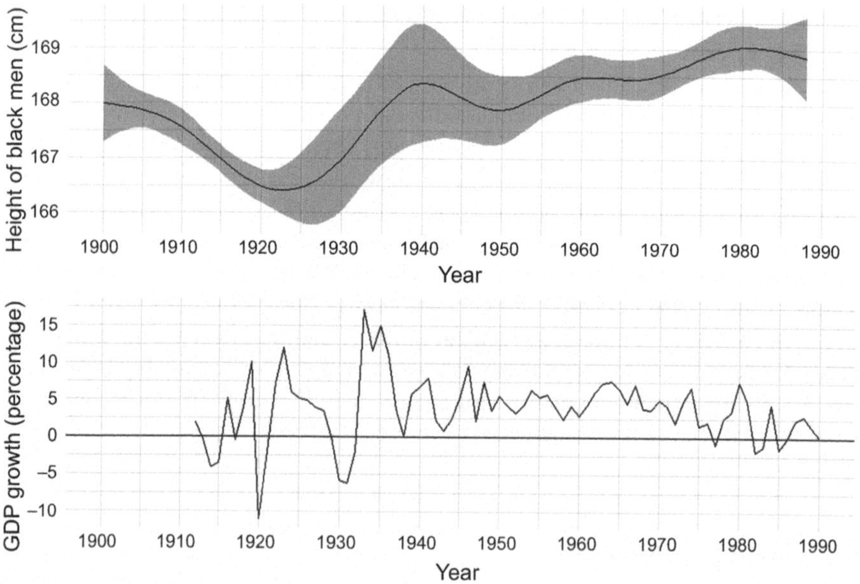

Fig. 6 Comparison of GDP growth and the height of black men, 1900–1990. Source: Mpeta et al. (2018); own calculations

South Africans. The turnaround seems to occur around the time that South Africa leaves the gold standard in December 1932, when growth accelerates to above 10% per annum for several years. This is the consequence of an expansion in mining and, importantly, as we show above, manufacturing. The expansion of gold mining in and around Johannesburg, for example, not only boosts mining employment for black men but also raises municipal revenues, allowing the city to improve housing and other infrastructure around the mines. Children born in those regions would have likely benefited, through better nutrition, from higher incomes (of their parents) and the healthier environment offered by better housing and other public goods.

Living standards continue to increase throughout the 1950s and 1960s, coupled with the positive economic growth rates we find, but then flattens off during the late 1970s and 1980s, when economic growth retracts. Although we cannot infer direct causation from GDP to living standards, Fig. 6 does provide some evidence that the two series correlate fairly closely across the twentieth century.

3 Cycles

Our GDP data set is also useful in providing a long-run view of business cycles and their relation to long-run structural change in South Africa. As noted before, the benefit of extending data to the period before 1946 is that it allows for a systematic comparison of economic behaviour—including cyclical properties—in the first half of the twentieth century and that of the 1960s and beyond. The latter has received the most attention from macroeconomists, in part due to the availability of data. In this section, we present some preliminary measures of the business cycle from 1911 onwards as well as some descriptive statistics to highlight changes in the volatility and co-movement properties of the business cycle over this period.

The cyclical analysis in this section follows the approach of Kydland and Prescott (1990), as applied by Burger (2009) to South African business cycles. The approach relies on a deviation cycle measure, which defines the business cycle as the deviation of output from an estimated output trend. The latter is typically identified by means of a time-series filter,[2] which involves smoothing, that is, the removal of high-frequency fluctuations (or 'noise') from data by various forms of averaging. A popular filter in business cycle analysis is the Hodrick–Prescott filter; Boshoff and McLean (2018) provides an assessment of the extent to which various filter-based business cycle measures correlate with demand and supply shocks in South Africa.

The Kydland and Prescott (1990) approach involves studying the volatility and co-movement characteristics of deviation cycles. We rely predominantly on standard deviations and correlation analysis to study the volatility and the co-movement of South African cycles, respectively.

[2]Time-series filters are statistical functions. In contrast, Du Plessis et al. (2008) and Boshoff and McLean (2018) investigate business cycles derived on the basis of structural economic models.

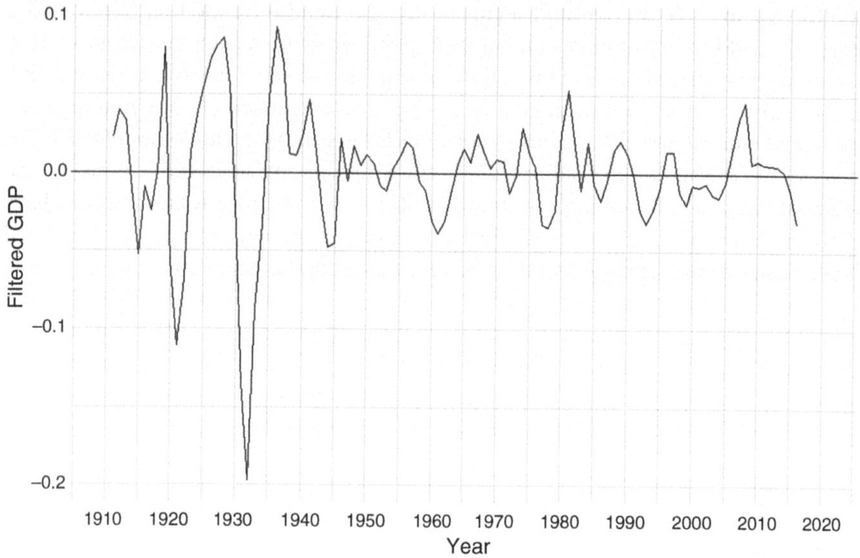

Fig. 7 Deviation cycles of South African GDP, with trend estimated using a Hodrick–Prescott filter. Source: Own calculations

3.1 Volatility

Figure 7 reports the deviation cycle for our new GDP measure. As noted in the review chapter of this book, cycles in GDP provide a sufficient approximation to the overall business cycle. We can therefore confidently assert that economic volatility declines substantially over the twentieth century: the standard deviation of the cycle declines from 7.1% for 1911–1940 to 2.1% for 1940–1970. Thereafter volatility is relatively stable, with a cycle standard deviation of 2.2% for 1970–1990 and 1.8% for 1990–2016. Note that the longer sample period 1990–2016 does mask the significantly lower volatility of the pre-crisis period.

One way to understand the interaction between cycles and structural change is to extract deviation cycles for individual sectors of the South African economy, as reported in Appendix 2. Table 1 reports the standard deviation of the sectoral cycles over the same four periods.

The standard deviation properties suggest a number of key cyclical patterns over the past 100 years. Firstly, a great many sectors (with the notable exception of government expenditure), experienced a decline in cyclical volatility in the second period (1940–1970) followed by an increase in the third period (1970–1990) and then a further moderation in the post-1990 period. The latter moderation is relatively well known and is evident from the results in Burger (2009) and Du Plessis and Kotzé (2010), who find a significant reduction in the volatility of South African business cycles from the period 1976–1994 to the period 1994–

Table 1 The standard deviation of the sectoral cycles, 1911–2016

	1911–1940	1940–1970	1970–1990	1990–2016
GDP (%)	7.1	2.1	2.2	1.8
Agriculture (%)	14.5	8.8	10.1	7.7
Transport (%)	6.4	3.4	3.6	5.0
Mining (%)	10.7	9.4	14.6	7.6
Manufacturing (%)	6.9	3.8	5.4	3.6
Construction (%)	19.3	13.7	9.9	9.9
Electricity (%)	4.8	4.6	10.1	9.1
Wholesale (%)	10.6	6.3	6.6	2.2
Finance (%)	6.4	6.3	6.2	2.9
Personal services (%)	5.6	2.8	4.1	2.6
Government (%)	9.2	12.0	3.8	3.3

2006. More interesting is the first moderation, which is likely due to accelerated trend growth (and hence reduced the importance of cyclical fluctuations) during 1940–1970. One could argue that political developments would have been key to the subsequent increase in volatility (refer to Laubscher's assessment, in a separate chapter, of cyclical experience since the 1980s). Mining—a key driver of cyclical activity since the early part of the twentieth century—experienced the most volatile of cycles in the 1970–1990 period. Secondly, and related, it is clear (as is often argued) that cycles in services sectors are significantly less volatile than those in the primary and secondary sectors. Even so, thirdly, it would seem that the traditionally more volatile primary and secondary sector cycles also moderated. For example, agriculture, which represented a major part of GDP in the early twentieth century, was characterized by volatile cyclical activity in the period before 1940, mostly owing to frequent droughts. The subsequent decline in volatility in 1940 to 1970 certainly contributed to the general moderation of our cyclical fluctuations; the benefits of technological improvements (drought-resistant crops) and infrastructure (dams) would help to explain this moderation. Finally, it is noteworthy that government expenditure has become one of the most stable in terms of cyclical volatility. In some ways, at least for the 1970–1990 period, it represents a constant increase in expenditure. Barring the trend though, this stability suggests that the government has not engaged in countercyclical policy to any significant extent since the 1970s. We return to this issue below.

3.2 Co-movement

Structural changes, as reflected in the relative ascendancy or decline of individual sectors, should be reflected in the correlation between the cycles of individual sectors and the aggregate business cycle. We study this changing correlation by calculating contemporaneous correlation coefficients for a rolling window of 20

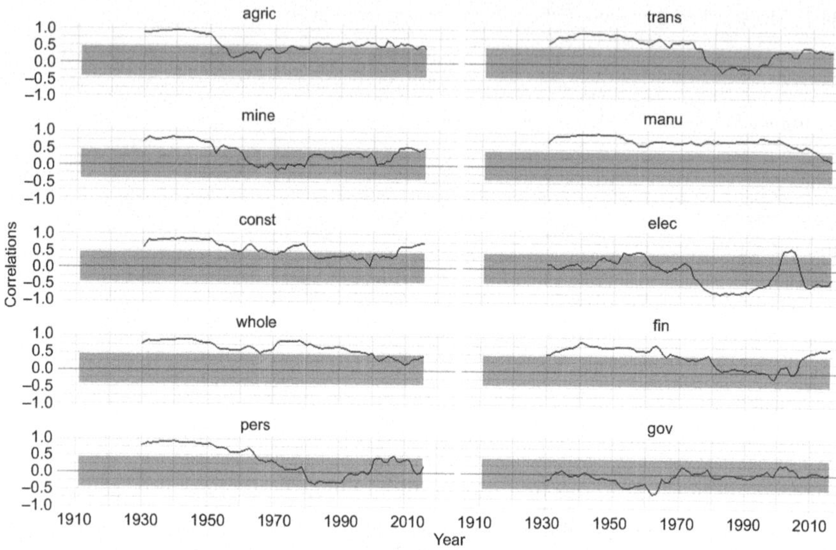

Fig. 8 20-year rolling correlations between cycles in GDP and those in other sectors

years and also perform a robustness check for a window of 40 years. For the 20-year rolling window (Fig. 8), the correlation coefficient at any given point in time must differ by at least 0.4 from a coefficient at another point in time, in order for the difference to be considered statistically significant (0.3 for a 40-year rolling period).[3] Table 2 also shows which sectoral cycles have significant rolling correlations with GDP cycles over various periods.

The correlation graphs offer a summary of the interplay between business cycles and structural transformation in the South African economy. The first rolling correlation, for 1930 (based on data from 1911 to 1930), shows that cycles in a great many sectors are correlated with cycles in GDP during the early parts of the twentieth century. Put differently, even before WWII, the South African economy has tightly co-moving sectors. The pervasive co-movement of the various sectors expands and persists until around 1960, after which it declines.

As structural transformation takes hold after 1960, the services sectors grow rapidly (and independent of cyclical developments) and the correlation of their cycles and those in GDP declines concomitantly (with the exception of wholesale services; as shown in the first column of Table 2). That is, as the rolling period moves on to include more data of the 1960s, the accompanying correlations decline towards zero; even as the economy becomes more service oriented, its cycles are—at

[3] $Tr^2\ \chi^2(1)$ with T the length of the window and r^2 the squared correlation coefficient implies that $r \sim \frac{1}{\sqrt{T}} z$ with $z\ N(0, 1)$. Therefore, a symmetric 95% confidence band for r would be calculated as $\pm\frac{1}{\sqrt{T}}1.96$ which equals approximately 0.4 for $T = 20$.

Table 2 Sectoral cycles with significant rolling correlations with GDP cycles, over various periods

	1911–1930	Between 1921–1940 and 1941–1960	Between 1941–1960 and 1961–1980	Between 1961–1980 and 1981–2000	Between 1981–2000 and 1998–2017
Agriculture	X	X	X	X	
Mining	X	X		X	
Manufacturing	X	X		X	
Construction		X			
Electricity				X	
Transport		X	X		X
Finance		X			X
Personal services	X	X	X		X
Wholesale	X	X	X	X	X
Government expenditure					

least until the 1980s—very much dominated by cycles in the primary and secondary sectors. The low correlation persists until around 2000. For finance, the decoupling appears to hold from 1960 until 2000,[4] for personal services from 1970 until 2000, and for transport from 1980 until 2000. After 2000, the correlations between the service sector cycles and the aggregate business cycle increase again.

The changes in correlations between sectoral and aggregate cycles are evident for the primary and secondary sectors. Reflecting the structural transformation of the economy, the correlation between business cycles and cycles in the primary sector grows weaker. For agriculture there is a gradual decline—so much so that the correlation between agricultural cycles and business cycles is significantly lower by the late 1990s compared to the period prior to the 1940s and become zero (or, not significantly different from zero) after 2000. The experience in mining is mixed: mining cycles are significantly correlated with business cycles until 1960, again over the period 1980–2000, and again in the post-2010 period.

As far as the secondary sector is concerned, the recent decline in the historically tight relationship between manufacturing and the business cycle is important. The manufacturing sector maintains a high and significant correlation with the larger business cycle from 1910 until 2000, after which the correlation declines rapidly. This would suggest weakening predictive power. The SARB's composite leading indicator of the South African business cycle does not include manufacturing-related variables. While Laubscher's (2014) multivariate approach includes manufacturing-related variables, manufacturing—in contrast to other variables in Laubscher's approach—often signals additional cycles after 2000 (see Boshoff and Du Plessis 2020).

[4]See the earlier chapter by Boshoff and Du Plessis (2020) for a review of the relationship between cycles in financial variables and the South African business cycle.

The rapid weakening of the relationship between manufacturing and the aggregate business cycle after 2000 is different from the gradual decline that is observed in the primary sector, especially for agriculture. The correlation between cycles in the construction sector and that of GDP cycles fluctuates significantly over the past 100 years. In addition, there is no consistent and significant correlation between cycles in electricity generation and GDP over most of the past 100 years, especially after 1960. There is, however, some evidence of counter-cyclicality: after 2005 (post the electricity crisis) electricity generation grows substantially (and arguably contra to economic growth).

All of these changes leave an economy, from the late 1990s, where the services sector cycles are tightly co-moving with aggregate business cycles, because of their dominance in GDP, while the primary and secondary sector follow their own cyclical patterns. Strikingly, and as alluded to earlier, there is virtually zero correlation between cycles in government expenditure and the aggregate business cycle over much of the past 100 years, with only the late 1970s suggesting some evidence of pro-cyclicality. The latter would be consistent with the results in an earlier chapter in this volume, where Boshoff and Du Plessis (2020) find that South African literature on fiscal cyclicality—at least literature based on deviation cycle concepts—generally favours concluding pro-cyclicality when relying on data after 1960. Even so, even this conclusion is dependent on the particular cyclical concept. It is noteworthy that our longer term results suggest that there was never a strong relationship between fiscal policy and the GDP cycle and that this relationship has remained weak, despite the rapid rise in the size of government expenditure over the past 40 years.

4 Conclusions

As our new GDP and sectoral series show, the South African economy has transformed over the course of the twentieth century. For the first time, it is possible to study systematically the impact that this has had on the business cycle—and its sectoral components. This systematic analysis produces two important insights. Firstly, the business cycle experienced two periods of moderation (one in the 1940–1970 period and one in the post-democracy period), both associated with strong economic growth. Secondly, the diffusion of the business cycle across sectors weakened substantially from the first part of the twentieth century, during which almost all sectoral cycles shared a tight correlation with the aggregate cycle. The transformation towards a services-based economy initially weakened the correlation between the various services cycles (including finance and retail), leaving much of the aggregate cycle related to fluctuations in agriculture, mining and manufacturing. After the 1990s, these traditional links break down, resulting in a business cycle strongly linked to various cycles in services. These descriptive insights represent but a first step in exploiting longer historical time-series data to understand South African economic changes.

Appendices

Appendix 1

Year	Nominal GDP at factor cost	Deflator	Real GDP at factor cost (constant 2010 prices)	GDP growth
1911	307	0.34	90,891	
1912	324	0.35	92,642	1.93
1913	326	0.35	92,263	−0.41
1914	311	0.35	88,504	−4.07
1915	315	0.37	85,345	−3.57
1916	352	0.39	89,787	5.20
1917	384	0.43	89,395	−0.44
1918	426	0.46	92,907	3.93
1919	519	0.51	102,284	10.09
1920	572	0.63	90,983	−11.05
1921	503	0.57	88,322	−2.92
1922	450	0.47	94,729	7.25
1923	489	0.46	106,135	12.04
1924	525	0.47	112,500	6.00
1925	550	0.47	118,270	5.13
1926	569	0.46	124,120	4.95
1927	595	0.46	129,049	3.97
1928	616	0.46	133,629	3.55
1929	614	0.46	133,559	−0.05
1930	565	0.45	125,807	−5.80
1931	510	0.43	117,965	−6.23
1932	478	0.41	115,642	−1.97
1933	545	0.40	135,522	17.19
1934	616	0.41	151,214	11.58
1935	705	0.41	173,865	14.98
1936	786	0.41	193,199	11.12
1937	834	0.42	200,370	3.71
1938	865	0.43	200,702	0.17
1939	914	0.43	212,204	5.73
1940	1011	0.45	226,790	6.87
1941	1142	0.47	244,847	7.96
1942	1267	0.51	250,492	2.31
1943	1355	0.54	252,608	0.84
1944	1437	0.56	258,779	2.44
1945	1552	0.57	272,314	5.23
1946	1696	0.57	298,523	9.62

(continued)

Year	Nominal GDP at factor cost	Deflator	Real GDP at factor cost (constant 2010 prices)	GDP growth
1947	1877	0.62	305,044	2.18
1948	2075	0.63	327,613	7.40
1949	2256	0.66	339,374	3.59
1950	2622	0.73	358,207	5.55
1951	2836	0.76	373,534	4.28
1952	3048	0.79	385,628	3.24
1953	3455	0.86	402,298	4.32
1954	3710	0.87	427,742	6.32
1955	3897	0.86	450,709	5.37
1956	4205	0.88	476,642	5.75
1957	4433	0.89	496,918	4.25
1958	4555	0.89	509,184	2.47
1959	4802	0.90	530,817	4.25
1960	5109	0.94	546,387	2.93
1961	5402	0.95	570,017	4.32
1962	5754	0.95	604,842	6.11
1963	6377	0.98	649,076	7.31
1964	6999	1.00	698,486	7.61
1965	7675	1.03	743,972	6.51
1966	8373	1.08	777,633	4.52
1967	9332	1.12	833,153	7.14
1968	10,062	1.16	865,459	3.88
1969	11,225	1.25	897,403	3.69
1970	12,303	1.30	943,146	5.10
1971	13,588	1.38	982,630	4.19
1972	15,384	1.54	1,001,764	1.95
1973	19,120	1.82	1,051,434	4.96
1974	23,655	2.11	1,122,023	6.71
1975	26,626	2.34	1,139,636	1.57
1976	30,027	2.58	1,163,713	2.11
1977	33,073	2.87	1,153,041	−0.92
1978	37,832	3.20	1,181,735	2.49
1979	45,072	3.68	1,223,546	3.54
1980	60,506	4.60	1,315,295	7.50
1981	69,917	5.07	1,380,023	4.92
1982	78,171	5.77	1,353,635	−1.91
1983	89,977	6.73	1,337,146	−1.22
1984	104,760	7.50	1,396,546	4.44
1985	120,568	8.76	1,375,918	−1.48
1986	141,146	10.27	1,374,922	−0.07
1987	165,210	11.75	1,405,789	2.24

(continued)

Year	Nominal GDP at factor cost	Deflator	Real GDP at factor cost (constant 2010 prices)	GDP growth
1988	195,819	13.53	1,447,029	2.93
1989	232,893	15.86	1,468,116	1.46
1990	269,242	18.32	1,469,775	0.11
1991	310,308	21.19	1,464,699	−0.35
1992	350,900	24.27	1,445,694	−1.30
1993	398,088	27.42	1,451,658	0.41
1994	447,241	30.03	1,489,067	2.58
1995	507,960	33.10	1,534,735	3.07
1996	573,226	35.71	1,605,142	4.59
1997	632,844	38.55	1,641,761	2.28
1998	681,321	41.54	1,640,112	−0.10
1999	743,852	44.48	1,672,371	1.97
2000	844,247	48.41	1,743,862	4.27
2001	936,503	52.09	1,797,714	3.09
2002	1,089,462	58.47	1,863,261	3.65
2003	1,184,333	61.86	1,914,592	2.75
2004	1,304,876	65.90	1,980,213	3.43
2005	1,440,741	69.49	2,073,413	4.71
2006	1,616,581	73.83	2,189,508	5.60
2007	1,857,779	80.37	2,311,623	5.58
2008	2,109,753	87.46	2,412,125	4.35
2009	2,245,638	94.03	2,388,258	−0.99
2010	2,459,568	100.00	2,459,568	2.99
2011	2,679,710	106.53	2,515,399	2.27
2012	2,884,767	112.16	2,572,007	2.25
2013	3,128,791	119.06	2,627,827	2.17
2014	3,351,263	125.67	2,666,752	1.48
2015	3,553,443	132.10	2,689,878	0.87
2016	3,803,374	141.05	2,696,419	0.24
2017	4,087,551	148.86	2,745,857	1.83

Appendix 2

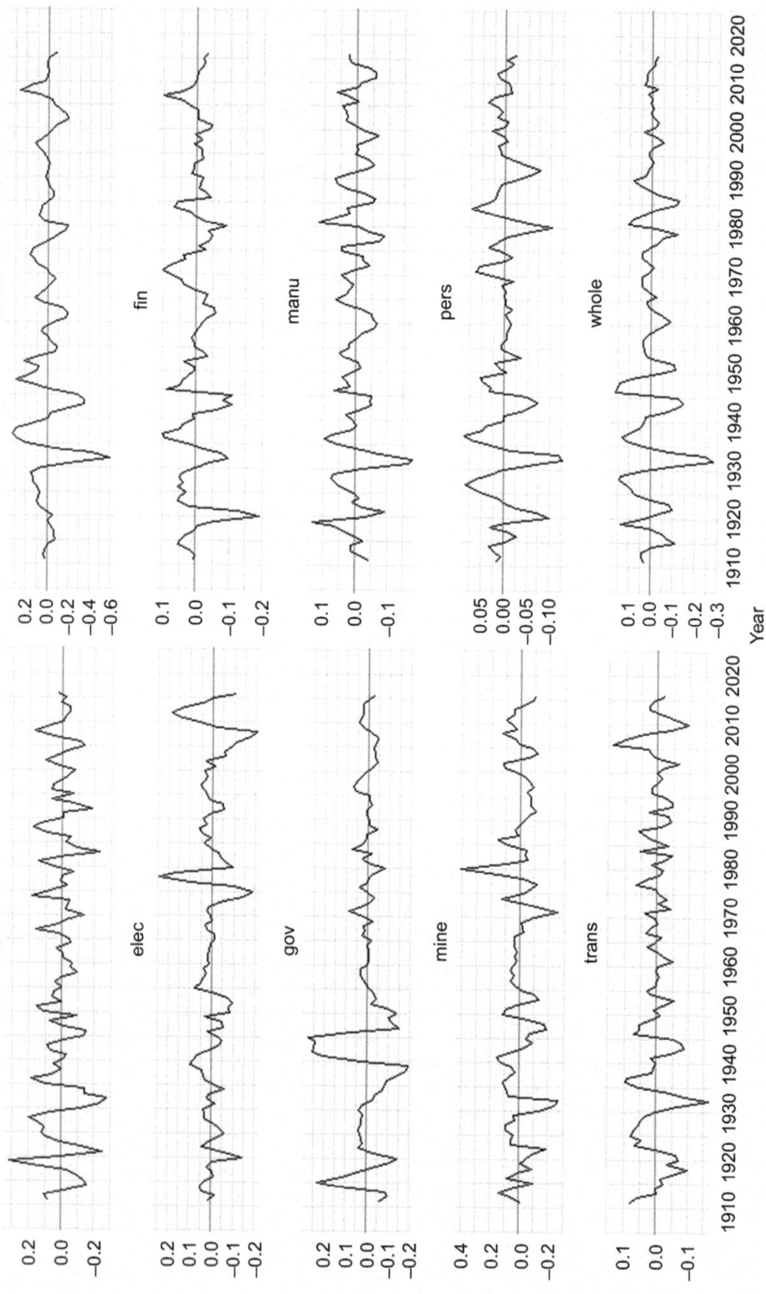
agric
elec
gov
mine
trans
const
fin
manu
pers
whole
1910 1920 1930 1940 1950 1960 1970 1980 1990 2000 2010 2020
Year

References

Bai, J., & Perron, P. (2003). Computation and analysis of multiple structural change models. *Journal of Applied Econometrics, 18*(1), 1–22.

Boshoff, W. H. (2008). Rethinking ASGISA and the Rand exchange rate. *South African Journal of Economic and Management Sciences, 11*(1), 113–118.

Boshoff, W. H., & du Plessis, S. A. (2020). *What do we know about the South African business cycle?* Heidelberg: Springer.

Boshoff, W. H., & McLean, L. (2018). What do deviation cycles measure? An analysis of the informational content of filter-based business cycles. *South African Journal of Economic and Management Sciences, 21*(1), 1–11.

Botha, D. P. J. (1968). *Report no. 09-10-01: Gross domestic product at factor cost.* Pretoria: Statistical Office.

Bureau for Census and Statistics. (1960). *Union statistics for fifty years. Jubilee issue.* Pretoria: Union of South Africa.

Burger, P. (2009). The South African business cycle: What has changed? *South African Journal of Economic and Management Sciences, 13*(1), 26–49.

Du Plessis, S., & Kotzé, K. (2010). The great moderation of the South African business cycle. *Economic History of Developing Regions, 25*(1), 105–125.

Du Plessis, S., & Smit, B. (2007). South Africa's growth revival after 1994. *Journal of African Economies, 16*(5), 668–704.

Du Plessis, S., & Smit, B. (2009). South Africa's growth revival after 1994. In J. Aron, B. Kahn, & G. Kingdon (Eds.), *South African economic policy under democracy* (pp. 28–57). Oxford: Oxford University Press.

Du Plessis, S., Smit, B., & Sutrzenegger, F. (2008). Identifying aggregate supply and demand shocks in South Africa. *Journal of African Economies, 17*(5), 765–793.

Fedderke, J., & Simkins, C. (2012). Economic growth in South Africa. *Economic History of Developing Regions, 27*(1), 176–208.

Fourie, J., & van Zanden, J.-L. (2013). GDP in the Dutch Cape Colony: The National Accounts of a slave-based society. *South African Journal of Economics, 81*(4), 467–490.

Greyling, L., & Verhoef, G. (2015). Slow growth, supply shocks and structural change: The GDP of the cape Colony in the late nineteenth century. *Economic History of Developing Regions, 30*(1), 23–43.

Hausmann, R. (2008). *Final recommendations of the international panel on growth.* Pretoria: National Treasury.

Herranz-Loncan, A., & Fourie, J. (2018). 'For the public benefit?' Railways in the British Cape Colony. *European Review of Economic History, 22*(1), 73–100.

Jones, S., & Müller, A. (1992). *The South African economy, 1910–1990.* London: Macmillan.

Kydland, F. E., & Prescott, E. C. (1990). "Business cycles: Real facts and a monetary myth." *Federal Reserve Bank of Minneapolis. Quarterly Review, 14*, 3–18.

Laubscher, P. (2014). *A new recession-dating algorithm for South Africa* (Stellenbosch Economic Working Papers 06/14).

Levy, P. I. (1999). Sanctions on South Africa: What did they do? *American Economic Review, 89*(2), 415–420.

Mpeta, B., Fourie, J., & Inwood, K. (2018). Black living standards in South Africa before democracy: New evidence from height. *South African Journal of Science, 114*(1–2), 1–8.

Nattrass, N., & Seekings, J. (2011). The economy and poverty in the twentieth century. In R. Ross, A. Mager, & B. Nasson (Eds.), *The Cambridge history of South Africa, 1885–1994* (Vol. 2, pp. 518–572). Cambridge: Cambridge University Press.

Ramela, O. A. (2018). *The evolution of occupational structures in South Africa 1875–1911: an analysis of the effects of the resource curse and blessing*. Masters dissertation, Stellenbosch: Stellenbosch Univeristy.

South African Reserve Bank (SARB). (2018). Online download facility. Accessed July 1, 2018, from www.resbank.co.za

Part II
The Financial Crisis and Its Impact on the Cycle

Business Cycle Recoveries: A Comparative View

W. H. Boshoff and L. H. Becker

The weak expansion, in many economies, following the Great Recession has shifted attention to understanding how financial crises and deep recessions affect subsequent business cycle expansions. One body of literature, drawing heavily on past US experience, studies the properties of the first stage of an expansion, called the recovery phase. Historically, US recovery phases have been characterised by strong, resurgent growth. The absence of such a resurgence following the global financial crisis has been seen as an important precursor of the subsequent lethargic growth in the USA.

The presence of a distinct recovery phase in US business cycles raises the general question of whether business cycles in most economies—including South Africa's—are also characterised by such distinct recovery phases. While South Africa escaped the worst of the financial crisis, the subsequent business cycle upswing was equally uninspiring. The preceding chapters have shown that South African business cycle expansions—with the exception of the pre-crisis expansion—have grown progressively weaker. Therefore, studying the properties of recoveries—and their relation to broader business expansions—within a broader international context may provide economists with a better understanding of the drivers of weak upswings in South Africa.

The following section sets out the literature on recoveries, suggesting an alternative method for recovery identification and outlining important properties of

W. H. Boshoff
Department of Economics, Stellenbosch University, Stellenbosch, South Africa
e-mail: wimpie2@sun.ac.za

L. H. Becker (✉)
Prescient Investment Management, Cape Town, South Africa
e-mail: louis.becker@prescient.co.za

W. H. Boshoff (ed.), *Business Cycles and Structural Change in South Africa*, Advances in African Economic, Social and Political Development,
https://doi.org/10.1007/978-3-030-35754-2_4

recoveries. A subsequent section introduces the methodology for identification and study of recoveries, followed by the South African results.

1 Recoveries

The aftermath of the financial crisis has prompted a response in business cycle research. The empirical literature prior to 2008 is fairly unanimous in finding that deep recessions tend to be followed by strong expansions—at least in the developed world. When the post-crisis expansion turned out to be weak, economists started questioning the stylized facts. One part of the recent academic effort is devoted to studying the first stage in business cycle expansions, called recoveries. Historically, business cycle recoveries in the USA are characterized by 'bounce-back' growth (Friedman 1969): deep recessions are followed by strong recoveries [for empirical work, see Zarnowitz (1992), Wynne and Balke (1992) and Sichel (1994)]. The recent recovery did not display this regularity, leading economists to investigate how a financial crisis may change the relationship between recession and recovery.

The literature on the business cycle effects of financial crises generally focuses on business cycle expansions as a whole, as opposed to only the initial recovery. Claessens et al. (2012), for example, find that expansions following recessions related to financial crises are generally weaker than other expansions. This finding, however, is sensitive to how much of the expansion is being considered. Bordo and Haubrich (2017) argue that the slow 2009 recovery, together with slow recoveries post-Depression and in the early 1990s, are exceptions: excluding these three, US recoveries since 1880 are typically stronger following recessions related to a financial crisis. Howard et al. (2011) find similarly positive support for bounce-back recoveries, based on a cross section of 59 countries since 1970. The choice of cycle phase (recovery versus entire expansion) therefore matters when determining stylized facts on the impact of financial crises on business cycles.

Bordo and Haubrich (2017) emphasise that their findings are sensitive to the particular definition of recovery: when recoveries are defined to last as long as preceding recessions, the 'bounce-back' result is stronger than when recoveries are defined to last for a fixed duration. In fact, the broader recovery literature employs a variety of definitions for recovery, which can be grouped into duration-based and trend-based definitions.

Duration-based definitions underlie regime-switching models for business cycle identification. Using Markov-switching models with a predetermined recovery duration of six quarters, Morley and Piger (2012) and Kim et al. (2005) model 'bounce-back' recoveries in the US. Fatás and Mihov (2013) use similar models, and additional post-crisis data, to argue that the behaviour of recoveries has changed. Furthermore, employing a different methodological approach, Howard et al. (2011) use a recovery duration of 3 years to delineate recoveries. In earlier work, Balke and Wynne (1995) follow a method similar to that employed by Burns and Mitchell,

Table 1 Average quarterly output growth (annualized) in South Africa and other economies in the first two quarters and subsequent four quarters of an official business cycle expansion, 1960–2015

	Full sample	Quarters 1–2 After recession	Quarters 3–6 After recession
South Africa[a]	3.1%	4.5%	4.5%
Number of cycles		10	9
United States[b]	3.1%	5.3%	4.1%
Number of cycles		8	7
United Kingdom[c]	2.4%	4.5%	3.4%
Number of cycles		13	10
Australia[d]	3.5%	3.1%	3.8%
Number of cycles		14	10

Notes: [a]Recessions identified by the South African Reserve Bank
[b]Recessions identified by the National Bureau of Economic Research
[c]Recessions identified by the OECD
[d]Recessions identified by the Melbourne Institute

dividing expansion phases into three equal parts and studying the initial part as recovery.

One of the limitations facing a duration-based analysis is its implicit assumption that the growth acceleration characterizing a recovery phase occurs immediately after the trough. This assumption, deriving from the US experience discussed earlier, may limit the ability to elucidate recoveries displaying different properties. Table 1 reports, for the period 1960 to 2015, average growth in each of the first eight quarters following a recession in South Africa, the USA, the UK and Australia. The 'bounce-back' behaviour of US (and, to an extent, UK) cycles are evident from this table: in these countries, growth in the first two quarters of an upswing is rapid relative to subsequent quarters.

In contrast, the earliest quarters of South African and Australian upswings are characterized by relatively moderate growth, suggesting that growth gains momentum more gradually in these countries. In fact, as discussed later, it would appear that the growth acceleration that ends recessions in South Africa peters out quickly after the trough, leading to a slow start to the recovery. Growth acceleration—if it materializes—often occurs a couple of quarters after a cyclical trough. An analysis based on a fixed duration for business cycle recoveries therefore underemphasises the heterogeneity of cyclical recoveries across economies. A duration-based analysis is also inconsistent with the finding in the empirical literature that cycles and cycle phases are not periodic.

Another part of the literature on recoveries relies on a trend-based definition: this approach views a recovery as a period during which output is returning to its long-run growth path. This body of literature distinguishes between return to peak output levels or to long-run output growth. In addition to using a duration-based definition of four quarters, Sichel (1994), Kannan et al. (2009) and Claessens et al. (2012), as well as Hall and McDermott (2016) define a recovery as the time required to return output to its peak level prior to the recession. Some studies adjust pre-crisis peak levels to reflect counterfactual trend growth (Fatás and Mihov 2013). An alternative approach defines recovery instead as the time it takes to return output to a long-run trend growth rate (Papell and Prodan 2012). This sets a lower benchmark, by accepting that recovery is achieved even if permanent output loss has occurred.

One challenge facing a trend-based definition is the difficulty of identifying the appropriate long-run counterfactual growth rate. In particular, recent work considers the impact of financial crises on potential output (Cerra and Saxena 2008).

A trend-based definition emphasises a particular property of recovery, namely recovery of recession output loss. This focus departs from the original Burns–Mitchell view of recovery as a revival stage in the expansion. In their original work, Burns and Mitchell (1946) identified three business cycle phases: recession, revival and prosperity. The revival phase was central to their view of the business cycle as a diffused phenomenon across various sectors—the revival stage is that initial stage of the cycle during which output growth is gathering momentum and spreading across sectors. In this view, it is diffusion and momentum that characterise a recovery, rather than its performance relative to a long-run growth benchmark. Such a view enables the identification and analysis of a broader set of recoveries—including weaker recoveries.

Consequently, this chapter proposes a definition of recovery that is neither duration nor trend dependent. In particular, as set out below, we define the recovery period as the period until the initial growth acceleration reaches its peak. This definition reaches back to the revival concept of Burns and Mitchell, discussed above, and emphasises the increased momentum of an economy 'building up speed' after the trough.

2 Methodology

A study of recovery phases requires, firstly, a method for the identification of such phases and, secondly, an approach to studying the properties of recovery phases. The following section discusses each in turn.

2.1 *Identification of Recovery Phases*

Following the cycle nomenclature introduced earlier in this book, our identification of recoveries relies on growth rate cycles. In particular, we are interested in the growth rate cycle coinciding with and following the trough. We seek specifically to identify the peak of this growth rate cycle (${x_t}^{GP}$), which can be identified using the following calculus rule:

$$\left\{ (\Delta x_{t-k}, \ldots, \Delta x_{t-1}) < \Delta {x_t}^{GP} > (\Delta x_{t+1}, \ldots, \Delta x_{t+k}) \right\}$$

A set of censoring rules is applied to the series of potential peaks. The censoring rules specify a minimum length of two quarters for a phase and five quarters for a cycle. These rules are similar to the ones conventionally applied to identify classical cycle turning points.

A recovery phase commences with the start of the upswing and ends when the growth rate cycle, coinciding with the start of the upswing, reaches a peak. In other words, the recovery phase is the period of accelerating growth following a business cycle trough. Formally, x_t is part of the recovery phase if it meets the following calculus rule:

$$\left\{ x_t : x^{T^-} < x_t < x^{\mathrm{GP}^+} \right\}$$

where x^{T^-} is the business cycle trough preceding x_t and x^{GP^+} is the first growth rate peak following x_t. As discussed in the results section, we will rely on official business cycle chronologies (such as the one generated by the SARB), to identify business cycle troughs and peaks.

We test the sensitivity of results to the particular definition by also considering a fixed-duration recovery, according to which the first four quarters of an expansion is defined as a recovery phase.

2.2 *Assessing Whether Recovery Is a Distinct Business Cycle Phase*

As 'recovery' denotes accelerated growth, the next step is to test formally whether mean growth during recovery is different from mean growth during the rest of the expansion. This can be achieved by a standard two-sided t-test. Alternatively, one may test whether recovery growth rates and growth rates for the remainder of an expansion are generated by the same probability distribution using a two-sample Kolmogorov–Smirnov (KS) test, utilising its asymptotic properties in finite samples (Conover 1971: 295–314).

2.3 *Analysis of Recovery Phases*

For those countries for which distinct recovery phases can be identified, we derive standard properties of such phases. Stylized facts about recoveries provide a historical standard against which to compare any particular recovery (Sichel 1994: 277). In particular, the turning point approach to the identification of cycle phases enables a descriptive analysis of recoveries using phase statistics, such as duration, amplitude and steepness. Phase statistics require the definition of an indicator variable, s_t^{recovery}, which equals unity when the cycle is in a recovery phase:

$$s_t^{\text{recovery}} = I\left\{x_t : x^{T^-} < x_t < x^{\text{GP}^+}\right\}$$

$$s_t^{\text{recovery}} = 0 \text{ otherwise}$$

Therefore, similar to previous chapters, the sample average duration of a recovery, $\hat{\boldsymbol{D}}^{\text{recovery}}$, is estimated as:

$$\hat{\boldsymbol{D}}^{\text{recovery}} = \boldsymbol{n}_{\text{recovery}}^{-1} \sum_{t=1}^{T} \boldsymbol{s}_t^{\text{recovery}}$$

with $\boldsymbol{n}_{\text{recovery}}$ the number of recovery phases in the sample period.

Similar statistics can be calculated for recession and prosperity phases. Information on duration is supplemented by sample measures of recovery phase amplitude ($\hat{\boldsymbol{A}}^{\text{recovery}}$) and steepness ($\hat{\boldsymbol{\Omega}}^{\text{recovery}}$):

$$\hat{\boldsymbol{A}}^{\text{recovery}} = \boldsymbol{n}_{\text{recovery}}^{-1} \sum_{t=1}^{T} \boldsymbol{s}_t^{\text{recovery}} \boldsymbol{\Delta}\left(\boldsymbol{x}_t\right)$$

$$\hat{\boldsymbol{\Omega}}^{\text{recovery}} = \frac{\hat{\boldsymbol{A}}^{\text{recovery}}}{\hat{\boldsymbol{D}}^{\text{recovery}}}$$

To understand why recoveries may differ, and what drives recoveries, this chapter also explores the behaviour of various components of aggregate expenditure in individual recoveries, i.e. that of consumption, investment, government consumption and net exports. Wynne and Balke (1992) show that durable consumption and residential investment in the USA show strong recovery features, with rapid growth during the early stages of an expansion. Hall and McDermott (2016) consider the behaviour of these components over the two most recent recoveries in New Zealand. They find that the stronger recovery of the 1990s was characterised by a combination of private investment and durable consumption, assisted by exports. In the South African context, Burger (2008, 2010) finds no significant role for inventories in explaining the reduced volatility of South African output. This may well be related to the behaviour of South African recoveries, which, as will be shown later, are not characterised by bounce-back growth.

To analyse the impact of components of aggregate expenditure on recoveries, we compare the internal properties of each recovery, as set out previously, with average growth in the various components.

3 Data

3.1 Data for Cross-Country Comparative Analysis

For the international comparative analysis, a GDP dataset is compiled from the International Monetary Fund's (IMF) International Financial Statistics (IFS 2016) database and from the Organisation for Economic Co-operation and Development's (OECD) Main Economic Indicators (MEI 2016) database.[1] Combining these two datasets provides a sizable set of countries that are readily examinable. In cases where GDP series for countries are present in both datasets, we have confirmed the substitutability of the series.[2]

The IFS database covers a group of 88 countries, while the MEI database includes series for the 34 OECD members and 7 non-member countries. The time series are of different lengths with GDP figures for the likes of Japan, Canada and the USA available as far back as 1958. Other countries such as those from South America, Africa and Asia typically have data available from the late 1990s (and later) only. South Africa is the exception to this group, having GDP data readily available from 1960. The length of the series for each country in the analysis set ranges from the first quarter for which it is available up until late 2015 or early 2016. Exception was made for a small combination of Latin American and African countries, along with Russia, for which GDP ranged up until the end of 2014. The longest series in the analysis set span 234 quarters, or just under 60 years. Countries with series spanning less than 15 years, or 60 quarters, are not considered.

The non-parametric approach to turning point identification, employed in this chapter, is invariant to the overall length of the series, in contrast to trend-fitting parametric techniques that are sensitive to the choice of sample period. Furthermore, in the analysis of recoveries, growth rates are pooled and tested for each individual country, which allows for consideration of time series of different lengths.

The IFS dataset boasts a bigger group of countries and longer series than the MEI dataset. However, some challenges emerge when scrutinizing the IFS dataset. Firstly, only 17 of the 88 IFS countries report seasonally adjusted GDP, whereas all the series in MEI have been seasonally adjusted. The IFS series are therefore adjusted, where appropriate, using the US Census Bureau's seasonal adjustment procedure.[3] After seasonal adjustment, the real GDP series for most countries appear well behaved, save for Denmark and Norway (for which we rely

[1]We access the data using the Quantec (2016) EasyData web portal. From IFS, indexed GDP volume series were downloaded, and from MEI the series named '*stock figures* at constant prices'.

[2]This is especially the case for countries with well-documented GDP data, including the USA, the UK and South Africa. For some countries present in both datasets, seasonal adjustment of GDP data was required. The two seasonally adjusted series were not always replicas of one other, but did show a high enough degree of concordance to justify treating them as substitutes.

[3]The X-12 procedure in EViews is employed, with the default multiplicative ARIMA(1,1,0) model specification.

on MEI data[4]). Secondly, data anomalies for Portugal and Greece IFS data require substitution with MEI data.[5]

The final dataset consists of 67 countries, of which 29 are developed countries and 38 are emerging market economies. The IFS source is used as the basis for the analysis and is augmented with MEI series for four countries as needed. A complete list of the countries in this dataset along with their sources is provided in Appendix 1.

Countries with longer series may experience more recoveries on average (as the expected number of cycles is higher), which increases the accuracy of the tests because of the larger number of observations. To allow for a comparison of the impact of the length of sample period, an arbitrary distinction is made between a 'long' dataset that contains countries whose series span 100 quarters or more and a 'short' dataset that contains countries whose series are shorter than 100 quarters. This distinction splits the broad dataset roughly in half with the long dataset containing 33 countries and the short dataset 34. As expected, most of the countries in the long data set are developed countries, with only six developed countries forming part of the short dataset. The long and short datasets, with their respective lengths and the number of recoveries identified for each country, are reported in Tables 7 and 8 in Appendix 2.

The analysis of components of South African output in the final section relies on macroeconomic data from the South African Reserve Bank's Quarterly Bulletin.

4 Results: Recovery Phases in Business Cycles Internationally

This section sets out the results for an international comparison of recovery phases, based on the IFS dataset of 67 countries discussed earlier.[6] As discussed, the aim is to test the first hypothesis, namely that post-recession bounce-back growth is a common feature of business cycles internationally. As shown in this section, the data strongly rejects this hypothesis, implying no statistical evidence to support the delineation of a separate recovery phase for most countries. The first subsection discusses how we compiled turning point chronologies for each country, while the second subsection presents the results for the recovery phases. A third section

[4]For both Denmark and Norway, we opt for the shorter MEI series. For Denmark, this accounts for a sharp initial divergence between the MEI and the longer IFS series, which is likely the result of the seasonal adjustment. The Norwegian IFS data appears more volatile, resulting in significantly different turning points.

[5]Portuguese IFS data shows a sharp plunge from the last quarter of 1998 to the first quarter of 1999, with no clear economic explanation. The Greek IFS series has missing data from the second quarter of 1991 up to the last quarter of 1998.

[6]This section draws on Becker (2017).

reports briefly on the recovery properties of those countries for which we find evidence of a separate recovery phase.

4.1 Turning Points

As recovery phases are defined by reference to business cycle troughs, there is a natural affinity between the analysis of recoveries and the traditional approach to business cycle analysis focused on turning points. This affinity therefore suggests that a study of recoveries fits well into this book, which has chosen turning point cycles as a primary tool for analysis of the South African cycle.

Official chronologies of business cycle turning points are readily available for the developed economies, as well as selected emerging markets, including South Africa. In the USA, it was the NBER that implemented and extended the Bry–Boschan approach—and extension of the original Burns–Mitchell methodology—to identify business cycle turning points in the USA. In South Africa, as discussed in earlier chapters, the SARB's business cycle research unit continuously monitors the economy for signals of turning points, using a similar approach. The Economic Cycle Research Institute (ECRI) identifies turning points using this method for all of the advanced economies and selected emerging markets. The ECRI turning points match the NBER and SARB dates well.

Turning point chronologies for a number of developed countries, as well as for most developing countries, are not available. Therefore, in order to extend the dataset to include these countries, we manually identify business cycle peaks and troughs for these countries using the BBQ methodology described in an earlier chapter.

The BBQ methodology is, of course, dependent on a single data series (GDP) and does not follow the data-rich approach underlying that of ECRI or any of the official institutions (including SARB). Even so, there is evidence that the BBQ algorithm can reasonably approximate business cycles identified using richer data. A comparison with SARB turning points for South Africa and NBER turning points for the USA suggests that, from the 1980s, the BBQ algorithms identify the same number of cycles as the official chronology, with turning points aligning relatively well between the two chronologies. This is consistent with the findings of Harding and Pagan (2002) for US cycles and Du Plessis (2006) for South African cycles. In the results below, we will indicate, for each country, which business cycle chronology is used.

4.2 Recoveries

Given business cycle turning points for each of the countries, we identify recovery phases using the methodology described earlier. As discussed, we identify recovery phases both on the basis of growth acceleration and using a fixed number of quarters (four) after the start of an expansion. We then conduct the statistical tests described earlier to test the null hypothesis that the identified recovery phases exhibit growth that is statistically significantly higher than growth in post-recovery expansion phases. To ensure robust inference, we set two conditions. Firstly, to reduce false positives, we only report results favouring a distinct recovery phase for those countries for which at least four recoveries could be identified during the sample period, as this number provided a sufficient number of growth observations to avoid small sample bias in both the *t*-test and the KS test (Noether 1963: 115–116; Kolmogorov 1933: 83–91). Secondly, to reduce false negatives, a country is deemed to have a statistically significant recovery phase if any two or more of the statistical tests across the two recovery definitions reject the null hypothesis. If both *t*-tests indicate distinct recovery phases, but the KS tests not, we would consider it sufficient evidence. The odd combination of significance for a fixed-duration KS test and a growth-based *t*-test is also allowed for.

The complete set of *t*- and KS test results for each of the 67 countries in our dataset is reported in Tables 7 and 8 in Appendix 2. These tables report the relevant business cycle turning point chronology used for each country, the relevant sample period for each, as well as the number of recoveries. Table 2 shows only the countries for which statistically significant recoveries were identified based on the above criteria. Note the evidence of bounce-back growth in recovery phases for the USA cycle, which is consistent with the literature.

The *t*-tests for both the fixed and the growth rate definitions show that mean growth is higher in the recovery phase than in the post-recovery phase. The same is true for the Kolmogorov–Smirnov tests, which indicate that US growth rates during recoveries are generated from a different distribution to those from the post-recovery expansions. These tests are all significant at a 90% confidence level.

The second observation is that a distinct recovery phase is not present in the business cycles of most countries. Only 11 countries, of which the USA and Australia are the only developed countries, experience distinct recovery phases. Even if the minimum number of recoveries criterion is relaxed to three (instead of four) recoveries, only Malaysia, Estonia and Turkey are added. This means that the standard approach to demarcating the cycles into two, rather than three, phases are appropriate for most countries. It also implies that the idea that business cycle 'bounce back' after recessions is limited to the USA and a few others.

In fact, another observation concerns the identity of the countries for which significant recoveries are identified. Many of these countries—especially those in Latin America (notably Brazil), as well as Botswana and Australia—are commodity based. Canada narrowly misses out on being included and *t*-tests applied to the OECD version of Canadian data support a distinct recovery phase, for both definitions of recovery. Unfortunately, other commodity producers, notably China and many African countries, are not included in the data set, because of the short length of its series. The only African countries included are South Africa, Morocco and Botswana, due to data constraints. In this sense, one could argue that South Africa, as a commodity producer, is special. South Africa's results robustly show,

Table 2 Countries with significant recovery phases

Country	Data characteristics			Kolmogorov-Smirnov test[a]		*t*-test (one-tailed)[a]	
	Period	Quarters	Recoveries	Fixed	GRP	Fixed	GRP
Americas							
United States	3/31/1958-6/30/2016	234	8	0.25 (0.064*)	0.25 (0.064*)	1.45 (0.077*)	1.67 (0.052*)
Mexico	3/31/1980-3/31/2016	145	6	0.29 (0.070*)	0.30 (0.030**)	1.67 (0.052*)	1.64 (0.054*)
Brazil	3/31/1995-6/30/2016	86	5	0.38 (0.033**)	0.36 (0.068*)	0.70 (0.245)	0.42 (0.34)
Chile	3/31/1980-6/30/2016	146	4	0.18 (0.683)	0.33 (0.046**)	0.25 (0.402)	1.80 (0.043**)
Ecuador	3/31/1991-3/31/2016	101	5	0.30 (0.126)	0.26 (0.226)	1.45 (0.078*)	1.37 (0.091*)
Paraguay	3/31/1994-12/31/2014	84	5	0.34 (0.092*)	0.38 (0.071*)	1.04 (0.153)	0.35 (0.363)
Europe							
Malta	3/31/1996-3/31/2016	81	5	0.20 (0.608)	0.21 (0.599)	1.35 (0.096*)	1.32 (0.099*)
Spain	3/31/1970-6/30/2016	186	3	0.49 (0.007***)	0.25 (0.439***)	−3.44 (0.999)	−0.71 (0.759)
Estonia	3/31/1993-3/31/2016	93	3	0.26 (0.460)	0.37 (0.056*)	0.56 (0.292)	1.76 (0.047**)
Asia-Pacific							
Australia	9/30/1959-6/30/2016	228	4	0.31 (0.088*)	0.41 (0.105)	1.56 (0.069*)	2.06 (0.037**)
Turkey	3/31/1987-3/31/2016	117	6	0.42 (0.003***)	0.50 (0.005***)	3.27 (0.001***)	3.16 (0.003***)
Malaysia	3/31/1988-3/31/2016	113	3	0.38 (0.092*)	0.43 (0.085*)	1.59 (0.069*)	1.23 (0.125)
Africa							
Morocco	3/31/1990-12/31/2014	100	6	0.26 (0.203)	0.32 (0.08*)	1.76 (0.043**)	0.86 (0.200)
Botswana	3/31/1994-3/31/2015	85	4	0.41 (0.058*)	0.43 (0.062*)	1.44 (0.085*)	1.01 (0.167)

[a] *P*-values are shown in brackets
*Significant at $\alpha = 0.1$; **Significant at $\alpha = 0.05$; ***Significant at $\alpha = 0.01$

across SARB, ECRI and BBQ turning points chronologies, that bounce-back growth is not characteristic of its business cycle. This is related to the slow response of investment to an initial boost in exports at the start of our cycles, which results in a relatively muted initial upswing. Subsequent chapters in this volume, by Laubscher (2020) and Hollander and Van Lill (2020), return to this theme.

4.3 Phase Statistics

Table 3 reports the phase statistics for the select countries for which a separate recovery phase is present. The average duration of recoveries in the Americas seems to be longer than the rest, with Mexico having the longest average duration. The maximum duration of recoveries is also similar to that of other countries, except for cycles in the USA and Mexico, both of which exhibit maximum recovery duration of 10 quarters. The maximum recovery duration for Canada, shown in Appendix 2, is nine quarters.

This gives a slight indication of the similarity between the business cycles of these economies. Furthermore, the average amplitude does not seem to vary much across countries, except for Botswana cycles, which exhibit high amplitude relative

Table 3 Recovery phase statistics for GRP (fixed[a]) definition

Country	Recovery quarters	Recoveries	Average duration	Maximum duration (GRP)	Average amplitude
Americas					
United States	32 (32)	8	4 (4)	10	0.05 (0.04)
Mexico	34 (24)	6	5.67 (4)	10	0.07 (0.05)
Brazil	16 (20)	5	3.2 (4)	5	0.04 (0.06)
Chile	19 (16)	4	4.75 (4)	6	0.09 (0.06)
Ecuador	20 (20)	5	4 (4)	5	0.06 (0.06)
Paraguay	15 (19)	5	3 (3.8)	6	0.06 (0.08)
Europe					
Malta	15 (18)	5	3 (3.6)	6	0.05 (0.07)
Spain	19 (12)	3	6.33 (4)	12	0.05 (0.02)
Estonia	16 (12)	3	5.33 (4)	7	0.12 (0.08)
Asia-Pacific					
Australia	8 (16)	4	2 (4)	4	0.03 (0.06)
Turkey	13 (24)	6	2.17 (4)	3	0.07 (0.11)
Malaysia	9 (12)	3	3 (4)	4	0.06 (0.08)
Africa					
Morocco	19 (22)	6	3.17 (3.67)	5	0.07 (0.1)
Botswana	11 (14)	4	2.75 (3.5)	5	0.1 (0.13)

[a]Results for the fixed definition are shown in brackets

to the rest. We also do not find much different results if average amplitude is considered for both definitions in the whole dataset, regardless of whether dated recoveries are statistically significant.

5 Further Disaggregated Results on South African Cyclical Recoveries

Business cycles in most countries—with the notable exception of the USA, as well as various commodity exporters—are not characterized by a distinct 'bounce back' recovery phase, during which growth accelerates very sharply. Recovery therefore gradually gathers pace, also in South Africa. This gradual acceleration is present even in subcomponents of South African output.

Table 4 shows a comparison of quarterly growth rates[7] (annualized) for consumption, investment, government expenditure and net exports in South Africa. The variance of the average growth rates is notably high, suggesting that averages over a longer period may be more informative. Even so, a comparison of average growth for the first two quarters to the subsequent four quarters does not suggest a clustering of high growth in earlier stages for most of the components. In addition, one may argue that a comparison among the first six quarters may not be illuminating, in that the recovery phase may itself span the entire six quarters. Consequently, it may be more informative to compare average growth during the entire identified recovery phase and the remainder of the expansion (the post-recovery expansion phase). Table 5 presents comparative results for the recovery and post-recovery expansion phases and confirms the earlier impression: consumption and government expenditure are generally similar for the two phases, while investment growth is systematically *lower*, not higher, in the earlier phase of an expansion. As attempted earlier, similar results are generated using a fixed-duration recovery definition (four quarters) instead of a methodology based on the growth momentum.

When considering the elements of consumption expenditure, it is striking that durable consumption expenditure appears to be higher later in South African recoveries, which is consistent with international findings. However, unlike the results for net exports discussed below, acceleration in durable consumption does not coincide with the earliest part of an economic recovery in South Africa. Semi-durable consumption does appear to accelerate but only really after the recovery, while non-durable consumption does not appear to change much.

Selected components of investment—specifically, investment by private enterprises, as well as residential building—show similar patterns to the overall investment figure: in both cases, growth rates accelerate later in South African recovery phases but only weakly so: investment remains at levels lower than investment during the rest of the expansion.

---

[7]Some of the growth rates may appear very high, due to annualization.

Table 4 Average quarterly output growth (annualized) in aggregate expenditure components in the first eight quarters of an official business cycle expansion, 1960–2017

Quarters after recessions	1	2	3	4	5	6	7	8	Full sample	Average quarters 1–2	Average quarters 3–6
Consumption (%)	1.9	5.6	4.2	5.2	5.7	6.0	4.9	6.7	3.6	3.7	5.5
Durable consumption (%)	−2.07	3.32	4.85	9.99	12.34	9.58	10.63	11.83	4.0	0.6	9.2
Semi-durable consumption (%)	0.8	2.4	3.1	3.9	5.7	5.8	6.7	7.1	5.0	1.6	4.6
Non-durable consumption (%)	1.8	3.3	2.9	3.00	3.9	3.7	3.6	4.6	2.9	2.6	3.4
Investment (%)	−2.5	−1.7	0.0	7.9	2.4	4.9	12.1	10.9	3.8	−2.1	6.4
Private enterprises (%)	−4.09	−2.13	−3.17	0.18	5.18	5.98	11.31	11.14	4.1	−3.1	2.0
Residential investment (%)	−4.71	−2.96	−4.68	−0.58	1.46	4.09	7.21	5.09	2.0	−3.8	0.1
Government (%)	6.5	0.4	4.7	8.7	2.7	7.0	−3.8	9.4	4.0	3.5	4.8
Net exports (%)	14.0	−6.6	−13.6	−20.9	−28.8	−4.3	−51.8	−3.8	15.6	3.7	−16.9
Net exports (year-on-year) (%)	28.32	17.39	11.55	−9.33	−16.88	−19.79	−26.57	−33.73	23.0	22.9	−8.6
Cycles	10	10	10	10	10	9	8	8			

Table 5 Comparison of average growth for recovery and post-recovery expansion phases in South African business cycle, 1960–2017

	Recovery identified using this chapter's methodology			Recovery of fixed duration (4 quarters)		
	Average growth Recovery (%)	Average growth Post-recovery expansion (%)	*t*-test result	Average growth Recovery (%)	Average growth Post-recovery expansion (%)	*t*-test result
Consumption	1.21	1.20	0.03	1.04	1.27	−0.92
Investment	0.88	2.10	−1.75**	0.22	1.98	−2.44***
Government	1.15	1.20	−0.06	1.24	1.15	0.10

**Reject at 5% significance level (critical value taken from a standard normal distribution, as degrees of freedom of *t*-distribution in each case exceed 100)
***Reject at 1%

Table 6 Kolmogorov–Smirnov test statistics (*P*-values in brackets), for the null hypothesis of equal distribution of growth rates in the components of aggregate expenditure, for different phases of the South African business cycle, 1960–2017

Component of aggregate expenditure	Recessions and expansions	Recoveries and post-recovery expansions
Consumption	0.451*** (0.000)	0.122 (0.620)
Investment	0.296*** (0.000)	0.269*** (0.008)
Government	0.169 (0.104)	0.158 (0.290)

***Reject at 1% significance level

More generally, Kolmogorov–Smirnov tests confirm that the distribution of growth rates of consumption and government expenditure is similar between recovery and post-recovery phases. The distribution of investment growth rates after the identified 'recovery' phases is actually centred around *higher* means than that of supposed 'recovery' phases. Consequently, to the extent that one wishes to refer to South African recoveries, they are clearly not investment -driven (Table 6).

The recovery experience of net exports suggests that it is the driving force that separates the earliest stage of South African expansions from recessions. Referring back to Table 4, it is clear that net exports accelerate very sharply in the first two to three quarters of a recovery. Much of this is driven by exports (not reported in the table), with imports accelerating later in the expansion, thus reversing the sharp initial increase in net exports. This acceleration is usually relatively short-lived and is masked when one considers the entire recovery phase, even if such a phase lasts only four to six quarters.

6 Conclusions

This chapter studies the initial quarters of business cycle expansions. In recent years, based on US experience, some economists have attempted to separate expansion phases into an earlier recovery phase and a subsequent post-recovery phase. Using a multi-country dataset, we show that distinct recovery phases cannot be identified for most countries, with the notable exception of the USA. That is, in most countries including South Africa, average growth during the first few quarters of expansion is not significantly higher than growth in subsequent quarters. This result is robust to the measure of recovery—fixed-duration recoveries exhibit similar behaviour. We conclude therefore that business cycle recovery is a gradual rather than an abrupt process—and South Africa is not alone in this experience. What is interesting about the South African experience is that we appear to be different from other commodity-producing countries.

Acknowledgements We thank Stan du Plessis for important insights, as well as audiences at Stellenbosch University, the University of Cape Town and participants at the 2019 Biennial Conference of the Economic Society of South Africa for valuable inputs on earlier versions of this chapter.

Appendix 1

Country	IFS identifier	MEI identifier	Database used
Argentina	IFS-I21399BVPZFQ		IFS
Australia	IFS-I19399BVRZFQ	MEI-AUS_NAEXKP01_STSAQ	IFS
Austria	IFS-I12299BVPZFQ	MEI-AUT_NAEXKP01_STSAQ	IFS
Belarus	IFS-I91399BVPZFQ		IFS
Belgium	IFS-I12499BVPZFQ	MEI-BEL_NAEXKP01_STSAQ	IFS
Bolivia	IFS-I21899BVPZFQ		IFS
Botswana	IFS-I61699BVPZFQ		IFS
Brazil	IFS-I22399BVPZFQ	MEI-BRA_NAEXKP01_STSAQ	IFS
Bulgaria	IFS-I91899BVPZFQ		IFS
Canada	IFS-I15699BVRZFQ	MEI-CAN_NAEXKP01_STSAQ	IFS
Chile	IFS-I22899BVPZFQ	MEI-CHL_NAEXKP01_STSAQ	IFS
Costa Rica	IFS-I23899BVPZFQ	MEI-CRI_NAEXKP01_STSAQ	IFS
Croatia	IFS-I96099BVPZFQ		IFS
Cyprus	IFS-I42399BVPZFQ		IFS
Czech Rep	IFS-I93599BVPZFQ	MEI-CZE_NAEXKP01_STSAQ	IFS
Denmark	IFS-I12899BVPZFQ	MEI-DNK_NAEXKP01_STSAQ	MEI
Ecuador	IFS-I24899BVPZFQ		IFS
Estonia	IFS-I93999BVPZFQ	MEI-EST_NAEXKP01_STSAQ	IFS
Finland	IFS-I17299BVPZFQ	MEI-FIN_NAEXKP01_STSAQ	IFS
France	IFS-I13299BVRZFQ	MEI-FRA_NAEXKP01_STSAQ	IFS
Georgia	IFS-I91599BVPZFQ		IFS
Germany	IFS-I13499BVRZFQ	MEI-DEU_NAEXKP01_STSAQ	IFS
Greece	IFS-I17499BVPZFQ	MEI-GRC_NAEXKP01_STSAQ	MEI
Guatemala	IFS-I25899BVPZFQ		IFS
Hong Kong	IFS-I53299BVPZFQ		IFS
Hungary	IFS-I94499BVPZFQ	MEI-HUN_NAEXKP01_STSAQ	IFS
Iceland	IFS-I17699BVPZFQ	MEI-ISL_NAEXKP01_STSAQ	IFS
India	IFS-I53499BVPZFQ	MEI-IND_NAEXKP01_STSAQ	IFS
Indonesia	IFS-I53699BVPZFQ	MEI-IDN_NAEXKP01_STSAQ	IFS
Ireland	IFS-I17899BVPZFQ	MEI-IRL_NAEXKP01_STSAQ	IFS
Israel	IFS-I43699BVPZFQ	MEI-ISR_NAEXKP01_STSAQ	IFS
Italy	IFS-I13699BVRZFQ	MEI-ITA_NAEXKP01_STSAQ	IFS
Jamaica	IFS-I34399BVPZFQ		IFS
Japan	IFS-I15899BVRZFQ	MEI-JPN_NAEXKP01_STSAQ	IFS

(continued)

Country	IFS identifier	MEI identifier	Database used
Korea	IFS-I54299BVPZFQ	MEI-KOR_NAEXKP01_STSAQ	IFS
Kyrgyz Rep	IFS-I91799BVPZFQ		IFS
Latvia	IFS-I94199BVPZFQ	MEI-LVA_NAEXKP01_STSAQ	IFS
Lithuania	IFS-I94699BVPZFQ	MEI-LTU_NAEXKP01_STSAQ	IFS
Macao	IFS-I54699BVPZFQ		IFS
Macedonia	IFS-I96299BVPZFQ		IFS
Malaysia	IFS-I68499BVPZFQ		IFS
Malta	IFS-I55699BVPZFQ		IFS
Mauritius	IFS-I18199BVPZFQ		IFS
Mexico	IFS-I27399BVRZFQ	MEI-MEX_NAEXKP01_STSAQ	IFS
Morocco	IFS-I68699BVPZFQ		IFS
Netherlands	IFS-I13899BVRZFQ	MEI-NLD_NAEXKP01_STSAQ	IFS
New Zealand	IFS-I19699BVRZFQ	MEI-NZL_NAEXKP01_STSAQ	IFS
Norway	IFS-I14299BVPZFQ	MEI-NOR_NAEXKP01_STSAQ	MEI
Paraguay	IFS-I28899BVPZFQ		IFS
Peru	IFS-I29399BVPZFQ		IFS
Philippines	IFS-I56699BVPZFQ		IFS
Poland	IFS-I96499BVPZFQ	MEI-POL_NAEXKP01_STSAQ	IFS
Portugal	IFS-I18299BVRZFQ	MEI-PRT_NAEXKP01_STSAQ	MEI
Romania	IFS-I96899BVPZFQ		IFS
Russia	IFS-I92299BVPZFQ		IFS
Serbia	IFS-I94299BVPZFQ		IFS
Singapore	IFS-I57699BVPZFQ		IFS
Slovak Rep	IFS-I93699BVPZFQ	MEI-SVK_NAEXKP01_STSAQ	IFS
Slovenia	IFS-I96199BVPZFQ	MEI-SVN_NAEXKP01_STSAQ	IFS
South Africa	IFS-I19999BVRZFQ	MEI-ZAF_NAEXKP01_STSAQ	IFS
Spain	IFS-I18499BVRZFQ	MEI-ESP_NAEXKP01_STSAQ	IFS
Sweden	IFS-I14499BVPZFQ	MEI-SWE_NAEXKP01_STSAQ	IFS
Switzerland	IFS-I14699BVRZFQ	MEI-CHE_NAEXKP01_STSAQ	IFS
Thailand	IFS-I57899BVPZFQ		IFS
Turkey	IFS-I18699BVPZFQ	MEI-TUR_NAEXKP01_STSAQ	IFS
United Kingdom	IFS-I11299BVRZFQ	MEI-GBR_NAEXKP01_STSAQ	IFS
United States	IFS-I11199BVRZFQ	MEI-USA_NAEXKP01_STSAQ	IFS

Appendix 2

Table 7 Long data set of countries, including descriptive information, the Kolmogorov–Smirnov and *t*-test results for various recovery definitions and the source of the underlying business cycle chronology

Country	Data characteristics			Kolmogorov-Smirnov test[a]		*t*-test[a] (one-tailed)		Chronology
	Period	Quarters	Recoveries	Fixed[b]	GRP[b]	Fixed[b]	GRP[b]	
Argentina	3/31/1990–6/30/2015	102	5	0.25 (0.339)	0.25 (0.339)	−1.13 (0.869)	−0.66 (0.745)	BBQ
Australia	9/30/1959–6/30/2016	228	4	0.31 (0.088*)	0.41 (0.105)	1.56 (0.069*)	2.06 (0.037**)	ECRI
Austria	3/31/1964–6/30/2016	210	6	0.13 (0.813)	0.10 (0.962)	0.01 (0.496)	0.01 (0.496)	ECRI
Belgium	3/31/1980–3/31/2016	145	6	0.19 (0.487)	0.14 (0.864)	0.03 (0.487)	0.12 (0.452)	BBQ
Bolivia	3/31/1990–12/31/2015	104	2	0.20 (0.922)	0.60 (0.089*)	0.79 (0.222)	2.41 (0.032**)	BBQ
Canada	3/31/1958–6/30/2016	234	3	0.26 (0.409)	0.26 (0.340)	1.19 (0.128)	1.60 (0.065*)	ECRI
Chile	3/31/1980–6/30/2016	146	4	0.18 (0.683)	0.33 (0.046**)	0.25 (0.402)	1.80 (0.043**)	BBQ
Ecuador	3/31/1991–3/31/2016	101	5	0.30 (0.126)	0.26 (0.226)	1.45 (0.078*)	1.37 (0.091*)	BBQ
Finland	3/31/1970–3/31/2016	185	7	0.11 (0.943)	0.14 (0.840)	−0.1 (0.541)	0.72 (0.239)	BBQ
France	3/31/1970–6/30/2016	186	7	0.13 (0.776)	0.11 (0.803)	−0.46 (0.677)	−0.20 (0.579)	ECRI
Germany	3/31/1960–6/30/2016	226	6	0.10 (0.975)	0.20 (0.296)	0.00 (0.500)	0.08 (0.466)	ECRI
Hong Kong	3/31/1973–6/30/2016	174	9	0.12 (0.811)	0.17 (0.293)	1.32 (0.096*)	1.13 (0.131)	BBQ
Israel	3/31/1980–3/31/2016	145	6	0.23 (0.232)	0.23 (0.232)	1.38 (0.089*)	0.91 (0.184)	BBQ
Italy	3/31/1980–6/30/2016	146	4	0.11 (0.984)	0.21 (0.313)	−0.21 (0.581)	0.92 (0.184)	ECRI
Japan	3/31/1958–3/31/2016	233	8	0.16 (0.506)	0.14 (0.729)	−1.08 (0.857)	−0.60 (0.723)	ECRI
Korea	3/31/1960–3/31/2016	225	4	0.28 (0.177)	0.23 (0.372)	1.18 (0.126)	−0.18 (0.571)	ECRI

(continued)

Table 7 (continued)

Country	Data characteristics			Kolmogorov-Smirnov test[a]		t-test[a] (one-tailed)		Chronology
	Period	Quarters	Recoveries	Fixed[b]	GRP[b]	Fixed[b]	GRP[b]	
Latvia	3/31/1990–3/31/2016	105	5	0.28 (0.187)	0.25 (0.275)	0.46 (0.326)	0.45 (0.328)	BBQ
Malaysia	3/31/1988–3/31/2016	113	3	0.38 (0.092*)	0.43 (0.085*)	1.59 (0.069*)	1.23 (0.125)	BBQ
Mexico	3/31/1980–3/31/2016	145	6	0.29 (0.070*)	0.30 (0.030**)	1.67 (0.052*)	1.64 (0.054*)	ECRI
Morocco	3/31/1990–12/31/2014	100	6	0.26 (0.203)	0.32 (0.080*)	1.76 (0.043**)	0.86 (0.200)	BBQ
Netherlands	3/31/1977–6/30/2016	158	6	0.20 (0.396)	0.18 (0.684)	0.51 (0.308)	0.88 (0.194)	BBQ
New Zealand	6/30/1982–6/30/2016	137	6	0.16 (0.668)	0.17 (0.605)	0.99 (0.166)	0.93 (0.181)	ECRI
Norway	3/31/1978–6/30/2016	154	8	0.14 (0.713)	0.15 (0.632)	1.00 (0.162)	0.88 (0.192)	BBQ
Peru	3/31/1979–3/31/2015	145	9	0.25 (0.083*)	0.19 (0.307)	1.17 (0.124)	0.64 (0.261)	BBQ
Philippines	3/31/1981–3/31/2016	141	4	0.30 (0.157)	0.31 (0.212)	−0.78 (0.779)	−0.75 (0.769)	BBQ
Singapore	3/31/1975–6/30/2015	162	4	0.12 (0.980)	0.21 (0.376)	0.82 (0.210)	1.88 (0.034**)	BBQ
South Africa	3/31/1960–3/31/2016	225	6	0.15 (0.781)	0.12 (0.857)	−0.68 (0.749)	−0.01 (0.504)	SARB/ECRI
Spain	3/31/1970–6/30/2016	186	3	0.49 (0.007***)	0.25 (0.439***)	−3.44 (0.999)	−0.71 (0.759)	ECRI
Sweden	3/31/1969–3/31/2016	189	5	0.24 (0.240)	0.26 (0.069*)	−0.130 (0.550)	1.28 (0.104)	ECRI
Switzerland	3/31/1965–6/30/2016	206	6	0.17 (0.594)	0.23 (0.251)	0.71 (0.242)	1.83 (0.039**)	ECRI
Turkey	3/31/1987–3/31/2016	117	6	0.42 (0.003***)	0.50 (0.005***)	3.27 (0.001***)	3.16 (0.003***)	BBQ
United Kingdom	3/31/1958–6/30/2016	234	4	0.22 (0.451)	0.15 (0.507)	−0.47 (0.678)	−0.54 (0.706)	ECRI
United States	3/31/1958–6/30/2016	234	8	0.25 (0.064*)	0.25 (0.064*)	1.45 (0.077*)	1.67 (0.052*)	NBER/ECRI

[a] *P*-values are shown in brackets
[b] GRP = growth rate peak definition; Fixed = fixed quarter definition
* Significant at $\alpha = 0.1$
** Significant at $\alpha = 0.05$
*** Significant at $\alpha = 0.01$

Table 8 Short data set of countries, including descriptive information, the Kolmogorov–Smirnov and *t*-test results for various recovery definitions and the source of the underlying business cycle chronology

Country	Data characteristics			Kolmogorov-Smirnov test[a]		*t*-test[a] (one-tailed)		Chronology
	Period	Quarters	Recoveries	Fixed[b]	GRP[b]	Fixed[b]	GRP[b]	
Belarus	3/31/1992–12/31/2015	96	4	0.33 (0.184)	0.17 (0.724)	−0.56 (0.711)	1.13 (0.131)	BBQ
Botswana	3/31/1994–3/31/2015	85	4	0.41 (0.058*)	0.43 (0.062*)	1.44 (0.085*)	1.01 (0.167)	BBQ
Brazil	3/31/1995–6/30/2016	86	5	0.38 (0.033**)	0.36 (0.068*)	0.70 (0.245)	0.42 (0.340)	ECRI
Bulgaria	3/31/1996–3/31/2016	81	3	0.40 (0.079*)	0.33 (0.530)	−0.53 (0.697)	0.76 (0.240)	BBQ
Costa Rica	3/31/2000–12/31/2014	60	2	0.22 (0.818)	0.24 (0.621)	−0.66 (0.738)	−1.27 (0.889)	BBQ
Croatia	3/31/1993–3/31/2016	93	4	0.20 (0.636)	0.24 (0.546)	0.85 (0.205)	−0.39 (0.649)	BBQ
Cyprus	3/31/1995–3/31/2016	85	4	0.21 (0.620)	0.24 (0.394)	−0.65 (0.740)	−0.87 (0.803)	BBQ
Czech Rep	3/31/1994–3/31/2016	89	4	0.35 (0.070*)	0.20 (0.641)	−0.44 (0.669)	−0.04 (0.514)	BBQ
Denmark	3/31/1995–6/30/2016	86	5	0.20 (0.647)	0.29 (0.174)	0.50 (0.312)	1.23 (0.113)	BBQ
Estonia	3/31/1993–3/31/2016	93	3	0.26 (0.460)	0.37 (0.056*)	0.56 (0.292)	1.76 (0.047**)	BBQ
Georgia	3/31/1996–6/30/2015	78	2	0.18 (0.962)	0.29 (0.754)	−0.34 (0.631)	1.14 (0.151)	BBQ
Greece	3/31/1995–6/30/2016	86	2	0.26 (0.960)	0.57 (0.237)	−0.08 (0.531)	−1.47 (0.911)	BBQ
Guatemala	3/31/2001–12/31/2015	60	1	0.25 (0.949)	0.68 (0.256)	0.05 (0.483)	1.26 (0.206)	BBQ
Hungary	3/31/1995–3/31/2016	85	5	0.16 (0.807)	0.20 (0.629)	−0.05 (0.52)	−0.32 (0.626)	BBQ
Iceland	3/31/1997–3/31/2016	77	4	0.20 (0.697)	0.17 (0.798)	−0.29 (0.612)	−0.13 (0.552)	BBQ
India	12/31/1996–12/31/2015	77	1	0.36 (0.620)	0.86 (0.049**)	0.84 (0.229)	2.99 (0.088*)	BBQ
Indonesia	3/31/1997–3/31/2016	77	1	0.57 (0.122)	0.39 (0.211)	−0.29 (0.604)	−0.13 (0.55)	BBQ
Ireland	3/31/1997–3/31/2016	77	3	0.23 (0.651)	0.24 (0.619)	0.45 (0.327)	0.37 (0.357)	BBQ
Jamaica	3/31/1996–3/31/2016	81	8	0.25 (0.347)	0.20 (0.629)	−0.07 (0.527)	−0.03 (0.512)	BBQ

(continued)

Table 8 (continued)

	Data characteristics			Kolmogorov-Smirnov test[a]		t-test[a] (one-tailed)		
Country	Period	Quarters	Recoveries	Fixed[b]	GRP[b]	Fixed[b]	GRP[b]	Chronology
Kyrgyz Rep	3/31/2000–12/31/2015	64	3	0.24 (0.621)	0.18 (0.826)	0.45 (0.327)	0.28 (0.391)	BBQ
Lithuania	3/31/1993–3/31/2016	93	3	0.27 (0.366)	0.27 (0.366)	−0.47 (0.678)	−0.07 (0.529)	BBQ
Macao	3/31/1998–3/31/2016	73	4	0.11 (0.994)	0.18 (0.747)	−0.13 (0.55)	−0.18 (0.572)	BBQ
Macedonia	3/31/2000–12/31/2015	64	4	0.46 (0.020**)	0.16 (0.871)	1.00 (0.166)	0.17 (0.432)	BBQ
Malta	3/31/1996–3/31/2016	81	5	0.20 (0.608)	0.21 (0.599)	1.35 (0.096*)	1.32 (0.099*)	BBQ
Mauritius	3/31/2000–12/31/2015	64	2	0.37 (0.432)	0.36 (0.570)	0.47 (0.322)	−0.29 (0.614)	BBQ
Paraguay	3/31/1994–12/31/2014	84	5	0.34 (0.092*)	0.38 (0.071*)	1.04 (0.153)	0.35 (0.363)	BBQ
Poland	3/31/1995–3/31/2015	81	3	0.26 (0.427)	0.37 (0.027**)	0.12 (0.452)	−0.46 (0.675)	BBQ
Portugal	3/31/1995–6/30/2016	86	2	0.48 (0.130)	0.34 (0.725)	1.42 (0.09*)	−0.02 (0.508)	BBQ
Romania	3/31/1998–3/31/2016	73	3	0.52 (0.011**)	0.32 (0.297)	−0.78 (0.775)	−0.03 (0.51)	BBQ
Russia	3/31/1995–12/31/2014	80	3	0.26 (0.429)	0.25 (0.272)	1.00 (0.166)	1.35 (0.093*)	ECRI
Serbia	3/31/1995–3/31/2016	85	6	0.23 (0.400)	0.21 (0.587)	1.68 (0.051*)	0.74 (0.232)	BBQ
Slovak Rep	3/31/1993–6/30/2016	94	3	0.19 (0.878)	0.31 (0.472)	0.68 (0.256)	1.2 (0.134)	BBQ
Slovenia	3/31/1992–3/31/2016	97	3	0.24 (0.506)	0.39 (0.062*)	−0.15 (0.558)	−1.86 (0.96)	BBQ
Thailand	3/31/1993–6/30/2016	94	2	0.74 (0.000***)	0.60 (0.006***)	2.69 (0.008***)	1.94 (0.038**)	BBQ

[a] P-values are shown in brackets
[b] GRP = growth rate peak definition; Fixed = fixed quarter definition
*Significant at $\alpha = 0.1$
**Significant at $\alpha = 0.05$
***Significant at $\alpha = 0.01$

References

Balke, N. S., & Wynne, M. A. (1995). Recessions and recoveries in real business cycle models. *Economic Inquiry, 33*(4), 640–663.

Becker, L. (2017). *Business cycles: Is the concept of a recovery phase*. M.Com. Thesis. Stellenbosch: Stellenbosch University.

Bordo, M. D., & Haubrich, J. G. (2017). Deep recessions, fast recoveries, and financial crises: Evidence from the American record. *Economic Inquiry, 55*(1), 527–541.

Burger, P. (2008). *The ups and downs of the South African economy: Rough seas or smooth sailing?* Inaugural lecture at University of the Free State.

Burger, P. (2010). The South African business cycle: What has changed? *South African Journal of Economic and Management Sciences, 13*(1), 26–49.

Burns, A. F., & Mitchell, W. C. (1946). *Measuring business cycles*. National Bureau of Economic Research: Washington, DC.

Cerra, V., & Saxena, S. C. (2008). Growth dynamics: The myth of economic recovery. *The American Economic Review, 98*(1), 439–457.

Claessens, S., Kose, M. A., & Terrones, M. E. (2012). How do business and financial cycles interact? *Journal of International Economics, 87*, 178–190.

Conover, J. (1971). *Practical nonparametric statistics* (1st ed.). New York: Wiley.

Du Plessis, S. A. (2006). Reconsidering the business cycle and stabilisation policies in South Africa. *Economic Modelling, 23*(5), 741–774.

Fatás, A. & Mihov, I. (2013). *Recoveries*. International Macroeconomics Discussion Paper No. 9551. Centre for Economic Policy Research.

Friedman, M. (1969). The monetary studies of the National Bureau. In *The optimum quantity of money and other essays*. Chicago: Aldine Publishing Company.

Hall, V. B., & McDermott, C. J. (2016). Recessions and recoveries in New Zealand's post-Second World War business cycles. *New Zealand Economic Papers, 50*(3), 261–280.

Harding, D., & Pagan, A. (2002). Dissecting the cycle: A methodological investigation. *Journal of Monetary Economics, 49*(2), 365–381.

Hollander, H., & van Lill, D. (2020). On the estimation and application of structural decompositions of the South African business cycle. In W. Boshoff (Ed.), *Business cycles and structural change in South Africa*. Heidelberg: Springer.

Howard, G., Martin, R., & Wilson, B. A. (2011). *Are recoveries from banking and financial crises really so different?* s.l.: International Finance Discussion Papers No. 1037. Washington, DC: Virginia Board of Governors of the Federal Reserve System.

IFS. (2016). *International statistics database*. [Online]. Retrieved May 11, 2019, from http://data.imf.org/?sk=5daba?2-c5ad-4d27-a175-1253419c02d1

Kannan, P., Scott, A., & Terrones, E. M. (2009). From recession to recovery: How soon and how strong? *World Economic Outlook*, 109–138.

Kim, C.-J., Morley, J., & Piger, J. (2005). Nonlinearity and the permanent effects of recessions. *Journal of Applied Econometrics, 20*(2), 291–309.

Kolmogorov, A. N. (1933). Sulla determinazione empirica di una legge di distribuzione. *Giornale dell'Istituto Italiano degli Attuari, 4*, 83–91.

Laubscher, P. (2020). A history of South Africa's modern business cycle. In W. Boshoff (Ed.), *Business cycles and structural change in South Africa*. Heidelberg: Springer.

MEI. (2016). *Main economic indicators*. [Online]. Retrieved May 11, 2019, from http://www.oecd.org/std/oecdmaineconomicindicatorsmei.htm

Morley, J., & Piger, J. (2012). The asymmetric business cycle. *The Review of Economics and Statistics, 94*(1), 208–221.

Noether, G. (1963). Note on the Kolmogorov statistic in the discrete case. *Metrika, 7*, 115–116.

Papell, D. H., & Prodan, R. (2012). The statistical behavior of GDP after financial crises and severe recessions. *The B.E. Journal of Macroeconomics, 12*(3), 1–31.

Quantec. (2016). Easy data, s.l.: s.n.

Sichel, D. E. (1994). Inventories and the first three phases of the business cycle. *Journal of Business, 12*(3), 269–277.

Wynne, M. A., & Balke, N. S. (1992). Are deep recessions followed by strong recoveries? *Economics Letters, 39*, 183–189.

Zarnowitz, V. (1992). What is a business cycle? In M. Belongia & M. Garfinkel (Eds.), *The business cycle: Theories and evidence, Proceedings of the 17th Annual Economic Policy Conference of the Federal Reserve Bank of St. Louis* (pp. 4–72). Boston: Kluwer Academic Publishers.

The Role of Institutional Structure in Mediating the Impact of the Financial Crisis on the South African Business Cycle

A. Freytag

1 Introduction

Ten years after the emergence of the worldwide financial and economic crisis, the geopolitical and global economic tensions are rising again. President Trump has started trade wars with most larger trading nations, China's miraculous growth path may come to an end, and other emerging economies, most notably Brazil, Turkey, Russia, and—not to be forgotten—South Africa are seriously struggling. The South African economy—just like other emerging economies—is dependent on global developments. After a long upswing after the end of Apartheid, the country was hit by the global financial crisis and, to a much smaller extent, the so-called Euro crisis. This chapter is interested in the mechanism of this contagious process.

Both crises, however, cannot be interpreted as typical recession events driven by the business cycle, but as supply-side driven. In the case of the worldwide financial and economic crisis, loose US monetary policy in combination with subsidizing homeowners beyond rationality and the attempt of the banks to sell the subprime loans as first class played key roles. The Euro crisis had its origin in unsustainable fiscal policies in almost all Eurozone member countries. The crisis and its effects also played a key role in the Euro crisis.

Regardless of the causes, small open economies such as South Africa are quite vulnerable to such economic crises abroad as the example of the worldwide financial and economic crisis 2008 made clear impressively. While at the outbreak of that

A. Freytag (✉)
Friedrich-Schiller-University Jena, Jena, Germany

Department of Economics, Stellenbosch University, Stellenbosch, South Africa

CESifo Research Network, Munich, Germany
e-mail: andreas.freytag@uni-jena.de

W. H. Boshoff (ed.), *Business Cycles and Structural Change in South Africa*, Advances in African Economic, Social and Political Development,
https://doi.org/10.1007/978-3-030-35754-2_5

crisis there still was some hope that the developing countries could eventually decouple themselves from the crisis, in 2009 it became obvious that this decoupling was not possible. Consequently, South Africa and other emerging countries—except for China and a few other Asian countries—were also drawn into this financial and economic crisis.

Given that the global economy today is at least as integrated as it was 10 years ago, it is unrealistic to assume that South Africa will be circumvented by future structural crises or severe recessions elsewhere. A brief analysis of the highly integrated world financial markets already shows the risks associated with deep integration; the opportunities offered by this integration not only seem worth the risk but also require a proper set of instruments to prepare the economy against crisis.

Indeed, the extent to which the emerging world suffered—both with respect to the deepness of the recession and its duration—depends first on the severity of the original crisis, second on domestic factors in the respective emerging economy itself, and third on feedback processes and reactions to the crisis. As already mentioned, not all countries suffered equally strong from the crisis.

These domestic factors are in the focus of this chapter. We concentrate on those institutions or governance elements that can help to insulate a country against crisis. By institutions we mean the formal and informal values, norms and rules that govern human interactions. They can both be created by political will or evolve spontaneously (North 1990).

Why could some Asian nations cushion themselves better against the crisis' impact than, for instance, South Africa? To understand this logic, we first develop an analytic framework to understand the transmission mechanisms of a global crisis to individual economies. In Sect. 3, we then briefly analyse how the South African economy was affected by the financial crisis. Section 4 is dedicated to an assessment of South Africa's ability to manage a potential future crisis. Conclusions round off the chapter.

2 The Transmission Mechanism of the Crisis

As many global crises before, the worldwide financial and economic crisis started in the OECD, this time in the USA and hit other OCD countries almost immediately after it started in 2007. By contrast, emerging economies (EMEs) suffered a delayed response to the crisis, with a number of EMEs not entering recession before 2009. That said, they could not insulate themselves against the crisis.

Figure 1 is an attempt to explain the complexity of the transition mechanisms of a crisis from industrialized countries} to EMEs dependent on EMEs' characteristics

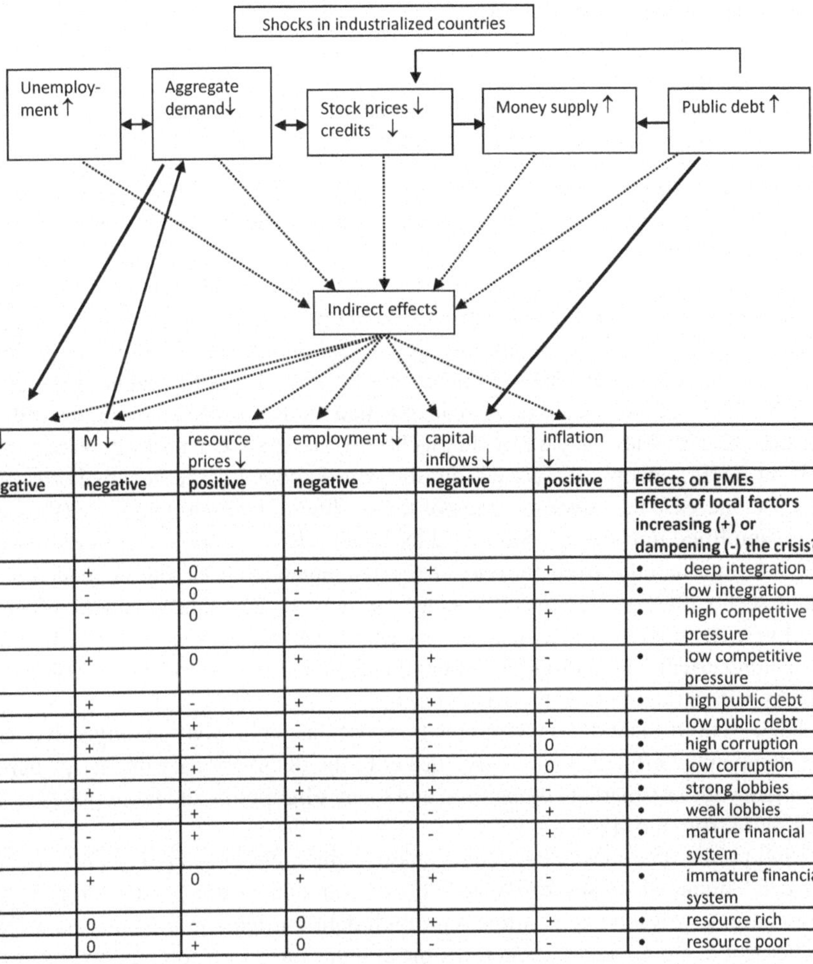

X↓	M↓	resource prices↓	employment↓	capital inflows↓	inflation ↓	
negative	**negative**	**positive**	**negative**	**negative**	**positive**	**Effects on EMEs**
						Effects of local factors increasing (+) or dampening (-) the crisis?
+	+	0	+	+	+	• deep integration
-	-	0	-	-	-	• low integration
-	-	0	-	-	+	• high competitive pressure
+	+	0	+	+	-	• low competitive pressure
+	+	-	+	+	-	• high public debt
-	-	+	-	-	+	• low public debt
+	+	-	+	-	0	• high corruption
-	-	+	-	+	0	• low corruption
+	+	-	+	+	-	• strong lobbies
-	-	+	-	-	+	• weak lobbies
-	-	+	-	-	+	• mature financial system
+	+	0	+	+	-	• immature financial system
0	0	-	0	+	+	• resource rich
0	0	+	0	-	-	• resource poor

Fig. 1 Transition mechanisms of the crisis from industrialized countries to emerging economies (Source: Freytag 2010: 230, own translation)

theoretically.[1] The upper part of Fig. 1 shows how the problems in industrialized countries affect the EMEs directly and indirectly.[2] These problems are a rise in unemployment associated with a fall in aggregate demand, a fall in prices on credit and stock markets and—partly as consequence of a policy response—an increase of money supply and rise in public debt. The broad outcomes included:

[1]See also Claessens et al. (2010).

[2]See Freytag (2010) for a detailed analysis.

- International trade (both exports and imports) was affected negatively
- Resource prices fell
- Employment decreased
- Capital inflows (and in part development aid payments) were reduced
- Inflation declined in the emerging world

The strongest, and in fact, direct influence of the crisis in industrialized countries on EMEs is probably the fall in aggregate demand and the rise in public debt in the OECD (indicated in bold arrows in the upper part of Fig. 1). The net effects are shown in the line "Effects on EMEs" (printed in bold). These transmission mechanisms are relatively uncontroversial. However, the second part is more revealing as it considers the amplifying (+) or dampening (−) effects of local factors in the individual EMEs. In other words: what drives the depth of the crisis in individual countries? Here, we can see that both macroeconomic, as well as institutional variables, play a role. Let us briefly discuss the macro variables.

If an EME is deeply integrated into the world economy, the negative effects of the crisis increase the adverse impact of the decline in international trade (thus a+, for an amplified impact). By contrast, a less integrated country will suffer less from the lower international trade (thus a−, for a dampened impact). The same directions can be seen with respect to the effects on employment, capital inflows, and inflation. The lower the degree of international integration of an EME, the lower will be the dampening effect on inflation. The effect on resource prices is independent from the country's integration in the global economy.

The extent of market competition is important as well. Highly competitive markets dampen the effects of the crisis (further to the disinflationary impact), whereas countries with less market competition and many oligopolies and monopolies suffer even more from the crisis.

High public debt makes the country more vulnerable tothe crisis as the country lacks the financial means to engage in demand-side programs. In addition, the potential to give social help is low with high debt burden. On the other hand, low public debt can dampen the effects, as the country has more potential to buffer the effects with the help of public spending.

As we know, these variables are not necessarily correlated with governance structures and institutions. However, in Fig. 1 there are some institutional variables, which may well be interpreted as proxies for the ability of countries to insulate themselves against global crises. We have concentrated on those institutions having clearly distinguished effects on economic welfare. These are corruption and vested interests (Olson 1982). We add the maturity of financial markets. The degree of corruption is the most relevant amongst these. We have chosen it because it can be measured and it can also be used as a proxy for other institutional variables, as it is highly correlated with a number of other institutional or governance indicators. One example is the World Bank indicator "Control of Corruption": it is correlated with all other World Bank indicators: "Voice and Accountability," "Political Stability and Absence of Violence," "Government Effectiveness," "Regulatory Quality," and

"Rule of Law" (World Bank 2018). In Sect. 3 we refer to the Corruption Perception Index (CPI) of Transparency International.

In Fig. 1 high corruption amplifies the negative and dampens the positive effects of the crisis respectively, which can be explained by the fact that corruption undermines the effectiveness of all policies, including economic policymaking.

Strong lobbies have a similar effect. In the attempt to maintain rents, they may have gained in the past, they are able to stop reforms that not only mitigate the crisis effects but also reduce exactly these.

A mature financial market will very likely dampen the negative effects of the crisis, in particular, when banks are healthy and ace only limited nonperforming loans. This helps the government to spend money in the real economy instead of rescuing banks.

A final word is justified with respect to natural resources. There is a vast literature that shows that the abundance of natural resources is a curse rather than a blessing in many countries, most of which are characterized by a high degree of corruption (Boschini et al. 2007). The Democratic Republic of Congo may serve as an example here. Therefore, we assume that the positive effects of the crisis dominate. However, given that governments are in short-term need for revenues, the consequences might well be negative in the short term.

Together, these theoretical considerations suggest that good institutions can dampen the effects of a crisis in an emerging or developing country. This is not surprising, given the large literature on institutions and economic welfare. Section 3 will explain the extent to which South Africa's institutions were supportive in cushioning the economy against the crisis effects.

In addition to these static effects, feedback effects that either strengthen or weaken the negative effects of the crisis have to be considered. If many developing and emerging economies are affected by the crisis, the recession in the "Global South" in turn further hurts the "Global North" (in addition to the initial effects). A vicious circle may start.

For an emerging economy such as South Africa, these feedback effects additionally depend on the reaction of all countries affected by the crisis. On the one hand, a strong protectionist impulse by the developed world as a reaction to the crisis would strengthen the negative consequences. On the other hand, fiscal programs in the developed world have the potential to increase demand also in the "Global South" if these fiscal impulses are not combined with protectionist measures.[3]

[3]The policies in Germany and the USA with respect to the car industry show the importance of this condition: Whereas the "cash-for-clunkers" program in the USA was restricted to American brands, the according program in Germany was applied to new cars of all bands. As a consequence, a Romanian producer experienced the highest sales growth (starting from a very low base) in Germany of all car producers in the world.

3 Historical Sketch: The Global Crisis and South Africa

South Africa was one of the most dynamic countries prior to the crisis, and at the outbreak of the crisis, it seemed that the country could decouple from the negative developments. This hope was fuelled by a prudent fiscal policy and a stability-oriented monetary policy since the end of Apartheid. In particular, the macroeconomic development in the first decade after 1994 was impressive (Du Plessis et al. 2008). The financial market has been among the most developed in the world, inflation was low.

However, already in 2008, the structural problems of the country were substantial, as analyses of the Harvard Group,[4] OECD (2008), as well as Draper and Freytag (2008), show[5]:

- Despite democratization and global integration, South Africa faced governance problems from the start of the new regime. The most relevant problem was a high degree of corruption, which has not declined since. It also comprises an ineffective public administration.
- In addition, it has been running an ineffective, unfair, and expensive education system. This system was weak in 2009 and has only slightly recovered since, if at all (World Bank Group 2018).
- Not least these education problems have led to other problems in the population, such as brain drain and epidemic diseases (HIV/AIDS).
- Finally, the issue of competition has to be discussed. First to mention are monopoly structures in network industries, the most relevant being electricity distribution. The South African parastatal electricity provider has experienced enormous difficulties and losses, which again hampers public policy responses to the crisis as well as leads to direct supply shortages. In addition, the railway system is monopolized and ineffective, causing high cost for those individuals who have to commute to work (World Bank Group 2018). Finally, fixed-line telephony was also a monopoly with high prices. This is not very important today, given the widespread use of mobile telephony, but was of relevance in 2008 (OECD 2008).
- In addition to these monopolies, there is also evidence for only moderate competition in other markets (Aghion et al. 2008).[6] Fedderke et al. (2018) can show rather high markups in the South African economy.

These problems already then contributed to high unemployment (then at around 25%) and continued constraints on the involvement of the historically disadvantaged

[4]The Harvard Group was a group of leading economists from Harvard, who in 2006, jointly with South African colleagues, wrote a number of economic policy-oriented studies on South Africa; see also https://www.hks.harvard.edu/centers/cid

[5]See also the contributions in Parsons (2009).

[6]For an alternative view, see Du Plessis et al. (2015a, b).

in the economy, despite a comprehensive Black Economic Empowerment (BEE) program.

Table 1 shows the development of important economic indicators between 2003 and today. Real GDP per capita growth before the crisis was rather substantial and fell dramatically just to recover a bit in 2010. The level of unemployment was rather modestly affected by the crisis. It has to be considered, however, that the official unemployment figures have to be taken with a grain of salt. The public budget was hit quite hard by the crisis and did not recover since.

In 2003, the South African current account turned into a deficit since savings did not suffice to finance investment. In 2008, this deficit could cautiously be interpreted as sustainable (Smit 2007; Draper and Freytag 2008). Over the crisis, it fell to be built up afterward again. According to the intertemporal approach to the balance of payments, a young country (such as South Africa) may well run a current account deficit if it reflects high levels of investment (Dluhosch et al. 1996).

Table 2 shows the indicators of governance quality in South Africa. The indicators discussed here are Human Development Indicator of the World Bank (HDI, between 0 und 1), the Index of Economic Freedom of the Fraser Institute (EF, between 0 and 10), as well as the Indicators of Freedom House about Civil Liberties (CL), and political Rights (PR). The latter are normed between 1 and 7, with1 documenting the highest level of liberties and rights.

Table 1 Important South African economic indicators, 2003–2017

	2003	2007	2010	2013	2015	2017
Real GDP per capita growth	3.1	4.8	1.8	1.0	−0.1	n.a.
Inflation	5.8	7.1	4.3.	5.8	4.6	5.3
Unemployment	28.0	24.2	24.7	24.6	25.2	27.7
Budget balance/GDP	−2.0	0.7	−5.4	−4.4	−4.1	−4.6
Public debt/GDP	35.4	30.0	34.7	44.1	49.3	53.1
Current account/GDP	−1.1	−6.5	−1.5	−5.9	−4.4	−2.3
Currency reserves in import months	1.6	3.5	4.6	4.3	5.5	n.a.

Source: Draper and Freytag (2008), own calculations and estimation on the basis of IMF (2018) and SARB (2010, 2018)

Table 2 Institutional indicators since 1990

		South Africa							
	African average 2007	1990	2000	2005	2007	2010	2013	2015	2017
HDI	0.51 (2005)	0.621	0.629	0.609	0.616	0.638	0.665	0.666	n.a.
CPI	2.9	n.a.	5.0	4.5	5.1	4.4	4.2	4.4	4.3
PR	4.3	6	1	1	2	1	2	2	2
CL	4.0	5	2	2	2	2	2	2	2
EF	5.7 (2005)	5.26	7.04	6.87	6.79	6.75	6.75	6.64	n.a

Source: Draper and Freytag (2008), World Bank (2018), Fraser Institute, Freedom House, Transparency International

Governance, as shown by all indicators used here, was dramatically improved after the end of Apartheid (see the numbers of 1990 in Italics), but did not show improvement between 1994 and the crisis. On the contrary, both economic freedom and the degree of corruption showed a slight change to the worse. In the period before 2008, the political situation was highly stable and the coherence of the South African population was still visible; the term "Rainbow Nation" was still justified, at least observed from the outside. This seems to have changed under the Presidency of Jakob Zuma.

These were the conditions when the country was hit by the financial crisis. We may now work through the economic aspects as displayed in Fig. 1, i.e., exports,

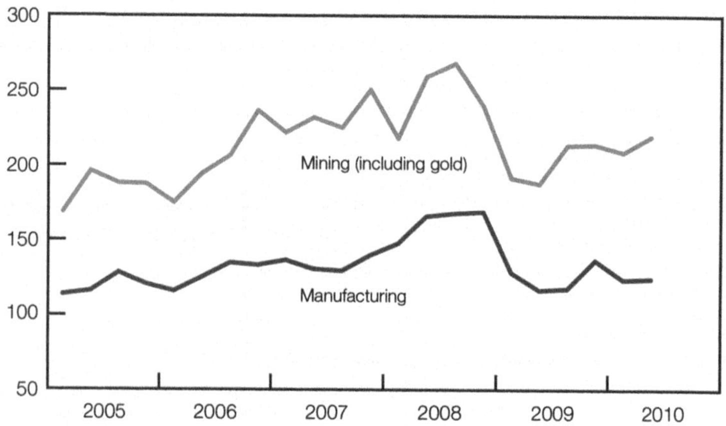

Fig. 2 Volume of South African exports (in Rand billion) prior to and following the financial crisis (2005–2010), seasonally adjusted and annualised, at constant 2005 prices (Source: SARB 2010)

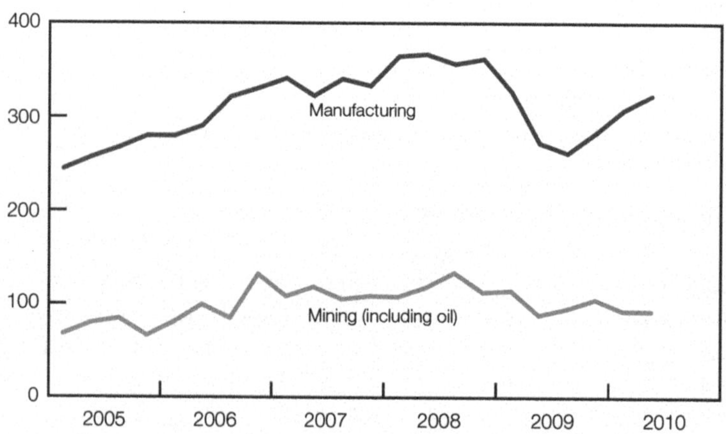

Fig. 3 Volume of South African imports (in Rand billion) prior to and following the financial crisis (2005–2010), seasonally adjusted and annualised, at constant 2005 (Source: SARB 2010)

imports, resources prices, capital inflows, and inflation, to show that the framework explains the course of the South African crisis quite well.

Export revenues and import spending fell (see Figs. 2 and 3) after a peak in the last quarter of 2008, which shows the deep integration of South Africa already in 2008. The interesting pattern, however, is that commodity exports fell much sharper than commodity imports, showing that the price and income elasticities of South Africa's commodity imports is lower that of its commodity exports. It is evident that South African resource prices fell just as resource prices declined globally. For the manufacturing sector, such difference cannot be seen. The secondary sector shrank by roughly 20% (Parliamentary Monitoring Group 2009). However, it has to be mentioned that deep integration and macroeconomic stability lead to the good situation of South Africa after 1990 and before the crisis (Edwards and Lawrence 2006; Hausmann and Klinger 2006).

As a consequence of the crisis, GDP per capita growth, employment, and business confidence (as a predictor of investment and, therefore, capital inflows) declined. Again, the secondary sector was particularly adversely affected (Parliamentary Monitoring Group 2009). It is not possible to infer to what extent the market power of individual firms has contributed to this decline, but one may argue that the overall low competitive pressure in South African markets, for goods, as well as services, had rather negative consequences. As a positive consequence, inflation was back in the band of 3–6%.

In sum, the South African economy reacted to the financial crisis as predicted by the model in Fig. 1. Compared to the Apartheid regime, improved governance structures in South Africa in combination with a rational policy response in the international economy mitigated this shock, ensuring that, after a couple of years, the world, as well as South Africa, was back on a growth path.[7]

4 How Well Is South Africa Prepared for a Future Crisis?

The analysis of the degree to which South Africa was hit by the worldwide financial and economic crisis of the year 2008 shows that the country was rather well prepared for it and could escape it quickly. Governance indicators signaled a quite favorable set of institutions, which was supported by a fair degree of political coherence. The macroeconomic situation was also supportive for a quick recovery. Low public debt and high growth prior to the crisis made it both economically and politically easy to establish a few measures to escape the crisis. For example, the public sector was able to increase employment until the end of 2009 by a higher rate than before (SARB

[7] Subsequent political and economic problems in South Africa are of structural nature and not caused in the world economy but by the government. These problems are not the subject of this chapter. See the analysis of the weak postcrisis recovery in the chapter by Boshoff and Becker (2020).

2017). This escape was enhanced by a rational policy response on the globe—in particular, by the almost entire absence of protectionist responses.

The comfortable economic setting as experienced by the end of 2008 cannot be observed in early 2018. This holds for both the economic situation and the governance structure, as well as the political stability, and peace.

Real per capita output has been stagnating for some years (see Table 1). Officially measured unemployment is three percentage points higher in 2017 than in 2007 prior to the last crisis. Inequality is also on a persistently high level (OECD 2017). This may imply a populace less patient with the short-term effects of crisis reforms.

Furthermore, the country's fiscal position at the time of writing (mid 2018) is worse than it was a decade earlier. Public debt has almost doubled in terms of GDP, and the annual fiscal deficit in recent years has been constantly around 4–5% of GDP. This would have negative consequences in a future crisis, limiting the potential for fiscal stimulus.

The already lower rate of inflation indicates that the South African Reserve Bank (SARB) has placed much emphasis on monetary stability, which can be interpreted as a positive sign. The other positive exception can be seen for aspects of external economic relations, as both the current account deficit as percent of GDP and the currency reserves measured in import months show: the current account deficit in 2007 was larger and the currency reserves smaller than in 2017.

Nevertheless, as for the institutional aspects, it appears that South African society is slightly worse prepared for a potential crisis than in 2008. On official metrics, the general political climate is comparable to that of 2007 (CL and PR in Table 2). Yet economic freedom has been declining ever since 2000.[8] The degree of corruption is higher than in 2008. The country, in addition, seems to suffer from a decline in social trust. In addition, the political climate has encouraged rating agencies to further downgrade, or at least consider downgrading, South African sovereign debt (OECD 2017: 22). In such a climate, the country's response to a shock such as the one of 2008 is likely to be weaker.

It may be argued that the decline in governance indicators took place slowly and that the differences compared to 2008 are minor. Even so, the decline in governance does not appear to have been arbitrarily small. It goes hand in hand with a number of political developments, including large-scale corruption under the Zuma administration, which has undermined trust. The high degree of corruption certainly undermines the country's resilience against future crises. It is also still to be seen whether the new presidency will be able to strengthen the firewalls against a potential new crisis. Therefore, it is indeed difficult not to conclude that the consequences of a potential worldwide crisis today would be more severe than a decade ago. This is bad news, since—as Boshoff and Becker (2020) show later in this volume—South Africa's speed of recovery has been relatively slow historically. This would indicate an even bigger problem in the wake of another recession.

[8] According to the Fraser Institute, a country is defined as economically free, if the index exceeds 7.5.

5 Conclusion

In a highly integrated world, South Africa cannot insulate itself from such crisis. It can, however, strengthen forces that mitigate external shocks for the South African economy, considering that the intensity of business cycle fluctuations is dependent on structural factors.

Unfortunately, the current economic and political situation in South Africa does not allow much optimism. In comparison to the period immediately after 2008, when the country was severely hit by the worldwide financial and economic crisis, the country is now structurally weaker. Its economic performance, in particular, with respect to employment and fiscal stability is significantly weaker than a decade ago. This implies that the policy response to a potential crisis might lack stamina. The situation is even worsened by governance problems—in particular, corruption has increased substantially since the mid-2000s.

It is the first and foremost task of the new administration to fight corruption and increase trust among the population. This is a general requirement for a fractionalized country such as South Africa. It would have the benefit to cushion the country against future crises.

References

Aghion, P., Braun, M., & Fedderke, J. (2008). Competition and productivity growth in South Africa. *The Economics of Transition, 16*, 741–768.

Boschini, A. D., Pettersson, J., & Roine, J. (2007). Resource curse or not: A question of appropriability. *Scandinavian Journal of Economics, 109*(3), 593–617.

Boshoff, W., & Becker, L. (2020). Business cycle recoveries: A comparative view. In W. Boshoff (Ed.), *Business cycles and structural change in South Africa*. Heidelberg: Springer.

Claessens, S., Dell'Ariccia, G., Igan, D., & Laeven, L. (2010, April). Cross-country experiences and policy implications from the global financial crisis. *Economic Policy*, 267–293.

Dluhosch, B., Freytag, A., & Krüger, M. (1996). *International competitiveness and the balance of payments*. Cheltenham: Edward Elgar.

Draper, P., & Freytag, A. (2008). *South Africa's current account deficit, trade policy report 25*. Johannesburg: SAIIA.

Du Plessis, S., Smit, B. & Sturzenegger, F. (2008). *The cyclicality of monetary and fiscal policy in South Africa since 1994*, CID Working Paper No. 163, Harvard University.

Du Plessis, S., Freytag, A., & Boshoff, W. (2015a). Deliberate recovery: The connection between policy, politics and the economic recovery from the international financial crisis. *Taiwan Journal of Democracy, 11*, 17–36.

Du Plessis, S., Katzke, N., Gilbert, E. & Hart, C. (2015b). *Mark-ups and competition: A comparison of the profitability of listed south African industrial companies*, Working Papers 02/2015, Stellenbosch University, Department of Economics.

Edwards, L. & Lawrence, R. (2006). *South African trade policy matters: Trade performance & trade policy*, CID Working Paper No. 135, Harvard University.

Fedderke, J., Obikili, N., & Viegi, N. (2018). Markups and concentration in south African manufacturing sectors: An analysis with administrative data. *South African Journal of Economics, 86*(S1), 120–140.

Fraser Institute. (2018). *Economic freedom in the world*. Retrieved April 25, 2018, from www.freetheworld.com

Freedom House. (2018). *Freedom in the world*. Retrieved April 25, 2018, from https://freedomhouse.org/report/freedom-world/freedom-world-2018

Freytag, A. (2010). Schwellenländer in der Weltwirtschaftskrise – Probleme und Reaktionen am Beispiel Südafrikas. In T. Theurl (Ed.), *Wirtschaftspolitische Konsequenzen der Finanz- und Wirtschaftskrise* (pp. 215–241). Berlin: Duncker & Humblot.

Hausmann, R. & Klinger, B. (2006, August). *South Africa's Export Predicament*, CID Working Paper No. 129, Harvard University.

International Monetary Fund. (2018, April). *IMF world economic outlook*, Washington, DC, quoted as IMF 2009.

North, D. C. (1990). *Institutions, institutional change and economic performance*. Cambridge: Cambridge University Press.

OECD. (2008). *South Africa – Economic assessment*, OECD Economic Surveys volume 2008/15, Paris.

OECD. (2017). *OECD economic surveys - South Africa*, Paris.

Olson, M. (1982). *The rise and decline of nations: Economic growth, stagflation, & social rigidities*. New Haven, CT: Yale University Press.

Parliamentary Monitoring Group. (2009). *South Africa's response to the global economic crisis: Ministerial briefing*. Retrieved September 1, 2009, from www.pmg.org.za

Parsons, R. (Ed.). (2009). *Zumanomics*. Sunnyside: Jacana Media.

Smit, B. (2007, September 10–12). The sustainability of South Africa's current account deficit. In *Paper Presented at the Biennial conference of the economic Society of South Africa*. Johannesburg.

South African Reserve Bank. (2010). *Quarterly bulletin*, September 2010, Pretoria quoted as SARB.

South African Reserve Bank. (2017) *Quarterly bulletin*, December 2017, Pretoria, quoted as SARB.

South African Reserve Bank. (2018). *Quarterly bulletin*, March 2018, Pretoria, quoted as SARB.

Transparency International. (2018). *Corruption perception index*. Retrieved April 25, 2018, from https://www.transparency.org/research/cpi/overview

World Bank. (2018). *Data*. Retrieved April 25, 2018, from https://data.worldbank.org/indicator

World Bank Group. (2018). *An incomplete transition. Overcoming the legacy of exclusion in Africa*. Washington, DC: Republic of South Africa Systematic Country Diagnosis

Part III
Key Drivers of the South African Business Cycle

A History of South Africa's Modern Business Cycle

P. Laubscher

1 Introduction

This chapter on South Africa's modern business cycle is motivated by the theme of Professor CGW Schumann's (1938) monograph, *Structural changes and business cycles in South Africa, 1806–1936*. At the time, this work contributed to economists' broader quest in unravelling the dynamics between long-run growth and short-run cyclical change. In similar vein, the current chapter seeks to provide a descriptive analysis of South African business cycles over the period since the mid-1970s.

In doing so, we note that, '*... we still face ... the same basic question as did Burns and Mitchell 50 years ago: how should one isolate the cyclical component of an economic time series? In particular, how should one separate business-cycle elements from slowly evolving secular trends, and rapidly varying seasonal or irregular components?*' (Baxter and King 1999). Sophisticated statistical methods are applied in modern business cycle research separating trends from cycles; however, in the process information regarding the underlying business cycle may be lost (see Harding and Pagan 2002, 2005; Zarnowitz and Ozyildirim 2001).

Zarnowitz and Ozyildirim (2001: 7–9) argue that de-trending becomes indispensable when studying long phases of high or low growth. That is, in addition to classical cycles, growth cycles may also be informative. During the post-war period of reconstruction in Germany and Japan (and, later, with structural reforms in India), these economies witnessed long periods of sustained positive growth, which generated the need to study growth cycles. Indeed, it may be useful to *study both*

P. Laubscher (✉)
Department of Economics, Stellenbosch University, Stellenbosch, South Africa

Bureau for Economic Research (BER), Stellenbosch University, Stellenbosch, South Africa
e-mail: p.laubscher@mweb.co.za

W. H. Boshoff (ed.), *Business Cycles and Structural Change in South Africa*,
Advances in African Economic, Social and Political Development,
https://doi.org/10.1007/978-3-030-35754-2_6

classical and growth cycles, as discussed in an earlier chapter by Boshoff and Du Plessis (2020).

Accepting that long-run growth and short-run cyclical change are intertwined, the objective will be to analyse how discrete structural changes interacted with the proverbial *'unceasing round of the business cycle'* in shaping SA's cyclical development. Factors, such as the triggers of (and propagating forces in) the various cycles, the influence of international business cycles, the role of political shocks and the changing pattern of cyclical diffusion, will be under consideration. The idea is to provide a descriptive narrative, as well as an introductory quantitative analysis, of the changing character of SA's modern business cycle.

The chapter has five main sections: First, some background is provided on the central theme of long-run growth versus short-run cyclicality. The issue of discrete change and endogenous business cycle momentum is considered. Second, an attempt is made to divide the period under investigation into sub-periods; the SARB's business cycle dating methodology is discussed in the context of alternative approaches. Given these elements, the main body of the chapter discusses each of the official six-and-a-half peak-to-peak business cycles from the mid-1970s to 2017 in the third section. In the fourth section, the quantitative analysis follows. The *final* section concludes with a synthesis.

2 The Relative Roles of Exogenous and Endogenous Drivers

In characterizing the modern SA business cycle, the identification of longer and shorter term growth trends is one of the first analytical challenges. Business cycle theories are usually differentiated in relation to the issue of exogeneity versus endogeneity at the source of business cycle fluctuations and the explanations have varied and evolved over time. Are business cycles caused/driven by *external shocks* (including policy errors) or is there some *endogenous 'law' of regularity* causing/driving the business cycle; or is it a combination of these two factors?

One of the fathers of business cycle research, Arthur Burns, believed that the *'business cycle has an unceasing round'*, where endogenous factors such as the evolution of economic variables (e.g. business capital spending, credit extension and levels of business and consumer confidence) interact in ways that lead to economic fluctuations. He viewed propagation forces in a market economy as powerful and typically overriding economic and public policy experiments.

The Economic Cycle Research Institute (ECRI), which continued working in the Burns tradition, developed a system of leading coincident indicators for various regions of the world and across time periods. A key condition for the ECRI indicators to have predictive content in any particular country is that a free market prevails and is not being overwhelmed by war, weather or political upheaval (Achuthan and Banerji 2004: 95). The implication is that while each business cycle, both in its expansion and contraction phase, is unique, there is a common thread even across countries and time periods, namely the existence of a free enterprise economy. Alternatively, when a market economy is subject to political upheaval, like South Africa during the apartheid era, exogenous factors may distort the operation of the business cycle.

Beyond non-market influences, however, the business cycle has an endogenous regularity and momentum. It does happen that during long periods of sustained growth (or subpar growth) that policymakers, analysts and business executives become convinced of the 'death of the business cycle'. It is true that improved expertise in macro-managing an economy (including the operation of automatic fiscal stabilisers), the impact of technological advances (e.g. the development of the Internet and just-in-time inventory management), the rise of the services economy and some aspects of globalization, the business cycle have been tamed to a large extent in the sense that the amplitude of cyclical developments were reduced. However, even in this regard, the 2008–2009 global financial crisis offered a sharp reminder of the 'unceasing round of the business cycle'.

There has been an important debate regarding the instability of the 1970s and 1980s with some economists emphasizing adverse structural factors explaining the fluctuations in economic activity and others arguing that—despite these exogenous shocks—the SA business cycle still possessed an underlying regularity [see, for example, Mohr and Rogers (1994: 298)]. As discussed later in this chapter, it is fair to conclude that the SA economy experienced major structural disruptions over the period since the 1970s, which must have had an important influence on the domestic business cycle. Even so, much evidence remains in support of Arthur Burns' quip regarding the '*unceasing round of the business cycle*'. Even the protracted 1989–1993 economic downturn (at the time of tumultuous political change) and the subsequent economic recovery (1993–1996) correlate closely with the G7 industrial production cycle, much in the same way as during the 1980s—see Fig. 1. We return to this particular issue later in this chapter.

3 Identifying Periods of Structural Change

South Africa is a small and open economy and it follows that international developments would have an important bearing on economic performance. Industrialisation commenced earlier than many other contemporary so-called emerging economies and even industrial economies, with maize farming and gold mining being developed as key platforms around the turn of the previous century, and assisting the development of secondary industry from the 1920s and 1930s [see Terreblanche and Nattrass (1990) and the earlier chapter in this book, by Boshoff and Fourie (2020)]. Even so, industrialization and modernization only really accelerated after the Second World War. Manufacturing as a share of GDP reached a peak in 1981 and has suffered a secular decline since, including over the past 24 years of democratic rule. SA's modernisation continued, with the economy being characterised by a growing services sector.

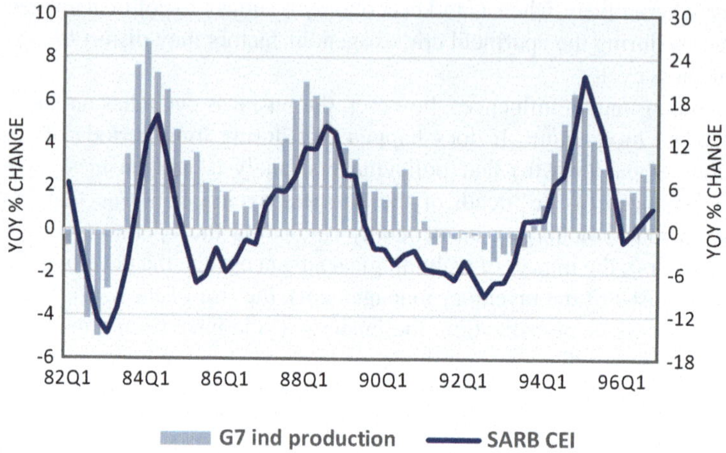

Fig. 1 SARB coincident indicator vs G7 countries' industrial production cycle. Source: Quantec Research and South African Reserve Bank

The modern business cycle in South Africa was therefore shaped during the post-war period, in line with most other emerging market economies. Furthermore, is it evident that the inflection point in the longer term growth of the world economy around the early 1970s, marked by the end of the Bretton Woods system of fixed exchange rates and the first international oil price shocks, also had a profound impact on the performance of the SA economy. Then there was South Africa's hamstrung political development, characterised by racial segregationist policies. The following quote from the SA historian, Charles Feinstein (quoted in McCarthy 2015: 17) suggests a structural break in the 1970s:

> From the 1920s to the 1970s an expanding industrial sector was supported by a combination of high profits and abundant foreign exchange derived from unlimited international demand for gold. There was then a dramatic structural break and the economy switched from apparently triumphant progress to distressing decline.

Internationally, post-war productivity growth in the major industrial countries declined from the early 1970s, mainly due to the higher energy costs. Level recessions also emerged in these countries confirming the onset of a new structural period (IMF 2002: 107). Romer (1999) and Basu and Taylor (1999) broadly agree with this identification in terms of business cycle research. Kose et al. (2005) studied the global business cycle and identified three structural periods (also consistent with the former-mentioned analyses), namely the Bretton Woods period (1960–1972), the period with common shocks (1972–1986) and the globalisation period (1986 and beyond).

Domestically, the combination of the oil shocks of 1973–1974 and its international repercussions, as well and the escalation of resistance to the country's racial segregation policies, which became embedded in the apartheid political system from 1948, fueled not only an economic downturn (1974–1977) but introduced structural change. SA's average real economic growth rate decelerated structurally from close to 5% per annum (1946–1973) to 1.5% per annum (1974–1993). It would seem that the long-term retreat of global growth, combined with the adverse domestic politics, explains SA's '*... dramatic structural break ... from apparently triumphant progress to distressing decline*'.

Provided this clear structural break in economic performance, this chapter revisits the analysis of SA's modern business cycle from the mid-1970s onwards. The chapter sub-divides this era into separate structural periods, which we will show are associated with unique business cycle features. Two major events stand out: the political transition to a full democracy (April 1994) and the Great Recession (2008–2009). Whereas real economic growth re-accelerated following the political transition to 3.2% per annum (1994–2017), the period following the Great Recession impact (2008–2017) witnessed significantly slower growth. These 'structural sub-periods' require further unpacking.

Previous analysis has shown how the characteristics of SA business cycles changed from that before the mid-1970s (see De Vries 1994: 18–21; Mohr and Rogers 1994: 294; Du Plessis and Smit 2002; Du Plessis 2006a, b; Laubscher 2016: 8–10).[1]

As noted, and also evident from other chapters in this book, the growth trend turned downwards over this period (Fig. 3) [see also Du Plessis and Smit (2005: 3–5)]. Not only did the downswing phases of the business cycle lengthen, but the amplitude of the fluctuations increased, implying greater economic instability. This is reflected in Fig. 2, showing a 10-year rolling standard deviation of real GDP growth in SA over the 1970–2017 period. Business cycle volatility increased sharply from the 1970s, peaked during the mid-1980s and remained high until the early 1990s whereafter it subsided. It increased again at the time of the Great Recession impact but tapered off thereafter.

[1]During the first structural period (1946–1973), a clear upward trajectory in the secular growth trend was observable, with SA witnessing nine complete (peak-to-peak) business cycles averaging 37.4 months in length over this period. Upswing phases lasted an average 24 months and downswing phases 13.4 months. In none of the calendar years over this period was negative real GDP growth registered. This changed from the mid-1970s. Over the 20-year period 1974–1993 no less than 4 calendar years of negative growth were registered, with the length of the business cycle increasing to 64.3 months on average, mainly due to much longer downswing phases, lengthening from 13.4 to 33 months.

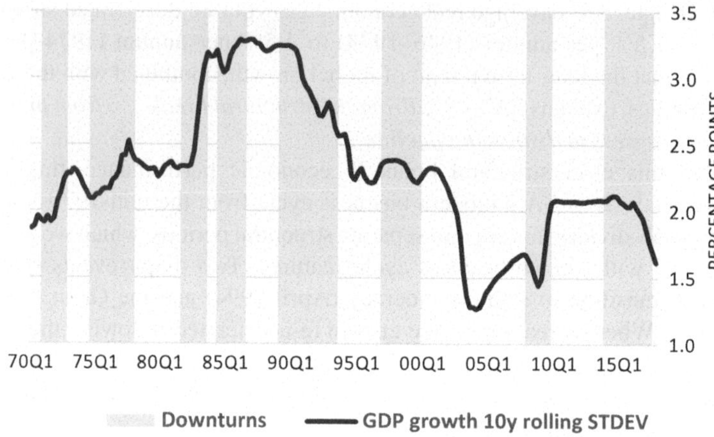

Fig. 2 Changing volatility of real GDP growth in SA, 1970–2017. Source: South African Reserve Bank; own calculations

The onset of the cyclical downturn in September 1974 has been regarded as the turning point of the structural economic downturn (De Vries 1994).[2] It makes intuitive sense that the upper turning point of a longer term cycle will coincide with that of the higher frequency business cycle development. Interestingly, this point is borne out by an analysis of business cycle properties over the longer term [see Boshoff and McLean (2018)]. Applying a bandpass filtering method, it appears that both the short-term (high-frequency) component of the SA business cycle and the long-term (medium-term frequency) component reached an upper turning point in 1974Q3, i.e. coinciding with the SARB's determination of the onset of the 1974–1977 economic downturn (See Fig. 3; the three structural turning points 74Q3, 92Q3 and—perhaps less convincing—07Q4, are indicated by the red circles).[3]

[2]The timing of the 'upper turning point' varies according to different analysts. Venter (2019: 16) prefers the onset of SA's longest post-war downturn at the time (January 1971). The USA announced the end of the dollar's convertibility into gold in August 1971 and in December of that year, a general re-alignment of international currencies was agreed upon (Smit and Van der Walt 1973: 36). Venter (2019) argues that the end of the Bretton Woods system of fixed exchange rates disrupted international pricing and production processes long before the onset of the oil-induced downturn in 1974. Burger (2010: 28–29) prefers the upper structural turning point to be when the 1974–1977 economic downturn developed into a full-blown recession following the June 1976 Soweto uprisings. August 1974 is right in between these two views.

[3]The methodology to determine SA's medium-term cycle followed that of Boshoff and McLean (2018). Both a high-frequency (short-term) business cycle component and a low-frequency (medium-term) cycle component were extracted by applying a Christiano & Fitzgerald bandpass filtering method. The short-term cycle is that component of (log-transformed) GDP that corresponds to a frequency range of 6–32 quarters; the medium-term frequency range was taken as 32–200 quarters (i.e. 8–50 years). The medium-term cycle depicted in Fig. 3 is calculated as the per cent deviation of the sum total of the short- and medium-term frequency components relative

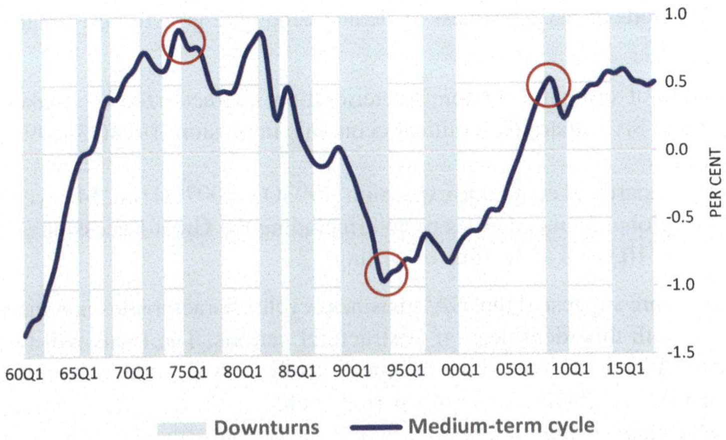

Fig. 3 SA's medium-term business cycle, 1960–2017

From that point onwards, the SA economy witnessed a gradual deterioration in growth performance until the late 1980s, when growth dropped below the long-term trend, as international sanctions and domestic political crises impacted the economy (Boshoff and McLean 2018). This deterioration reached a nadir at the end of the longest post-war downturn (1989–1993), which was marred by deep sociopolitical unrest in the run-up to South Africa's first democratic election.

Subsequently, growth performance improved. The recovery was assisted by the global economy exiting the non-synchronised downturn of the early 1990s (overshadowed by the impact of German unification and Japanese decline, amongst others). However, the recovery was fundamentally being driven by the post-election lift in domestic business and consumer confidence, marking the onset of SA's first post-apartheid expansion (see a later chapter by Binge (2020), on business confidence in South Africa). This period witnessed significant shorter term fluctuations in economic activity, but the longer term trend was unambiguously upwards, culminating in SA's record post-war expansion (1999–2007).

Once more, considering Fig. 3, it would appear as if the 2007Q4 upper turning point in both this (higher frequency) expansion and SA's medium-term cycle coincide. This seems to introduce a new structural period, i.e. the global financial crisis and subsequent Great Recession, 2008–2009, which had a lingering impact, both globally and domestically. As such, it may be possible to identify three

to the trend. The 07Q4 (structural) upper turning point is contentious and difficult to date, as it is relatively recent; the end of 2014 also seems to present itself as a possible upper turning point in this regard. It is only from 2015 that SA's real economic growth slowed more visibly.

structural periods in SA's business cycle and economic growth performance from the mid-1970s:

- The period of structural economic deterioration, characterized by weaker global growth and SA's apartheid political-economic implosion, 1974Q3–1993Q2 (i.e. 19 years)
- SA's post-apartheid economic expansion, 1993Q3–2007Q4 (i.e. 14½ years); and
- The post-global financial crisis period (including the Great Recession), 2008Q1 to date (i.e. 10 years at the time of writing).

It is therefore suggested that SA's business cycle characteristics are analysed in accordance with this identification of structural periods. The focus will be on the post-Bretton Woods period, asking the question of how SA's modern business cycle was influenced and changed over this period, including the post-2007 period. Some econometric analysis may only be feasible if the post-apartheid expansion and the post-2007 periods are combined, culminating in the question of how SA's business cycle changed from before to after the first full democratic elections in the post-Bretton Woods period (see Burger 2010, applying a similar research question).

4 A Narrative Analysis of the South Africa Business Cycle

From the foregoing analysis, it is evident that international developments and SA's political development exercised a strong bearing on the performance and cyclical development of the SA economy. This is not unique to SA. As Zarnowitz (1992: 357) puts it: 'How the economy moves over time depends on its structure, institutions and policies, all of which are subject to large historical changes'. Yet, equally significant is the tendency in free enterprise economies for '... business cycles ... [to] ... retain a high degree of continuity, which shows up most clearly in the co-movements and timing sequences among the main cyclical processes'. To account for the rich political and economic context of South African' business cycles from the mid-1970s, this section presents a narrative dissection of each cycle. This narrative history is followed by a descriptive quantitative analysis in the next section.

4.1 The Mid-1970s Economic Downturn Had Long-Term Features

The early and mid-1970s represents a period of far-reaching change, both at the international and domestic levels. *At the international level*, the creation of a free gold market and the end of the Bretton Woods era of fixed exchange rates introduced substantial strains in the pricing and production processes of the major industrial countries during the course of 1973–1974 (Smit and Van der Walt 1982: 43). When the first oil embargo arrived at the end of 1973, the impact was substantial. Combined, these changes did not only induce a world economic downturn, described as particularly severe,[4] but had long-term implications as it introduced a structural break in the trend growth rates of the major industrial countries (Rasche and Tatom 1977: 10).

SA only moved to a system of floating exchange rates in 1979. However, apart from the oil shocks, the early 1970s also marked the onset of intensified internal sociopolitical protest against the apartheid state (see De Vries 1994: 21; Giliomee 2004: 530; Terreblanche 2002: 307).[5] The political independence of SA's neighbouring countries (backed by communist states) threatened the apartheid state and involved the country in a low-intensity war on the Angolan border. The economic downturn that ensued from August 1974 was moderate and gradual at first until the unsettling political developments (including the June 1976 Soweto uprising) triggered a more serious outright recession, 1976–1977.

It is agreed that the onset of economic downturns in most countries during the mid-1970s also announced the onset of longer term growth retardations (Zarnowitz 1992: 241). In symphony with international developments and impacted by the lengthy reform and death of the apartheid state, SA's trend growth also lowered after 1974.

Downturn: September 1974 to December 1977 The mid-1970s downturn had external origins, being the impact of the first oil price shock. This was transmitted to SA via slower export growth and weaker non-gold terms of trade. Real exports declined sharply by 18% from 1972Q4 to 1975Q1, which mirrored the close to 15% contraction in mining GDP over the period 1973Q1–1975Q3. The non-gold terms of trade also deteriorated by 15% between the end of 1973 and the end of 1975. The initial impact met with resilient real domestic expenditure due to expansionary macroeconomic policies (negative real interest rates and robust fiscal expansion). Both government consumption expenditure (driven, amongst others, by defence spending) and capital expenditure were buoyant.[6]

[4]During the first oil price shock at the end of 1973, the US dollar price of crude jumped by 175% and during the second, successive increases from early 1979 saw the price another 165% higher by the middle of 1980. G7-countries' real GDP was down more than 2% between late 1973 and early 1975; and again down 1.5% during the first three quarters of 1980.

[5]Following the Sharpeville event (March 1960), black political protest was severely repressed for more than a decade. Apart from the emergence of the black consciousness movement, no real political protest ensued until the African labour strikes in 1973 in Durban (see Terreblanche 2002: 307, 356). Terreblanche traces the onset of political change in SA to the Durban labour protests. During the first quarter of the year, around 61,000 African workers struck in 160 strikes, impacting 146 firms in the area (Fisher 1993: 211).

[6]This period witnessed major public sector investment projects (e.g. the development of the Richards Bay and Saldanha Bay harbours, the expansion of Eskom's electricity supply capacity, the start of the second and third phases of the Sasol coal-to-fuel plants, the building of the Sishen–Saldanha and Richards Bay railway lines, the containerisation programme of the transport sector

It took the external and internal (political) shocks to stop the buoyant domestic market in its tracks; countercyclical monetary policy also played some role (see De Kock 1974: 6–7). The confidence shock caused a sharp pullback in investment, which cascaded throughout the economy.[7] Therefore, the economic downturn traversed two phases. During the initial phase (1974Q3 to end-1975) growth slowed down and during the second phase (1976–1977), a full-blown recession unfolded. Real GDP growth receded from above 6% in 1974 to 2.3% in 1976 and −0.1% in 1977 (real GDE contracted by more than 5% during 1976–1977). The economic downturn lasted 40 months, exceeding the post-war average of 14 months (Smit and Van der Walt 1982: 54). The lengthened economic downturn hinted toward a structural break in the post-war economic growth trend. However, it needs to be emphasized that this economic downturn was a so-called *growth recession*, i.e. the absolute level of real GDP continued to expand (by 2.9%) over the full recessionary period.

Expansion: January 1978 to August 1981 The late 1970s upswing was preceded by the world economy emerging from the downturn following the oil price shocks of 1973–1974. Stimulatory fiscal and monetary policies added fuel to the recovery in real domestic expenditure, particularly the replenishment of inventory levels. The expansion reached an inflection point mid-1979. Before that point, i.e. the first 18 months of the recovery, growth was weak. Thereafter growth accelerated notably (second half of 1979 to end-1981). The acceleration of real domestic expenditure was quite dramatic, increasing from 3.2% per annum over the period 1978 to mid-1979 to double-digit levels subsequently up to the third quarter of 1980 (Fig. 4, left).

The earlier recessionary contraction in investment and therefore, imports, drove an improvement on the current account of the balance of payments, with a surplus registered during 1977 at the trough of the business cycle (Fig. 5, right). The subsequent increase in the gold price (from around \$200 in 1979 to above \$600 in 1980) drove the current account surplus further, reaching 14% of GDP by the first quarter of 1980. While this high current account surplus facilitated higher growth, the current account deteriorated sharply again as fixed and inventory investment recovered (1980–1981), imports surged and the gold price and terms of trade collapsed—by the end of the economic expansion (1981) the current account deficit measured above 8% of GDP. Exports (and the mining sector) were also hit by the second oil price shock (1979), which sent the major industrial countries

and various water infrastructure developments by the Department of Water Affairs) — see Smit and Van der Walt (1982: 48).

[7]Fixed investment contracted by 17% between the end of 1975 and the end of 1977, while the lagged adjustment in cumulative inventory investment amounted close to 50% over the 3-year period, end-1975 to end-1978. Whereas the prime overdraft interest rate drifted 4.5% points higher between the end of 1973 and during the course of 1974, this was not sufficient to compensate for the oil-induced (and demand-pull) increase in inflation over this period. Real consumer spending did contract eventually (by close to 4% over the 18-month period, end-1975 to middle-1977).

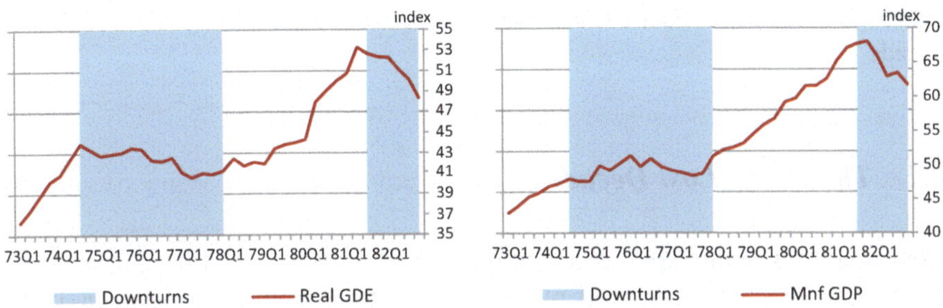

Fig. 4 Strong real domestic spending and import replacement benefiting manufacturing. Source: South African Reserve Bank and Statistics SA

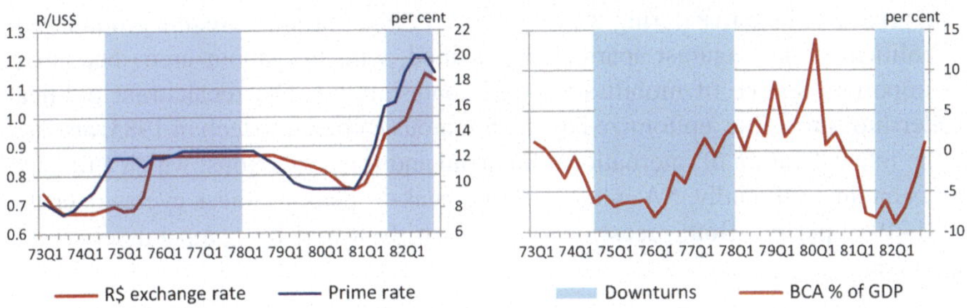

Fig. 5 Monetary policy, the rand exchange rate and balance on the current account, 1974–1981. Source: South African Reserve Bank and own calculations

into recession (early 1980s). All of these were reflected in a substantially weaker exchange rate from 1981 onwards (Fig. 5, left).

The higher gold price (and that of substitutes for oil, i.e. uranium and coal) countered the adverse terms of trade impact tied to the higher oil price. Furthermore, infrastructure projects began bearing fruit by boosting SA's export capacity; import replacement policies also stimulated the manufacturing sector. Manufacturing real value added expanded by close to 40% from trough to peak, i.e. much stronger (22%) compared to the corresponding expansion of real GDP (refer to Fig. 4, right).

The 1978–1981 economic recovery can be described as average in the context of the post-1974 business cycles; however, it was weaker compared to the preceding post-war economic recoveries. The downturn phase lengthened notably and combined with the less robust economic recovery, the 1974–1981 business cycle is regarded as the first in a period of structurally weaker economic growth in SA. Another notable feature of this business cycle was the sharp swings in fixed and inventory investment (being transmitted to the current account of the balance of payments via fluctuating imports). This introduced a measure of increased volatility in the overall growth pattern, a tendency that was destined to amplify in the 1980s. The high gold price at the time and a buoyant mood on the back of the 1978–1981 economic recovery generated expectations of enduring prosperity. These expectations turned out to be spectacularly misplaced. Intensifying sociopolitical unrest and increased international isolation became the story of the 1980s lost decade.

4.2 The 1980s Lost Decade

Gold was SA's main export commodity during the 1970s and 1980s, accounting for 50% of merchandise export revenues at the peak of the gold price in 1980. The high gold price and SA's embedded position as a leading commodity exporter gave rise to high expectations regarding general economic prospects.[8] These did not materialise. Apart from bouts of improvements, the long-term trend in the gold price was negative during the 1980s and 1990s. Furthermore, the groundswell of political protest against apartheid intensified, with the labour arena becoming an important source of mobilisation and contestation.[9] The recalcitrant political leadership at the time, epitomized by the infamous Rubicon speech in 1985, also led to the intensification of international financial and trade sanctions, which strangled the economy. Officially, SA witnessed two peak-to-peak business cycles over the 1981–1989 period. Both recessions were deep, followed by comparatively weak recoveries.

The 1981–1984 Cycle The first economic downturn unfolded when the gold price declined (1981–1982) from the peak achieved during 1980. It occurred shortly after the second international oil price shock, leaving the South African economy exposed, also having to contend with the impact of the Third World debt crisis and the associated capital outflows from risky capital markets (1981–1982). The economy consequently suffered a painful downturn during the early 1980s.

The onset of the economic downturn was export-led; G7 industrial production declined by 7.5% between the first quarter of 1980 and end-1982, which is correlated with the 21% contraction in South African real exports over the corresponding period. Mining real value added also declined over the 1979–1981 period (by close to 5%). Combined with a sharp fall in the terms of trade (in line with the gold price decline) the current account deficit, which developed towards the end of 1980 (following a surplus measuring 14% of GDP in 1980Q1) had to be addressed. In only 18 months, from the end of 1980, domestic interest rates increased by more than 10 percentage points. Economic activity peaked in September 1981 and

[8]It needs to be emphasised that SA's mining sector became diversified: SA was the third-largest minerals producer in the world in 1980, being the lead producer of gold, platinum and gem diamonds, as well as steel and alloy mineral commodities, chrome, manganese and vanadium; SA was also one of the top three suppliers of coal and uranium (see Venter 2019: 17).

[9]African unionism was suppressed during the 1950s and 1960s. From the early 1970s African unionism began to grow with 26 independent African unions (and a membership of 120,000) by 1976. Legislative changes (1979) saw African unionization growing further and this culminated in the formation of *The Congress of South African Trade Unions* (COSATU) in 1985, uniting 33 independent unions (Venter 2019: 18–19).

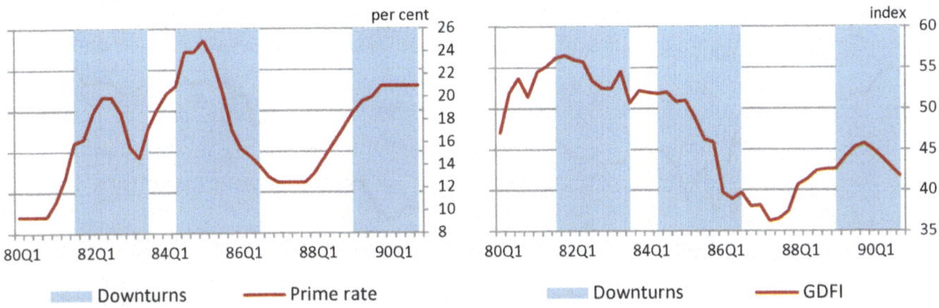

Fig. 6 Prime interest rate and fixed investment spending over the 1981–1989 period. Source: South African Reserve Bank and own calculations

reached a trough 19 months later, in March 1983. The economic downturn was of short duration, but the deepest in the post-war period (Van der Walt 1989: 41). While fixed investment only contracted by 10% (1981Q4–1983Q2), it did not recover (Fig. 6, right). The decline continued subsequently, with fixed investment contracting by a further 30% over the mid-1984–1987 period. This followed tighter monetary policy following the political interference in interest rates in 1982 (Fig. 6, left).[10] This triggered the second leg of the economic downturn (see below).

The 1983–1984 recovery was wholly consumption driven. Real household consumption accelerated by 13% between 1983Q2 and 1984Q2 and was accompanied by strong expansionary fiscal policy, reflected in real government consumption growth of 17% over the expansion; the ratio of government spending to GDP rose by 6½ percentage points over the complete 1981–1986 period (Fig. 7, right). However, the consumption recovery failed to translate into a wider recovery.[11]

The 1984–1989 Cycle Judging by the behaviour of fixed investment expenditure, the economic downturn actually continued throughout 1981–1986. Adverse domestic factors, specifically the Rubicon speech in August 1985 and the events leading up to this speech (including a state of emergency in response to political protests) deepened the economic downturn. Prime overdraft rates were hiked by 11 percentage points from March 1983 to August 1984. This, combined with the business confidence shock,[12] induced a precipitous decline in real fixed investment spending

[10]The prime overdraft interest rate was cut by no less than 6% points between October 1982 and March 1983 in a development which became known as the 'Primrose prime', with former President PW Botha intervening in the decision for political reasons (a by-election at the time in the Primrose constituency).

[11]Only 60% of the time series' growth rates in the SARB's diffusion index exceeded the long-term average towards the end of 1983 compared to more than 80% doing so during the previous expansion, 1978–1981 (Van der Walt 1988: 34).

[12]The RMB/BER business confidence index plunged by 65 points between September 1980 and December 1982, recovered by 26 points up to mid-1984, whereafter it plunged another 36 index points to a low level of 10 points reached during the third quarter of 1985 at the time of the Rubicon speech impact.

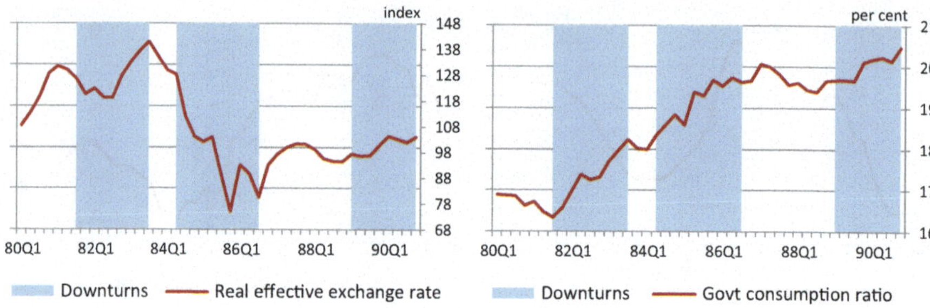

Fig. 7 Real effective rand and fiscal policy stance over the 1981–1989 period. Source: South African Reserve Bank and own calculations

(30% from peak to trough, 1984–1986), which propagated the recessionary spiral in the economy (Fig. 6). Expansionary fiscal policy (Fig. 7, right) and a sharp depreciation of the rand (falling by close to 50% in real terms between 1983Q1 and 1985Q3)[13] did counter recessionary forces in the economy somewhat (Fig. 7, left).

The early 1980s economic downturn reached a trough only in 1986.[14] While the first leg of the prolonged downturn was externally induced, its second leg had domestic origins—real exports only shrunk by 1% during this time period, while real GDE shrunk by close to 8%. This followed an almost 12% contraction over the first leg of the downturn. The contraction of the domestic economy is explained by the knock-on effects of the global economic downturn and the sharp subsequent tightening of interest rates. The intervening period also reflected a policy error, resulting in a temporary consumption boost, which had to be aborted in view of the overall balance of payments condition and the currency-induced inflation spiral. Consumer inflation spiralled upwards to 18% by the end of 1985 (from 10% early 1984).

Volatility was a key feature of the 1981–1989 business cycles. The 1970s already brought greater business cycle volatility. This volatility increased in the 1980s, with the emergence of so-called stop-go business cycles. The sharp and continuous capital outflows in the wake of the debt standstill and restructuring (1985) forced the policy authorities to maintain a surplus on the current account of the balance of payments. This placed a serious balance of payments constraint on economic growth, which influenced business cycle developments. The 1986–1989 economic recovery was impacted by major uncertainty, the imposition of trade and financial

[13]After a period of stability, the rand exchange rate fell sharply following the introduction of a floating exchange rate in January 1979 and the subsequent balance of payments pressures.

[14]During the first quarter of 1986, the level of real GDP was still below that of end-1981, despite the intervening brief economic recovery, 1983–1984.

sanctions and sociopolitical unrest. A defining characteristic of this recovery was its slow start, its comparatively low peak and slow speed.[15]

The recovery did develop some momentum during 1987–1988. It appears government and household consumption expenditure led the recovery, with its onset characterised by deep negative real interest rates (Inflation peaked around 18% following the rand exchange rate fallout in 1985 and nominal rates were cut at five occasions through 1986). Furthermore, the export sector benefited from improving growth in SA's main trading partner economies—real G7-country GDP expanded by more than 12% over the 1986–1989 domestic upswing phase of the business cycle and SA's real exports recovered by 20–30% over the corresponding period. In time, these demand factors stimulated fixed and inventory investment, which assisted the recovery. Fiscal policy was also loosened in 1986 and early 1987.

The 1980s must count as the darkest period, economically speaking, of the apartheid political order. The period 1985–1993 recorded real GDP growth averaging 0.5% per annum.

4.3 The 1989–1996 Cycle: Green Shoots of New Beginnings

The 1989–1996 peak-to-peak business cycle spans the run-up to SA's first full democratic elections (April 1994) and the economic upswing that ensued (1993–1996). On the one hand, the tumultuous political changeover seems to have dictated a prolonged economic downturn over the period 1989–1993, followed by a post-election increase in business and consumer confidence and, therefore, economic revival. On the other hand, the continuity between the business cycles of the 1980s and the 1989–1996 business cycle is striking. Witness the close link with the G7-countries' industrial production cycle over the 1980s, which continued during the early 1990s (Fig. 1). This correlation over a period of tumultuous exogenous influences (sociopolitical unrest, trade and financial sanctions and its scrapping, financial volatility and a protracted drought in agriculture) is remarkable. Nonetheless, the economy experienced its longest post-war downturn in the run-up to the elections. While the 1980s balance of payments constraint was slow to lift, the ensuing recovery carried green shoots of new beginnings.

Record Downturn: March 1989–May 1993 The onset of a somewhat protracted—and unsynchronised—world economic downturn, the tightening of monetary policy, responding to inflationary pressures and balance of payments concerns, and a deterioration in the terms of trade, ushered in the domestic economic downturn. Exports only contracted by 11.2% from peak to trough, bottoming early

[15] The speed of adjustment over the 12-quarter recovery period measured a relatively mild 2.8% and dispersion was low. Only around 65% of economic activity growth exceeded the long-term average (compared with 80% during the 1978–1981 expansion) (see Van der Walt and Pretorius 1995: 31).

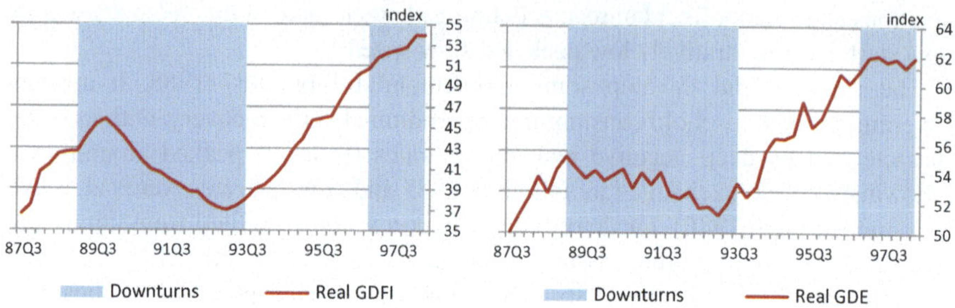

Fig. 8 1989–1996 cycle: prolonged contraction in GDFI and GDE, followed by post-election recovery. Source: South African Reserve Bank and own calculations

1991 as the USA and some other economies emerged from their downturns. The downturn became more protracted as world economic growth remained hesitant.[16] Furthermore, the economic downturn was deepened by a serious agricultural drought (1992) and the sociopolitical upheaval in the run-up to SA's first full democratic elections (April 1994) (Fig. 8).

South Africa also experienced its Paul Volcker moment in 1989, with monetary policy being tightened under the hand of the then new Governor of the SARB, Dr. Chris Stals. He favoured positive real interest rates, protecting the value of the rand and driving inflation down. This had the typical cyclical consequences[17] but also had longer term implications for inflation and domestic spending. The outstanding feature of the economic downturn was its length (51 months) being the longest in SA's post-WWII history and comparable to the Great Depression of the 1930s (Van der Walt and Pretorius 1995: 36–38). What made the economic downturn particularly bad was that it came at the end of a period of poor secular growth coupled with major political uncertainty.

Expansion: June 1993–November 1996 Improved export growth during the second half of 1993 on the back of the world economic recovery, as well as a strong recovery in agricultural conditions, led the expansion. From 1994, the political change bolstered business and consumer confidence, with the end of financial and economic sanctions, the phasing out of exchange control (e.g. the scrapping of the financial rand mechanism, March 1995) and lower inflation (Fig. 9, left) being key growth-supporting factors. A strong improvement in SA's terms of trade tied to an improvement in international commodity prices was a key feature of the improving economic conditions during 1994–1995. Financial deepening also saw sharp growth

[16]The business cycles of the G3 economies were unsynchronised due to the impact of German unification and the malaise of the Japanese economy.

[17]Real household consumption expenditure contracted by 3.4% and real gross domestic fixed investment by 19.1% (Fig. 8, left), resulting in an overall contraction of no less than 7.2% in real gross domestic spending (Fig. 8, right). The slump in investment was also related to low business confidence due to the intense uncertainty in the run-up to the April 1994 elections.

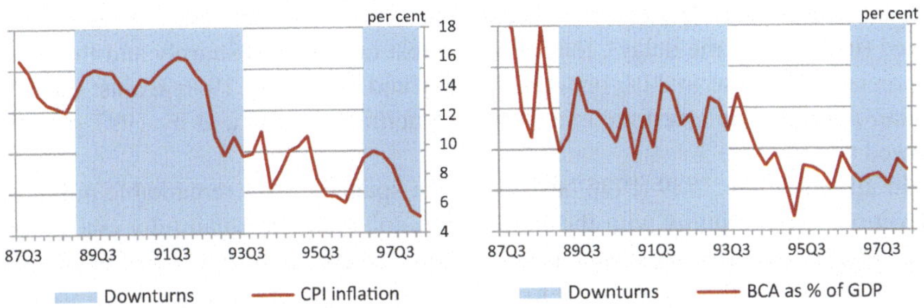

Fig. 9 The 1990s characterized by lower inflation and smaller BoP surpluses. Source: South African Reserve Bank

in credit spending as many households entered the credit markets for the first time in the post-apartheid era. The monetary growth increased inflation expectations, and interest rates were hiked in September 1994 and again in February and June 1995.

Fixed investment was also a strong component of the upswing, bolstered by mega investment projects (e.g. big steel-related investments such as Alusaf and Columbus). These public sector projects were an important catalyst in the fixed investment revival, which became broader based during 1995. Strong pent-up demand for capital spending was also a key driver of renewed growth. Unfortunately, it was evident that the domestic private sector still faced important structural constraints, not to mention SA's *'baptism-of-fire'* re-entering the international financial markets.

The improvement in business confidence was closely linked to the cyclical improvement in domestic demand conditions. Fixed investment growth petered out during the second quarter of 1996. The initial improvement in household consumption expenditure was moderate compared with the business cycle upswing phases of the 1980s, due to positive real interest rates (Pretorius et al. 1999: 41). Government consumption, which initially added to the growth momentum, slowed as fiscal policy was tightened in line with the GEAR longer term growth strategy (implemented in February 1996 in response to extreme financial volatility).

The current account of the balance of payments accumulated a deficit during the second half of 1994, due to strong capital inflows from the middle of that year and particularly during 1995, following the end of the dual exchange rate system (Fig. 9, right). The classical balance of payments constraint on growth asserted itself when the capital inflows reversed in February 1996 and again during the third quarter of 1996. It became evident that in a financially integrated global market place domestic economic policy was not independent (see Basu and Taylor 1999).

The SARB's policy was to rebuild the country's foreign exchange reserves, to gradually relax exchange controls and to restructure the market for foreign exchange, including the forward market. In the words of the then Governor: 'Good progress was made … during 1994 and 1995, but the country was surely not yet in a position to withstand the adverse developments of early 1996 … ' (Stals 1997: 3). The financial volatility in 1996 also provided the first indications of things to come. The structural shortcoming, namely insufficient balance of payments reserves, resurfaced. Net reserves declined in 1996, short-term interest rates were hiked (including some delay), long-term interest rates spiked sharply and the rand depreciated by close to 22% between January and December 1996 against the US dollar. All these signalled the end of the economic upswing and by 1997 growth slowed down.

In all, while the 1989–1996 business cycle spanned SA's remarkable political transition, the continuity with the 1980s 'stop-go' cycles was painfully evident as SA's first post-apartheid expansion ended. The reprieve on the balance of payments was short-lived and too little for it to be labelled as structural change. Even so, the 1994–1995 current account deficit certainly signalled a new beginning. Whereas the fixed investment ratio merely recovered to its pre-recession level during the expansion phase of the cycle, this recovery continued even during the subsequent economic downturn (1997–1999) and beyond.

4.4 The 1997–2007 Cycle: Encouraging Evidence of Structural Advances

The SA economy underwent key structural changes from the early 1990s. *Firstly,* an aggressive trade liberalisation policy was implemented to comply with the 1994 GATT. This exposed the SA industry to the winds of international competition. *Secondly,* the seminal political transition created new opportunities for the previously disadvantaged, including improved access to credit, employment and ownership and also opportunities to participate in the broader economic policymaking process. *Thirdly,* SA's financial integration with the world economy received further support with the scrapping of the dual exchange rate mechanism (March 1995) and the relaxation of exchange controls. Initially, capital inflows were slow to react. This changed gradually and South Africa became a favoured beneficiary of international portfolio capital, including for some inward direct investment. These structural changes were slow to permeate the economy and, as noted, the first post-apartheid economic expansion remained closely related to those of the 1980s. However, closer inspection of both the 1997–1999 economic downturn and the 1999–2007 expansion provides some indication of the underlying structural changes taking hold.

Downturn: January 1997–August 1999 The economic downturn which commenced towards the closing stages of 1996 and ended in August 1999 was the first post-apartheid economic downturn and was a noticeable period. *For one*, it was impacted by the East Asian financial crisis in 1997–1998, which tended to prolong the recessionary period (Venter and Pretorius 2001: 68). *Secondly*, the real economic growth rate only tapered off to below its long-term average, being the first *growth recession* witnessed since the 1970s.[18] Provided the prevailing macroeconomic

[18]The 1993–2007 period witnessed sustained positive growth, i.e. with no *level recession*. This characteristic does change when testing for *growth cycles* explaining the SARB's determination.

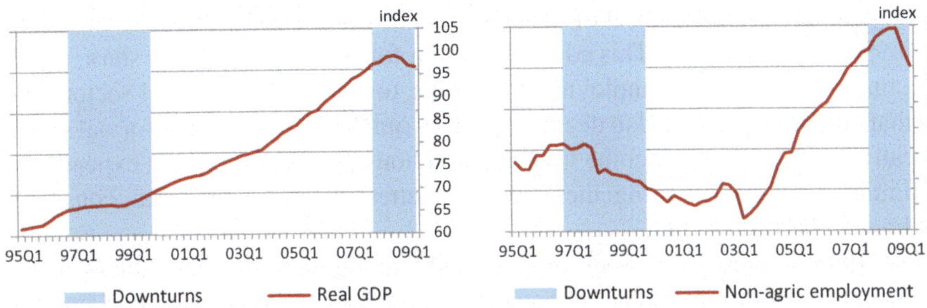

Fig. 10 Record expansion in GDP reverses adverse post-apartheid tendency in employment. Source: South African Reserve Bank

conditions (with prime rates reaching 25% in August 1998), this could be interpreted as encouraging evidence of structural improvements in the economy. This statement requires some unpacking.

The slowdown in real domestic expenditure, commencing during the second half of 1996 in response to restrictive macroeconomic policies,[19] was desirable in restoring the current account imbalance that developed during SA's first post-apartheid expansion. Initially, SA weathered the financial contagion from the East Asian financial crisis well with the rand remaining stable. Early during 1998, the domestic economy was starting to move beyond the recessionary phase; the decline in business confidence stabilised, interest rates declined (October 1997 and March 1998) and most economic indicators pointed to an imminent recovery.

Unfortunately, the East Asian contagion spread to Russia in 1998, with international investor risk aversion reaching extreme levels (April/May 1998). The rand came under pressure as portfolio capital flowed out from the country. A sharp increase in interest rates followed from April to August 1998 (with prime rates reaching 25%). These events delayed the economic recovery and prolonged the downward phase of the business cycle.

Amidst evidence of increased domestic economic resilience, the higher levels of uncertainty and reduced business confidence[20] and fixed investment spending, the contractionary fiscal policy and structural changes in the local labour market combine in explaining a precipitous fall a formal sector employment, measuring 7.5% over the course of the economic downturn (end-1996 to 1999Q3; Fig. 10, right). The decline in formal sector (non-agricultural) employment began much earlier; the contraction amounts to 15% between early 1995 and mid-2003, i.e. 2

[19]Prime rates increased by 5% points between 1994Q1 and 1996Q4. Fiscal policy was also tightened in procyclical manner following the implementation of the GEAR strategy (1996). Real government consumption expenditure contracted by an almost unprecedented 3.8% between 1996Q4 and 1998Q4.

[20]The RMB/BER business confidence index declined by more than 50 points from the end of 1995–1998Q4, i.e. at the apex of the impact of the Russian LTCM bankruptcy in the wake of the East Asian economic crisis.

calendar years before the onset of the economic downturn and 4 calendar years into the 1999–2007 expansion. This adverse trend in formal employment is stark, partly reflecting a huge shift of employment from the formal to the informal sector. The fact that employment tended to decline or shift from the formal to the informal sector typically involving some income loss, and real household consumption expenditure continuing to expand during the downturn, attest to the extent that consumer purchases relied on credit.

The 1998 interest rate shock at the height of household indebtedness had a significant impact on consumer behaviour. Consumers' propensity to consume on credit tapered noticeably after 1998. Interest rates declined to levels before the 1998 shock by mid-1999, but real domestic spending was slow to gather renewed speed. Cost-cutting and downsizing continued in the corporate sector and austere macroeconomic policies constrained the momentum. Yet, these proved to be the building blocks for an unusual expansion.

Record Expansion: September 1999 to November 2007 The second post-apartheid economic recovery was supported by an improvement in world economic activity following the East Asian crisis. The initial phase of the economic recovery will be remembered for two developments. *Firstly*, the notable decline in business and consumer confidence levels during calendar 2000 as markets reacted negatively to a number of non-economic factors (e.g. the Zimbabwean political-economic crisis and the HIV/AIDS debate). *Secondly*, the sharp depreciation of the rand exchange rate from the beginning of 2000 but more substantially towards the end of 2001 following the World Trade Center attacks in the USA. The subsequent spike in inflation invited 400 basis points of interest rate hikes during 2002, which caused recessionary conditions in key sectors (Venter 2005). Therefore, the first phase of the 1999–2007 expansion delivered moderate economic growth rates; however, there were signs of increased economic resilience.[21]

Export growth slowed down in response to the world economic downturn during 2001, however, the eventual real GDP growth rate of 2.8% for 2001 came in at the higher end of expectations. The resilience in domestic economic growth in the face of the world economic downturn was in sharp contrast to earlier periods of equally weak world economic conditions (e.g. 1981–1983 and 1991–1993).

The steady recovery in real household expenditure was central in the general economic recovery. The combination of steady growth in household income, low inflation and personal tax relief contributed to firmer growth in personal disposable incomes, exceeding the growth in credit extension to households, leading to reduced household indebtedness. This made consumers less vulnerable to the impact of the increase in interest rates during 2002. The improved demand conditions formed the basis for the recovery in fixed investment.

[21]The SARB identified two distinct phases during this record long expansion: the first stretched from 1999 to 2003 and the second from 2004 to 2007. The latter period delivered robust economic growth (Venter 2009: 65).

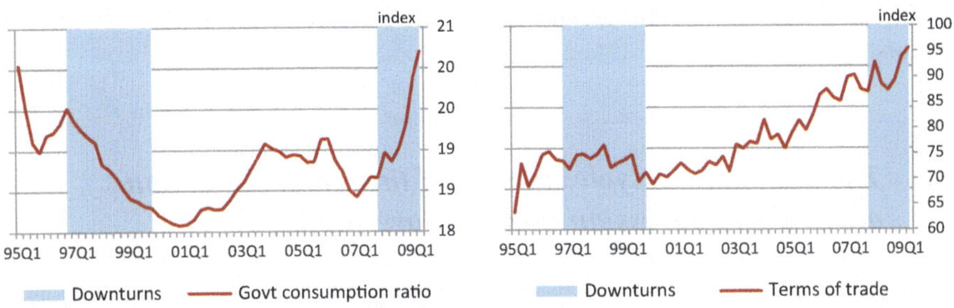

Fig. 11 Record 1999–2007 expansion benefits from looser fiscal policy and boost in terms of trade. Source: SA Reserve Bank and own calculations

The fixed investment revival was supported by public sector capital spending plans (infrastructure fixed investment) and export growth. The investment revival became the backbone of the economic recovery during calendar 2002. Improved profitability and productivity levels in the corporate sector following years of cost-cutting, downsizing and rationalisation, also boosted business confidence and fixed investment spending; from 2002 it appeared that the corporate sector embarked upon a period of 'upsizing,' which augured well for the economic expansion. Uninterrupted real economic growth, accelerating from around 2002–2003, is depicted in Fig. 10, left. The adverse trend in formal employment began reversing (Fig. 10) on the back of faster economic growth.

The greater economic resilience was embodied in a reduced contra-cyclical contribution to GDP growth from net exports (Fig. 11, right),[22] as well as a more stable macroeconomic environment enhancing steady growth in after-tax real disposable incomes. The fiscus could embark upon a more expansionary route (circa 2002) (Fig. 11, left). This probably encapsulates the essence of the structural improvements. The economy registered its longest post-war expansion. The 'second' phase of this expansion was characterised by strong growth, appreciably higher business and consumer confidence, as well as lively global growth and commodity prices. Real GDP growth averaged above 5% per annum between 2003 and 2007.

Important to note, however, the external financial sector lagged this structural improvement, reflected in a volatile currency. The rebuilding of the country's foreign exchange reserves was a longer term process. SA benefited mainly from portfolio investment inflows, which heightened the risk of financial volatility. SA's international competitiveness also lagged, reflected in the current account deficit in excess of 6% of GDP at the peak of the cycle. This implied that SA's export improvement was far from complete. The current account deficit made SA vulnerable to the impact of the 2007 US sub-prime financial crisis, which sparked

[22]Due to SA's re-integration with the world economy, particularly manufactured exports to African countries performed well during the second half of the 1990s. Exports continued to expand while imports declined, causing net exports to add to GDP growth in the face of global setbacks (e.g. during 1997–1998 and 2001).

the Great Recession worldwide, terminating SA's record expansion. SA's political leadership also changed.

4.5 *The 2007–2013 Cycle: Impact of the Great Recession and the Retrogression in SA's Governance*

As noted earlier in this book (see Boshoff and Becker 2020), the SA economy did not suffer a major financial impact from the global financial crisis which sparked the Great Recession. The country witnessed some capital flight and the rand exchange rate came under some pressure, but the broader financial conditions remained largely unaffected. The main impact arrived via the *trade channel* as all its trading partner economies suffered recessionary impacts, which caused the demand for exports to shrink. Commodity prices also tumbled temporarily; however, the big commodity price collapse only happened later when China's growth slowed down (2011–2015). The *real economic impact* was therefore more meaningful, including a contraction in real GDP and, more seriously, steep net job losses. The latter measured more than a million formal jobs by the end of 2010, effectively reversing close to half of the net jobs created over the 5 calendar years preceding the economic downturn. The contraction in real GDP was less serious in a historical context.[23] *The main feature of the 2007–2013 business cycle was the poor recovery phase.* As discussed by Boshoff and Becker, the aftermath of the Great Recession and the change in political leadership (2007 and 2009) left an indelible mark on the economy.

Downturn: December 2007 to August 2009 The 2008–2009 domestic economic downturn will be remembered for the fact that it embodied an abrupt end to SA's record expansion. The recession impact is best reflected in the 23.5% drop in the level of exports (2007Q4–2009Q3) coinciding with the full length of the domestic downturn. The shock impact on the export side is mirrored in a close to 15% drop in the export-oriented manufacturing output and a 14.5% drop in mining output. It also explains (with a three quarter time lag) the bulk of the 4.5% decline in non-agricultural formal sector employment, which then spilled over to household consumer spending. Real household consumption expenditure contracted by 2.4% (peak-to-trough).

Fixed investment spending contracted by 11.5%, being driven by the collapse in business confidence (62 points in all peak to trough, 44 points from the onset of the economic downturn). This, in turn, occurred mainly not only as a result of intense uncertainty in the wake of the global financial crisis but also due to falling production capacity utilisation as the demand conditions in particular the export sectors waned. The decline in fixed investment spending mainly comprised machinery

[23]The average contraction of real GDP during post-1974 economic downturns was 4.1%.

and equipment spending (including transport equipment) as the construction sector was boosted by the infrastructure spending associated with the World Soccer Cup in 2010; in fact, the construction sector avoided absolute contraction during the full period of the economic downturn—it was only towards the end of 2009 when most of the mega construction projects linked to the event began tapering off that the sector registered contractions in the level of real value add, i.e. 1.3% in all during 2010 (Venter 2011: 65–66).

The domestic market impact of the global economic downturn was countered by strong countercyclical fiscal policy as real government consumption expenditure continued to grow (by 10.1%) over the course of the 18-month economic downturn. This also softened the adverse impact on aggregate employment and household income. Real gross domestic expenditure contracted by 3% (peak to trough) and real GDP by 2.7%. The sharp fall in exports was countered by an equally sharp 22% drop in real import volumes, causing net exports to trend sideways during the economic downturn.

Expansion: September 2009 to November 2013 Close inspection of the expansion, which lasted 51 months (peaking in November 2013), reveals an inflection point around the middle of 2011, i.e. seven to eight quarters from the onset of the economic recovery. The initial period, 2010/2011, was characterized by a rebound in business confidence and economic activity from the recessionary slump in 2008–2009. *Firstly*, continued growth in China and India drove an immediate recovery in commodity prices, extending the commodity (super) cycle to 2011. *Secondly*, on the domestic front, strong countercyclical fiscal policy throughout the economic downturn and after (Fig. 12, left), witnessed sharp increases in public sector employment and real wage rates—the latter also spilling over to the private sector. This, combined with lower inflation in 2010, generally low interest rates (Fig. 12, right), a boom in unsecured lending (2010/2011) and the recovery on the JSE and higher property prices, boosted household consumption expenditure. Hence, the expansion may be classified as being consumption driven.

During the *second phase*, the export recovery was hampered by the sovereign debt crisis in SA's largest trading partner, the EU, which experienced a second leg of

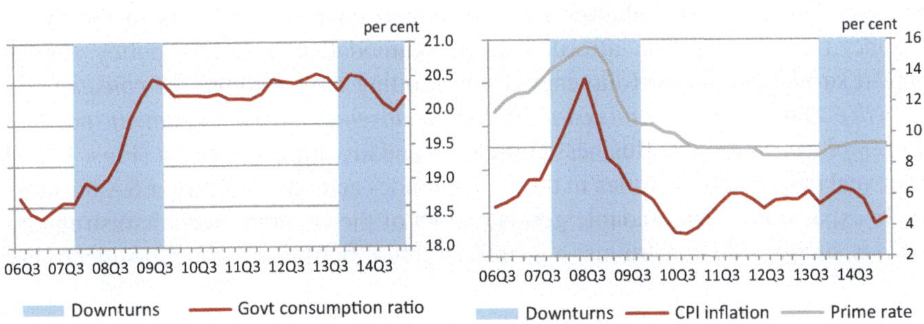

Fig. 12 The 2009–2013 expansion: fiscal stimulus, low inflation and interest rates. Source: South African Reserve Bank and Statistics SA

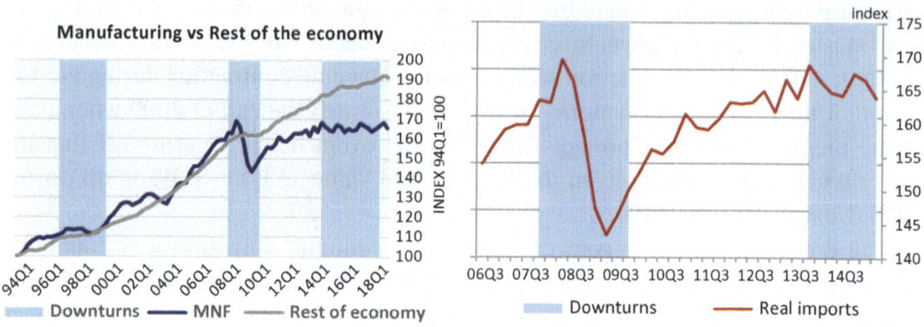

Fig. 13 The 2009–2013 expansion: manufacturing lags, imports surge. Source: South African Reserve Bank

the Great Recession (2010–2012). Furthermore, the (rebalancing) Chinese economy slowed, sparking a collapse in commodity prices (2011–2015) and a deterioration in SA's terms of trade over the period mid-2011 to end-2013; the global backdrop remained *'unfavourable and turbulent'* (Venter 2016: 107). Lower productivity growth, ageing populations, high indebtedness, poor business sentiment and fixed investment were all characteristic of economic growth in the advanced economies.

From 2011 onwards, domestic business confidence oscillated around weak levels and growth decelerated notably *'... as the weak global economy, domestic structural constraints and later also slowing domestic consumer demand all contributed to the demise of the upward phase in the business cycle'* (Venter 2016: 110). The typical flashpoints—or endogenous business cycle factors—sparking the upper turning point in the cycle were absent. No overcapacity, no undue wage pressures, no credit overextension, etc. While the current account deficit reached a shocking 6% of GDP mid-2013, this was handsomely financed; furthermore, the deficit was a direct result of the deteriorating terms of trade and a high import intensity, in turn, linked to a deteriorated manufacturing performance (Laubscher 2016: 14) (see Fig. 13).

Each business cycle has its peculiarities. The main narrative of the 2009–2013 expansion was that it was consumption led, with strong procyclical fiscal policy.[24] Whereas low inflation and zero-bound interest rate levels in the major advanced economies also afforded an accommodative monetary policy stance, amidst strong inward portfolio capital flows, oiling the spending, *the consumption growth eventually became unsustainable in the absence of fixed investment spending and employment growth.* Business confidence and investment were flat (Figs. 14 and 15 reveal the weak trajectories in these magnitudes compared to earlier SA business cycle expansions). The tradable goods sectors of the economy were hamstrung by serious supply-side constraints, e.g. infrastructure bottlenecks (such as electricity

[24]The expansionary fiscal stance produced budget deficits measuring above 5% of GDP in 2012/2013 and 2013/2014, inducing fiscal consolidation from 2012 onwards in procyclical fashion.

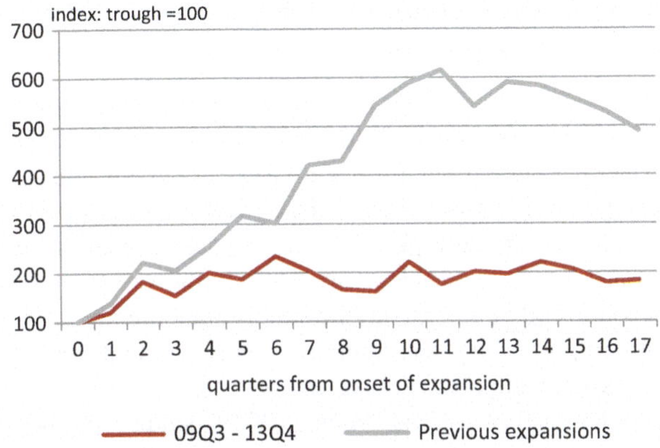

Fig. 14 Business confidence. Source: Bureau for Economic Research and South African Reserve Bank

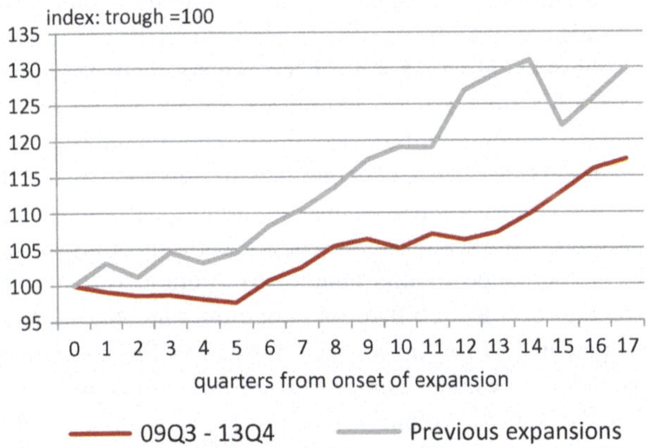

Fig. 15 Fixed investment. Source: Bureau for Economic Research and South African Reserve Bank

outages), disruptive labour market developments and prevailing economic policy uncertainty.[25] The latter aspect was directly linked to governance issues and associated regulatory uncertainties in key sectors (e.g. agriculture and mining). Slow credit growth also meant an important propagating factor in the business cycle momentum was absent.

[25]By the end of 2013, neither the level of real exports nor manufacturing and mining real value added had recovered to their pre-recession levels. The mining sector was also impacted by serious labour market instability, notably the tragic Marikana incident in the platinum sector (August 2012).

4.6 The 2013 to Date Economic Downturn—Resilience in Spending Become Unsustainable

From the former brief analysis, it is evident that the SA economy embarked upon an unusual business cycle exiting from the Great Recession impact in 2009. As noted, the absence of higher business confidence and growing fixed investment was a prominent feature. The mature phase of the expansion also did not deliver the typical overheating business cycle elements. The economy drifted into an economic downturn towards the end of 2013 from the supply side, mainly due to weak global growth, domestic supply-side constraints and deep economic policy uncertainty. This was in sharp contrast to previous cycles.

In a later chapter in this volume, Venter (2019) studies the behaviour of the SARB's composite leading business cycle indicator over the course of this unusual business cycle phase. The analysis shows that the leading indicator provided a reliable early signal of the end-2013 economic downturn. An equally pronounced and pervasive lower turning point signal (April 2016) initially indicated the possible onset of an economic recovery (from 17Q2). Unfortunately, the anticipated upward phase of the business cycle was not sufficiently persistent. Idiosyncratic factors, namely economic policy uncertainty and political developments, impacted business confidence adversely, which continued to inhibit investment. The SARB's leading indicator peaked in February 2018 and continued to trend downwards by mid-2019. The post-2009 absence of a revival in business confidence and investment continued. This rendered the surprising resilience in real domestic spending unsustainable.

It is outside of the scope of this chapter to attempt to quantify the adverse impact of the general political climate on economic outcomes. Economic growth appears to have ranked low on the list of priorities of the governing party under the leadership of former president Zuma, who assumed office in May 2009 (see the Freytag (2020) analysis in this volume). This low priority was evident in the serious weakening of governance of public institutions. Apart from internal divisions and corruption (including so-called 'state-capture'), inconsistent policy pronouncements and serious regulatory concerns in key sectors generated a climate of intense economic policy uncertainty. In addition, the lingering uncertainty in the wake of the Great Recession aggravated strained economic conditions. Figure 16 shows the constraining influence of the general political climate, as measured by the BER in a survey of manufacturing executives.[26] Weak trends in fixed investment were found to be inversely correlated to the extreme levels of general political uncertainty impacting business. Yet, this was not the only story of the 2013-to date economic downturn.

The preceding expansion exhibited a small amplitude due to the flat trajectory of business confidence and fixed investment (and exports). The interesting point is that

[26] This indicator reached a historical peak in 2017 in the run-up to the governing political party's leadership conference (December).

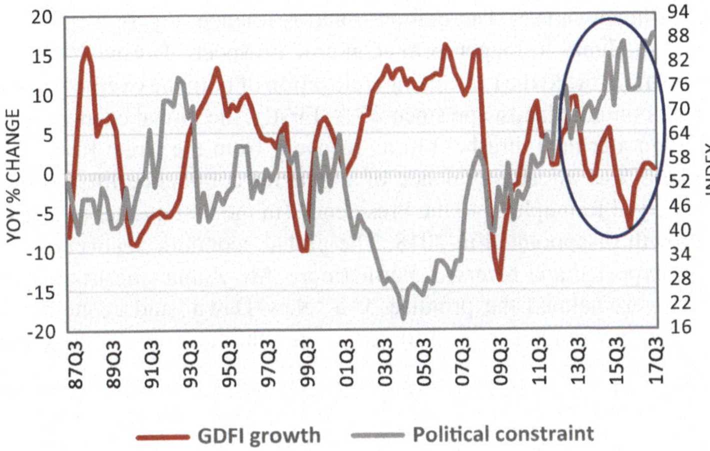

Fig. 16 Fixed investment spending versus general political uncertainty. Source: South African Reserve Bank and Bureau for Economic Research

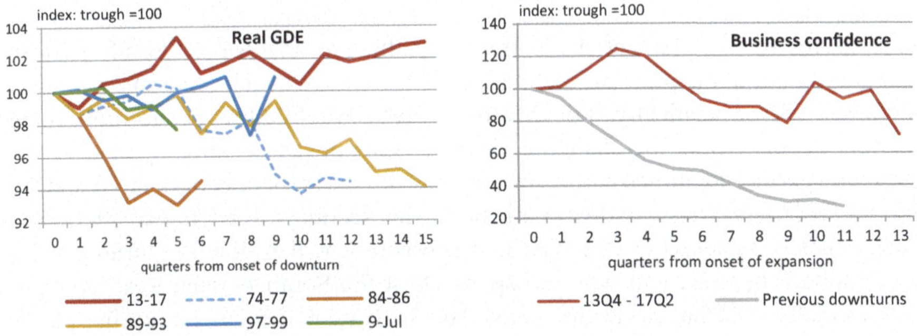

Fig. 17 Real domestic spending and business confidence during downturns. Source: South African Reserve Bank, Bureau for Economic Research and own calculations

the same remained true during the downturn. Real economic growth continued to slow down (and business confidence fell sharper in 2017), but as Fig. 17 (right) reveals, the tendency in business confidence held up much better compared to previous downturns. The resilience in business confidence was not spurious. It is explained by what may be characterised as an important feature of the downturn, i.e. the resilience in real gross domestic expenditure (GDE). Household expenditure provided the backbone, government consumption was relatively well behaved (and largely neutral in terms of its impact) and investment spending actually held up well in a historical context and in view of all the headwinds. This pattern was very different compared to previous economic downturns (Fig. 17, left).

Business confidence did not rise during the expansion, but it also did not fall as sharp during the economic downturn like the pattern usually tended to be. This trend translates into unexpected resilience during an economic downturn, which faced serious headwinds.[27] The demonstrated resilience augurs well in terms of the country's medium- to longer term economic prospects. During 2017 and early 2018, South Africa faced the (promising) relaxation of both the overpowering trends affecting the economic landscape since 2009. Firstly, the global economy appeared to have crossed a critical threshold in its recovery from the Great Recession; and, secondly, there was already evidence of a general confidence lift following the ascension of Cyril Ramaphosa to the Presidency (in the first quarter of 2018). Even so, SA's growth disappointed in 2018. The global economic recovery turned out weaker than expected and reversed. Furthermore, Mr. Zuma's destructive legacies have so far overwhelmed the promise of a 'New Dawn' and economic revival. While the economy remains poised for faster growth, the structural headwinds are formidable.

5 Descriptive Analysis of Properties of South African Business Cycles

It is useful to complement the narrative qualitative analysis of South African business cycles in the previous section with a descriptive quantitative analysis since the mid-1970s. Specifically, a descriptive analysis would allow one to draw some inferences concerning the changing characteristics of the business cycle over the structural periods identified earlier. In keeping with the taxonomy of Boshoff and Du Plessis (2020), presented earlier in this book, this section will adopt two alternative approaches to business cycles. The first subsection will follow the turning point cycle approach, consistent with the approach of the South African Reserve Bank and a number of chapters in this book. The analysis will focus on turning points identified by the Bank as well as a set of independently identified turning points, using the BBQ method, as discussed by Boshoff and Du Plessis (2020). In following a turning point approach to business cycles, the emphasis will be on various phase properties, including phase duration, amplitude, steepness, the shape of the cycle and cumulative change over the cycle or phase. The analysis will rely on overall GDP, the expenditure components of GDP as well as the broad sectors included in GDP. The second subsection will follow the modern approach to business cycles, which view cycles as 'serially correlated deviations from trend'. Therefore, the emphasis in this the second part will be on volatility and co-movement analysis over all three structural periods, in respect of the same variables as investigated under the

[27] An alternative interpretation is that of the late Cees Bruggemans, who warned in 2014 that SA's business cycle was being suspended due to the momentous societal changes, combining with the post-2009 global uncertainties. The usual business cycle dynamics became absent, with no real lift in business confidence and economic growth, but in its place, a 'wait-and-see' attitude in the private sector. This turned out to be a remarkable insight (Bruggemans 2014). As it turned out, the economy hardly expanded and, subsequently, hardly slowed down.

turning point cycle approach, as well as other key economic indicators, including interest rates, inflation, money and credit supply and the exchange rate. All data is of a quarterly frequency.

5.1 *Key Characteristics of Turning Point Cycles*

The methods applied to describe the various business cycle characteristics rely mainly on existing work. The chapters by Boshoff and Du Plessis (2020) as well as Boshoff and Becker (2020) already cover the concepts of duration, amplitude and steepness.

In addition, we define the shape of the cycle as follows:

$$\nu_i = 1/\left(d_i/2\right)\left\{\sum_{k}^{\frac{d_i}{2}}\left(y_{k+t_i} - y_{k+t_{i-1}}\right) - \sum_{k=\left(\frac{d_i}{2}\right)}^{d_i}\left(y_{k+t_{i-1}}\right)\right\} \tag{1}$$

where:

d_i = duration of the *i*th business cycle phase

ν_i = the average difference between the cumulative change during the first half of the *i*th phase of the cycle and that during the second half of the phase.

The shape of the cycle is an indication of the non-linearity of the cycle: a positive (negative) value for the metric ν_i indicates a stronger expansion (contraction) during the first half of the phase compared to the second half; conversely, a negative (positive) value indicates a stronger second half of the expansion (contraction). A measure for the *average shape of the cycle* over the sample period can be obtained according to a weight equal to the duration of the *i*th phase (d_i) relative to the total sample period duration, *N*, and averaging over $\{\nu_i\}$, as indicated in Eq. (2).

$$= \frac{1}{N}\sum_{i}\left(\frac{d_i}{N}\right)\nu_i \tag{2}$$

Duration Characteristics

As noted, the duration characteristics of the SA business cycle were investigated over the period 1974–2017, considering both the SARB's official dating of the business cycle turning points, as well as with the application of the BBQ dating algorithm. We have already noted the changes in the duration characteristics of SA's modern business cycle from the post-war period (1946–1973) to the subsequent period (1974–1993 and beyond). A key change relates to the lengthening of the business cycle, which was an international phenomenon (IMF 2007b: 68–69). In

SA's case the lengthening occurred mainly due to substantially longer economic downturns (Venter 2019: 11–20).

In keeping with the narrative analysis, we do not consider the first three decades after the Second World War (1946–1973) (please refer to the chapter by Boshoff and Fourie (2020) for a longer term view of South African cycles in the twentieth century). The focus of the current study is on the period from the mid-1970s, which was subdivided into three structural periods, i.e. 1974–1993, 1993–2007 and 2008–2017. Unfortunately, an 'end-point' of the third period has not been identified. We have witnessed only one-and-a-half complete peak-to-peak business cycles (i.e. 2007–2013, as well as the 2013-to date economic downturn). Therefore, an investigation of the duration and other phase statistics over this period is not feasible. Consequently, following the approach adopted by Burger (2010), this chapter compares the business cycle duration (and other) characteristics over the pre-1994 and post-1994 periods. The results are displayed in Table 1.

The results confirm that the SA business cycle lengthened over the sample period (1974–2017) compared to the post-war period (1946–1973). The full business cycle lengthened to 26 quarters (or 79 months) from 12½ quarters (37.4 months) according to the SARB determination (Venter 2019: 12). Even applying the BBQ algorithm (measuring seven peak-to-peak business cycles compared to the six official cycles over the 1974–2017 period), suggests cycles lengthened to 21 quarters (63 months). The lengthening occurred due to both longer downturns, i.e. from 4½ quarters to 11 quarters (SARB) or 9 quarters (BBQ), and due to longer expansions, i.e. from 8 quarters to 16 quarters (SARB) or 12 quarters (BBQ).

Table 1 The SA business cycle: duration characteristics—SARB vs BBQ dating: 1974–2017

	SARB official determination			BBQ algorithm		
Statistic	Downturns	Expansions	Cycle	Downturns	Expansions	Cycle
Post-war (1946–1973)#	**4½**	**8**	**12½**	–	–	–
Ave duration:	**11**	**16**	**26**	**9**	**12**	**21**
74Q3–93Q2	11	12	22	11	8	17
93Q3–17Q4	11	25	34	8	16	25
Full sample:						
Max	17	33	44	15	17	31
Min	6	5	11	5	4	10
Median	11	15	26	10	14	23
Proportion:	45.0%	55.0%	–	46.0%	54.0%	–
74Q3–93Q2	60.0%	40.0%	–	62.3%	37.7%	–
93Q3–17Q4	33.3%	66.7%	–	33.7%	66.3%	–
E/C ratio:	–	1.56	–	–	1.59	–
74Q3–93Q2	–	1.03	–	–	0.83	–
93Q3–17Q4	–	2.08	–	–	2.16	–

Bold indicates totals
#Source: Venter (2019: 12); own calculations

When considering the differentiation between the pre-1994 and post-1994 periods, it is evident from Table 1 that the lengthening of the business cycle from the mid-1970s was mainly due to notably longer expansions during the post-1994 period: according to the SARB chronology, the length of downturns remained unchanged at 11 quarters over both sub-periods, whereas expansions doubled from 12 quarters to 25 quarters. The full business cycle therefore lengthened even further during the post-1994 period to 34 quarters (102 months). Over the post-1994 period, the economy spent two-thirds of the time in expansion compared to only 40% of the time during the pre-1994 period. These proportion statistics are mirrored in the BBQ-based turning point chronology. According to this dating method, the duration of expansions actually remained unchanged at eight quarters during the pre-1994 period and compared to the post-war period (1946–1973). Thereafter duration of expansions doubled (similar to the official determination) to 16 quarters (and the full cycle to 25 quarters). The expansion/contraction ratio (E/C ratio) also reflects stronger expansions during the post-1994 period, for both business cycle-dating methodologies.

In all, while the post-war trend of longer business cycles continued over the period from the mid-1970s (from 37.4 months during the 1946–1973 period to 102 months during the post-1994 period), the disruptions caused by the implosion of the apartheid state (1974–1993), characterized by recurrent sociopolitical crises and intensifying international isolation, had the effect of dampening this trend; the duration of expansions only lengthened moderately (or remained unchanged), while downturns lengthened noticeably. The 1994 political transition brought a doubling in the length of expansions, while downturns tended to shorten.

Other Business Cycle Characteristics

Other business cycle characteristics, including amplitude, steepness and shape of the cycle, were also measured and compared between the pre- and post-1994 periods, as reported in Table 2.

Both the SARB's determination and the BBQ algorithm suggest that expansions had a substantially larger average *amplitude* compared to downturns. Furthermore, the amplitude of expansions increased noticeably in the post-1994 period. This result is consistent with the duration statistics. Whereas the amplitude of downturns is negative in respect to the pre-1994 period, it turned positive in the post-1994 period. This reveals the presence of *growth recessions* during the post-1994 period compared to absolute contractions in the pre-1994 period.[28] Regarding expansions, their amplitude increased notably during the post-1994 period. In this regard, the record 1999–2007 expansion is a clear outlier, as the amplitudes of the 1993–1996 and the 2009–2013 expansions were in line with those of the pre-1994 period.

The steepness statistics reveal interesting characteristics of SA's modern business cycle. Firstly, mirroring the amplitude statistics, relatively shallow absolute

[28]During both the 1997–1999 and 2013-to date economic downturns, real GDP continued to expand in absolute terms, which contrasted with the classic recessions witnessed during the 1980s 'stop-go' business cycles.

Table 2 The SA business cycle: other characteristics—SARB vs BBQ dating: 1974–2017

	SARB official determination			BBQ algorithm		
Characteristic	Downturns	Expansions	Cycle	Downturns	Expansions	Cycle
Ave amplitude (%):	**0.00**	**0.16**	–	**0.00**	**0.13**	–
74Q3–93Q2	−0.02	0.12	–	−0.02	0.09	–
93Q3–17Q4	0.02	0.24	–	0.02	0.15	–
Steepness:	**0.000**	**0.010**	–	**0.000**	**0.010**	–
74Q3–93Q2	−0.002	0.010	–	−0.002	0.012	–
93Q3–17Q4	0.002	0.009	–	0.003	0.009	–
Shape of cycle:	**0.001**	**−0.007**	–	**0.000**	**0.001**	–
74Q3–93Q2	0.002	−0.005	–	−0.001	−0.001	–
93Q3–17Q4	0.000	−0.010	–	0.001	0.002	–
Ave GDP growth (% pa)	**−0.3**	**4.6**	**2.4**	**0.0**	**4.5**	**2.4**
74Q3–93Q2	−0.8	5.5	1.5	−1.0	5.3	2.2
93Q3–17Q4	0.7	3.7	3.2	1.0	3.8	2.6
Ave GDP growth[a]	**−0.1**	**4.2**	–	**0.1**	**4.1**	–
74Q3–93Q2	−0.5	4.9	–	−0.6	4.5	–
93Q3–17Q4	0.9	3.8	–	1.1	4.0	–

Bold indicates totals
Source: South African Reserve Bank and own calculations
[a]Real GDP growth weighted by the duration of the business cycle phase relative to the total time during the full sample period spent in expansion (contraction)

contractions during the pre-1994 period were followed by relatively shallow growth recessions during the post-1994 period. Secondly, expansions tended to be notably steeper compared to the downturns, however, the steepness of expansions receded during the post-1994 period. The steepness of expansions receded not because of weaker growth (that accelerated), but due to longer duration. Once more, the record 1999–2007 expansion played a disproportionate role in this regard. These results are consistent between both business cycle-dating methods. The pre-1994 period was characterised by absolute contractions and shorter, but steeper, expansions true to the 'stop-go' business cycles of the 1970s and 1980s.

In terms of the shape of the South African business cycle, results are somewhat mixed. Most results suggest (marginal) non-linearity over the period from the mid-1970s. According to the SARB determination, downturns tend to be linear over the first and second halves of the business cycle, albeit evident that some differentiation is visible considering the sub-periods. Downturns tend to gather momentum during the second part of the business cycle phase over the pre-1994 period, whereas, they tended to be linear over the post-1994 period. Expansions, on the other hand, appear to gather significantly more momentum during the second half of the business cycle phase. This is true regarding both sub-periods, albeit evidently more so regarding the post-1994 period.[29] These results are somewhat contradicted by the BBQ results.[30] One has to conclude that the 'shape of the cycle' results is inconclusive, except regarding expansions. This agrees with the marginal results obtained in a previous similar study of SA's business cycle characteristics over the early 1970s to early 2000s period (see Du Plessis 2006a: 8, 20).

Finally, considering the growth momentum during business cycle phases, the results indicate that real GDP growth was relatively rapid during expansion phases (4.5% per annum) and being followed by relatively shallow downturns (zero to −0.3% real GDP growth per annum). The contrast was sharper during the pre-1994 period, with growth varying from −1% per annum during contractions to +5.5% per annum during expansions. The higher growth during expansions in the pre-1994 period compared to that during the post-1994 period reflects the degree of 'rebound' from absolute contractions. From a full business cycle perspective, real GDP growth averaged significantly faster during the post-1994 period (3% per annum) compared to the pre-1994 period (1.5% per annum). These results do not change when the growth rates are weighted by the duration of the business cycle phases (i.e. according to a larger weight to business cycle phases with longer durations).

Business Cycle Characteristics at the Disaggregated Level

The foregoing business cycle characteristics were also investigated in respect of the main expenditure components of GDP, as well as the broad non-agricultural sectors of the economy.[31] Interesting patterns emerge. While the average duration, amplitude, steepness and GDP growth momentum are considered in respect of each expenditure component and broad sector in GDP, only the steepness results are displayed in Figs. 18, 19 and 20. The detailed results are shown in the Appendix.

From Fig. 18 it is clear that sharp contractions in fixed and inventory investment and, to a lesser extent, exports played an important part in economic downturns. The influence of contracting inventories receded during the post-1994 period but remained—along with fixed investment and exports—the steepest expenditure component of GDP. Imports also contracted steeply, which countered the contraction in GDP. Also see Fig. 20, where an analysis was made of the *growth cycles* in the

[29]SA's record expansion (1999–2007) was characterised by a slow start (2000–2003), evolving into rapid growth during the second part of the upturn (2004–2007). This largely explains the non-linearity of expansions over the post-1994 period.

[30]The disagreement between the SARB determination and that of the BBQ algorithm can be explained. Whereas the SARB identified a record long post-apartheid expansion (1999–2007), which gathered a substantial faster pace during the second half, the BBQ algorithm actually identified a 'growth recession' during the slower first half of the expansion (2002Q3–2004Q1). According to the BBQ algorithm, both downturns and expansions were slightly faster during the first part of the phases in contrast to the shape of the cycle according to the SARB determination.

[31]The expenditure and gross value added components of GDP were analysed in their (natural log) levels, applying the BBQ algorithm in determining turning points. Alternatively, classical cycles were investigated. Where possible, the results were corroborated with a growth cycle analysis and no contradictions were found.

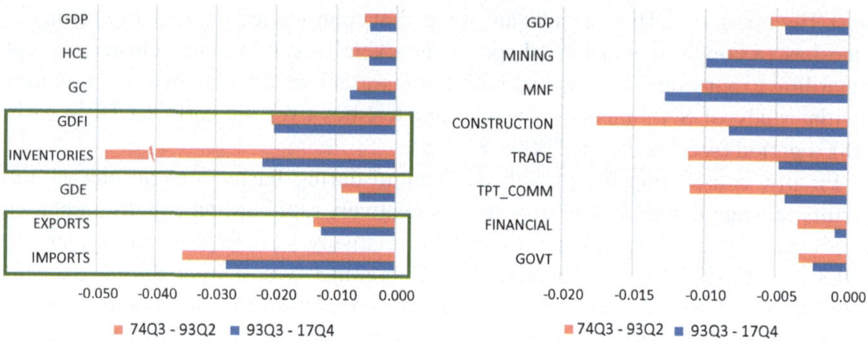

Fig. 18 SA business cycle—steepness of economic downturns: pre-1994 vs post-1994

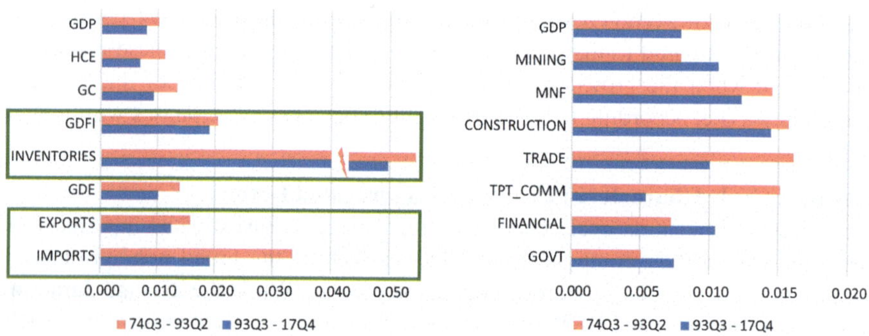

Fig. 19 South African business cycle—steepness of expansions: pre-1994 vs post-1994

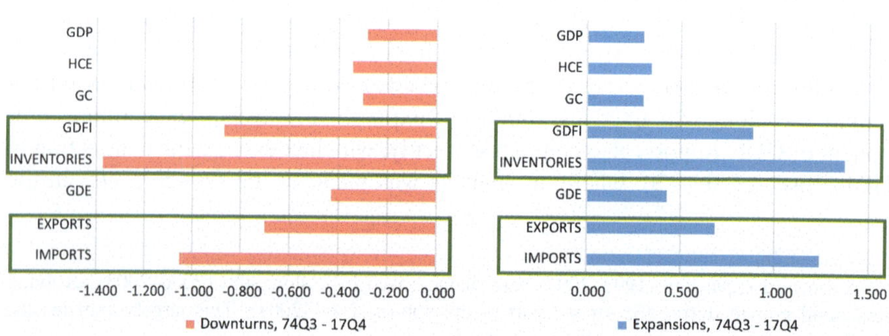

Fig. 20 The steepness of South African growth cycles over the full sample period, 1974Q3–2017Q4

GDP expenditure components over the full sample period. The steepness of the contraction in most expenditure components receded during the post-1994 period. However, this was not related to the longer duration of economic downturns in the post-1994 period (downturns shortened) but was due to shallower contractions.

Therefore, economic downturns both shortened and became shallower during the post-1994 period and this is true regarding most expenditure components of GDP.

Regarding the broad economic sectors, there are interesting diverging patterns between the two periods. Contractions in construction activity were particularly steep during the pre-1994 period, as were those of mining, manufacturing, internal trade and transport and communication, i.e. all the cyclical sectors of the economy. This changed during the post-1994 period. Whereas contractions in construction activity remained steep, this receded noticeably compared to the pre-1994 period. Both mining and manufacturing emerge as the key drivers of economic downturns in the post-1994 period, i.e. more so compared to the pre-1994 period. The impact of the 2008–2009 Great Recession may have had a disproportionate influence in this regard. The services sectors (internal trade, transport and communication, financial and business services and the general government) played a much smaller cyclical role in the economic downturns over the post-1994 period.

Regarding expansions, it is also clear that the accumulation of inventories plays an important part, both during the pre- and post-1994 periods; its steepness did recede during the post-1994 period. The steepness of all expenditure components of GDP was higher during the pre-1994 period; however, this was the result of a shorter duration. As noted, business cycles were characterised by deeper contractions and sharper rebounds over this period, giving rise to the 'stop-go' cycle description. The results are consistent with the foregoing analysis of the duration and other business cycle characteristics. In terms of 'driving' the expansions, it is evident that fixed and inventory investment and exports played the leading roles, including the associated and counterbalancing swings in imports (see Laubscher 2019: 469–470).[32] This pattern displays clearer in Fig. 20, where an analysis was made of the growth cycles in the GDP expenditure components over the full sample period.[33]

As far as *sectoral patterns are concerned*, manufacturing, construction, internal trade and transport and communication expansions tended to be steeper during the pre-1994 period; however, their steepness receded during the post-1994 period, particularly that of the internal trade and transport and communication sectors. The strongest sectoral 'drivers' of the post-1994 expansions were construction, manufacturing and mining. It is also interesting that the steepness of the financial and government sector expansions increased notably during the post-1994 period, hinting towards an increased 'driving' role—an issue to which this book returns in

[32]It needs to be emphasized that these results need to be tested for statistical significance and causality. To state that a variable *drives* the expansion or contraction is loaded. Here, it is simply assumed from basic theoretical premises that a steeper trajectory of an economic magnitude gives it some driving property in terms of the business cycle development. However, more research is required.

[33]The (natural log-transformed) value of each seasonally adjusted expenditure component and GDP at constant prices was de-trended applying a Christiano-Fitzgerald bandpass filter (see Boshoff and McLean 2018). The turning points in the resultant cycle component of each time series were then determined using the BBQ algorithm, which also calculated the business cycle statistics such as duration, average amplitude and steepness.

the chapter by Hollander and Van Lill (2020). Manufacturing and construction, on the other hand, lost some of their 'driving' role in expansions compared to the pre-1994 period. The poor growth of manufacturing during the post-2009 period is a well-documented fact.

In all, whereas the SA business cycle (officially) lengthened to 34 quarters (102 months) during the post-1994 period from 12½ quarters (37.4 months) during the post-war period (1946–1973), the intervening period witnessed only a modest increase in the duration of expansions and downturns. Business cycle volatility tended to increase over this period, reflected by steeper changes in the expenditure and sector components of GDP. Whereas the average steepness and growth tended to be higher during the pre-1994 period, the duration of expansions doubled during the post-1994 period and downturns tended to stabilise (or shorten). This resulted in higher peak-to-peak economic growth during the post-1994 period. The economy spent 60% of the time in *a downturn* over the pre-1994 period compared to only a third of the time during the post-1994 period. However, it is clear that the record 1999–2007 expansion had a disproportionate influence in this regard. Including the weak post-2009 expansion in the sample period, the distinction between the two periods becomes less apparent, particularly when the disaggregated sectoral and spending components of GDP are considered.

What does stand out *on the demand side* during both the pre- and post-1994 periods, is the important cyclical role of fixed and inventory investment, as well as exports (and imports). Sharp contractions in fixed and inventory investment (driving counterbalancing imports) played the strongest role in economic downturns, whereas slowly improving fixed and inventory investment that gathers speed during the second half of the upturn appears to be a key feature of expansions. *On the supply side*, manufacturing, mining and construction and–to a lesser extent—internal trade appeared to play a stronger role in the business cycle, both during expansions and downturns. This is what one would expect. More nuances emerge from an analysis of volatility and co-movement, as attempted in the next section.

5.2 Business Cycle Volatility and Co-movement

In an earlier chapter, Boshoff and Du Plessis (2020) discussed an alternative approach to business cycle identification, which does not focus on turning points. This alternative approach, which dominates modern business cycle research, views cycles as 'serially correlated deviations from trend'. As noted in that chapter, two of the key variables of interest in this literature relate to volatility and co-movement.

Figure 2, presented earlier, depicts the changing volatility of South Africa's real GDP growth, with a 10-year rolling standard deviation. This figure illustrates the increase in volatility of real economic growth over the 1980s and how it subsided from the mid-1990s and beyond. The volatility of real GDP growth can also be seen as a measure of SA's business cycle volatility, given the scope of the aggregate GDP variable. The aim of this section is to investigate the volatility and co-movement of

GDP and its expenditure and sectoral components, as well as other key economic indicators.

Volatility will be assessed by considering the standard deviation of the cyclical component of each variable (after log transformation and applying a CF bandpass filtering methodology) during each identified structural period. The standard deviation during each structural period is expressed in relative terms to the standard deviation of the cyclical component of the relevant variable during the full sample period. The absolute value of the standard deviation of the cycle component of each variable (i.e. only the expenditure and sector components of GDP) is also shown, both independently and in relation to that of GDP.

To measure co-movement, cross-correlation coefficients are calculated between the business cycle component of GDP and those of all the other economic time series, at different lag intervals (i.e. contemporaneous, as well as in periods $t-1$ to $t-4$ and $t+1$ to $t+4$). The business cycle component is again obtained by de-trending each economic time series using a bandpass filter (following Agresti and Mojon in their study of the characteristics of the Euro area business cycle, 2001; also see the study by Burger (2010) of South Africa's business cycle characteristics across structural time periods).[34,35] All economic time series were transformed into their natural logarithms before de-trending, except for the CPI inflation rate, the different interest rates and the yield curve. While the volatility results are reported separately from the co-movement results, they should be read in conjunction as displayed in the Appendix.

The Evolution of Business Cycle Volatility

Table 3 displays the volatility of real GDP and its expenditure and sectoral components across the three structural sub-periods, i.e. 1974Q3–1993Q2 (the demise of apartheid period), 1993Q3–2007Q4 (the post-apartheid expansion period) and 2008Q1–2017Q4 (the post-global financial crisis period). Hereafter, these periods will be referred to as the first, second and third period, respectively. Subdivision of the post-1994 period is feasible in terms of duration. Furthermore, the study of the post-2007 period, spanning the impact and aftermath of the 2008 global financial crisis, tends to reveal significant and useful results.

[34] Analysts differ in their choice of de-trending method. Zarnowitz and Ozyildirim (2001) motivate, for instance, why the Phase Average Trend (PAT) method tends to deliver superior results compared to other frequency filter smoothing methods. Other researchers have found the opposite; the OECD actually moved from the PAT filtering method to a (double) Hodrick–Prescott (HP) filtering method in the compilation of the OECD's composite business cycle indictors (Nilsson and Gyomai 2011). This institution rates the HP and Christiano & Fitzgerald (CF) bandpass filtering methods above PAT.

[35] Agresti & Mojon applied a marginally adjusted version of the Baxter and King (1999) (BK) bandpass filter (2001: 6–7). In the current study, the Christiano & Fitzgerald (CF) version was chosen as it avoided the truncation of end-points problem encountered in the BK version. The objective is to investigate co-movement across structural sub-periods, which rendered the BK method of de-trending problematic. Burger (2010) used the Hodrick Prescott (HP) filter; however, this filter is also known to possess an end-point problem (see Zarnowitz and Ozyildirim 2001).

Table 3 Business cycle volatility: GDP demand and supply, 1974–2017

Variable	1974Q3–2017Q4 Standard deviation		1974Q3–1993Q2	1993Q3–2007Q4	2008Q1–2017Q4
			Standard deviation scaled with full sample		
	Absolute	Relative/ GDP	Relative	Relative	Relative
GDP	0.014	(1.0)	1.16	0.70	0.56
Expenditure:					
Consumption	0.020	(1.5)	1.09	0.62	0.73
Govt consumption	0.016	(1.1)	1.17	1.00	0.43
Investment	0.051	(3.6)	1.21	0.44	0.67
Cum inventories	0.300	(21.5)	0.61	1.45	0.13
GDE	0.024	(1.8)	1.27	0.47	0.52
Exports	0.032	(2.3)	0.82	0.73	1.21
Imports	0.067	(4.8)	1.29	0.42	0.81
Sectors:					
Mining	0.019	(1.4)	1.02	0.66	1.11
Manufacturing	0.030	(2.1)	1.03	0.79	0.91
Construction	0.035	(2.5)	1.20	0.68	0.52
Trade	0.028	(2.0)	1.27	0.76	0.39
Transport/communications	0.021	(1.5)	1.32	0.79	0.28
Financial	0.011	(0.8)	0.80	1.32	0.52
Government	0.009	(0.6)	1.22	0.57	0.56

A number of observations can be made regarding the results contained in Table 3. Firstly, considering the demand side of the economy, the volatility of GDP was significantly higher during the first period, highlighted by the number of shaded cells indicating a relative value higher than unity. This is consistent with Fig. 2 noted above. In the previous section, the origin of SA's boom–bust business cycles was discussed being the second half of the 1970s. These cycles became more pronounced during the 1980s and continued in an important way up to the mid-1990s. GDP volatility receded noticeably during the second period and even further during the third period. The volatility of government consumption spending and private inventory investment remained average or above average during the second period. Export volatility picked up strongly in period three; however, the big slump and rebound at the time of the Great Recession impact (2008–2009) played an overbearing role in this short structural period.

Secondly, the more volatile expenditure components of GDP are fixed and inventory investment. Over the full sample period, fixed investment is 3½ times as volatile as GDP; and inventory investment substantially more so. Furthermore, exports and imports are between 2.3 and 4.8 times as volatile as GDP. These results agree with the steepness business cycle characteristics and the suggestion that investment, exports and countervailing imports play an important role as momentum drivers in SA's business cycle. Not shown in Table 3, is a notable increase in the relative volatility of household consumption expenditure, i.e. from being as volatile as GDP during the first period to being double GDP's volatility during the third period (see the Appendix, Table 12). This hints towards a stronger cyclical role for household consumption spending during the third period [compare Burger (2010)].

From a sectoral perspective, it is evident that the volatility of manufacturing and construction real value added is higher (between 2 and 2½ times that of GDP), followed by internal trade (double) and the other services sectors (e.g. transport and communication). Financial and business services and the general government are the only two sectors being less volatile compared to aggregate GDP. However, notice the increased relative volatility of financial services during the second period. This is consistent with SA's financial re-integration with the world economy and the accompanying financial volatility witnessed during the 1990s.

Table 4 shows the (relative) volatility of a range of key policy and financial economic variables. Again, it is clear that the first period witnessed the highest volatility, with inflation, money supply and interest rate volatility being well above average over this period. The most significant result is the reduced volatility of interest rates across the three structural periods, i.e. both the nominal and real prime overdraft rate, 10-year government bond yields and the yield curve. A similar tendency is evident in the case of the three monetary aggregates and credit supply. Inflation volatility picked up during the second period. This volatility was presumably transmitted by the more volatile currency over this period, also

Table 4 Business cycle volatility: policy and other financial variables, 1974–2017

	1974Q3–2017Q4		1974Q3–1993Q2	1993Q3–2007Q4	2008Q1–2017Q4
	Standard deviation		Standard deviation scaled with full sample		
Variable	Absolute	Relative/GDP	Relative	Relative	Relative
Policy variables:					
CPI inflation	1.989	–	0.88	1.13	0.67
CPI index	0.016	–	1.12	1.25	0.73
Prime_nom	2.147	–	1.19	0.82	0.34
Prime_real	2.649	–	1.29	0.65	0.29
GC_ratio	0.315	–	0.89	0.99	0.68
Money supply:					
M1	0.053	–	1.24	0.66	0.32
M2	0.041	–	1.24	0.45	0.33
M3	0.031	–	1.17	0.66	0.34
Credit supply	0.032	–	1.13	0.69	0.40
Financial variables:					
Neer	0.084	–	0.77	1.01	0.82
Reer	0.068	–	0.88	0.90	0.83
10y bond	0.769	–	1.12	1.04	0.43
Yield curve	2.109	–	1.19	0.87	0.36

explaining the volatility of the financial sector noted above and the fact that the volatility in bond yields remained above-average during the second period.

Money supply volatility remained sticky at a high level during the second period (not shown, but around 2–3½ times the volatility of GDP). This pattern coincided with the tendency in the volatility of CPI inflation. The government only moved to a system of direct inflation targeting in February 2000. These volatility results are interesting in the context of SA's version of the Great Moderation (see Du Plessis and Kotze 2012) and should be read in conjunction with the narrative analysis of this period, presented earlier.

A Cross-Correlation Analysis of Key Macroeconomic Magnitudes
The cross-correlations between various lag intervals of GDP and its expenditure and sectoral components, as well as some other key economic indicators were calculated. The calculations were done after transforming each variable to its natural logarithm (excluding the inflation and interest rates) and extracting the 'business cycle component' of each time series applying a CF bandpass filter. The detailed results are shown in the Appendix in respect of each structural sub-period. The results contained in Tables 5 and 6 only show the peak correlation coefficient and its lead (+) or lag (−).[36]

Regarding the expenditure components of GDP, all reveal a close *procyclical* correlation with GDP, except exports during the first period. The correlation between real household consumption and GDP tends to be contemporaneous to marginally leading (also see the Appendix), while changes in fixed and inventory investment tend to lag changes in GDP. While some analysts tend to interpret this result as if consumption drives the SA business cycle, with investment having a secondary role, this is of course not true. Further testing is required, but the higher variance of fixed and inventory investment spending (also reflected in the steepness statistics) suggests that these variables exert a stronger cyclical influence in *driving* the cycle even though they respond to a (leading) pick up in household consumption. The momentum factor is stronger in the case of fixed and inventory investment, which suggests a stronger driving property (compared to consumption, for instance).

It is not clear what drives the pick up in household consumption. In the first period, actual inflation (and price levels) typically declined one to two quarters before the pick up in GDP, which suggests real disposable income could be a factor. In this period, exports were uncorrelated with changes in GDP.[37] During the second and third periods, the (contemporaneous) correlation of exports improved, most

[36]The cross-correlation coefficient is calculated between GDP$(t + k)$, $k = -4, \ldots, 4$, and the relevant economic indicator at time period t. A lead relation is therefore indicated when $k = 1, \ldots, 4$ and a lag relation is indicated when $k = -1, \ldots, -4$. This follows the method in Agresti and Mojon (2001) and is contrary to that of Burger (2010).

[37]This poor correlation between the cyclical components of exports and GDP was reported in other studies as well (see Du Plessis 2006a; Burger 2010). The impact of trade sanctions and other exogenous shocks on the political and economic policy terrain probably assist in explaining it. The current study shows that the pro-cyclical influence of exports improved over the post-1994 period (compare Burger 2010).

Table 5 Cross-correlation analysis: expenditure components and sectors with GDP, 1974–2017

Variable(t)	1974Q3–1993Q2		1993Q3–2007Q4		2008Q1–2017Q4	
	Peak cross correlation with GDP($t + k$)[a]					
	Correlation	Lag(−)/lead(+)	Correlation	Lag(−)/lead(+)	Correlation	Lag(−)/lead(+)
GDP	1.00	0	1.00	0	1.00	0
Expenditure:						
Consumption	0.80	0.5	0.86	0	0.87	0
Govt consumption	0.51	0	−0.47	−4	0.60	−4
Investment	0.76	0	0.55	−2	0.72	−2
Cum inventories	0.82	−1	0.42	−1	0.68	−1
GDE	0.95	0	0.83	0	0.89	0
Exports	−0.14	−2	0.72	−1	0.87	0
Imports	0.85	1	0.57	0	0.91	0
Sectors:						
Mining	−0.34	4	−0.52	3	0.62	1
Manufacturing	0.93	1	0.83	0	0.89	0
Construction	0.77	−1	0.87	−1	−0.84	0
Trade	0.82	0	0.79	2	0.70	1
Tpt & comm	0.74	0	0.65	−2	0.79	−1
Financial	0.77	1	0.70	0	0.48	−2
Government	0.06	1	0.42	4	0.43	2

[a]Contra-cyclical correlations with GDP are indicated in red

likely being a force in GDP changes via improved incomes in the export sector spilling over to the consumer sector and spurring increased fixed and inventory investment. Over these periods, real interest rate changes became countercyclical (as monetary policy should aim for). This occurred in the era of positive real interest rates, initiated by the then Governor of the SARB, Dr. Chris Stals, during the early 1990s, i.e. as noted, SA's Paul Volcker moment.

These results are consistent with the description of the structural advances in the SA economy becoming evident in the post-1994 period (specifically during the 1997–2007 business cycle, see our earlier discussion of this cycle). In this regard, the countercyclical behaviour of the government consumption ratio throughout the full sample period is interesting. The inverse correlation with GDP is not high, particularly during the first period. Furthermore, it led to changes in GDP with four quarters during the second period, suggesting fiscal policy was out of synch with the business cycle over this period. During the third period, it returned to a contemporaneous inverse correlation, suggesting fiscal policy was countercyclical (as one would like it to be). The countercyclical nature of fiscal

Table 6 Cross-correlation analysis: policy and financial variables with GDP, 1974–2017

Variable	1974Q3–1993Q2		1993Q3–2007Q4		2008Q1–2017Q4	
	Peak cross correlation with GDP($t+k$)[a]					
	Correlation	Lag(−)/lead(+)	Correlation	Lag(−)/lead(+)	Correlation	Lag(−)/lead(+)
GDP	1.00	0	1.00	0	1.00	0
Policy variables:						
CPI inflation	−0.27	2	0.51	−1.5	0.52	−2
CPI index	−0.34	1	0.50	−2	−0.57	0
Prime nominal	0.59	−2	−0.43	−4	0.55	4
Prime real	0.39	−1	−0.55	0	−0.54	−4
GC ratio	−0.36	0	−0.55	3.5	−0.86	0
Money supply:						
M1	0.57	0	0.33	1	0.84	2
M2	0.46	−2	0.27	−4	−0.75	3
M3	0.46	−1	0.45	−4	−0.69	3
Credit supply	0.59	−2	0.49	3	−0.75	3
Financial variables:						
Nominal effective R	0.51	3	−0.49	0.5	0.67	3
Real effective R	0.47	3	−0.48	1.5	−0.66	−4
10y bond	0.69	−2	0.11	−4	−0.33	−2
Yield curve	−0.44	−2	−0.69	−4	−0.66	−1

[a]Contra-cyclical correlations with GDP are indicated in red

policy at the time of the Great Recession impact was noted earlier. However, there is evidence that fiscal policy became pro-cyclical in the ensuing expansion (2010–2013), with the large-scale expansion of public sector employment and high real wage increases. When low economic growth constrained the fiscal revenues, causing high budget deficits (in excess of 5% of GDP), fiscal consolidation had to be implemented during the economic downturn (2013–2017). More research is required regarding the cyclical role of fiscal policy—see the summary of South African research in the earlier chapter by Boshoff and Du Plessis (2020).

Regarding the sector components of GDP, the very strong (and leading) relation between changes in manufacturing real value added and aggregate GDP stand out. It is evident that the manufacturing sector plays a critical role in SA's business cycle fluctuations and this is despite the reduced role of the sector in aggregate GDP in recent years. This can be explained by the wide backward and forward linkages of this sector with the rest of the economy. In contrast, the mining sector reveals a weak inverse (and leading) correlation with GDP during the first two periods. The relation between changes in mining real value added and GDP does not make theoretical sense, suggesting other factors at play. This also ties in with the export relation to GDP (at least during the first period, characterised by trade sanctions, for instance).

During the third period, the correlation became positive and contemporaneous; however, the Great Recession impact may have had a disproportionate influence over this period. More research is required to disentangle the export relation to GDP changes. Whereas the construction cycle lagged the GDP cycle during the first two periods, it became inverse and contemporaneous during the third period. The impact of the construction phase linked to the World Cup Soccer event in the run-up to and in the wake of 2010 are well known and assist in explaining the contemporaneous inverse correlation; under normal conditions one would expect a pro-cyclical, but lagging, relation with changes in aggregate GDP, in line with the evidence during the first two periods (Table 5).

The leading and positive correlation between the internal trade sector and GDP during the post-1994 period is notable and agrees with the foregoing analysis on the demand side of the economy. The correlation of the transport and communication as well as financial and business services sectors are significant and cyclical changes in these sectors tend to lag that of aggregate GDP. The reduced correlation of financial services with GDP during the post-financial crisis period is, however, notable.

Regarding the money supply (and credit) aggregates, it is evident from Table 6 that all aggregates are weakly pro-cyclical, with the narrow money supply leading, and the broader monetary aggregates lagging, changes in GDP. This is in line with the international evidence (see Agresti and Mojon 2001; Zimmerman 2005; see also Boshoff (2005) for South African conclusions). Only during the third period, the broader definitions of the money supply, as well as credit, became inversely correlated with (and also leading) changes in GDP. During the first two periods, the broader monetary aggregates tended to lag the changes in GDP. In contrast, the leading characteristic of M1 is evident, with it increasing during the third period and the correlation with GDP also becoming stronger.[38] The weaker tendencies in the correlation between the monetary aggregates and GDP during the second period may be related to the higher volatility of these aggregates during this period.

Regarding changes in the nominal and real effective exchange rate and their correlation with changes in GDP, no systematic relationship is identifiable. A similar comment can be made regarding 10-year government bond yields. Whereas the yield curve (i.e. the difference between the 10-year government bond yield and a short-term money market interest rate) clearly displays a countercyclical relation with changes in GDP as one would expect, the lag relationship during the first two periods is counter-intuitive. Our findings concerning the leading indicator properties of financial variables—including weak support for interest and exchange rates and stronger support for the yield curve—mirror extant literature, as described in the chapter by Boshoff and Du Plessis (2020).

[38]The real M1 money supply is a component in the SA Reserve Bank's composite leading business cycle indicator.

In general, the bivariate correlation analysis suggests that it is indeed limiting to focus on specific indicators when attempting to assess or forecast cyclical turning points. As discussed by Boshoff and Du Plessis (2020), an alternative would be to rely on a multivariate approach, combining various indicators. Such an approach is consistent with that of the SARB, as described by Venter (2019) in a later chapter on turning point forecasts.

6 Synthesis and Conclusions

The business cycle is not observable and its measurement is not a straightforward matter. Sophisticated mathematics, meticulous observation and dissection of economic time series and econometric modelling are often involved with the objective of identifying the cyclical element in broad economic activity. A complicating matter, of central importance to this book, is the interaction between long-term growth trends and short-term business cycle movements.

The descriptive part of the current study follows the SARB's (official) business cycle chronology. As this method involves the de-trending of economic time series and it essentially being a growth cycle approach, the quantitative analysis was augmented with a consideration of an alternative dating method (i.e. the BBQ method). This heeds the foregoing recommendations in terms of considering both the classical and the growth cycle, with the focus being on the successive periods of expansion and contraction, in general, economic activity. The quantitative analysis proved robust when both business cycle dating approaches were considered.

Whereas South Africa's modernisation has its origins in the 1920s and 1930s, it really only got off the ground after WWII. This period coincided with the so-called 'golden era' of high and sustained world economic growth, during which South Africa benefited as a supplier of basic commodities (initially mainly gold and maize and in time a more diversified range). This period also coincided (from 1948) with the institution of the apartheid system, which generated untold strife in SA's modern development. While the immediate post-war period (1946–1973) was characterized by rapid industrialization and urbanization and sustained high economic growth, its business cycle development did not come under the spotlight in the current study. Partly due to data constraints and partly due to the fact that it has been covered elsewhere in this book, it was decided to focus on the period from the early 1970s, being a period of deep structural change, both internationally and domestically.

From this point (circa 1973), the end of the 'golden era' of global growth and the onset of a broader resistance to apartheid embodied the broad parameters for SA's modern business cycle development. The upper turning point of this structural downturn in the SA economy was timed as the onset of the 1974–1977 economic downturn, i.e. 1974Q3.

Both the narrative and the descriptive quantitative analysis relied mainly on previous work in discussing the modern SA business cycle. Its novelty lies in the fuller description of each of the six-and-a-half (peak-to-peak) business cycles, also including the post-2009 period, i.e. in offering an understanding of the impact of the Great Recession and the decline of political governance in SA under former president Zuma. The objective is to reveal the business cycle triggers and underlying propagating factors, the impact of international business cycle influences, as well as that of political (and other) shocks and the changing diffusion of the business cycle.

The noticeable lengthening of the economic downturn in 1974–1977, combined with a recovery, which was less robust compared to those of the post-war period (1946–1973), announced the 'stop-go' business cycles in SA, which intensified during the 1980s (read: higher amplitude and increased volatility). The impact of sociopolitical instability also intensified during the 1980s, with the roots of open resistance and the reform of the apartheid state traced back to the early 1970s (e.g. the 1973 Durban strikes). To be true, the economic instability was not unique to SA. The period 1973–1986 is described as one of common global shocks (IMF 2007a, b; Kose et al. 2005; also compare the analysis of the synchronicity of SA's business cycle with the global business cycle, Botha 2010).

Business cycle volatility continued beyond the 1980s, with the country experiencing its 'Volcker moment' only in 1989 and its political transition during the first half of the 1990s. During this interim period, the link between the South African business cycle and the G7 industrial production cycle remained remarkably strong. This linkage spans the nadir of SA's 'lost decade' (1985–1993), culminating in the country's worst and longest post-war economic downturn (51 months), as well as the first post-apartheid expansion and SA's re-integration with the world economy. The continuity of SA's business cycle, particularly over the 1989–1996 peak-to-peak business cycle, is remarkable in view of the extreme exogenous influences at the time.

Throughout the sample period, the economy was impacted by sociopolitical and global shocks—the oil price shocks and the political shocks of the mid-1970s, the severe early 1980s global economic downturn and the collapse of the gold price, the state of emergency (July 1985) and the impact of the Rubicon speech, the early 1990s drought, protracted global economic downturn and the sociopolitical unrest in the run-up to the April 1994 first full democratic elections; the 1990s financial volatility; the impact of the Great Recession, 2008–2009; 'Nenegate' (December 2015) and the run-up to the ANC leadership conference (December 2017). This list is not exhaustive.

The continuity of the connection with SA's trading partners' growth may, somewhat paradoxically, be explained by SA's stop-go business cycle mechanics. The quantitative analysis shows that the export connection in the fluctuation of GDP disappeared over the 1974–1993 period; the volatility of interest rates was the highest over this period and real economic growth deteriorated also being exceptionally volatile (with growth oscillating between −1% per annum during downturns and +5.5% per annum during rebounds). Inflation patterns and their link with GDP fluctuations are tricky, being distorted by exchange rate swings. Inflation was high, as was exchange rate volatility. Yet, a stable relationship with the G7 industrial production cycle remained.

One of the defining business cycle issues since the mid-1970s was that South African monetary and fiscal policies were often subject to non-economic factors and contributed to economic fluctuations. Fiscal policy tended to be expansive due to the demands of defence spending and the policy conviction regarding Keynesian demand management in stimulating economic growth. Budget deficits were monetised, which contributed to excessive growth in bank credit utilisation and real domestic expenditure and imports. This, in turn, led to both inflation and balance of payments bottlenecks and consequent sharp adjustments in monetary policy and the attendant stop-go business cycles. The balance of payments constraint was the South African economy's Achilles' heel. When the growth in G7 industrial production and international commodity prices was high, SA's economic policy mavericks could be tolerated, however, for only as long as the balance of payments could absorb the consequences.

South Africa's financial re-entry to the world economy was a baptism of fire and the growth improvement was slow to get off the ground (Du Plessis and Smit 2005). Capital flows were volatile at first; the second half of the 1990s was characterized by significant financial volatility. The balance of payments constraint was only relieved when portfolio capital inflows became more substantial, particularly in the wake of the loosening of monetary policies in the major advanced economies during the 2000s and strong growth globally (2003–2007), boosted by the growth of China and other emerging economies.

Whereas the current account deficit that was registered during the second half of 1994 signalled change, the macroeconomic policy reforms were slow to show up in economic outcomes. The 1996–2007 business cycle was special in this context. The implementation of the GEAR policy framework (February 1996), which achieved unambiguous success in the macroeconomic policy department, contributed not only to the 1997–1999 growth recession but also proved to be building blocks for SA's record 1999–2007 expansion. The improvement in the domestic economy was embodied in a more stable macroeconomic environment enhancing steady growth in after-tax real disposable incomes and affording the fiscus to embark on a more expansionary route (circa 2002). Fixed investment responded strongly to the improved demand conditions and net exports made a stronger contribution to growth on the back of new export markets and a more competitive currency. The export improvement has to be qualified though, as discussed below.

The high inflation of the 1980s and early 1990s was tamed and business cycle volatility receded. Currency volatility remained high throughout the full sample period (and beyond), albeit somewhat muted compared to the 1980s. The 1990s reform of macroeconomic policies succeeded in reducing inflation and interest rate volatility, but the improvement in the export sector lagged, rendering the currency vulnerable. It also rendered the economy vulnerable to the impact of the 2007 global financial crisis. The impact of the ensuing Great Recession, and—

Table 7 Cross-correlation between SA's exports and trading partner business cycles

Exports	Std deviation Absolute	Relative/ GDP	Cross-correlation with TP CEI($t+k$) k −4	−3	−2	−1	0	1	2	3	4
74Q3–17Q4	0.032	2.32	0.12	0.30	0.49	0.64	**0.71**	**0.69**	0.56	0.37	0.17
74Q3–93Q2	0.027	1.65	0.40	0.49	**0.55**	**0.56**	**0.50**	0.42	0.31	0.17	0.04
93Q3–07Q4	0.024	2.44	0.15	0.34	0.49	0.62	**0.72**	**0.70**	0.64	0.52	0.35
08Q1–17Q4	0.039	5.06	−0.32	−0.06	0.30	0.67	**0.91**	**0.84**	0.58	0.22	−0.08
11Q3–17Q4	0.017	2.32	−0.09	0.02	0.18	0.35	**0.47**	0.49	0.47	**0.47**	**0.53**

Bold indicates the contemporaneous correlation coefficient, as well as the maximum values
Source: South African Reserve Bank (2018, March)
TP CEI SA's trading partners' composite coincident economic indicator

unknown at the time—SA's governance retrogression under new political leadership overtook the record expansion and some of the structural improvements on the policy front.[39]

The quantitative analysis showed the importance of investment and export growth as momentum drivers in the fluctuations of GDP. Sharp contractions in investment accompanied the economic downturns over both the pre-1994 period and the post-1994 period; likewise, sharp increases in investment (often towards the second half) of economic expansions. While the steepness of household consumption spending increased, particularly over the post-2007 period, it is fair to conclude that the endogenous continuity of SA's business cycle has to be located in the investment and export departments (obviously, with the countervailing associated swings in imports being part of the equation).

While the export connection broke down during the pre-1994 period (reflected in exports being uncorrelated with GDP and only weakly correlated with the business cycles of SA's trading partners), it remains critical in SA's business cycle development. Table 7 shows the changing correlation between export fluctuations and that of SA's trading partner economies' business cycle over the various periods under investigation in the current study. The correlation is pro-cyclical and high, except over the 1974Q3–1993Q2 period, when it receded to 0.55 and tended to lag the business cycle of SA's trading partner economies; during the other periods, the export fluctuations appear to be contemporaneous. Of concern, is the return to a weaker correlation (equivalent to that during the pre-1994 period) between mid-2011 and end-2017, i.e. excluding the impact of the 2008–2009 economic downturn and rebound. This is consistent with other findings regarding poor export growth during the post-2009 period and in response to the improvement in global growth, particularly from the middle of 2016.

The 2009–2013 expansion was unusual in that the economy drifted into an economic downturn from the supply side, without the typical triggers at the peak of

[39]With hindsight, even the record 1999–2007 expansion was not great by SA's own and international peer-group standards (Du Plessis and Smit 2005: 39).

the business cycle. The notable feature of this cycle was the weak fixed investment tendency, tied to poor business confidence levels. This gave the expansion a flat trajectory. Another notable feature was the lagging manufacturing performance, which contributed to the high current account deficit in 2013 despite lacklustre growth. Household spending, supported by government consumption was an important component of the expansion, which became unsustainable due to insufficient investment and employment growth.

While these weak business cycle dynamics were present, explaining the weak expansion, the 2013-to date economic downturn, in turn, produced unexpected resilience initially. The backbone of this resilience can be traced to steady real domestic expenditure, mainly household consumption. The growth of SA's middle class during the post-1994 period is arguably at the bottom of this development, which is encouraging. In this context, the change in political leadership early 2018 and the initial associated lift in business and consumer confidence bode well. Unfortunately, the lingering adverse effects of the Zuma Presidency is proving a major challenge and are at the source of economic growth disappointments during the course of 2018 and the first half of 2019. The global economy also slowed over this period. The strength of any future expansion and business cycles to come will depend on the extent to which South Africa can capitalise on the new-found resilience of domestic spending, by addressing the structural shortcomings in fixed investment and exports.

Appendix

Table 8 The SA business cycle: other properties—Expenditure on GDP (BBQ level): 1974–2017

	HCE			GC			GDFI			CUM_Inventories			GDE			Exports			Imports			GDP		
Characteristic	PT	TP	PTP	PT	TP	PTP	PT	TP	PTP	PT	TP	PTP	PT	TP	PTP	PT	TP	PTP	PT	TP	PTP	PT	TP	PTP
Ave duration:	**6**	**27**	**36**	**6**	**25**	**31**	**8**	**14**	**21**	**13**	**19**	**33**	**7**	**17**	**25**	**6**	**14**	**20**	**8**	**17**	**25**	**5**	**19**	**25**
74Q3–93Q2	6	26	32	6	24	30	11	13	23	20	8	29	10	13	23	6	13	20	10	13	23	6	11	15
93Q3–17Q4	8	32	40	6	26	31	5	15	19	6	26	35	4	23	27	6	14	20	5	21	27	4	31	38
Ave amplitude:	**−0.04**	**0.28**	–	**−0.04**	**0.28**	–	**−0.15**	**0.27**	–	**−1.06**	**1.51**	–	**−0.06**	**0.20**	–	**−0.08**	**0.20**	–	**−0.27**	**0.43**	–	**−0.03**	**0.17**	–
74Q3–93Q2	−0.04	0.29	–	−0.04	0.32	–	−0.22	0.26	–	−1.99	0.74	–	−0.09	0.18	–	−0.08	0.21	–	−0.35	0.44	–	−0.03	0.11	–
93Q3–17Q4	−0.04	0.22	–	−0.04	0.24	–	−0.09	0.28	–	−0.13	2.02	–	−0.02	0.24	–	−0.07	0.18	–	−0.15	0.41	–	−0.02	0.25	–
Steepness:	**−0.007**	**0.010**	–	**−0.007**	**0.011**	–	**−0.020**	**0.020**	–	**−0.082**	**0.081**	–	**−0.008**	**0.012**	–	**−0.013**	**0.014**	–	**−0.033**	**0.026**	–	**−0.005**	**0.009**	–
74Q3–93Q2	−0.007	0.011	–	−0.007	0.013	–	−0.021	0.020	–	−0.100	0.099	–	−0.009	0.014	–	−0.014	0.016	–	−0.035	0.033	–	−0.005	0.010	–
93Q3–17Q4	−0.005	0.007	–	−0.008	0.009	–	−0.020	0.019	–	−0.022	0.078	–	−0.006	0.010	–	−0.012	0.012	–	−0.028	0.019	–	−0.004	0.008	–
Ave growth	**−2.6**	**4.9**	**2.9**	**−3.3**	**5.3**	**2.5**	**−7.7**	**6.9**	**0.9**	**−20.3**	**61.9**	**2.6**	**−3.4**	**5.2**	**1.7**	**−6.0**	**6.3**	**1.7**	**−13.1**	**12.8**	**1.4**	**−2.2**	**3.6**	**1.9**
74Q3–93Q2	−2.8	5.4	3.2	−3.8	6.0	3.8	−7.8	7.8	−0.1	−31.4	43.6	−3.4	−4.2	6.3	1.2	−5.6	7.2	1.5	−14.1	17.0	0.4	−2.3	4.4	1.9
93Q3–17Q4	−1.8	2.8	1.8	−2.8	4.6	1.3	−7.6	6.1	1.9	−9.2	74.1	6.6	−2.3	3.7	2.4	−6.5	5.2	2.0	−11.7	7.1	2.8	−1.9	2.7	1.8

Table 9 The SA business cycle: other properties—Sectors (BBQ level): 1974–2017

	Mining			Manufacturing			Construction			Internal trade			TPT & COMM			Financial			Government			GDP		
Characteristic	PT	TP 1	PTP	PT	TP	PTP	PT	TP 1	PTP	PT	1 TP	PTP	PT	TP	PTP	PT	TP	PTP	PT	TP	PTP	PT	TP	PTP
Ave duration:	**9**	**9**	**17**	**5**	**9**	**14**	**8**	**16**	**24**	**5**	**15**	**20**	**4**	**23**	**27**	**2**	**53**	**55**	**8**	**36**	**44**	**6**	**22**	**28**
74Q3–93Q2	9	11	20	6	9	16	10	8	16	6	9	14	5	20	25	2	59	61	3	47	50	7	12	17
93Q3–17Q4	8	7	16	4	9	13	5	27	36	4	36	40	2	34	36	2	50	52	11	31	42	4	31	38
Ave amplitude:	**−0.08**	**0.08**	–	**−0.06**	**0.12**	–	**−0.12**	**0.23**	–	**−0.05**	**0.19**	–	**−0.05**	**0.29**	–	**−0.01**	**0.49**	–	**−0.02**	**0.23**	–	**−0.03**	**0.18**	–
74Q3–93Q2	−0.08	0.08	–	−0.06	0.14	–	−0.17	0.12	–	−0.07	0.14	–	−0.05	0.31	–	−0.01	0.43	–	−0.01	0.24	–	−0.04	0.12	–
93Q3–17Q4	−0.08	0.08	–	−0.05	0.11	–	−0.04	0.39	–	−0.02	0.35	–	−0.01	0.18	–	0.00	0.52	–	−0.02	0.23	–	−0.02	0.25	–
Steepness:	**−0.009**	**0.009**	–	**−0.011**	**0.013**	–	**−0.015**	**0.015**	–	**−0.010**	**0.013**	–	**−0.011**	**0.013**	–	**−0.003**	**0.009**	–	**−0.002**	**0.006**	–	**−0.005**	**0.008**	–
74Q3–93Q2	−0.008	0.008	–	−0.010	0.015	–	−0.018	0.016	–	−0.011	0.016	–	−0.011	0.015	–	−0.003	0.007	–	−0.003	0.005	–	−0.005	0.010	–
93Q3–17Q4	−0.010	0.011	–	−0.013	0.012	–	−0.008	0.014	–	−0.005	0.010	–	−0.004	0.005	–	−0.001	0.010	–	−0.002	0.007	–	−0.004	0.008	–
Ave growth	**−4.1**	**4.3**	**−0.1**	**−4.3**	**5.5**	**1.7**	**−5.3**	**6.3**	**0.7**	**−3.6**	**6.2**	**2.5**	**−3.6**	**6.4**	**3.5**	**−1.0**	**3.5**	**3.4**	**−1.1**	**2.1**	**1.3**	**−2.2**	**3.6**	**1.9**
74Q3–93Q2	−3.7	3.5	0.1	−3.8	6.5	2.1	−6.7	7.2	−0.8	−4.4	6.9	2.2	−4.0	7.3	3.8	−1.4	2.9	2.8	−1.3	2.0	1.8	−2.3	4.5	2.0
93Q3–17Q4	−4.5	4.8	−0.2	−4.9	4.5	1.3	−2.9	5.0	2.6	−2.1	3.9	3.2	−1.7	2.2	2.0	−0.3	3.9	3.7	−1.1	2.2	1.1	−1.9	2.7	1.8

Table 10 Business cycle volatility and cross-correlation analysis: 1974–1993[a]

	Standard deviation			Cross correlation with GDP(*t*+*k*): 1974Q3–1993Q2								
Variable(*t*)	Absolute	Relative/GDP	*k*	−4	−3	−2	−1	0	1	2	3	4
GDP	0.016	1.0		0.04	0.35	0.67	0.91	**1.00**	0.91	0.67	0.35	0.04
Expenditure:												
Consumption	0.022	1.4		0.05	0.23	0.45	0.67	**0.80**	**0.80**	0.67	0.43	0.15
Govt consumption	0.019	1.1		−0.15	0.06	0.28	0.45	**0.51**	**0.45**	0.32	0.16	0.02
Investment	0.061	3.8		0.35	0.53	0.67	**0.75**	**0.76**	0.69	0.54	0.34	0.11
Cum inventories	0.184	11.4		0.50	0.67	**0.78**	**0.82**	0.76	0.61	0.39	0.15	−0.07
GDE	0.031	1.9		−0.08	0.23	0.56	0.82	**0.95**	**0.91**	0.73	0.47	0.18
Exports	0.027	1.6		−0.13	−0.14	−0.14	−0.11	−0.07	−0.04	−0.05	−0.07	−0.06
Imports	0.087	5.4		−0.26	0.05	0.38	0.66	**0.83**	**0.85**	0.73	0.52	0.27
Sectors:												
Mining	0.020	1.2		−0.01	0.02	0.01	−0.03	−0.10	−0.20	−0.28	**−0.33**	**−0.34**
Manufacturing	0.030	1.9		−0.13	0.16	0.48	0.74	**0.91**	**0.93**	0.80	0.57	0.30
Construction	0.042	2.6		0.42	0.59	0.72	**0.77**	**0.73**	0.59	0.39	0.16	−0.08
Trade	0.035	2.2		0.04	0.24	0.48	0.69	**0.82**	**0.80**	0.64	0.38	0.07
Tpt & comm	0.027	1.7		−0.10	0.15	0.42	0.63	**0.74**	**0.71**	0.53	0.29	0.05
Financial	0.009	0.5		−0.09	0.13	0.37	0.59	**0.73**	**0.77**	0.70	0.53	0.32
Government	0.011	0.7		−0.17	−0.16	−0.09	−0.02	0.04	0.06	0.04	−0.01	−0.06
Policy variables:												
CPI inflation	1.751	-		0.25	0.23	0.14	0.01	−0.12	−0.23	**−0.27**	**−0.25**	−0.18
CPI index	0.017	1.1		0.03	−0.06	−0.17	−0.26	−0.32	**−0.34**	**−0.32**	−0.28	−0.21
Prime_nom	2.546	-		0.44	**0.56**	**0.59**	0.53	0.35	0.09	−0.20	−0.43	−0.59
Prime_real	3.429	-		0.20	0.30	**0.37**	**0.39**	0.32	0.18	−0.01	−0.20	−0.34
GC_ratio	0.280	-		0.01	−0.13	−0.25	−0.33	**−0.36**	**−0.34**	−0.30	−0.25	−0.19
Money supply:												
M1	0.065	4.0		0.03	0.23	0.41	0.52	**0.57**	**0.55**	0.45	0.30	0.10
M2	0.051	3.2		0.31	0.40	**0.46**	**0.46**	0.41	0.30	0.14	−0.05	−0.27
M3	0.036	2.3		0.27	0.36	0.43	**0.46**	**0.45**	0.39	0.27	0.10	−0.12
Credit supply	0.036	2.2		0.43	0.53	**0.59**	**0.58**	0.49	0.32	0.09	−0.18	−0.44
Financial variables:												
Neer	0.064	4.0		−0.12	−0.08	−0.01	0.11	0.25	0.39	**0.49**	**0.51**	0.44
Reer	0.060	3.7		−0.11	−0.14	−0.12	−0.05	0.08	0.24	0.39	**0.47**	**0.44**
10y bond	0.862	-		0.45	0.60	**0.69**	**0.68**	0.54	0.28	−0.05	−0.37	−0.62
Yield curve	2.514	-		−0.33	**−0.41**	**−0.44**	−0.39	−0.26	−0.08	0.12	0.29	0.40

[a]Correlation coefficients coloured in red indicate peak correlation; the cells shaded in grey indicate statistical significance at a 5% confidence level

Table 11 Business cycle volatility and cross-correlation analysis: 1993–2007[a]

	Standard deviation			Cross correlation with GDP(t+k): 1993Q3–2007Q4								
Variable(t)	Absolute	Relative/GDP	k	−4	−3	−2	−1	0	1	2	3	4
GDP	0.010	1.0		0.12	0.38	0.66	0.89	**1.00**	0.89	0.66	0.38	0.12
Expenditure:												
Consumption	0.013	1.3		0.16	0.37	0.58	0.75	**0.86**	**0.83**	0.72	0.55	0.35
Govt consumption	0.016	1.6		**−0.47**	**−0.30**	−0.09	0.11	0.23	0.25	0.22	0.19	0.20
Investment	0.022	2.3		0.47	**0.53**	**0.55**	0.49	0.36	0.13	−0.10	−0.28	−0.37
Cum inventories	0.434	44.7		0.05	0.19	0.34	**0.42**	**0.40**	0.31	0.20	0.12	0.09
GDE	0.012	1.2		0.11	0.27	0.49	0.70	**0.83**	**0.76**	0.54	0.26	0.00
Exports	0.024	2.4		0.22	0.47	0.65	**0.72**	**0.70**	0.59	0.45	0.31	0.18
Imports	0.028	2.9		0.19	0.32	0.44	**0.54**	**0.57**	0.49	0.33	0.14	−0.02
Sectors:												
Mining	0.013	1.3		0.01	−0.14	−0.30	−0.42	−0.51	−0.51	−0.510	**−0.52**	**−0.51**
Manufacturing	0.023	2.4		0.05	0.33	0.58	0.76	**0.83**	**0.76**	0.62	0.45	0.31
Construction	0.024	2.4		0.44	0.66	0.81	**0.87**	**0.83**	0.62	0.35	0.07	−0.14
Trade	0.021	2.2		−0.39	−0.14	0.14	0.40	0.62	0.74	**0.79**	**0.77**	0.70
Tpt & comm	0.016	1.7		0.48	0.59	**0.65**	**0.63**	0.56	0.37	0.16	−0.03	−0.18
Financial	0.014	1.5		0.36	0.43	0.54	**0.64**	**0.70**	0.63	0.47	0.26	0.02
Government	0.005	0.5		0.19	0.29	0.38	0.42	0.36	0.13	−0.13	**−0.35**	**−0.48**
Policy variables:												
CPI inflation	2.254	-		0.28	0.42	**0.51**	**0.51**	0.40	0.20	0.00	−0.14	−0.21
CPI index	0.019	2.0		0.43	**0.48**	**0.50**	0.46	0.35	0.13	−0.11	−0.29	−0.39
Prime_nom	1.757	-		**0.48**	**0.42**	0.31	0.15	−0.04	−0.23	−0.37	−0.43	−0.43
Prime_real	1.730	-		0.13	−0.12	−0.36	**−0.51**	**−0.55**	−0.49	−0.38	−0.25	−0.17
GC_ratio	0.311	-		0.13	−0.02	−0.17	−0.28	−0.38	−0.45	−0.51	**−0.55**	**−0.55**
Money supply:												
M1	0.035	3.6		−0.02	−0.14	−0.13	0.02	0.22	**0.33**	**0.32**	0.18	−0.01
M2	0.019	1.9		**0.27**	0.16	0.10	0.13	0.20	0.18	0.10	−0.04	−0.19
M3	0.021	2.1		**0.45**	**0.39**	0.34	0.34	0.37	0.32	0.22	0.08	−0.09
Credit supply	0.022	2.3		0.02	0.13	0.21	0.29	0.37	0.42	**0.47**	**0.49**	0.46
Financial variables:												
Neer	0.085	8.7		−0.25	−0.28	−0.34	−0.42	**−0.49**	**−0.49**	−0.41	−0.28	−0.11
Reer	0.061	6.3		−0.10	−0.12	−0.19	−0.31	−0.42	**−0.48**	**−0.48**	−0.40	−0.27
10y bond	0.800	-		**−0.46**	**−0.43**	−0.28	−0.10	**0.04**	0.07	0.06	0.06	0.11
Yield curve	1.828	-		**−0.69**	**−0.65**	−0.54	−0.34	**−0.11**	0.13	0.30	0.41	0.46

[a]Correlation coefficients coloured in red indicate peak correlation; the cells shaded in grey indicate statistical significance at a 5% confidence level

Table 12 Business cycle volatility and cross-correlation analysis: 2008–2017[a]

	Standard deviation			Cross correlation with GDP(*t*+*k*): 2008Q1–2017Q4								
Variable(*t*)	Absolute	Relative/GDP	*k*	−4	−3	−2	−1	0	1	2	3	4
GDP	0.008	1.0		−0.13	0.17	0.55	0.87	**1.00**	0.87	0.55	0.17	−0.13
Expenditure:												
Consumption	0.015	1.9		−0.02	0.27	0.57	0.79	0.87	0.76	0.53	0.26	0.04
Govt consumption	0.007	0.9		0.60	0.38	0.06	−0.24	−0.43	−0.46	−0.38	−0.24	−0.09
Investment	0.034	4.4		0.48	0.64	0.72	0.65	0.40	0.02	−0.36	−0.62	−0.70
Cum inventories	0.038	4.9		0.43	0.54	0.64	0.68	**0.62**	0.40	0.09	−0.23	−0.47
GDE	0.013	1.6		0.07	0.30	0.56	0.78	0.89	0.79	0.55	0.26	0.01
Exports	0.039	5.1		−0.15	0.07	0.40	0.72	0.87	0.72	0.37	−0.04	−0.37
Imports	0.054	7.0		−0.03	0.20	0.50	0.78	0.91	0.79	0.48	0.10	−0.20
Sectors:												
Mining	0.021	2.8		−0.56	−0.29	0.07	0.41	0.61	0.62	0.46	0.22	−0.02
Manufacturing	0.027	3.5		−0.19	−0.01	0.30	0.65	0.89	0.87	0.62	0.25	−0.10
Construction	0.018	2.3		0.05	−0.19	−0.45	−0.69	−0.84	−0.80	−0.62	−0.33	−0.04
Trade	0.011	1.4		−0.15	0.06	0.30	0.53	0.68	0.70	0.61	0.44	0.25
Tpt & comm	0.006	0.8		0.16	0.42	0.65	0.79	0.77	0.56	0.25	−0.07	−0.31
Financial	0.006	0.7		0.37	0.45	0.48	0.45	0.35	0.18	0.01	−0.09	−0.10
Government	0.005	0.6		0.14	0.36	0.43	0.31	0.02	−0.22	−0.33	−0.26	−0.08
Policy variables:												
CPI inflation	1.334	-		0.47	0.50	0.52	0.48	0.35	0.12	−0.17	−0.42	−0.56
CPI index	0.011	1.5		−0.25	−0.36	−0.47	−0.55	−0.57	−0.46	−0.23	0.07	0.35
Prime_nom	0.733	-		0.28	0.43	0.55	0.54	0.35	0.02	−0.35	−0.63	−0.75
Prime_real	0.769	-		−0.54	−0.47	−0.38	−0.32	−0.28	−0.19	−0.04	0.13	0.26
GC_ratio	0.215	-		−0.01	−0.26	−0.55	−0.78	−0.86	−0.69	−0.35	0.06	0.38
Money supply:												
M1	0.017	2.2		−0.41	−0.25	−0.01	0.31	0.64	0.83	0.84	0.67	0.40
M2	0.014	1.8		0.39	0.60	0.66	0.50	0.15	−0.27	−0.60	−0.75	−0.73
M3	0.011	1.4		0.24	0.51	0.63	0.51	0.16	−0.25	−0.57	−0.69	−0.62
Credit supply	0.013	1.7		0.45	0.62	0.66	0.50	0.17	−0.23	−0.57	−0.75	−0.75
Financial variables:												
Neer	0.068	8.8		−0.56	−0.51	−0.35	−0.10	0.21	0.49	0.65	0.67	0.57
Reer	0.057	7.3		−0.66	−0.63	−0.50	−0.29	−0.03	0.23	0.43	0.52	0.51
10y bond	0.328	-		−0.17	−0.28	−0.33	−0.28	−0.16	−0.06	0.00	0.01	−0.02
Yield curve	0.753	-		−0.21	−0.38	−0.57	−0.66	−0.55	−0.25	0.13	0.47	0.66

[a]Correlation coefficients coloured in red indicate peak correlation; the cells shaded in grey indicate statistical significance at a 5% confidence level

References

Achuthan, L., & Banerji, A. (2004). *Beating the business cycle: How to predict and profit from turning points in the economy*. New York: Currency Doubleday.

Agresti, A. M., & Mojon, B. (2001). *Some stylized facts on the euro area business cycle* (ECB Working Paper, No. 95). European Central Bank.

Basu, S., & Taylor, A. M. (1999). Business cycles in international historical perspective. *Journal of Economic Perspectives, 13*(2), 45–68.

Baxter, M., & King, R. G. (1999). Measuring business cycles: Approximate band-pass filters for economic time series. *Review of Economics & Statistics, 81*(November), 575–593.

Binge, L. (2020). Business confidence and the business cycle in South Africa. In W. Boshoff (Ed.), *Business cycles and structural change in South Africa*. Heidelberg: Springer.

Boshoff, W. H. (2005). The properties of cycles in South African financial variables and their relation to the business cycle. *South African Journal of Economics, 73*(4), 796–804.
Boshoff, W. H. & McLean, L. (2018). What do deviation cycles measure? An analysis of the informational content of filter-based business cycles. *South African Journal of Economic and Management Sciences, 21*(1), a1689. https://doi.org/ 10.4102/sajems.v21i1.1689.
Boshoff, W., & Becker, L. (2020). Business cycle recoveries: A comparative view. In W. Boshoff (Ed.), *Business cycles and structural change in South Africa*. Heidelberg: Springer.
Boshoff, W., & du Plessis, S. (2020). What do we know about the South African business cycle? In W. Boshoff (Ed.), *Business cycles and structural change in South Africa*. Heidelberg: Springer.
Boshoff, W., & Fourie, J. (2020). The South African economy in the twentieth century. In W. Boshoff (Ed.), *Business cycles and structural change in South Africa*. Heidelberg: Springer.
Botha, I. (2010). A comparative analysis of the synchronisation of business cycles for developed and developing economies with the world business cycle. *The South African Journal of Economics (SAJE), 78*(2), 192–207.
Bruggemans, C. (2014, March 6). *Suspending the SA business cycle*. Accessed from http://www.fnb.co.za
Burger, P. (2010). The South African business cycle: What has changed? *South African Journal of Economics & Management Sciences, 13*(1), 26–47.
De Kock, G. (1974, November). *The business cycle in South Africa – Recent tendencies*. Address delivered at the School of Business Leadership, University of South Africa (UNISA).
De Vries, A. J. M. (1994). Die Suid-Afrikaanse Ekonomie, 1944–1994. In *Gedenkbundel van die Buro vir Ekonomiese Ondersoek*. Stellenbosch: US Printers.
Du Plessis, S. A. (2006a). Reconsidering the business cycle and stabilization policies in South Africa. *Economic Modelling, 23*(5), 761–774.
Du Plessis, S. A. (2006b). *Business cycles in emerging market economies: A new view of the stylised facts* (Stellenbosch Economic Working Papers, 02/06). The Department of Economics and the Bureau for Economic Research, University of Stellenbosch.
Du Plessis, S. A., & Kotze, K. (2012). *Trends and structural changes in South African macroeconomic volatility*. ERSA Working Paper 297. http://econrsa.org/home/index.php?option=com_download$gid=441&Itemid=67
Du Plessis, S. A., & Smit, B. W. (2002). *Stretching the South-African business cycle*. Paper delivered at the 7th Annual Conference on Econometric Modelling for Africa, Kruger National Park.
Du Plessis, S. A., & Smit B. W. (2005, October 28–29). *Economic growth in South Africa since 1994*. Paper delivered at the Conference, Economic Policy Under Democracy: A Ten Year Review, Stellenbosch.
Fisher, F. (1993). Class consciousness among colonized workers in South Africa. In L. Schlemmer & E. Webster (Eds.), *Change, reform and economic growth in South Africa*. Johannesburg: Ravan Press.
Freytag, A. (2020). The role of institutional structure in mediating the impact of the financial crisis on the South African business cycle. In W. Boshoff (Ed.), *Business cycles and structural change in South Africa*. Heidelberg: Springer.
Giliomee, H. (2004). *Die Afrikaners: 'n Biografie*. Cape Town: Tafelberg.
Harding, D., & Pagan, A. (2002). Dissecting the cycle: A methodological investigation. *Journal of Monetary Economics, 49*(2), 365–381.
Harding, D., & Pagan, A. (2005). A suggested framework for classifying the modes of cycle research. *Journal of Applied Econometrics, 20*(2), 151–159. Accessed from http://www.jstor.org.ez.sun.ac.za/stable/25146349.
Hollander, H., & van Lill, D. (2020). On the estimation and application of structural decompositions of the South African business cycle. In W. Boshoff (Ed.), *Business cycles and structural change in South Africa*. Heidelberg: Springer.

International Monetary Fund (IMF). (2002, April). Chapter 3: Recessions and recoveries. In *World economic outlook*. Washington, DC: IMF.
International Monetary Fund (IMF). (2007a, April). Chapter 4: Decoupling the train: Spillovers and cycles in the global economy. In *World economic outlook*. Washington, DC: IMF.
International Monetary Fund (IMF). (2007b, October). Chapter 5: The changing dynamics of the global business cycle. In *World economic outlook*. Washington, DC: IMF.
Kose, M. A., Otrok, C., & Whiteman, C. H. (2005). *Understanding the evolution of world business cycles* (IMF Working Paper 05/211). International Monetary Fund.
Laubscher, P. (2016). *Salient features of SA's post-2009 business cycle* (BER Research Note, 2016, No 1). University of Stellenbosch.
Laubscher, P. (2019). Forecasting business cycles in South Africa. In A. Ozyildirim, P. Pichetti, & S. Smirnov (Eds.), *Business cycles in BRICS* (pp. 465–495). Cham: Springer.
McCarthy, C. L. (2015). *South African trade policy: What can it achieve given supply-side stumbling blocks*. Stellenbosch: Tralac.
Mohr, P., & Rogers, C. (1994). *Macro economics* (3rd ed.). Isando: Lexicon.
Nilsson, R., & Gyomai, G. (2011). *Cycle extraction: A comparison of the phase-average trend method, the Hodrick-Prescott and Christiano-Fitzgerald filters*. Accessed May 11, 2018, from https://www.oecd-ilibrary.org/economics/cycle-extraction-a-comparison-of-the-phase-average-trend-method-the-hodrick-prescott-and-christiano-fitzgerald-filters_5kg9srt7f8g0-en
Pretorius, W. S., Venter, J. C., & Weideman, P. E. (1999, September). *Business cycles in South Africa during the period 1993 to 1997*. Pretoria: SA Reserve Bank Quarterly Bulletin.
Rasche, R. H., & Tatom, J. A. (1977). The effects of the new energy regime on economic capacity, production, and prices. *Federal Reserve Bank of St. Louis Review, 59*(4), 2–12.
Romer, C. (1999). Changes in business cycles: Evidence and explanations. *Journal of Economic Perspectives, 13*(2), 23–44.
SA Reserve Bank. (2018, March). *Quarterly bulletin*. Accessed from http://www.resbank.co.za.
Schumann, C. G. W. (1938). *Structural changes and business cycles in South Africa, 1806–1936*. New York: Wiley.
Smit, D. J., & Van der Walt, B. E. (1973, June). *Business cycles in South Africa during the period 1968 to 1972*. Pretoria: SA Reserve Bank Quarterly Bulletin.
Smit, D. J., & Van der Walt, B. E. (1982, June). *Growth trends and business cycles in the south African economy, 1972 to 1981* (pp. 41–57). Pretoria: SA Reserve Bank Quarterly Bulletin.
Stals, C. (1997). *Monetary policy: Options and strategies*. Governor of the SA reserve Bank address at the Twentieth Annual Investment Conference of Societe Generale Frankel Pollak (Pty) Ltd, Johannesburg. Accessed from http://www.resebank.co.za.
Terreblanche, S. J. (2002). *A history of inequality in South Africa, 1652–2002*. Pietermaritzburg: University of Natal Press.
Terreblanche, S. J., & Nattrass, N. (1990). A periodization of the political economy from 1910. In N. Nattrass & E. Ardington (Eds.), *The political economy of South Africa*. Cape Town: Oxford University Press.
Van der Walt, B. E. (1989, March). *Business cycles in South Africa during the period 1981 to 1987* (pp. 33–42). Pretoria: SA Reserve Bank Quarterly Bulletin.
Van der Walt, B. E., & Pretorius, W. S. (1995, March). *Business cycles in South Africa during the period 1986 to 1993*. Pretoria: SA Reserve Bank Quarterly Bulletin.
Venter, J. C. (2005, September). *Reference turning points in the south African business cycle: Recent developments* (pp. 61–70). Pretoria: SA Reserve Bank Quarterly Bulletin.
Venter, J. C. (2009, September). *Business cycles in South Africa during the period 1999 to 2007* (pp. 61–69). Pretoria: SA Reserve Bank Quarterly Bulletin.
Venter, J. C. (2011, June). *Business cycles in South Africa during the period 2007 to 2009* (pp. 61–66). Pretoria: SA Reserve Bank Quarterly Bulletin.
Venter, J. C. (2016, March). *Business cycles in South Africa from 2009 to 2013* (pp. 102–112). Pretoria: SA Reserve Bank Quarterly Bulletin.

Venter, J. C. (2019). A brief history of business cycle measurement in South Africa. In A. Ozyildirim, P. Pichetti, & S. Smirnov (Eds.), *Business cycles in BRICS* (pp. 184–211). Cham: Springer.

Venter, J. C., & Pretorius, W. S. (2001, September). *A note on the business cycle in South Africa during the period 1997 to 1999*. Pretoria: SA Reserve Bank Quarterly Bulletin.

Zarnowitz, V. (1992). *Business cycles: Theory, history, indicators and forecasting*. Chicago: University of Chicago Press.

Zarnowitz, V., & Ozyildirim, A. (2001). *Time series decomposition and measurement of business cycles, trends and growth cycles* (Economics Program Working Paper Series, EPWP #01-03). Conference Board, USA.

Zimmerman, C. (2005). *Business cycle measurement*. Department of Economics, University of Connecticut, Unpublished mimeo.

On the Estimation and Application of Structural Decompositions of the South African Business Cycle

H. Hollander and D. van Lill

1 Introduction

South African business cycle dynamics have been fairly well-documented within the empirical econometric literature (see, e.g., Moolman 2004; du Plessis 2004, 2006; du Plessis et al. 2008; Burger 2008, 2010; du Plessis and Kotzé 2010; Bosch and Ruch 2013; Venter 2017; Vermeulen et al. 2017). While econometric models can be used effectively to delineate the determinants of movements in the business cycle, theoretically derived dynamic general equilibrium models can provide more-detailed underlying structural dynamics of an economy (Ohanian et al. 2009). Indeed, over the last two decades, dynamic stochastic general equilibrium (DSGE) models became the most widely adopted methodological approach in macroeconomic policymaking (Tovar 2009; Lindé et al. 2016). This family of models, most notably, allows for more intricate characterizations of economic decision-making through the establishment of rigorous microfoundations.[1]

A theoretical framework that embraces microfoundations has a number of unique benefits. First, it allows the researcher to decompose variables into the likely factors driving their evolution over time. These factors include both endogenous frictions and exogenous shocks. Second, it paves the way for causal inference, allowing

[1] In particular, microfoundations relay the ability of these models to incorporate forward-looking, policy invariant, and heterogeneous agent behaviour (see, e.g., Ohanian et al. 2009). However, these models are not without their drawbacks. In the next section a discussion is undertaken to describe the current role for these type of models and the extensions that need to be incorporated to keep them relevant to the underlying economic environment.

H. Hollander (✉) · D. van Lill
Department of Economics, Stellenbosch University, Stellenbosch, South Africa
e-mail: hylton@sun.ac.za; dvanlill@sun.ac.za

W. H. Boshoff (ed.), *Business Cycles and Structural Change in South Africa*, Advances in African Economic, Social and Political Development,
https://doi.org/10.1007/978-3-030-35754-2_7

macroeconomic relationships to be generated from microeconomic principles. Finally, it opens up the possibility for welfare analysis, affording practitioners the ability to make informed judgements surrounding the implications of a particular policy or policy rule.

DSGE models typically form part of a suite of methodologies in the toolkit of policymakers—especially central banks (Tovar 2009). These central bank models rely heavily on the benchmark New-Keynesian DSGE framework for policy analysis and forecasting (see, e.g., Lindé et al. 2016; Botha et al. 2017). While DSGE models have a greater degree of theoretical coherence, econometric models often showcase greater empirical coherence (Wren-Lewis 2018).[2] As such, it is not the explicit goal of this chapter to forecast future values of key indicators. Instead, we focus on reproducing and detailing conditions of the South African business cycle environment.

Documenting the business cycle dynamics in South Africa using modern techniques of dynamic stochastic general equilibrium (DSGE) models has recently become more popular (see Steinbach et al. 2009, 2014; Alpanda et al. 2010; Paetz and Gupta 2016; Hollander et al. 2019),[3] but is still in its infancy compared to more traditional econometric methods. The various DSGE models developed for the South African economy primarily include features that have become standard in the small open-economy literature. Generally, these frictions attempt to reproduce empirical regularities built-up from microfounded motivations, such as staggered price- and wage-setting; price- and wage-indexation to past inflation; habit formation in consumption; incomplete international risk sharing through asset diversification; incomplete exchange rate pass-through to domestic inflation; and Taylor-type rules to describe monetary policy. Financial frictions (i.e., financial sector components in DSGE models) are another important dimension that has experienced increased attention in the domestic literature. In addition, a number of models (including hybrid DSGE-VARs) have been used explicitly for forecasting purposes (Liu and Gupta 2007; Liu et al. 2009; Alpanda et al. 2011; Gupta and Steinbach 2013; Balcilar et al. 2015, 2017) or explicitly for fiscal and monetary policy analysis (e.g., Jooste et al. 2013; Liu 2013)—although relatively little attention has been paid to fiscal rules.[4]

The specific goal of this chapter is to unify the important contributions in the literature through the use of nested macroeconomic DSGE models. In particular, we first consider the benchmark closed economy New-Keynesian DSGE (NKDSGE) model, as presented by Smets and Wouters (2003, 2007). This benchmark model is

[2]The role for DSGE models in providing accurate forecasts of macroeconomic indicators is not so clear cut. Although DSGE models can be used in conjunction with other macroeconometric tools, this is not its strong suit, and traditional econometric models might perform better in this regard. See, for example, the discussion in Blanchard (2018) about the relevance of DSGE models when it comes to predicting events or the path of macroeconomic indicators.

[3]Kotzé's (2014) PhD thesis provides a detailed discussion and application of DSGE approaches similar to the objective of this chapter.

[4]Works-in-progress incl. Kotzé (2017) and Kemp (PhD).

then extended along two dimensions. First, in order to address criticisms launched against the DSGE modelling paradigm in the wake of the financial crisis, financial frictions are incorporated through a non-trivial financial sector (see, e.g., Gerali et al. 2010). Specifically, we incorporate a role for monopolistically competitive retail banking, bank balance sheet management, and stock market wealth effects (Hollander and Liu 2016a,b). Second, open economy features are introduced to more accurately reflect the prevailing economic conditions in the South African economy (see, e.g., Adolfson et al. 2007; Steinbach et al. 2009; Hollander et al. 2019). Incorporating these non-trivial, yet tractable, extensions will help the model capture important business cycle moments. South Africa is, for example, particularly exposed to movements in international markets and therefore it is important to present a small open economy dynamic stochastic general equilibrium (SOE-NKDSGE) model. In the next section we frame the debate among macroeconomists as to the theoretical and empirical relevance of DSGE models.

2 The DSGE Framework as a Modelling Paradigm

Kuhn (1996) argued that for a paradigm shift to occur there needs to be a core failure in the prevailing paradigm and that a persuasive new path must clearly emerge. The failure of New-Keynesian DSGE models to accurately predict the financial crisis has generated sharp criticism of the consensus model, with several pundits unequivocally pronouncing the demise of this modelling framework (Korinek 2017; Stiglitz 2017). As a result of this perceived failure, it is argued that macroeconomic modelling is now primed for a paradigm shift.[5] Taking these criticisms into consideration, we discuss the role that DSGE models have played in the past and possible extensions that would allow it to become a core component of the new path for macroeconomic modelling following the financial crisis.

2.1 *The Current State of DSGE*

The two decades preceding the Great Financial Crisis (GFC) were marked by an unprecedented consensus on the intellectual and institutional framework for macroeconomic policymaking (Bernanke 2012). At the heart of the consensus is the dynamic general equilibrium framework, which was pioneered by Leeper and Sims (1994) and Schorfheide (2000). It was then further propelled into the mainstream by the seminal contributions of, among others, Woodford (2003), Smets and Wouters (2003, 2007), and Christiano et al. (2005). This macroeconometric

[5]According to Krugman (2018) the big new idea that will reshape macroeconomics has not yet arrived. Many ideas have been forwarded, but none is taking the profession by storm.

modelling paradigm has been implemented universally by policymakers, who were able to utilize the models successfully to understand the consequences of policy actions better, and thereby achieve macroeconomic stability. However, these models were not equipped to forestall financial market failure.

Economics, as a discipline, has developed with the use of theoretical frameworks that often ignore knotty real-world frictions in order to remain tractable and computationally feasible (De Walque et al. 2010). Theorists make assumptions that reduce complex real-world interactions into digestible mathematical equations. Some of these assumptions have been questioned in the wake of the international financial crisis. A particular concern is the idea that financial markets are perfect and complete, with the implication that financial shocks are irrelevant to real economic outcomes (Roger and Vlcek 2012). There was a commonly held belief that finance, in the first approximation, was irrelevant to business cycle movements (Woodford 2003). However, owing to recent events, it has been acknowledged that the financial crisis originated from a collapse of financial intermediation, which has cemented the idea that credit market frictions have real implications (Ahn and Tsomocos 2013). The shortcomings of macroeconomic models revealed during the crisis have led many critics, such as Kirman (2010), Caballero (2010), Stiglitz (2011, 2017), Krugman (2011), DeLong (2011), Kay (2012), Romer (2016), and Korinek (2017) to question the underlying assumptions of DSGE models.

This leads one to question whether the entire DSGE modelling framework needs to be rebuilt from scratch or simply restructured. Fortunately, as argued by Wright (2018) and Vines and Wills (2018), most macroeconomists side with the idea that DSGE models only need moderate modifications. Blanchard (2018) points out that there is broad-scale agreement on a few specific propositions when it comes to DSGE modelling. He emphasizes that while DSGE is about general equilibrium modelling, it is important to acknowledge partial equilibrium models, those without general equilibrium closure. These models can provide significant understanding of particular mechanisms. Once these dynamics are understood, they can be incorporated, in an almost modular fashion, into broader general equilibrium frameworks.[6] For example, Wright (2018) argues that monetary search models that bring together the interaction of money and financial markets in a partial equilibrium setting need to be incorporated into a DSGE framework and would address many of the current shortcomings in monetary economics.

While the lack of financial frictions is usually forwarded as the most severe shortcoming in the current DSGE setup, other important shortcomings have also been identified. The most important of these, as listed in a recent survey by Vines and Wills (2018), are the development of better microfoundations that relax the focus on rational expectations (e.g., bounded rationality) and the introduction of heterogeneous agents. In this chapter we extend the core DSGE framework to include financial market components, but refrain from addressing the multitude

[6]Blanchard (2018) compares DSGE models to a Meccano set, a platform that can easily integrate new elements developed outside the general equilibrium setting.

of extensions proposed above as little consensus exists at present on how to incorporate these components. It is exciting to postulate the possible directions that macroeconomics might take in the immediate future, but for the purpose of exposition we will only focus on financial frictions, as this literature is significantly more mature and would allow us to better model key features of the business cycle.

3 The Benchmark DSGE Model Framework

In this section, we introduce a stylized New-Keynesian framework that embodies all the core features of the models used in this chapter (Christiano et al. 2005; Smets and Wouters 2007). The model consists of a number of frictions to both real and nominal variables and seven exogenous shocks. These features are primarily included to match empirical regularities observed in the data and to provide a non-negligible role for monetary policy (Fuhrer 2000; Smets and Wouters 2003; Christiano et al. 2005).[7] The key feature of New-Keynesian models is that of monopolistic markets in price and wage setting, the so-called nominal rigidities or sticky prices and wages.[8] The stochastic components of the DSGE framework allow for deviations from a deterministic steady-state growth path.[9] The model is therefore only concerned with deviations of variables from their steady-state, where these deviations are generated by exogenous stochastic components. As such, we are concerned with estimating and evaluating a structural decomposition of the South African business cycle.

Following Smets and Wouters (2003, 2007), all models incorporate the implied flexible price and wage ("efficient") equilibrium conditions to derive a model-consistent output gap. The output gap is important for identifying the dynamic inefficiencies of demand shocks for policy evaluation. In this setting, the goal of policy is to stabilize (or smooth) the business cycle fluctuations arising from inflation and output gap variability. Importantly, when we extend the model to an open economy setup, with incomplete and rigid import price adjustment and exchange rate pass-through, the stabilization of domestic prices (total headline inflation) may no longer be optimal (Smets and Wouters 2002). Additionally, we find that the effect of monetary policy is severely constrained by introducing a risk

[7]That is, the model extends directly from the real business cycle (RBC) framework.

[8]The distinction between Calvo-type (fixed probability of adjustment) and Rotemberg-type (quadratic adjustment costs) price setting is unimportant at first-order approximation (Ireland 2004, 2007), and therefore our discussions in this paper will limit the details of alternative modelling approaches that deliver similar first-order outcomes. There are, however, important non-linear effects on adjustment dynamics and welfare (see, e.g., Leith and Liu 2016).

[9]Again, at a first-order approximation, the distinction of a deterministic (constant) growth or level steady-state is unimportant for our business cycle analysis here. Although, estimations will be sensitive to the specification and treatment of observational variables in the estimation of models (see Pfeifer 2018).

premium on borrowing. This raises serious identification issues for macroeconomic policy analysis in a strict interest rate targeting framework—and even more so when the model is extended to include credit frictions and financial wealth effects.

3.1 The Household Sector and Equilibrium Conditions

Households maximize utility subject to a budget constraint. Utility is modelled to exhibit a constant elasticity between current and future consumption (i.e., a constant coefficient of relative risk aversion) and to include external habit formation so that households change consumption gradually over time.[10] Household preferences are separable in consumption $C_{j,t}$, labour $N_{j,t}$, and real money balances $\mathcal{M}_{j,t}/P_t$, such that each household j maximizes their discounted lifetime utility function

$$E_0 \sum_{t=0}^{\infty} \beta^t \left[\frac{(C_{j,t} - \phi C_{t-1})^{1-\sigma_c}}{1-\sigma_c} - \frac{(N_{j,t})^{1+\sigma_n}}{1+\sigma_n} + \frac{a}{1-\sigma_m} \left(\frac{\mathcal{M}_{j,t}}{P_t} \right)^{1-\sigma_m} \right], \tag{1}$$

where β^t is the household's discount factor. Utility depends positively on the consumption of goods and negatively on the supply of labour hours, N_t. The coefficient of relative risk aversion σ_c measures the curvature of the household's utility function with respect to its argument $C_{j,t} - \phi C_{t-1}$, where external habit formation is parameterized by ϕ. It also measures the inverse of the intertemporal elasticity of substitution in consumption. σ_n is the inverse of the elasticity of hours worked to the real wage. Households derive direct value from the liquidity services of real money holdings, where σ_m is the interest elasticity of money demand.

Households have access to two types of assets: money $\mathcal{M}_{j,t}$ and bonds $B_{j,t}$, where bonds pay a gross nominal rate of return $(1 + i_t^b)$. Notably, we assume that each household j owns an equal portion of all firms in the economy, and the household outsources its labour decision to labour unions who determine their wage rate. The representative household j therefore allocates periodic income from wages (W_t), bonds, dividends, and cash balances to current consumption and new financial wealth holdings:

$$P_t C_{j,t} + Q_t B_{j,t} + \mathcal{M}_{j,t} \leq B_{j,t-1} + \mathcal{M}_{j,t-1} + W_t N_{j,t} + \Pi_{j,t}^H + T_{j,t}, \tag{2}$$

where Q_t is the discount on one-period bond purchases such that the pay-off at maturity is the short-term nominal interest rate $I_t^b \mu_t^b$. The stochastic disturbance term μ_t^b represents the domestic risk premium (spread) over the monetary policy

[10] For tractability, we simplify the model as much as possible and therefore ignore the more complex intertemporal modelling of internal habit formation (see Fuhrer 2000). Again, the distinction between internal (time non-separable) and external (exogenous) habit formation becomes important for higher-order approximations (e.g., uncertainty) or regime changes.

rate. $\Pi^H_{j,t}$ are dividends/profits received from domestic firms, and $T_{j,t}$ represents lump-sum net transfers from government.

Consumption and Savings Behaviour

Households optimize their consumption-savings decision by maximizing Eq. 1 subject to Eq. 2. The aggregated first-order conditions for bonds give the standard Euler equation governing intertemporal consumption dynamics:

$$1 = \beta E_t \left[\frac{\Lambda_{t+1}}{\Lambda_t} \frac{P_t}{P_{t+1}} I_t^b \mu_t^b \right], \tag{3}$$

where $\Lambda_t = (C_t - \phi C_{t-1})^{-\sigma_c}$ is the marginal utility of consumption and the Lagrangian multiplier of the budget constraint. The first-order condition for money follows as

$$\frac{\Lambda_{m,t}}{\Lambda_t} = 1 - \beta E_t \left[\frac{\Lambda_{t+1}}{\Lambda_t} \frac{1}{\Pi_{t+1}} \right], \tag{4}$$

where $\Pi_{t+1} = P_{t+1}/P_t$ is gross inflation, $\Lambda_{m,t} = a(\mathcal{M}_t/P_t)^{-\sigma_m}$ is the liquidity services from holding real money balances. Equation 4 captures the household's demand for real money balances. In equilibrium, the money supply process is such that seigniorage revenue equals lump-sum net transfers: $\mathcal{M}_t - \mathcal{M}_{t-1} = T_t$.

Labour Supply Decisions and the Wage-Setting Equation

Monopolistically competitive unions determine the optimal wage for households for a given labour demand schedule. There is a continuum of unions, and each union represents workers of a certain type τ. The labour demand schedule that each household type τ faces is determined by

$$N_t^\tau = \left(\frac{W_t^\tau}{W_t} \right)^{-\xi_t^w} N_t \,, \tag{5}$$

where ξ_t^w is the stochastic wage elasticity of substitution across different types of households.

Following Calvo-type price setting, only a random fraction $(1 - \theta_w)$ of unions have the opportunity to reset their wages $(\tilde{W}_t)$ each period. Whereas those unions that cannot reset their wages simply index to the lagged wage rate. The aggregate wage index is given by

$$W_t^{1-\xi_t^w} = \theta_w (\Gamma_t W_{t-1})^{1-\xi_t^w} + (1 - \theta_w)(\tilde{W}_t)^{1-\xi_t^w} \,, \tag{6}$$

where $\Gamma_t = \Pi_{t-1}^{\gamma_w} = (P_{t-1}/P_{t-2})^{\gamma_w}$ and γ_w is the degree of wage indexation. The re-optimizing union's problem is to therefore choose $\tilde{W}_t$ to maximize the consumption-weighted wage income:

$$\max_{\tilde{W}_t} E_t \sum_{i=0}^{\infty} (\theta_w \beta)^i \left[\frac{\Gamma_{t+i} \tilde{W}_t N_{t+i}^{\tau}}{P_{t+i}(C_{t+i} - \phi C_{t-1+i})^{\sigma_c}} - \frac{(N_{t+i}^{\tau})^{1+\sigma_n}}{1+\sigma_n} \right], \tag{7}$$

subject to the labour demand schedule in Eq. 5. Solving and linearizing the optimization problem and combining it with Eq. 6 gives the forward-looking New-Keynesian wage-setting equation.

3.2 Decision Problems of Firms and Equilibrium Conditions

The domestic goods-producing sector is made up of a continuum of infinitely lived firms indexed by $j \in [0,1]$. The decision problem can be characterized by two stages. First, firm j minimizes the total cost of production subject to the production constraint. Second, each firm j maximizes its profit function subject to a domestic demand schedule. Following Calvo (1983), all firms face a probability θ_p of not being able to optimally adjust prices. In this market, final goods producers are monopolistically competitive.

Various alternative approaches can be taken where, for example, households also rent physical capital to intermediate goods producing firms which earns a rate of return equal to its marginal product. They may also own firms but there exists a separate physical capital producing sector (see, e.g., Bernanke et al. 1999). We, however, treat investment and capital goods production as a wholly-separate competitive sector with an implied "shadow" value (Iacoviello 2005).

Capital Goods Producers

The representative capital goods producing firm chooses a path for investment (V_t) that maximizes the present value of its profits:

$$\max_{K_{t+1}, V_t} E_t \sum_{i=0}^{\infty} \Lambda_{t,t+i} \left[R_{t+i}^k K_{t+i} - V_{t+i} - \Phi\left(\frac{V_{t+i}}{K_{t+i}}\right) K_{t+i} \right] \tag{8}$$

subject to the capital accumulation equation given by

$$K_{t+1} \leq (1-\delta) K_t + \xi_t^{v} V_t \,, \tag{9}$$

where δ measures the depreciation rate of capital, and K_t represents the physical capital stock at the beginning of period t. ξ_t^v is an investment-specific efficiency shock. R_t^k is the gross (real) return on rented capital holdings, and $\Phi(\cdot)$ captures the adjustment cost of capital installation.[11] We assume that the prices of consumption goods and investment goods coincide ($P_t = P_t^V$). $\Lambda_{t,t+i}$ denotes the consumption-based relevant discount factor for real profits, i-periods ahead, given by $\Lambda_{t,t+i} \equiv \beta^i(\Lambda_{t+i}/\Lambda_t)$.

The first-order conditions for the capital goods producer problem are

$$Q_t^k = E_t\left\{\Lambda_{t,t+1}\left[R_{t+1}^k + Q_{t+1}^k(1-\delta) + \Phi_{t+1}^v V_{t+1} - \Phi_{t+1}\right]\right\} \tag{10}$$

$$\xi_t^v Q_t^k = 1 + \Phi_t^v K_t\ , \tag{11}$$

where $\Phi_t^v = (\kappa_v/\delta)(V_t/K_t - \delta)(1/K_t)$ and Q_t^k is the marginal value of an additional unit of capital. That is, Q_t^k is the "shadow value" of the capital accumulation constraint (11) and equals the present discounted value of the marginal profits of an additional unit of capital (10).

Intermediate Goods Producers

In the intermediate goods production stage, each firm j combines factor inputs, labour ($N_{j,t}$), and capital ($K_{j,t}$), to produce intermediate goods for final goods production with the following Cobb–Douglas production technology: $Y_{j,t} = \xi_t^a(K_{j,t})^\alpha(N_{j,t})^{(1-\alpha)}$, where α captures the share of physical capital in production and ξ_t^a represents total factor productivity that follows an auto-regressive stochastic process of order one (the technology shock). The decision problem is to therefore select the optimal combination of factor inputs—labour and capital—to minimize the total cost of production, taking prices as given:

$$\min_{\{N_{j,t},K_{j,t}\}} TC_{j,t} + \lambda_t(Y_{j,t} - \xi_t^a(K_{j,t})^\alpha(N_{j,t})^{(1-\alpha)})\ , \tag{12}$$

where $TC_{j,t} = \frac{W_t}{P_t^h}N_{j,t} + R_t^k K_{j,t}$ is the total real cost of production. The aggregate first-order efficiency conditions for labour and capital are

$$\frac{W_t}{P_t} = \lambda_t\frac{\partial Y_t}{\partial N_t} = (1-\alpha)\lambda_t\frac{Y_t}{N_t} \tag{13}$$

$$R_t^k = \lambda_t\frac{\partial Y_t}{\partial K_t} = \alpha\lambda_t\frac{Y_t}{K_t}\ , \tag{14}$$

[11] $\Phi' > 0$, $\Phi'' < 0$, $\Phi'(\delta) = 0$, $\Phi(\delta) = 0$. Specifically, $\Phi(V_t/K_t)K_t = (\kappa_v/2\delta)(V_t/K_t - \delta)^2K_t$.

where λ_t is the real marginal cost of production and the Lagrangian multiplier of the production function.

Final Goods Sector

In the final goods (retail) production stage, each firm j is monopolistically competitive in its intermediate good $Y_{j,t}$. The firm is able to brand and sell its retail good at a mark-up P_t over marginal cost, taking into account their individual demand curves from consumers. We assume that only a random fraction $(1-\theta_p)$ of firms can adjust their retail price in each period. Therefore, each firm j faces the following decision problem:

$$\max_{\{\tilde{P}_t\}} E_t \sum_{i=0}^{\infty} \theta_p^i \Lambda_{t,t+i} \left[\left(\frac{\Pi_{t+i-1}^{\gamma_p} \tilde{P}_{j,t}}{P_{t+i}} - \lambda_{t+i} \right) Y_{j,t+i} \right] \tag{15}$$

subject to the consumer demand schedule for goods

$$Y_{j,t+i} = \left(\frac{\tilde{P}_{j,t}}{P_{t+i}} \right)^{-\xi_t^p} Y_{t+i}, \tag{16}$$

where ξ_t^p is the stochastic price elasticity of demand for intermediate good Y_t. $\tilde{P}_t$ denotes the optimal price set by firms who are able to adjust the price in period t, and λ_t is the real marginal cost of production. The aggregate price level is determined by

$$(P_t)^{1-\xi_t^p} = \theta_p \left(\left[\frac{P_{t-1}}{P_{t-2}} \right]^{\gamma_p} P_{t-1} \right)^{1-\xi_t^p} + (1-\theta_p)(\tilde{P}_t)^{1-\xi_t^p}, \tag{17}$$

where γ_p determines the degree of price indexation for non-optimizing retailers. Solving and linearizing the optimization problem and combining it with Eq. 17 gives the forward-looking New-Keynesian Phillips curve.

Government and Market Clearing

The short-term interest rate is determined by a Taylor-type reaction function that describes monetary policy decisions:

$$I_t = (I_{t-1})^{\rho_i} \left(\frac{\Pi_t}{\Pi^{target}} \right)^{\kappa_\pi (1-\rho_i)} \left(\frac{\Delta Y_t}{Y} \right)^{\kappa_y (1-\rho_i)} \xi_t^i, \tag{18}$$

where ρ_i is the weight on the lagged policy rate, κ_π is the weight on inflation, and κ_y is the weight on output growth, $\Delta Y_t = Y_t/Y_{t-1}$. ξ_t^i captures exogenous innovations to the short-term interest—typically identified as independent and identically distributed monetary policy shocks. The short-term nominal interest rate therefore rises (falls) whenever inflation and output growth rise above (fall below) their average, or steady-state. All markets clear and, in the symmetric equilibrium, all representative agents make identical decisions. To close the model we include the aggregate resource constraint:

$$Y_t = C_t + V_t + \xi_t^g , \tag{19}$$

where the final goods market is in equilibrium if production equals demand for consumption and investment plus an exogenous expenditure component, ξ_t^g, which captures both government spending and the trade balance.[12]

Exogenous Shocks

There are seven exogenous shocks in the benchmark Smets and Wouters (2007) framework that follow AR(1) processes with independent and identically distributed standard deviations. The three core New-Keynesian shocks are the technology shock (ξ_t^a), the price mark-up shock (ξ_t^p), and the monetary policy shock (ξ_t^i).[13] The supply-side of the real economy includes a wage mark-up shock (ξ_t^w) which distorts the labour market. On the demand side, we have an investment-specific efficiency shock (ξ_t^v), a risk premium shock (ξ_t^b) and, as mentioned in the previous section, an exogenous expenditure component (ξ_t^g) in the aggregate resource constraint.

4 The Linearized System of Equilibrium Conditions

In addition to the benchmark New-Keynesian model based on Smets and Wouters (2007) (*SW-NK* hereafter), we develop three alternative models. First, a "naive" New-Keynesian model of the three-equation type based on Ireland (2011) (*Naive-NK* hereafter): an IS curve, a Phillips curve, and a monetary policy rule. Second, a standard small open economy New-Keynesian model based on Hollander, Gupta, and Wohar (2019) (*SOE-NK* hereafter), and third, a New-Keynesian model extended to include a retail and wholesale banking sector and a role for equity in household

---

[12]Given that Y_t, C_t, and V_t are observed data inputted into the model for estimation, the AR(1) stochastic process ξ_t^g is included, as in Smets and Wouters (2007), to avoid stochastic singularity and to reduce estimation bias toward the other structural shocks.

[13]ρ_i in the monetary policy rule (18) captures the persistence of innovations to ξ_t^i. In this context, it captures the degree of interest rate smoothing by the monetary authorities.

wealth, firm creditworthiness, and bank capital dynamics, based on Hollander and Liu (2016a) (*FF-NK* hereafter). Appendices 1–3 give the complete list of linearized equilibrium conditions.

As far as possible, we stick to the canonical approach adopted in Smets and Wouters (2003, 2007) for each of the four models described. That is, we synchronize the structural framework, structural shocks, and estimation procedures as far as possible to ensure an appropriate evaluation and comparison of the results from each model. Here, we show the core New-Keynesian framework and highlight the key equations for each extended version of the nested model. In what follows, lower-case variables with a hat, $\hat{x}_t$, represent log-deviations from a steady-state or trend.

4.1 The Core New-Keynesian Specification

We begin with Ireland's small-scale model:

$$\text{IS curve}: \hat{y}_t = \frac{1}{(1+\phi)}\hat{y}_{t+1} + \frac{\phi}{(1+\phi)}\hat{y}_{t-1} - \frac{(1-\phi)}{\sigma_c(1+\phi)}(\hat{i}_t - E_t[\hat{\pi}_{t+1}]) \tag{20}$$

$$\text{NK Phillips curve}: \hat{\pi}_t = \frac{\gamma_p}{(1+\gamma_p\beta)}\hat{\pi}_{t-1} + \frac{\beta}{(1+\gamma_p\beta)}E_t[\hat{\pi}_{t+1}] + \tilde{\kappa}\tilde{y}_t \tag{21}$$

$$\text{Monetary policy rule}: \hat{i}_t = \rho_i\hat{i}_{t-1} + (1-\rho_i)(\kappa_\pi\hat{\pi}_t + \kappa_y\Delta\hat{y}_t) + \epsilon_t^i \tag{22}$$

where $\tilde{y}_t = (\sigma_c/(1-\phi) + \sigma_n)\hat{y}_t + (\sigma_c\phi)/(1-\phi)\hat{y}_{t-1} + (1+\sigma_n)\hat{\xi}_t^a$ is the real marginal cost of production, $\Delta\hat{y}_t = \hat{y}_t - \hat{y}_{t-1}$, and $\tilde{\kappa} = (1-\theta_p)(1-\theta_p\beta)/(\theta_p(1+\gamma_p\beta))$.[14] For expositional reasons we ignore the slightly different specifications for the shock variables across the models. The key reason being that the technology shock and price mark-up shock are collinear in a *Naive-NK* model as presented above. On the aggregate supply-side, Ireland (2011) distinguishes a price mark-up shock in the New-Keynesian Phillips curve from the technology shock to the *growth rate* of output. On the demand side, in addition to the monetary policy shock, Ireland's model includes a preference shock that has an analogous role as the risk premium shock in the benchmark Smets and Wouters model (see Sect. 6.1).

[14]Ireland (2011) assumes log preferences ($\sigma_c = 1$) and linear disutility of hours worked ($\sigma_n = 0$). In addition, to enrich the dynamics of the model, habit formation is endogenous to the representative household (internal). This specification is shown in Appendix 1. Note that the three-equation New-Keynesian model presented here follows very similarly to the three-equation model specification for the foreign economy in Hollander et al. (2019).

The Smets and Wouters model presented in Sect. 3 (*SW-NK* hereafter) extends the *Naive-NK* model to include labour market frictions and capital goods market frictions, namely sticky wage-setting and adjustment costs to physical capital accumulation. These two frictions generate imperfect adjustment in factor inputs for production and hence help replicate empirical features observed in the data. The investment schedule with adjustment costs follows as:

$$\hat{v}_t - \hat{k}_t = \beta E_t(\hat{v}_{t+1} - \hat{k}_{t+1}) + \frac{\beta R^k}{\kappa_v} E_t(\hat{r}^k_{t+1}) + \frac{\sigma_c}{\kappa_v}(\hat{c}_t - \hat{c}_{t+1}) , \quad (23)$$

where $R^k = 1/\beta - (1 - \delta)$. And the nominal wage inflation process follows from the optimal (real) wage-setting equation of unions as:

$$\hat{\pi}^w_t - \gamma_w \hat{\pi}_{t-1} = \beta E_t \hat{\pi}^w_{t+1} - \theta_w \beta \gamma_w \hat{\pi}_t + \Omega^*(\hat{mrs}_t - \hat{w}_t) , \quad (24)$$

where $\Omega^* = \frac{(1-\theta_w)(1-\theta_w\beta)}{\theta_w(1+\xi^w\sigma_n)}$ and $\hat{mrs}_t = \frac{\sigma_c}{1-\phi}(\hat{c}_t - \phi\hat{c}_{t-1}) + \sigma_n\hat{n}_t$.[15]

4.2 *Extending the Model to the Open Economy*

It is straightforward to extend the described New-Keynesian framework to include open economy dynamics. Here, we follow the approach of the small open economy models of Steinbach et al. (2009), Alpanda et al. (2010) and Hollander et al. (2019) applied to the South African economy. These models all incorporate access to a foreign-currency denominated asset, domestic importing retailers (sticky import price setting), and deviations from purchasing power of parity, which captures short-run incomplete nominal exchange rate pass-through observed in the data (Burstein and Gopinath 2014).[16] As such, exchange rate overshooting is an outcome of the

[15]Log-linearizing the optimality condition for wage-setting and solving for $\tilde{w}_t$ gives the optimal reset wage equation:

$$\tilde{w}_t = \frac{(1 - \theta_w\beta)}{(1 + \xi^w\sigma_n)} E_t \sum_{i=0}^{\infty} (\theta_w\beta)^i \left(\chi mrs_{t+i} + \xi^w \sigma_n w_{t+i} + p_{t+i} - \gamma_w \pi_{t+i-1} \right), \quad (25)$$

where $\chi \equiv \frac{W}{MRS^s \mu^w}$. Combining (25) with the log-linearized wage index equation gives the aggregate sticky real wage ($\hat{w}_t = w_t - p_t$) equation:

$$\begin{aligned} \hat{w}_t &= \Omega\beta E_t \hat{w}_{t+1} + \Omega\hat{w}_{t-1} + \Omega\Omega^*(\hat{mrs}_t - \hat{w}_t) \\ &\quad + \Omega\beta E_t \hat{\pi}_{t+1} - \Omega\hat{\pi}_t - \Omega\theta_w\beta\gamma_w\hat{\pi}_t + \Omega\gamma_w\hat{\pi}_{t-1} , \end{aligned} \quad (26)$$

where $\Omega = \frac{1}{(1+\beta)}$. Equation 26 can be re-written in nominal wage inflation form as Eq. 24.

[16]For a given exchange rate, domestic importing retailers are import "price-takers", but face a downward sloping domestic demand curve.

model where international risk sharing in consumption allows for asset markets to clear, and therefore interest rates to adjust, more rapidly than price adjustments in the goods sector.

Specifically, complete international consumption risk sharing implies complete international asset markets. The optimality conditions for domestic- and foreign-currency denominated assets therefore give the standard uncovered interest parity (UIP) condition:

$$\hat{i}_t^b = \hat{i}_t^{b*} + E_t[\Delta\hat{\varepsilon}_{t+1}] + \hat{\Phi}_t \,, \tag{27}$$

where $\hat{i}_t^b$ and $\hat{i}_t^{b*}$ are the domestic and foreign short-term nominal interest rates, $\hat{\varepsilon}_t$ is the nominal effective exchange rate (direct quoting), and $\hat{\Phi}_t$ is the prevailing stochastic risk premium for the domestic economy ($\hat{\mu}_t^b - \hat{\mu}_t^{b*}$). A positive shock to $\hat{\Phi}_t$, equivalent to a negative demand shock, raises the return on domestic currency bonds relative to foreign currency bonds and reduces current consumption (Smets and Wouters 2007; Steinbach et al. 2009). The *nominal* exchange rate is therefore the market clearing price for domestic and foreign asset demand derived optimally from the domestic household's consumption Euler equations.

The evolution of the *real* exchange rate (RER) represents a measure of trade competitiveness: the value of a basket of domestic goods in terms of a similar basket of foreign goods. It is rising in the domestic real interest rate ($i_t - E_t[\pi_{t+1}]$) and falling in the foreign real interest rate ($i_t^* - E_t[\pi_{t+1}^{f*}]$). A positive shock to the prevailing stochastic risk premium ($\hat{\Phi}_t$) reduces the real exchange rate of the domestic economy. The assumption here is that purchasing power parity must either hold in steady-state (if import price mark-ups are zero), or revert to a constant level. Any *long-run* deviations from PPP, as a result of productivity differentials or changes in the structure of the non-tradable goods sector, are therefore not accounted for by the model.

This implies that the *real* exchange rate adjusts to consumption dynamics between the domestic and foreign sectors.[17] Specifically, we can combine the definition of the real exchange rate: $rer_t \equiv \hat{\varepsilon}_t + \hat{pr}^{f*}$, where $\hat{pr}^{f*} = \hat{p}_t^{f*} - \hat{p}_t$ is the foreign-domestic relative price level, with the UIP condition (27) to describe the equation of motion for the relative purchasing power parity condition (i.e., the real exchange rate):

$$\hat{rer}_{t+1} = \hat{rer}_t + E_t[\Delta\hat{\varepsilon}_{t+1}] + \hat{\pi}_{t+1}^{f*} - \hat{\pi}_{t+1} \,. \tag{28}$$

The terms-of-trade follows as the price of imports relative to the price of domestically produced goods (denominated in domestic currency). The assumption here is that domestic firms cannot price discriminate across markets and that the

---

[17] I.e., RER equates the marginal utilities of consumption between the domestic and foreign households.

law of one price (l.o.p) holds for domestic export prices. This also implies that the share of domestic goods in the foreign economy consumption bundle is negligible. A first-order approximation expresses the terms-of-trade as the difference between the relative prices of foreign and domestic goods: $\hat{s}_t = \hat{pr}_t^f - \hat{pr}_t^h$, where $\hat{pr}_t^i = \hat{p}_t^i - \hat{p}_t$ for $i = h, f$. The trade balance follows as the difference between exports ($\hat{x}_t$) and imports ($\hat{m}_t$): $\hat{x}_t = \hat{y}_t^* - \xi^{f*}(\hat{pr}_t^h - \hat{rer}_t)$ and $\hat{m}_t = \hat{c}_t^f$, where $\hat{y}_t^*$ is foreign demand and ξ^{f*} is the foreign (export) price elasticity of demand for domestic goods,[18] and $\hat{c}_t^f$ is the consumption of foreign goods.

4.3 Extending the Model to the Financial Sector

Our financial model is based on Hollander and Liu (2016a) (*FF-NK* hereafter) which incorporates the monopolistically competitive banking sector structure of Gerali et al. (2010) (sticky interest rate adjustment) with the equity price channel developed in Hollander and Liu (2016b). In this model, households have access to credit as well as savings. Their savings portfolio is allocated between "safe-assets" and investment in the equity market. The price of equity is determined by households' demand for equity investment. Both banks and firms issue equity, and as a result, the value of equity influences credit spreads through both the bank capital channel and the financial accelerator channel (Hollander and Liu 2016a,b). For example, an equity price collapse reduces borrower creditworthiness, which puts upward pressure on retail credit spreads from the demand side. On the supply-side, a fall in the bank capital-to-asset ratio, due to the equity price collapse, induces financial distress in over-leveraged banks. As a result, interbank spreads widen and net interest margins between funding (short-term) and lending (long-term) rates narrow to the extent that interest rate pass-through is incomplete. Figure 1 highlights this relationship between the bank capital-to-asset ratio of South African deposit-taking institutions and both the retail (term) spread and the interbank spread. Over the period 1995:01–2018:05, the term spread (top panel) is strongly positively correlated (0.57), and the interbank spread (bottom panel) is strongly negatively correlated (−0.50).[19]

Banks operate in both the commercial (retail) and investment (wholesale) sectors. In the monopolistically competitive retail sector, they supply credit to both households and firms. Retail loan rate setting is symmetric for households and firms

[18] I.e., the change in foreign demand for domestic goods given the foreign price of domestic goods relative to the foreign price of foreign goods can be expressed as: $\hat{pr}_t^{h*} - \hat{pr}_t^{f*} = \hat{pr}_t^h - \hat{rer}_t$.

[19] Recent empirical evidence suggests that bank capital adequacy ratios in South Africa are procyclical (see, e.g., Akinsola and Ikhide 2017; Maredza 2015). For now, we abstract from measuring the extent of this endogenous procyclicality by requiring banks to target a non-binding capital-asset ratio that is subject to precautionary/regulatory shocks.

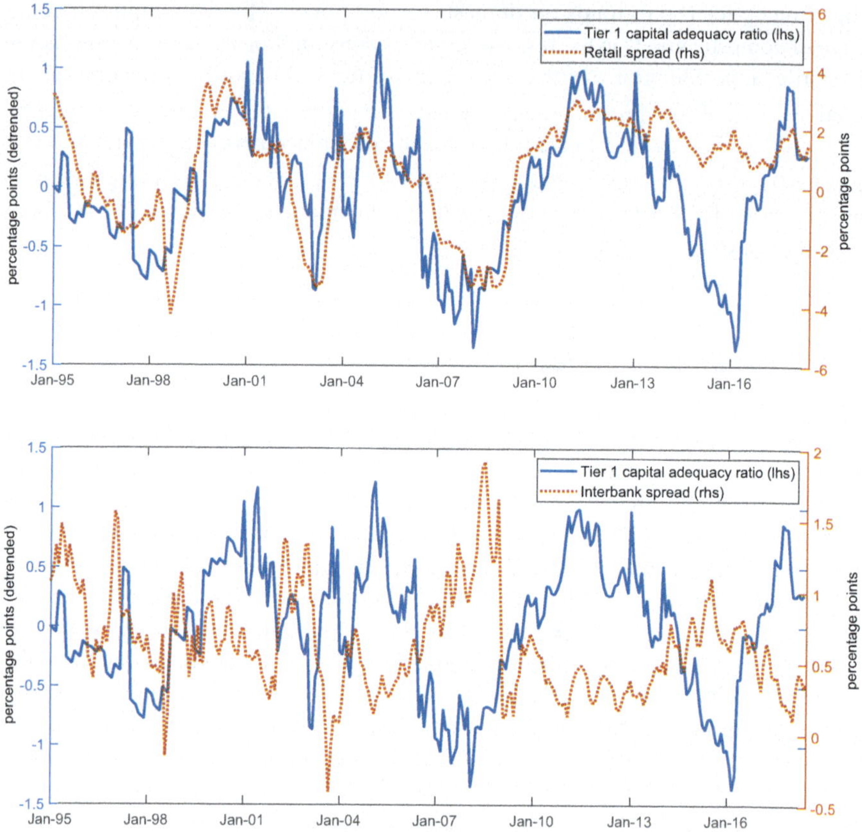

Fig. 1 Correlation between linearly detrended tier 1 bank capital adequacy ratio for South African deposit-taking institutions and interest rate spreads. The term spread is the difference between 10-year and 3-month treasury bonds (top panel). The interbank spread (bottom panel). The interbank spread is the difference between 3-month negotiable certificates of deposit and the 3-month treasury bill rate

$(z = h, f)$ and is described by the following retail credit spread between the retail loan rate and the interbank loan rate:

$$\hat{i}_t^z - \hat{i}_t^c = \frac{\kappa_z}{\kappa_z^*}\hat{i}_{t-1}^z + \frac{\beta_B \kappa_z}{\kappa_z^*}E_t\hat{i}_{t+1}^z + \frac{(1+\nu_B)(\varepsilon^z - 1) - (1+\beta_B)\kappa_z}{\kappa_z^*}\hat{i}_t^c + \frac{(1-\nu_B)(\varepsilon^z - 1)}{\kappa_z^*}\mu_t^z, \quad (29)$$

where μ_t^z is the stochastic process for retail rate mark-ups imposed by commercial banks, and $\kappa_z^* = (1-\nu_B)(\varepsilon^z - 1) + (1+\beta_B)\kappa_z$. Equation (29) shows that household and firm loan rate setting depends on the stochastic markup, past and expected future loan rates, and the wholesale interbank funding rate ($\hat{i}_t^c$), which depends on the policy rate and the balance sheet position of the bank. A positive adjustment of the interbank rate puts upward pressure on retail loan rates. As $\nu_B \rightarrow 1$, the influence of the interbank rate over retail rate setting increases, while the influence of the stochastic markup decreases. In contrast, a higher adjustment cost (κ_z) smooths the adjustment of retail loan rates and hence retail credit spreads.

In the competitive wholesale sector, the interbank credit spread between the interbank loan rate and the policy rate follows as:

$$\hat{i}_t^c - \hat{i}_t = -\kappa_k \tau^3 (\hat{k}_t^B - \hat{l}_t - \hat{\tau}_t), \tag{30}$$

where $\hat{k}^B$ is the total bank capital which accumulates gradually through common equity stock valuation changes and retained earnings.[20] Market clearing in the credit market ensures that $\hat{l}_t$ equals the aggregate of household and firm loans. The coefficient κ_k captures the adjustment cost of contemporaneous deviations of the capital-to-asset ratio from a target capital requirement ratio, which we assume to follow an exogenous stochastic process: $\hat{\tau}_t = \ln(\tau_t) = (1 - \rho_\tau) \ln \tau + \rho_\tau \ln \tau_{t-1} + \epsilon_{\tau,t}$. This banking sector setup allows for procyclical interbank credit spread variability based on aggregate bank balance sheet adjustments. That is, bank leverage drives a wedge between the policy rate and other market rates. To the extent that leverage is procyclical (Adrian and Shin 2010, 2013) the effectiveness of monetary policy over longer-term retail rates declines (Hollander and Liu 2016a). For example, during stress episodes the interbank credit spread immediately widens with a deterioration of bank capital-asset positions. Thereafter, the interbank credit spread narrows as banks accumulate larger capital buffers and the capital-to-asset ratio converges on the target τ_t.

The bank capital accumulation is as follows

$$\hat{k}_t^B = (1 - \delta_B)\hat{k}_{t-1}^B + \delta_B \hat{\pi}_{\psi,t-1}^B + \phi_\psi (\hat{q}_t^{\psi,b} - \hat{q}_{t-1}^{\psi,b}) - (1 - \phi_\psi)\hat{\pi}_t \,, \tag{31}$$

$\hat{q}_t^{\psi,b}$ is the equity price and ϕ_ψ measures the pass-through effect of equity price changes on total bank capital and δ_B is the bank capital depreciation rate, capturing management costs for banks.[21] Retained earnings $(\hat{\pi}_{\psi,t-1}^B)$ are bank profits net of dividend payments. Equation 31 therefore provides a role for the market capitalization of bank equity in the formation of total bank capital, which, in turn, influences the feasible supply of credit. This reflects both the recent regulatory emphasis on common equity as a buffer to bank balance sheet shocks and the recent

---

[20] Adrian and Shin (2010, 2013) show that banks (in the USA) tend to actively manage their capital-assets ratios through debt rather than equity. As such, bank capital accumulation is persistent (for a more-detailed discussion see, e.g., Hollander 2017). In addition, we assume that the market value of bank equity influences the book value of common (or tier 1) bank equity (Adrian and Shin 2010, 2013).

[21] We assume that the stock of equity shares are fixed, thus $\hat{\psi} = \hat{\psi}^b + \hat{\psi}^f = 0$.

observed rise in the ratio of bank capital to assets in South Africa (see Fig. 1). From January 2008 to June 2017 regulatory tier 1 bank capital to risk-weighted assets (of which common equity forms the majority) rose steadily from 8.9% to 13.5%, and total capital adequacy ratios rose from 11.8% to 16.5%. Prior to the global financial crisis, tier 1 capital adequacy ratios rose in two successive waves from 6.5% (March 1994) to 9.5% at the end of 2007, peaking twice in May 2001 (9.5%) and January 2005 (10.6%).

Households and firms are credit constrained by their creditworthiness (Hollander and Liu 2016a). This generates a financial accelerator mechanism that propagates not only financial sector disturbances, but also demand (nominal) and supply (real) shocks originating outside of the financial sector (Bernanke et al. 1999; Kiyotaki and Moore 1997). Creditworthiness depends on household wealth (wage income and equity assets) and firm assets and net worth (physical capital and equity). Factor inputs in production (labour and physical capital) therefore serve as a measure of creditworthiness for loans. The equity price channel, in addition, provides a distinct dynamic interaction between asset prices (wealth and net worth) and credit limits. The first-order approximations of these two constraints follow as:

$$\hat{l}_t^f = \frac{\phi_k}{R^f}(\hat{q}_t^k + \hat{k}_{t-1}) + \frac{(1-\phi_k)}{R^f}\hat{q}_t^{\psi,f} - \hat{i}_t^f + \frac{1}{R^f}\hat{\nu}_t^f , \tag{32}$$

$$\hat{l}_t^h = \frac{\phi_w}{R^h}(\hat{w}_t + \hat{n}_t) + \frac{(1-\phi_w)}{R^h}\hat{q}_t^{\psi,h} - \hat{i}_t^h + \frac{1}{R^h}\hat{\nu}_t^h , \tag{33}$$

where $\phi_k \in (0, 1)$ is the weight on physical capital stock. $\hat{q}_t^k$ is the real price of physical capital, $\hat{\nu}_t^f$ is a stochastic loan-to-value (LTV) ratio, and $\hat{i}_t^f$ is the nominal interest rate on firm loans ($\hat{l}_t^f$). The market value of physical capital ($\hat{q}_t^k + \hat{k}_{t-1}$) and firm equity ($\hat{q}_t^{\psi,f} + \hat{\psi}_{t=0}^f$) serve as a measure of creditworthiness. In other words, they serve as a market-based signal for firm's net worth and hence collateral. The equity market is introduced into the production sector in such a way that it has an impact on the firm's resource allocation and, in turn, the productivity of the economy. The household's wage income together with its investment in the equity market represents creditworthiness and serves as collateral, where $\phi_w \in (0, 1)$ is the weight on wage income. $\hat{\nu}_t^h$ is a stochastic LTV ratio and, correspondingly, in cases of default $1 - \hat{\nu}_t^h$ can be interpreted as the proportional transaction cost for the bank's repossession of the borrower's collateral. Following the literature (e.g., Iacoviello 2005), we assume that the size of shocks is small enough that the borrowing constraint is always binding.

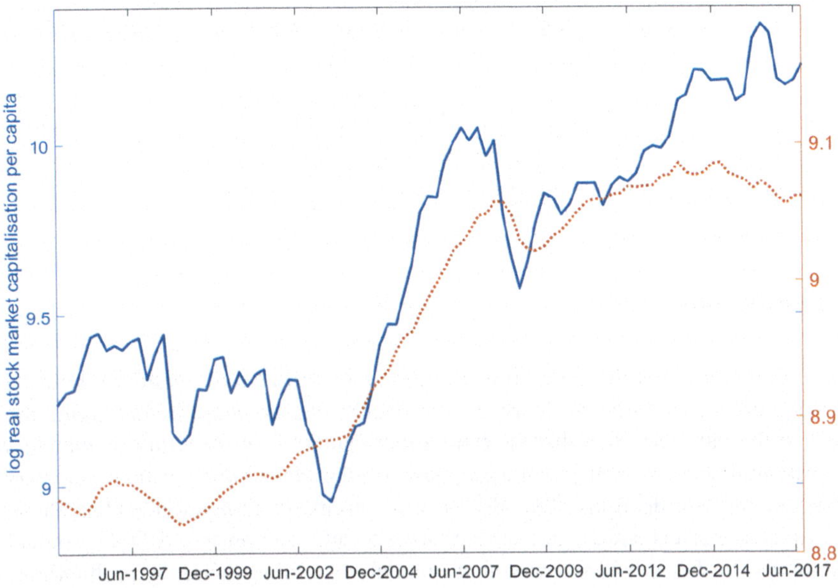

Fig. 2 Correlation between log real stock market capitalization per capita (left axis) and log real GDP per capita (right axis)

Equity prices follow a standard consumption-based asset-pricing equation from the households optimality condition for equity investment (ψ_t)[22]:

$$\hat{q}_t^{\psi} = E_t[\hat{q}_{t+1}^{\psi} - \frac{\sigma_c}{1-\phi}(\hat{c}_{t+1} - \phi\hat{c}_t)] + \frac{\sigma_c}{(1-\Gamma_\psi)(1-\phi)}(\hat{c}_t - \phi\hat{c}_{t-1})$$
$$+ \frac{\Gamma_\psi}{1-\Gamma_\psi}(\hat{\lambda}_t^h + \hat{\upsilon}_t^h) - \hat{\xi}_t^{\psi}, \tag{34}$$

where the Lagrangian multiplier, $\hat{\lambda}_t^h$, is the marginal utility of an additional unit of loans, and $\Gamma_\psi = ((1/R^h) - \beta_h)\upsilon_h(1-\phi_w)$. Arbitrage ensures that $\hat{q}_t^{\psi} = \hat{q}_t^{\psi,i}\ \forall\ i = h, b, f$ (see, e.g., Hollander 2017, for a more-detailed exposition). Figure 2 highlights the procyclicality of the equity price.

We introduce six shocks in the financial sector. On the supply-side of credit, we have two retail loan rate mark-up shocks to household loans ($\hat{\mu}_t^h$) and firm loans ($\hat{\mu}_t^f$). On the demand side of the credit market, household loans and firm loans are subject to loan-to-value ratio shocks ($\hat{\upsilon}_t^h$ and $\hat{\upsilon}_t^f$). Households' demand

[22]We do not distinguish between saver and borrower households as in Hollander and Liu (2016b) which allows for a demand and supply interaction for equity investment. Instead, we follow Hollander and Liu (2016a) and the problem simplifies to a dynamic asset-pricing equation (see, e.g., Cochrane 2008).

for safe-asset holdings is subject to an exogenous shock ($\hat{\xi}_t^b$)—which replaces the risk premium shock in the *SW-NK* model. Therefore, this safe-asset demand shock captures the aggregate demand for monetary aggregates with respect to intertemporal consumption decisions of households. Finally, an equity price shock ($\hat{\xi}_t^\psi$) simultaneously affects consumption, production, and bank lending activities through the equity price channel as described in Hollander and Liu (2016a,b).

5 Estimation

This section discusses the estimation methodology and results. First, we describe the estimation procedure and the parameter restrictions we adopt before taking the model to the data. We then discuss estimation results of the structural parameters and structural shocks, with specific emphasis on the plausibility of the parameters and economic implications. We also test for weak identification and evaluate the empirical performance against alternative South African-based DSGE model estimations. In this sense, we care about model uncertainty whereby probabilities are prespecified but outcomes are unknown—i.e., "inside uncertainty" or "risk within a model" (Hansen 2014, 2017).

In order to distinguish between relevant model specifications we estimate our three alternative models in addition to the benchmark New-Keynesian model (*SW-NK*) based on Smets and Wouters (2007). As a reminder, our "naive" New-Keynesian model (*Naive-NK*) contains an IS curve, a Phillips curve, and a monetary policy rule. We then extend the *SW-NK* model in two directions: first, to a standard small open economy New-Keynesian model (*SOE-NK*) based on Hollander, Gupta, and Wohar (2019); second, to a model with a detailed financial sector (*FF-NK*) based on Hollander and Liu (2016a), that includes a retail and wholesale banking sector and a role for the equity market in financial wealth, borrower creditworthiness, and bank capital dynamics. Here, model specification is important for discriminating between different business cycle models, their estimated responses to identified structural shocks, and the inferences we make regarding their policy responses (Nakamura and Steinsson 2018)—what Hansen (2014, 2017) refers to as "outside uncertainty" or "ambiguity about a model [among a family of alternatives]". We specifically look at the robustness of model specification in Sect. 6.[23]

[23]A third component of uncertainty relates to potential model *mis*specification (Hansen 2014, 2017).

5.1 Estimation Methodology

The model is estimated using Dynare, a MATLAB pre-processor that allows for Bayesian estimation of dynamic stochastic general equilibrium (DSGE) models (http://www.dynare.org/). The estimation procedure use the Metropolis–Hastings (MH) Markov-chain Monte Carlo (MCMC) algorithm with 200,000 draws for three chains (with a burn-in of 0.5). To ensure that the tails of the posterior mode are identified, the scale used for the jumping distribution is adjusted to ensure an acceptance rate of approximately 25%.[24]

We estimate the benchmark model, and the respective extensions, using data over the period 1995Q1–2017Q2. The sample size of 90 observations covers the post-Apartheid period of South Africa and conforms with reasonable sample sizes used in Bayesian estimation of DSGE models (An and Schorfheide 2007; Steinbach et al. 2009). There are seven key macroeconomic variables: real gross domestic product (GDP), real consumption, real investment, headline consumer price index (CPI) inflation, real wages, employment, and the nominal interest rate.[25] For the *FF-NK* model (which develops a richer financial sector) we include observable variables for household assets, household loans, firm loans, the aggregate bank capital adequacy ratio, as well as the stock market index for South Africa.[26] For the *SOE-NK* model we calculate the foreign economy macroeconomic data using a trade-weighted average for the USA, UK, Euro area, and Japan. Combined, we have the foreign GDP, the foreign total CPI inflation, and the foreign 3-month treasury bill (government securities) rate. All data are log-differenced except interest rates—which are in quarterly terms. All quantity variables, except employment, are expressed in per capita terms.[27]

The choice of the prior distribution can have significant implications for the estimated models. Our focus is to align our parameter restrictions with that of the existing literature, whilst ensuring the initial conditions and restrictions are as

---

[24]See An and Schorfheide (2007) for a review of Bayesian methods for evaluating DSGE models.

[25]See the Appendix for data and sources.

[26]Aggregate tier 1 bank capital adequacy ratio data is used to proxy regulatory/precautionary capital requirement shocks (τ_t). Quarterly tier 1 capital adequacy data can be compiled from the SARB's BA700 and DI400 bank statistics for the entire sample period. This measure therefore includes the risk-adjusted exposure of banks and describes the contemporaneous regulatory/precautionary "target". Due to data constraints, we have not included aggregate retail interest rates to households and firms. For households, the predominate mortgage rate is benchmarked to prime lending rates which tracks the short-term rate very closely. Interestingly, we obtain a very similar result if we derive the effective rate from the aggregate bank income statement statistics collected by the SARB. For firms, there is no immediate way to weight corporate bonds listed on the JSE. It is likely, however, that long-term corporate yields are benchmarked to the 10-year government bond rate, but this requires a stricter assumption of the role of monetary policy over the term structure in our model setup (see Hollander and Liu 2016a).

[27]For a useful guide on the treatment of observational variables in the estimation of DSGE models see Pfeifer (2018).

consistent as possible across all model estimations. We therefore calibrate relatively few parameters to allow for flexibility when estimating the alternative model specifications (see Table 6). Notably, the household discount factor β is normalized to be 0.99 across all models, which implies an annualized real rate of return of 4% for safe-assets. The capital-output share α is set to 0.30, and the physical capital depreciation rate δ is set to 0.03. A steady-state price elasticities of demand for retail goods (ξ^p) and for different types of labour (ξ^w) are 11 and 5, which imply steady-state gross mark-ups of 10% ($\xi^p/(\xi^p - 1)$) and 25% ($\xi^w/(\xi^w - 1)$). We use the value of ρ_g from Steinbach et al. (2014), who separately estimate and then fix the exogenous spending persistence parameter. Remaining parameters follow directly from the models implied steady-state, and in a few cases are calibrated to the averages of South African macroeconomic data.

5.2 Parameter Estimates

Tables 1 and 2 provide the means, standard deviations, and shapes that describe the prior and posterior marginal distributions for the estimated parameters from the benchmark *SW-NK* model. In this section, we focus the discussion of our results in terms of the extant literature. Table 3 compares the estimated parameters from the *SW-NK* model to the estimations from the five recent South African-based NK-DSGE models identified: Steinbach, Mathuloe, and Smit (*SMS09*); Steinbach, du Plessis, and Smit (*SPS14*); Alpanda, Kotzé, and Woglom (*AKW10*)—which includes *SMS09* replication; Paetz and Gupta (*PG16*)—which includes a nested NK model; and the nested Hollander, Gupta, and Wohar (*HGW19*) model without oil.

Table 1 Structural parameters

Parameter	Description	Prior distribution			Posterior distribution			
		Type	Mean	Std. dev	Mean	Median	90% HPD int.	
Preferences								
ϕ	Habit formation	Beta	0.70	0.10	0.795	0.798	0.735	0.858
σ_c	Relative risk aversion	Inv.Gam	1.50	0.50	1.197	1.182	0.893	1.489
σ_n	Inverse elasticity of lab.	Inv.Gam	1.50	0.50	2.616	2.275	1.010	4.342
Firms and price setting								
κ_v	Phys. capital adj. costs	Inv.Gam	5.00	0.50	6.469	6.398	5.232	7.697
θ_p	Sticky price adjustment	Beta	0.70	0.10	0.810	0.811	0.763	0.856
γ_p	Domestic price indexation	Beta	0.30	0.10	0.231	0.226	0.110	0.345
θ_w	Sticky wage adjustment	Beta	0.70	0.10	0.647	0.650	0.542	0.753
γ_w	Wage indexation	Beta	0.30	0.10	0.342	0.338	0.178	0.503
Monetary policy rule								
κ_π	Weight on inflation	Gam	1.50	0.10	1.521	1.518	1.366	1.671
κ_y	Weight on output	Gam	0.50	0.10	0.502	0.497	0.349	0.652

Table 2 Exogenous processes

	Parameter	Prior distribution Type	Mean	Std. dev	Posterior distribution Mean	Median	90% HPD interval	
AR coefficients								
ρ_a	Technology	Beta	0.50	0.10	0.897	0.898	0.865	0.931
ρ_b	Risk premium	Beta	0.50	0.10	0.565	0.567	0.481	0.653
$\rho_{g,y}$	Cross-corr. w/ tech.	Beta	0.50	0.10	0.453	0.451	0.295	0.608
ρ_v	Investment specific	Beta	0.50	0.10	0.539	0.539	0.412	0.664
ρ_i	Monetary policy	Beta	0.50	0.10	0.849	0.849	0.825	0.872
ρ_p	Price mark-up	Beta	0.50	0.10	0.465	0.466	0.343	0.591
ρ_w	Wage mark-up	Beta	0.50	0.10	0.409	0.408	0.280	0.550
Standard deviations								
ϵ_a	Technology	Inv.Gam	0.01	Inf	0.010	0.010	0.008	0.011
ϵ_b	Risk premium	Inv.Gam	0.01	Inf	0.002	0.002	0.001	0.002
ϵ_g	Exogenous spending	Inv.Gam	0.01	Inf	0.030	0.029	0.026	0.033
ϵ_v	Investment specific	Inv.Gam	0.01	Inf	0.006	0.006	0.005	0.007
ϵ_i	Monetary policy	Inv.Gam	0.01	Inf	0.002	0.002	0.002	0.002
ϵ_π	Price mark-up	Inv.Gam	0.01	Inf	0.005	0.005	0.004	0.006
ϵ_w	Wage mark-up	Inv.Gam	0.01	Inf	0.008	0.007	0.006	0.009

The parameter estimates for each alternative model specification (i.e., *Naive-NK*, *SOE-NK* and *FF-NK*) are shown in Table 4.[28]

For the preference parameters, a value of 0.795 for the degree of habit formation is analogous to the estimated value found in *SPS14*, and is only slightly above the calibrated value of 0.70 often adopted in the literature. Similarly, at 1.20, the coefficient of relative risk aversion follows closely to the estimates in *SMS09* and *AKW10-SMS*, which also corresponds to the log-utility specifications ($\sigma_c = 1$) in *SPS14*, *PG16*, and *PG16-NK*. In contrast, *AKW10* and *HGW19* find values of 0.58 and 3.92. Both of these models extend the *SW-NK* framework to a small open economy. *AKW10* attribute their *stronger* response of aggregate consumption to the real interest rate (i.e., where the intertemporal (interest) elasticity of consumption is $1/\sigma_c$) to their incomplete international risk sharing specification and the inclusion of the nominal exchange rate as an observable variable in estimation (*AKW10*, pp. 175–178). Whereas, in *HGW19*, intertemporal consumption decisions of households are more muted but falls within the range of plausible estimates in the international literature. Both papers note that the burden of adjustment falls on σ_c estimates to capture movements in the data—especially since the other two key preference parameters, ϕ and σ_n, are fixed.[29] Another consideration is that the sample periods

[28]The respective prior and posterior distribution statistics for the alternative models—as well as convergence statistics—reported in the technical appendix are available upon request.

[29]Laubscher provides a detailed discussion of South African business cycle fluctuations in Chap. 6 in this book. Notably, household consumption expenditure from 1974Q3 to 2017Q4 was more

Table 3 Estimated parameter comparisons from alternative South African-based DSGE models

	Posterior estimates							
	SW-NK	*SMS09*	*SPS14*	*AKW10*[a]	*AKW10-SMS*	*PG16*	*PG16-NK*	*HGW19*
Data sample	95Q1–17Q2	90Q1–07Q4	00Q1–12Q4	90Q1–07Q4	90Q1–07Q4	71Q1–13Q1	71Q1–13Q1	95Q1–17Q2
Preferences								
ϕ	0.80	0.70[b]	0.81	0.70[b]	0.70[b]	–	–	0.70[b]
σ_c	1.20	1.03	1[b]	0.58	0.99	1[b]	1[b]	3.92
σ_n	2.62	3[b]	5[b]	3[b]	3[b]	1.90	1.45	3[b]
Firms and price setting								
κ_v	6.47	–	10.5	–	–	–	–	0.25[b]
θ_p	0.81	0.54	0.70	0.46	0.49	0.81	0.79	0.50
γ_p	0.23	0.25[b]	0.50	0.25[b]	0.25[b]	0.43	0.45	0.55
θ_w	0.65	0.50[b]	0.69[b]	0.50[b]	0.50[b]	0.64	0.65	0.75[b]
γ_w	0.34	0.70	0.50[b]	0.70	0.70	0.39	0.46	0.50[b]
Monetary policy rule								
κ_π	1.52	1.39	1.73	1.48	1.37	1.24	1.19	1.41
κ_y	0.50	0.63	0.25	0.48	0.59	1.19[c]	1.43[c]	0.73
AR coefficients								
ρ_a	0.90	0.73	0.77	0.74	0.81	0.74	0.75	0.862
ρ_b[d]	0.57	0.64	0.70	0.65	0.65	0.83	0.83	0.867
ρ_g	0.815[a]	–	0.815[a]	–	–	0.65	0.67	–
$\rho_{g,y}$	0.45	–	–	–	–	–	–	–
ρ_v	0.54	–	0.79	–	–	–	–	–
ρ_i	0.85	0.73[a]	0.83	0.73[a]	0.73[a]	0.41	0.39	0.85
ρ_p	0.47	0.74	0.65	0.75	0.80	0.53	0.51	0.63
ρ_w	0.41	0.80[a]	0.49	0.80[a]	0.80[a]	0.43	0.41	–

Standard deviations								
ϵ_a	0.010	0.015	0.015	0.008	0.008	0.025	0.017	0.014
ϵ_b[d]	0.002	0.005	0.001	0.006	0.005	0.056	0.045	0.003
ϵ_g	0.030	–	?	–	–	0.005	0.005	–
ϵ_v	0.006	–	0.003	–	–	–	–	–
ϵ_i	0.002	0.004	0.001	0.004	0.004	0.003	0.003	0.002
ϵ_p	0.005	0.020	0.006	0.016	0.017	0.001	0.002	0.015
ϵ_w	0.008	0.014	0.004	0.009	0.009	0.015	0.002	–
Obs. var.	7	6	15	7	6	8	8	6
# est. shocks	7	9	12	6	5	10	10	7
# est. param.	24	24	40	17	15	29	27	26

[a]Posterior mode "similar" to posterior mean (p. 177). List of parameters only include those corresponding to *SW-NK*
[b]Fixed (calibrated) parameters
[c]Output gap, not output growth, used in MP-reaction function
[d]Either risk premium or preference shock

Table 4 Alternative model parameter estimates

	Posterior distribution means					Posterior distribution means			
	SW-NK	*Naive-NK*	*SOE-NK*	*FF-NK*		*SW-NK*	*Naive-NK*	*SOE-NK*	*FF-NK*
Marginal density	2088.04	1050.22	2939.0	2597.79					
Preferences					*AR coefficients*				
ϕ	0.795	0.611	0.792	0.726	ρ_a[a]	0.897	1.000	0.673	0.487
σ_c	1.197	–	1.197	1.246	ρ_b[b]	0.565	0.808	0.598	0.896
σ_n	2.616	–	2.885	0.501	ρ_g	–	–	–	–
Firms and price setting					$\rho_{g,y}$	0.453	–	0.367	0.537
κ_v	6.469	–	0.305	9.049	ρ_v	0.539	–	0.610	0.580
θ_p	0.810	0.586	0.709	0.858	ρ_i	0.849	0.853	0.854	0.860
γ_p	0.231	0.376	0.315	0.158	ρ_p	0.465	0.452	0.667	0.384
θ_w	0.647	–	0.777	0.748	ρ_w	0.409	–	0.394	0.185
γ_w	0.342	–	0.203	0.185	ρ_e	–	–	–	0.699
Monetary policy rule					ρ_h	–	–	–	0.702
κ_π	1.521	2.101	1.559	1.527	ρ_{ν^h}	–	–	–	0.874
κ_y	0.502	1.856	0.546	0.565	ρ_{ν^e}	–	–	–	0.600
Credit demand					ρ_ψ	–	–	–	0.813
ϕ_w	–	–	–	0.969	*Standard deviations*				
ν^h	–	–	–	0.871	ϵ_a	0.010	0.010	0.016	0.012
ϕ_k	–	–	–	0.596	ϵ_b[b]	0.002	0.019	0.014	0.028
ν^f	–	–	–	0.784	ϵ_g	0.030	–	0.012	0.005
Credit supply and bank balance sheet					ϵ_v	0.006	–	0.012	0.003
κ_k	–	–	–	0.784	ϵ_i	0.002	0.003	0.002	0.002
κ_f	–	–	–	0.339	ϵ_p	0.005	0.008	0.068	0.005
κ_h	–	–	–	6.698	ϵ_w	0.008	–	0.012	0.018
ϕ_ψ	–	–	–	1.070	ϵ_f	–	–	–	0.068
ν_B	–	–	–	0.499	ϵ_h	–	–	–	0.099
					ϵ_{ν^h}	–	–	–	0.032
					ϵ_{ν^f}	–	–	–	0.076
					ϵ_ψ	–	–	–	0.049
					ϵ_τ	–	–	–	0.033
Obs. var.	7	3	10	12					
# shocks	7	4	10	13					
# param.	24	12	41	46					

[a] *Naive-NK* estimates a growth-rate shock to output. This table excludes open economy parameters
[b] *Naive-NK* = preference shock. *FF-NK* = safe-asset demand shock

and observable variables of these models do not fully coincide. That said, it is evident from Table 4—comparing *SW-NK*, *Naive-NK*, *SOE-NK*, and *FF-NK*—that household preference parameters σ_c and ϕ are robust to the specification of alternative models given consistent priors—in other words, the restrictions on certain parameters and different exogenous shocks not related to the core household sub-block. Similarly, the elasticity of labour supply $(1/\sigma_n)$ is consistent with calibrated values in the literature, but also appears sensitive to model specifications—most notably, *FF-NK* (the consequences of which are clearly evident in Sect. 6, Fig. 13).

Domestic prices and wages tend to be adjusted every 2–4 quarters $(1/(1-\theta))$. This implies a sticky price- and wage-setting parameter (θ_p and θ_w) range of 0.5–0.75. For closed economy models in particular, θ_p estimates tend to imply that prices are set yearly which is consistent with what we find in *SW-NK*. For open economy model estimates, prices tend to be adjusted more frequently—usually between 2 and 4 quarters. Our results correspond closely to that of *PG16* and *PG16-NK*, which is in line with the calibration approach in the literature. That is, with the exception of *SMS09* (which informed the calibrated parameters in *AKW10*), the weight applied to historical inflation (i.e., indexation parameters γ_p and γ_w) tends to be 50% or less. Firm-specific physical capital adjustment costs exhibit the weakest consistency across models. Such high capital/investment adjustment costs—that imply an elasticity of investment of approximately 0.1–0.15 in response to a 1% change in the price (shadow value) of installed capital (see Eq. 44)—are generally inconsistent with the international literature. *HGW19* (p. 8, ft. 7) provide some motivation for fixing κ_v when identification may be an issue, which is addressed further in the identification section below.[30]

Turning to the monetary policy reaction function, the majority of model estimates (both from the literature in Table 3 and from the alternative specifications in Table 4) find a larger weight on inflation stabilization than that on output. This not only corroborates the South African Reserve Bank's (SARB's) official commencement of its inflation targeting monetary regime in February 2000,[31] but is consistent with the SARB's policy trajectory as described by the Taylor-rule specification from the 1970s through to 2006 (see, e.g., Ortiz and Sturzenegger 2007): that is, a fairly strong and consistent anti-inflation bias and a more recent emphasis on output deviations.[32]

---

volatile than output, and it experienced noticeably steeper contractions and expansions from 1974Q3 to 1993Q2.

[30]Nakamura and Steinsson (2018) note how, in such cases, moments estimated from microeconomic data can "help to discipline models" (p. 62). In our analysis, the investment sub-block of the DSGE model does not have an outsized influence on the dynamics of the model. This, however, should not be brushed under the rug. As micro data informs parameterization of the Phillips curve for monetary policy analysis, investment/capital price elasticities should inform calibration of country specific estimations where investment adjustments are applicable to the question at hand.

[31]The official announcement came in August 1999.

[32]For the period 1995Q4–2005Q3, specifically, (Ortiz and Sturzenegger 2007, p. 671) find: $\kappa_\pi = 1.36$ [1.02, 1.67]; $\kappa_y = 0.42$ [0.18, 0.65]; $\rho_i = 0.68$, [0.59, 0.77]. The authors also find negligible

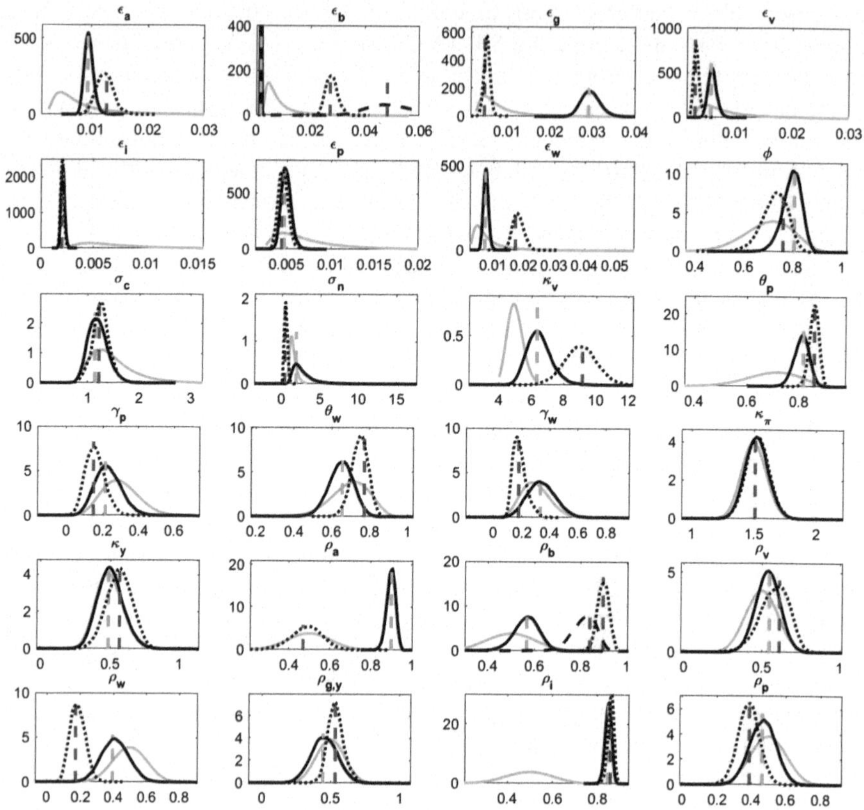

Fig. 3 Prior (grey), *SW-NK* posterior (solid black), and *FF-NK* posterior (dotted black) distribution statistics with posterior modes (dashed green and red vertical lines). Distributions for ϵ_b and ρ_b include equity price ψ (dashed black)

The persistence of shocks vary somewhat across the models. Most consistently, technology shocks are more persistent than estimated supply-side shocks to prices and wages. With the introduction of a broad set of financial frictions (*FF-NK*), however, the persistence of "traditional" supply-side shocks drop considerably. Demand-side persistence parameters seem to be more sensitive to alternative specifications (for example, ρ_b) and sample size ($PG16$ and $PG16 - NK$). Section 6 evaluates the contribution of the structural shocks in more detail.

Figure 3 provides a visual representation of the posterior estimates. For a number of parameters, the prior and posterior distributions are quite similar. This may indicate that the priors drive the posterior results and that the data is uninformative

relevance for any "fear of floating" bias (interest rate reactions in response to nominal exchange rate fluctuations) but admit that the Taylor-rule specification likely understates the relative importance of controls on capital flows or forward market interventions, pre-2000.

for estimating that parameter (see, e.g., Canova 2007). It could also be the case that the prior is a good initial approximation of the possible distribution of parameter values. This is often the case, as we have just discussed, for parameters such as κ_π and κ_y—the weights on inflation and output in the monetary policy reaction function (for a similar comparison, see *SPS14*, Fig. 3, pp. 42–44). That is, in some situations, one would question more-carefully the empirical result that did not conform to the prior which rests on a substantial body of literature (e.g., the value of κ_y for *PG16* in Table 4, or more generally the variability in κ_υ across models). This logic follows when comparing across model specifications with the same given prior (*SW-NK* vs *FF-NK* in Fig. 3). Figure 3 shows the greatest variation between the two model specifications for the exogenous shock processes, which suggests that the core New-Keynesian model blocks are robust to additional model features.[33] On the surface, this result reiterates a general finding in the literature that the magnitude and persistence of shocks (see exogenous process in Tables 2, 3, and 4) tend to be the main factors adjusting, and therefore explaining, business cycle variation over time, rather than estimated changes to structural parameters (Stock and Watson 2003; Sims and Zha 2006; Smets and Wouters 2007; Ireland 2011; Hollander and Liu 2016a). Section 5.3 looks into identification and model sensitivity.

5.3 *Identification and Model Sensitivity*

This section provides a discussion on the comparison of the prior and posterior statistics and performs a formal identification analysis of the benchmark *SW-NK* model. Instead of shutting off each friction individually, as in Smets and Wouters (2003), we look at identification tests of pairwise collinearity to infer the importance of specific structural parameters. This procedure allows us to identify which endogenous frictions are empirically important.

We follow Ratto (2008) and Ratto and Iskrev (2011) to perform the identification analysis for the baseline *SW-NK* model.[34] Weak identification implies that changes in a particular parameter are compensated for by linear combinations of one or more other parameters (Iskrev 2010); or changes in a particular parameter have a negligible effect on the moments of the model (Andrle 2010). Identification patterns are shown by taking the singular value decomposition of the Jacobian matrix and displaying the eigenvectors corresponding to the smallest (or highest) singular values (see Ratto and Iskrev 2011, p. 34). The smallest singular value indicates the particular parameter with the weakest identifiable pattern.

---

[33]Figure 21 shows the prior and posterior distributions for the remaining *FF-NK* parameters not corresponding to *SW-NK*.

[34]This is easily implemented in Dynare using the `identification` command.

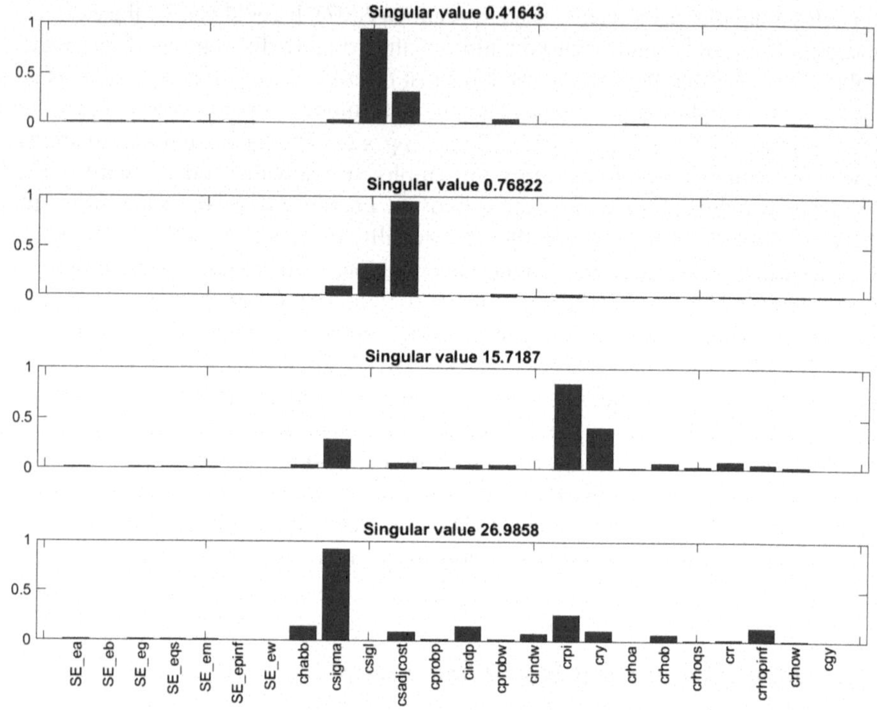

Fig. 4 Identification patterns at posterior mean (lowest singular value)

Our identification analysis, from Figs. 4, 5, and 6, shows that all parameters are identified in the model at the posterior mean. Specifically, Fig. 5 plots the identification strength at the posterior mean. Parameters are ranked in increasing order of identification strength. From the top panel in Fig. 5, we see that all parameters are identified. The bottom panel suggests that all parameters have a non-negligible effect on the first- and second-order moments. However, we observe a desirable outcome that the relatively weaker identified parameters have a lesser effect on the moments of the model.

Figure 4 identifies weakest patterns for σ_n and κ_v. Given that we highlight these two parameters in the previous section as being the most sensitive across alternative model estimations, it is not surprising. This finding, however, does not appear to raise any serious identification issues. Firstly, as shown in Fig. 3, the data provides non-negligible information of the mean and/or distribution of at least 17 of the 24 estimated parameters. The parameters that exhibit very similar prior and posterior means and distributions are: $\{\sigma_n, \gamma_w, \kappa_\pi, \kappa_y, \rho_v, \rho_{g,y}, \rho_\pi\}$. With the exception of σ_n, it is clear that the identification of persistence parameters has a trade-off with the identification of structural parameters. For example, price stickiness and price indexation help identify persistence in inflation data that would otherwise

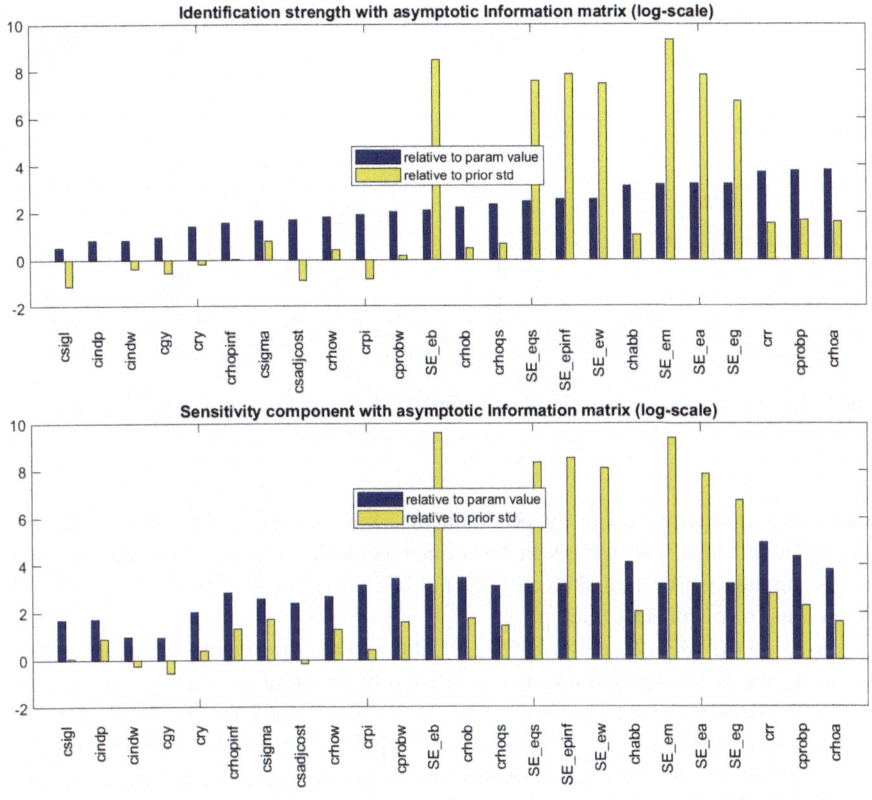

Fig. 5 Identification strength at posterior mean

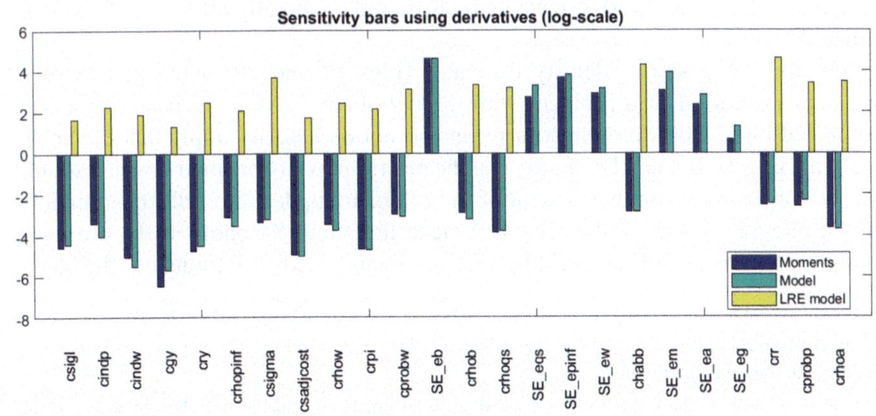

Fig. 6 Sensitivity analysis at posterior mean

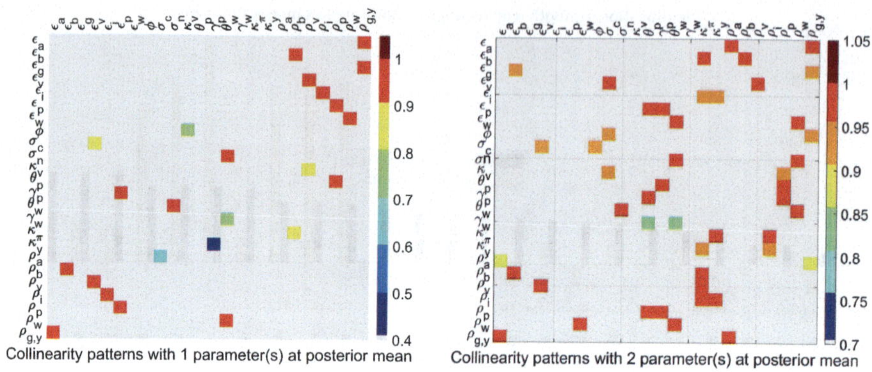

Fig. 7 Collinearity patterns with parameter(s) for *SW-NK* at posterior mean. Note: Dark red equals perfect collinearity

arise from estimating a highly persistent Markov process.[35] In contrast, and as already mentioned, parameters in the monetary policy reaction function (κ_π and κ_y) are already well established and it is not likely that we would expect significant deviations from well-informed priors.

Based on collinearity patterns (Fig. 7), the identification analysis suggests that adjusting the prior distribution of σ_n will likely be offset by changes in θ_w and ρ_w (wage stickiness and the persistence of the wage mark-up shock process). In other words, the sensitivity of the labour supply schedule to wage changes is weakly identified by parameters identifying other processes in the labour market. We observe this clearly when these parameters or shocks are fixed or excluded in the models from Tables 3 and 4. For the capital installation adjustment cost parameter (κ_v), we observe pairwise collinearity patterns with ρ_v (0.84) and multicollinearity patterns with σ_c and ρ_p (0.95), where both ρ_v and σ_c directly affect the investment schedule.

Finally, the posterior density estimates (Figs. 19 and 20) show that there is no clear indication of a problem with the optimizer.[36] As such, posterior means estimated to be close to their prior means do not necessarily imply that the priors drive the results. It could be, firstly, that the priors are well-specified—which should not be surprising given that several of the priors are updated to reflect estimations in the international as well as South African literature. Secondly, if the prior and posterior means are the same, this does not mean the distributions are the same.

[35]Information on collinearity patters showing this is observable in Fig. 7. Similar relationships are found with the other parameters.

[36]Figures 19 and 20 show the log-posterior likelihood functions and log-likelihood kernels. If the estimated mode is the local mode, it should be at the maximum of the posterior likelihood. We also look at the Markov-chain Monte Carlo diagnostics from the Metropolis–Hastings algorithm of the corresponding parameters. Here, we observe convergence of the estimates which eliminates bimodal or poorly identified parameter distributions (see Figs. 22, 23, and 24 on the multivariate and univariate convergence diagnostic statistics).

Figure 3 shows that the second-, third-, and fourth-moments of the parameters are quite different at times. Moreover, the consistency of the prior distributions and posterior estimations across alternative models suggests that the posterior estimates are robust.

Such diagnostics, as discussed in its entirety above, will be particularly useful for model extensions not established in the literature, and should guide researchers to weaknesses in their model specifications that may need to be addressed or help researchers to identify entirely erroneous specifications. For example, perfect collinearity occurs when both a technology shock to output (not *output growth* as in *Naive-NK*) and a mark-up (price) shock to marginal cost are included in the foreign economy block of the *SOE-NK* model (see Eqs. 60–63).

6 What Structural Shocks Drive the South African Economy?

In this section we evaluate the individual contribution of important structural shocks that may be used to explain behaviour of key variables in the South African economy. We also look at the property of robustness by comparing "identified moments" from our nested models (Nakamura and Steinsson 2018); that is, we identify the consistency (or not) of estimated responses to identified structural shocks. In doing so, we draw particular attention to monetary policy inference and the selection of exogenous shocks under alternative model specifications.

6.1 Impulse Response Analysis

Figures 8, 9, 10, 11, 12, and 13 plot the impulse responses for the different models. Figure 8 indicates the impact of a positive technology (or productivity) shock. This positive supply-side innovation results in the standard hump-shaped increase in output, consumption, and investment while bringing about a significant reduction in inflation. In reaction to the generated disinflation and widening output gap the reaction function of the central bank prompts a decrease in the interest rate. The quantitative impact of this shock is felt most strongly in the macroeconomic indicators related to the sticky prices and wages model. The accommodative monetary policy response has a persistent effect on consumption and investment, significantly greater than that of the *FF-NK* model and *SOE-NK* model, which sees the affected variables taking longer to return back to their steady-states. Notably, in the financial frictions model with sticky retail interest rate adjustment, the monetary policy response is to tighten credit conditions by raising the short-term nominal interest rate. The fall in employment (labour) as a result of the productivity shock is consistent with evidence in the literature.

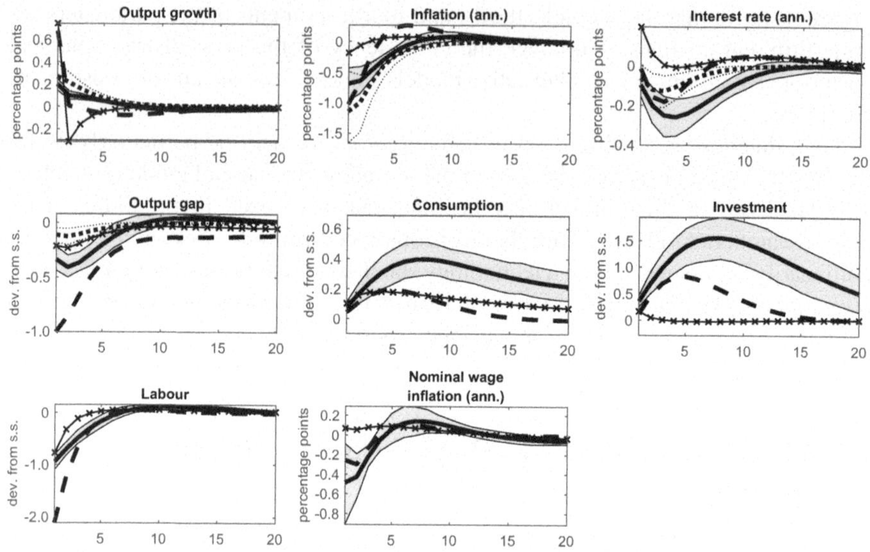

Fig. 8 IRF to a technology shock. Solid line: Sticky prices and wages (*SW-NK*) model. Dotted line: three-equation New-Keynesian (*Naive-NK*) model. Dashed line: Small open economy (*SOE-NK*) model. Cross-marker line: Financial frictions (*FF-NK*)

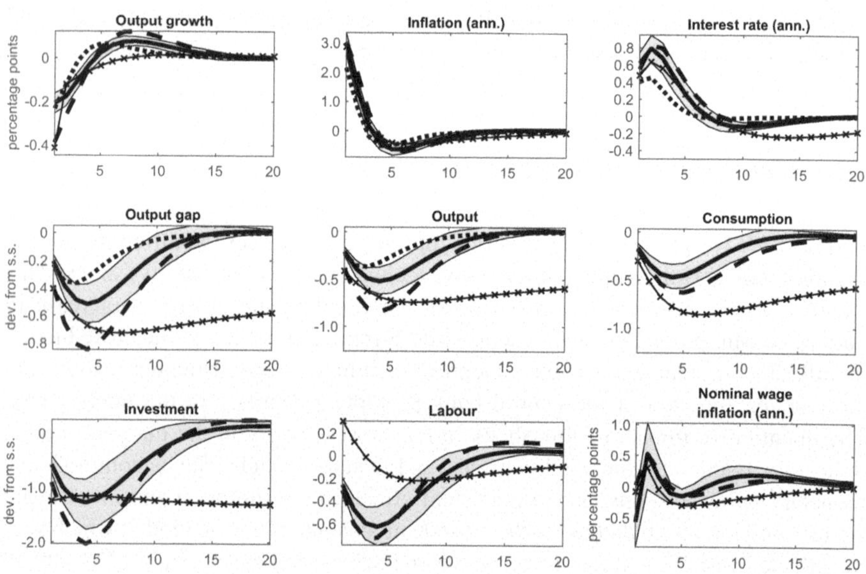

Fig. 9 IRF to a price mark-up shock. Solid line: *SW-NK* model. Dotted line: *Naive-NK* model. Dashed line: *SOE-NK* model. Cross-marker line: *FF-NK* model

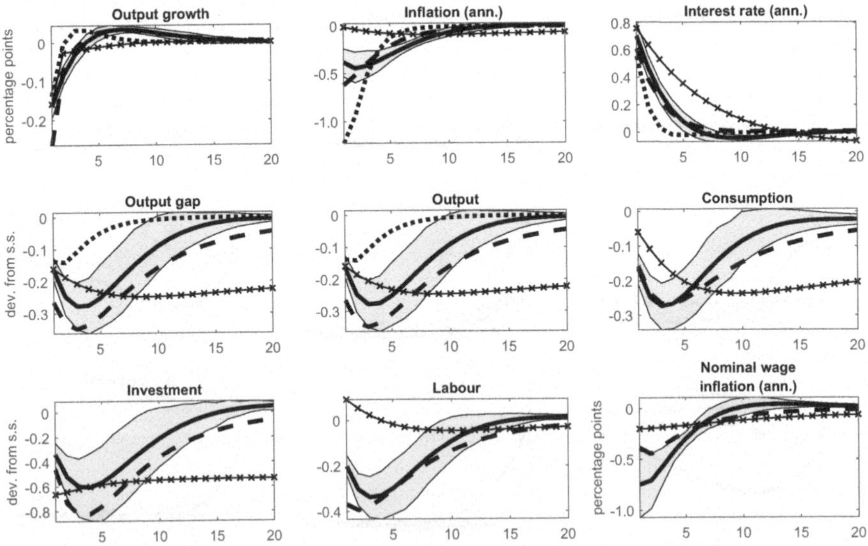

Fig. 10 IRF to a monetary policy shock. Solid line: *SW-NK* model. Dotted line: *Naive-NK* model. Dashed line: *SOE-NK* model. Cross-marker line: *FF-NK* model

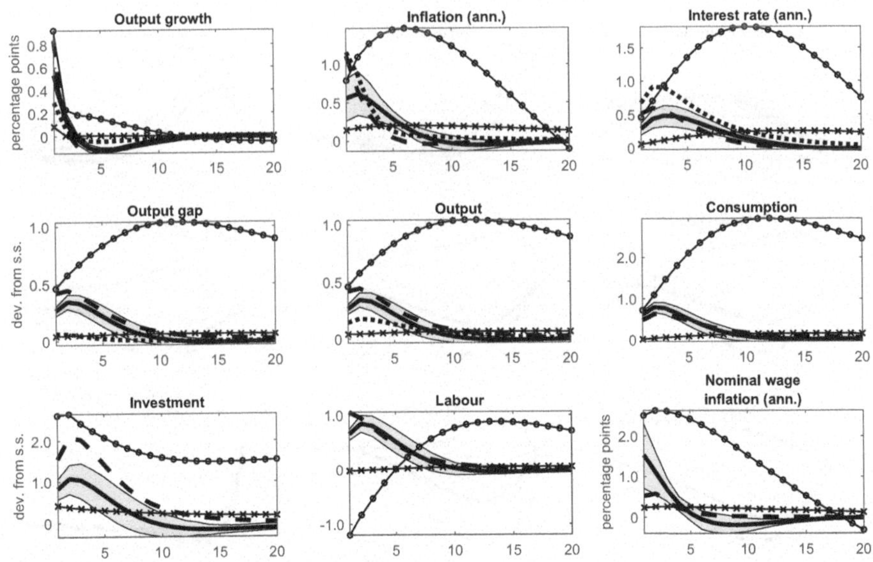

Fig. 11 IRF to a risk premium shock. Solid line: *SW-NK* model. Dotted line: *Naive-NK* model (preference shock). Dashed line: *SOE-NK* model. Cross-marker line: *FF-NK* model (safe-asset demand shock). Circle-marker line: *FF-NK* model (equity price shock)

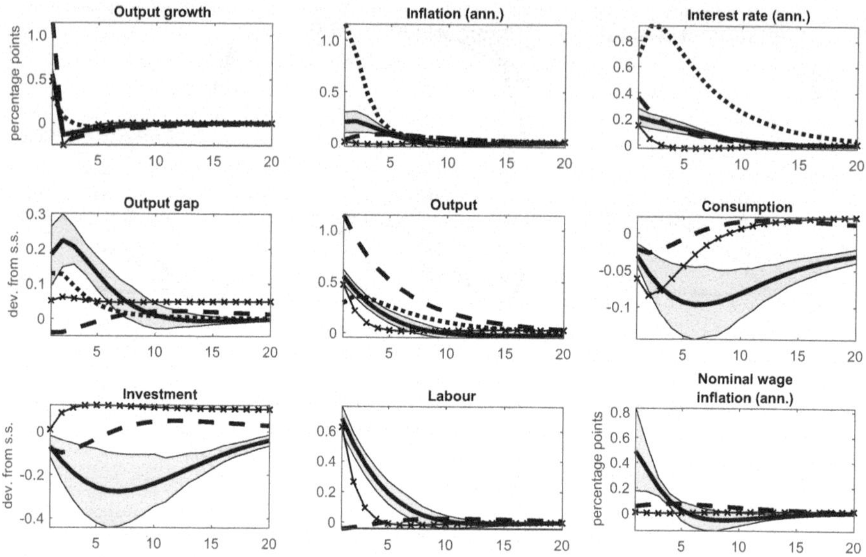

Fig. 12 IRF to an exogenous spending shock. Solid line: *SW-NK* model. Dotted line: *Naive-NK* model (preference shock). Dashed line: *SOE-NK* model. Cross-marker line: *FF-NK* model

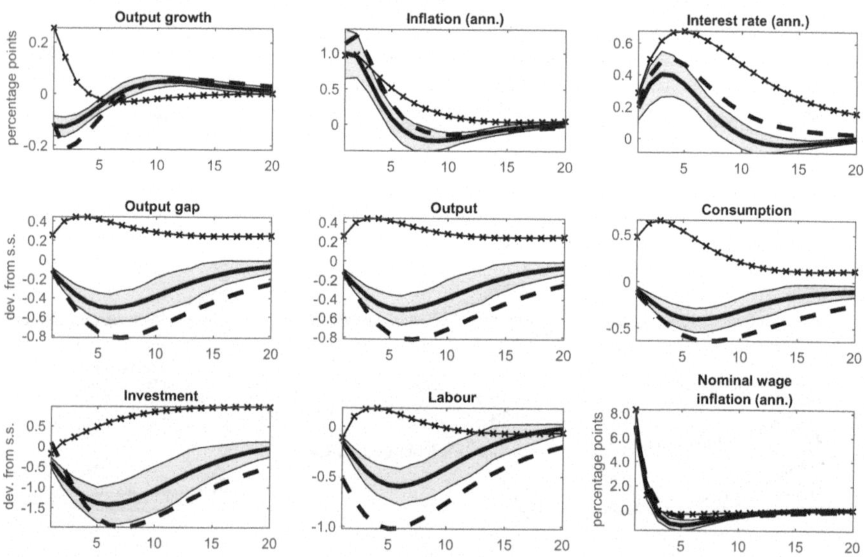

Fig. 13 IRF to a wage mark-up shock. Solid line: Sticky prices and wages (SW) model. Dashed line: Small open economy. Cross-marker line: Financial frictions

The price mark-up shock observed in Fig. 9 leads to a decrease in output, consumption, investment, and labour. Inflationary pressure created by this price shock generates similar interest rate increases for all four of the models, which leads to a quick convergence of inflation back to the steady-state at the expense of a prolonged recovery to real economic activity. Regarding output, consumption, investment, and labour, the *FF-NK* model again appears to be the significant outlier—especially with respect to labour. Two important mechanisms are at play. On the one hand, the financial frictions model predicts a more prolonged contraction due to monopolistic competition in the banking sector that generates a persistent tightening of credit conditions. On the other hand, the income effect of the initial wage increase on household wealth and creditworthiness offsets the cost-push effect on firm input costs, profits and therefore inflation. The lack of a clear trade-off between nominal wages and labour reflects high labour market rigidities. However, the response of nominal wages is barely significant and it is difficult to make definitive statements in this regard. As such, we briefly turn to the wage mark-up shock in Fig. 13 which more clearly bares witness to this second channel in the *FF-NK* model: here, we observe qualitatively similar results to that of the price mark-up shock, where, instead, the positive effect on wages is much more pronounced. As a result, the income effect of the wage increase on household wealth and creditworthiness far outweighs the cost-push effect on firm input costs, profits and therefore inflation.

Figure 10 represents the typical demand shock relevant for policy analysis. One can see that disturbances to the monetary policy reaction function (or, monetary policy "surprises") are largest in the case of the small open economy model and weakest in the model that incorporates financial frictions. This contractionary policy shock results in a persistent decline across output, consumption, investment, and labour—where, again, we see the clear effect of sticky retail interest rate adjustment. Notably, the response of inflation is quite varied, unlike the supply-side shocks, and ranges between 0 and 1.25 percentage points. The *Naive-NK* model in this instance shows the greatest inflation response, with inflation in all models returning to steady-state within 10 quarters. The effectiveness of the monetary policy transmission is clearly dampened by the presence of additional demand shocks in the *SW-NK*, *SOE-NK*, and *FF-NK* models. For example, greater aggregate demand from a decline in the risk premium on domestic assets, as presented in Fig. 11, reveals a typical procyclical demand shock. The impact of this shock, together with demand- and supply-side factors and disturbances in the *FF-NK* model, disrupts the monetary transmission mechanism which warrants cautious interpretation of interest rate policy in a stylized three-equation New-Keynesian model.

Figure 11 includes both the safe-asset demand shock and the equity price shock from the *FF-NK* model. As we will see in Sect. 6.2, the equity price shock has a far larger and more persistent influence on all of the key variables. Specification of the sources of financial shocks (as opposed more traditional "demand shocks") appears crucial to understanding demand-side stabilization policies. In this light, it is also important to note that the more-credible a central bank becomes (or is), the less likely we would observe "surprises" to the rule specifying their policy reactions.

That is, we may well observe that fluctuations to the short-term nominal interest rate coincide with increasingly stronger mean reversion of inflation to the target set by monetary authorities. Such an experience seems to be true for the South African Reserve Bank (SARB) (Ortiz and Sturzenegger 2007). In fact, Table 3 suggests a stronger anti-inflation bias when comparing models estimated over different sample periods. This implies that the *Naive-NK* model, and even the *SW-NK* model, likely overstate the "effectiveness" of the demand shock relevant for policy analysis. This does not, however, automatically imply that any model with financial frictions, including the *FF-NK* model here, is better specified or more useful for forecasting and counterfactual policy analysis.

Figure 12 captures demand-side factors (the so-called exogenous spending shocks) in the aggregate resource constraint not captured by the model framework—where *Naive-NK*, instead, includes the preference shock following Ireland (2011).[37] Ireland (2011) finds a strong role for demand-side preference shocks (to the household's discount factor) in the Great Recession episode of the USA. On the one hand, the *Naive-NK* model is useful to tease-out the heuristics of the business cycle in a transparent manner. But clearly, there exists a trade-off with the selection of shocks that generate business cycle fluctuations and the adequate interpretation thereof. Comparing the *SOE-NK* model IRFs to the *SW-NK* model shows how including open economy dynamics dampens the general importance of exogenous spending shocks (as expected) and brings into question their interpretation. For example, the response of output is largest in the *SOE-NK* model which means that most of the persistence is attributable to the exogenous shock process and not the internal propagation mechanisms of the model. This is possibly due to the additional foreign economy data and model parameters used in estimation (see Table 4). An obvious shortcoming is to include the trade balance (or the real exchange rate) as an observable variable in the estimation of the open economy model. This would require either relaxing the restrictive assumption of complete asset markets (international risk sharing in consumption) or introducing trade frictions (see, e.g., Canova and Ravn 1996; Obstfeld and Rogoff 2000; Eaton et al. 2016a,b).

6.2 Variance Decomposition

Table 5 reports the forecast error variance decomposition (FEVD) results from the benchmark *SW-NK* model. This shows the contribution of the structural shocks' innovations to the variance of gross domestic product (output) per capita, headline CPI (total) inflation, and the short-term nominal interest rate. We also include the

[37] As noted in Sect. 3.2, following Smets and Wouters (2007) and Steinbach et al. (2014), the measurement error is included to avoid stochastic singularity in the aggregate resource constraint given that output, consumption, and investment are all observable variables. The models therefore exclude government and net exports (with the exception of *SOE-NK*), as well as genuine measurement errors from the data.

Table 5 Forecast error variance decomposition of output, total inflation, and nominal interest rate

Description	Shocks	*SW-NK*: time horizons				*FF-NK*: time horizons			
		1-Quarter	1-Year	2-Years	5-Years	1-Quarter	1-Year	2-Years	5-Years
Forecast error variance decomposition of output									
Technology	ϵ_a	4.95	10.58	19.6	30.53	24.27	23.84	23.17	22.79
Risk premium	ϵ_b	34.95	32.52	22.55	17.02	0.32	0.26	0.25	0.25
Exogenous spending	ϵ_g	37.22	13.46	7.95	5.98	9.63	10.4	10.08	9.91
Investment specific	ϵ_v	12.26	14.16	12.11	10.29	1.29	1.28	1.24	1.22
Monetary policy	ϵ_i	3.27	5.16	4.91	4.02	1.08	0.9	0.88	0.86
Price mark-up	ϵ_p	5.39	15.24	16.41	13.22	6.95	6.38	6.23	6.19
Wage mark-up	ϵ_w	1.95	8.89	16.47	18.95	3.24	3.41	3.41	3.41
Credit supply	$\epsilon_\tau; \epsilon_{h,e}$	–	–	–	–	6.58	7.7	8.03	8.64
Credit demand	ϵ_{ν_h,ν_e}	–	–	–	–	12.02	14.29	14.27	14.27
Equity	ϵ_ψ	–	–	–	–	34.61	31.53	32.43	32.47
Forecast error variance decomposition of total inflation									
Technology	ϵ_a	4.33	6.87	6.45	6.56	0.32	0.2	0.21	0.19
Risk premium	ϵ_b	2.94	6.71	6.81	6.79	0.22	0.62	0.9	1.5
Exogenous spending	ϵ_g	0.39	0.8	0.8	0.79	0	0	0	0.01
Investment specific	ϵ_v	0.64	1.54	1.62	1.7	0.04	0.06	0.06	0.05
Monetary policy	ϵ_i	1.34	3.79	4.55	4.56	0.01	0.05	0.12	0.27
Price mark-up	ϵ_p	81.2	65.99	66.13	65.34	76.73	46.02	32.88	26.01
Wage mark-up	ϵ_w	9.16	14.31	13.64	14.27	8.83	13.78	11.15	8.82
Credit supply	$\epsilon_\tau; \epsilon_{h,e}$	–	–	–	–	6.3	12.02	11.07	9.28
Credit demand	ϵ_{ν_h,ν_e}	–	-	-	–	0.47	1.41	2.09	4.93
Equity	ϵ_ψ	–	–	–	–	7.07	25.85	41.53	48.93

(continued)

Table 5 (continued)

Description	Shocks	*SW-NK*: time horizons				*FF-NK*: time horizons			
		1-Quarter	1-Year	2-Years	5-Years	1-Quarter	1-Year	2-Years	5-Years
Forecast error variance decomposition of nominal interest rate									
Technology	ϵ_a	0.94	4.16	5.93	6.1	3.31	0.58	0.23	0.12
Risk premium	ϵ_b	7.84	16.92	21.84	22.3	0.28	0.6	0.93	1.79
Exogenous spending	ϵ_g	4.32	3.09	3.1	3.08	1.88	0.33	0.13	0.06
Investment specific	ϵ_v	2.23	4.98	6.75	7.08	0.37	0.13	0.08	0.05
Monetary policy	ϵ_i	45.55	19.69	15.71	15.22	46.24	18.54	8.3	3.57
Price mark-up	ϵ_p	35.65	40.11	33.44	33.14	19.1	14.59	5.95	3.38
Wage mark-up	ϵ_w	3.46	11.04	13.21	13.1	6.7	14.63	13.12	8.53
Credit supply	$\epsilon_\tau; \epsilon_{h,e}$	–	-	–	–	2.83	10.79	11.5	7.66
Credit demand	ϵ_{ν_h,ν_e}	–	–	–	–	2.24	4.08	4.55	5.07
Equity	ϵ_ψ	–	–	–	–	17.06	35.73	55.21	69.78
Forecast error variance decomposition of output gap									
Technology	ϵ_a	21	13.74	9.69	8.7	2.95	1.27	0.52	0.21
Risk premium	ϵ_b	53.64	40.66	30.72	26.99	0.48	0.29	0.25	0.27
Exogenous spending	ϵ_g	6.35	4.35	3.26	2.9	0.16	0.09	0.06	0.04
Investment specific	ϵ_v	2.7	4.46	4.59	4.28	0.34	0.15	0.18	0.22
Monetary policy	ϵ_i	5.02	6.45	6.66	6.29	1.63	1.16	1.02	0.94
Price mark-up	ϵ_p	8.3	19.14	22.45	21.02	10.42	9.72	8.89	7.4
Wage mark-up	ϵ_w	3	11.2	22.64	29.82	4.8	5.37	3.75	2.29
Credit supply	$\epsilon_\tau; \epsilon_{h,e}$	–	–	–	–	9.86	10.52	8.07	5.99
Credit demand	ϵ_{ν_h,ν_e}	–	–	–	–	17.89	25.06	26.33	24.26
Equity	ϵ_ψ	–	–	–	–	51.46	46.38	50.93	58.37

decomposition of the model implied output gap measure. We compare these results to the literature, as well as the *FF-NK* model, to highlight how model specification and the selection of exogenous sources of variation affect our understanding of business cycle fluctuations. The short-run is defined as 1-quarter to 1-year, the medium-run 2-years, and the long-run 5-years.

Output variability is driven mainly by supply-side factors in the long-run. Most notably, technology makes up 30.53% after 5-years. In the short-run, we observe over two-thirds contribution from the risk premium and exogenous spending shocks after 1-quarter. The effect of ϵ_g dampens quickly, whereas the effect of the risk premium shock persists strongly into the medium- and long-run. Supply-side mark-up shocks to domestic prices and wages account for the bulk of the variance in total inflation. Monetary policy innovations contribute relatively little to output and inflation variance (1–6%), but make up almost a half (45.55%) of first quarter short-term nominal interest rate movements. The medium- to long-run interest rate contribution dampens significantly with the rising contribution of exogenous risk premium and price mark-up factors. Interestingly, the large and persistent role for cost-push shocks suggests a non-negligible inflation-output trade-off for monetary authorities (see also, *HGW19*). That is, cost-push shocks drive a wedge between the output gap and inflation stabilizing objectives of the monetary authority (see, e.g., Hollander and Christensen 2018, Section 6.3).

On the domestic front, this overall picture conforms strongly with the literature.[38] That is, demand-side shocks dominate output and output gap fluctuations in the short- to medium-run, whereas supply-side shocks dominate aggregate real economic activity in the medium- to long-run. Further, total (headline) inflation is driven mainly by cost-push shocks, and due to the endogenous response of the monetary policy reaction function, these cost-push shocks, together with monetary policy and risk premium innovations, contribute non-negligibly to nominal interest rate variability.

All the alternative models presented in Tables 3 and 4, with the exception of *PG16* (discussed below), show that accounting for the foreign economy with traditional New-Keynesian specifications has only a marginal effect on the contributions of the domestic shocks. Even in Ortiz and Sturzenegger's estimated small (five-equation) open economy NK-DSGE model of South Africa (following Gali and Monacelli (2005)), terms-of-trade shocks play a relatively smaller role than technology or monetary policy innovations, and account mostly for nominal exchange rate fluctuations (Ortiz and Sturzenegger 2007, Fig. 4, p. 670). This should not be seen as a "failure" of the open economy structure, but rather the "success" of the New-Keynesian design to fit the data and provide plausible estimations of business cycle moments. For a large, relatively closed economy such as the USA or

[38] *SPS14*, in contrast, find that domestic labour supply shocks, not specified here, contribute a significant portion towards variation in all three variables along with domestic price mark-up shocks. For *SPS14*, it is not possible to decompose the short- versus long-run contributions of each shock as only the unconditional (infinite horizon) FEVD results are presented. The short- to medium-run likely exhibits results more directly comparable.

the Euro area, such a framework may provide a satisfactory structural decomposition of the business cycle (Smets and Wouters 2003, 2007). For a small open economy, such as South Africa, the domestic business cycle may often be the global trend.

Notably, we see that simple extensions to the open economy specifications can substantially alter the estimated responses to domestic shocks. For example, in the open economy model of *SPS14*, mark-up shocks to imported consumption goods inflation (that has a New-Keynesian Phillips Curve specification) contribute approximately one-third of the unconditional FEVD of CPI inflation and the interest rate. Moreover, *HGW19* show that accounting for commodity shocks can significantly reduce the relevance of domestic price mark-up shocks in headline inflation figures. In the *HGW19* model, oil (energy) imports are used in the firm's production process as a factor input and enter directly into the household's consumption basket. These model extensions are question-specific, and it is unclear how a policy-maker should weight each of the implied dynamic responses to a particular shock (e.g., the degree and scope of sticky import prices) or the sources of estimated responses altogether (commodity trade shocks).

In other open economy models with New-Keynesian features, stricter underlying assumptions can drastically change how the estimated model allocates weight to foreign economy shocks to the domestic business cycle. Following the model in Funke et al. (2011), *PG16* show a large effect for "foreign demand" on output and inflation variance. This is due to the specification of the model where foreign demand/output ($\hat{y}^*$), domestic technology ($\hat{\xi}^a$), and a household preference shock ($\hat{\xi}^b$) drive natural output (i.e., the flexible price equilibrium)—and therefore the natural real interest rate (*PG16*, p. 176, Eqs. A.37 and A.39). Specifically, international risk sharing under log utility implies that domestic output is a function of foreign output and terms-of-trade ($\hat{s}_t$): $\hat{y}_t = \hat{y}_t^* + \Phi^s \hat{s}_t$ (Funke et al. 2011, p. 322, Eq. 36), where $\hat{s}_t$ evolves according to the real interest rate differential between the domestic economy and the foreign economy (Funke et al. 2011, p. 320, Eq. 17). In addition, the production technology ($\hat{y}_t$) is assumed to be linear in labour (Funke et al. 2011, pp. 321 and 323), and $\hat{y}^*$ follows a stochastic auto-regressive process. In contrast, the greater contribution of $\hat{\xi}^b$ to output and interest rate deviations mimics that of the *Naive-NK* model developed by Ireland (2011) for his decomposition of the 2007–2009 Great Recession episode in the USA. This does not, however, imply that household preference shocks are robust and domestic technology innovations are not.[39]

Introducing financial frictions into the model has a similar significant impact on the estimated responses of all the main macroeconomic variables to the identified

[39] Unfortunately, it is not clear which data series are used to estimate the model, making inference difficult regarding the source or specification of the foreign economy. In addition, model misspecification is likely if the preference shock contributes significantly to the variance of output and interest rate but either has little explanatory power for other key macroeconomic variables (inflation, stock prices, consumption, or investment) or the FEVD of key macrovariables appear to be each individually driven by one particular shock; this appears to be the case (see *PG16*, Table 2, p. 172).

structural shocks. Table 5 shows a very large and persistent role for equity price shocks on all the main macroeconomic variables: approximately one-third for output and one-half for the output gap across all horizons.[40] For the nominal interest rate and total inflation, equity prices generate strong co-movement in the medium- to long-run. Interestingly, price mark-up shocks are still important, especially in the short- and medium-run, for total inflation and, to a much lesser degree, nominal interest rate. Similarly, shocks to the monetary policy rule are important in the short-run for nominal interest rate variance, but are negligible for the total inflation FEVD. This would, on the surface, suggest a relatively minor role for demand-side intervention by the monetary authorities. Here, it is important to consider the endogeneity of monetary policy as being the important business cycle stabilization factor, rather than identified moments based on estimated exogenous shocks to the short-term interest rate—which may be completely unrelated to the monetary authorities or simply due to the overly restrictive Taylor-rule specification of the monetary policy reaction function.

Another interesting observation from Table 5 is that demand-side shocks in the *SW-NK* model ($\epsilon_b, \epsilon_g, \epsilon_v$) become subservient to financial factors. Equity price shocks, as noted above, garner a significant portion of the variance decompositions. Aside, credit supply shocks are also an important driver of variance for all of the variables: between 8% and 12% at 1- and 2-year horizons. Credit demand shocks (the loan-to-value ratios in the household and firm borrowing constraints) contribute one-quarter and one-eighth to output gap and output, respectively. This exercise serves to highlight the narrative throughout this section that careful consideration should be taken when attempting to provide a structural decomposition of the business cycle. Counterfactual analyses, the identification ("effectiveness") of monetary policy and forecasting—all relevant for policy analysis—may deliver quite different results under different specifications. For example, the results from the *FF-NK* model suggests an influential role for macroprudential policy in credit demand and supply, not at all observable from the *SW-NK* model. The *SW-NK* model, in contrast, identifies financial distortions solely through an exogenous risk premium that monetary policy can directly offset. In the following section we give a brief discussion on the contribution of shocks to each observed point in the data.

[40]Figure 2 suggests that the historically strong procyclicality between equity prices and output diminished since 2013. In fact, Venter, in Chap. 9 of this book, points out that "this indicator [equity prices] disconnected somewhat from domestic economic developments and was removed as a component series of the composite leading business cycle indicator in 2015". Here, it is important to note that the SARB's atheoretical indicator aims to achieve empirical accuracy alone, whereas the DSGE framework attempts to match theory and data. That is, the strict theoretical assumptions of the DSGE model promote a large and persistent role for equity prices. Furthermore, because the monthly leading indicator components are revised over time, the stock market may well be included in the future.

6.3 Historical Decomposition

Figures 14, 15, 16, and 17 present the historical variance decomposition of output growth, output gap, interest rate, and headline inflation over the estimated sample period 1995Q1–2017Q2. The decomposition is based on the benchmark *SW-NK* model. We avoid attempting to make strong inferences regarding the individual shocks and instead group the seven shocks into their demand-side ($\epsilon_b, \epsilon_v, \epsilon_i$) and supply-side ($\epsilon_a, \epsilon_p, \epsilon_i$) origins.[41] Although Smets and Wouters (2007) refer to the exogenous spending shock (ϵ_g) as an exogenous *government* spending shock and therefore demand-side in nature, it actually includes demand- and supply-side (trade) factors as well as possible measurement errors in the aggregate resource constraint, not accounted for by consumption and investment data. There is also a non-negligible estimated cross-correlation component with the technology shock. We therefore keep this component separate.

First, in Fig. 14, it is interesting to compare the main sources of the recessions or downward phases over this period (see, e.g., Bosch and Ruch 2013, for comparison of alternative business cycle dating procedures). Output growth was negative and persistent from 1997Q1 until 1998Q4 with an unclear pattern of both supply and demand factors as contributing factors. The mild recession of 2001Q2–2001Q3 and

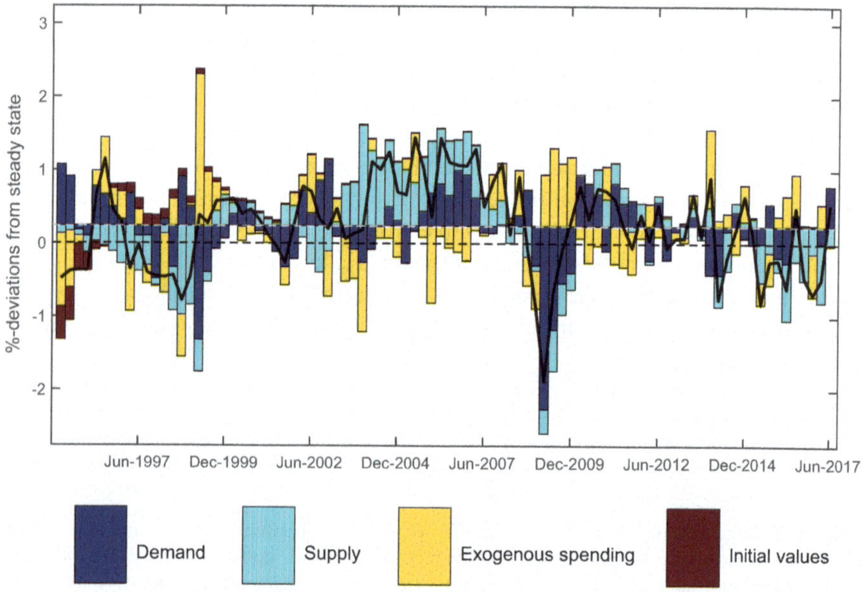

Fig. 14 Historical decomposition of output growth. Period: 1995Q1–2017Q2

[41]Table 5 gives an indication of the relative importance of these demand- and supply-side components. Detailed historical decomposition figures are available upon request.

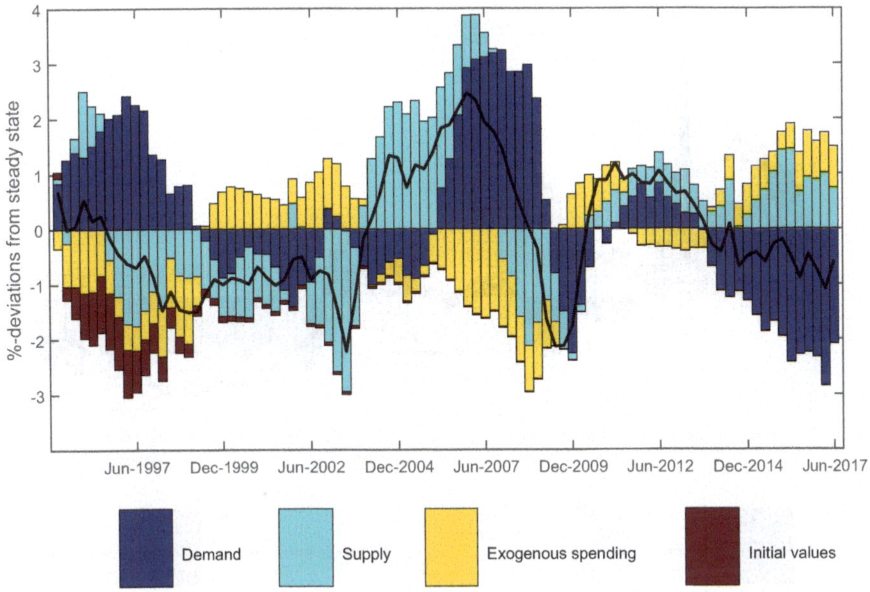

Fig. 15 Historical decomposition of output gap. Period: 1995Q1–2017Q2

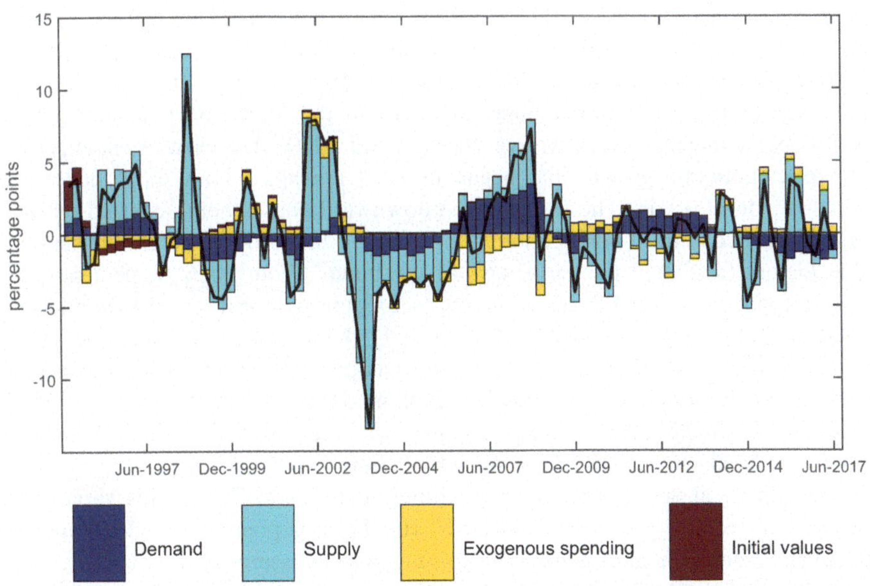

Fig. 16 Historical decomposition of headline inflation (annualized). Period: 1995Q1–2017Q2

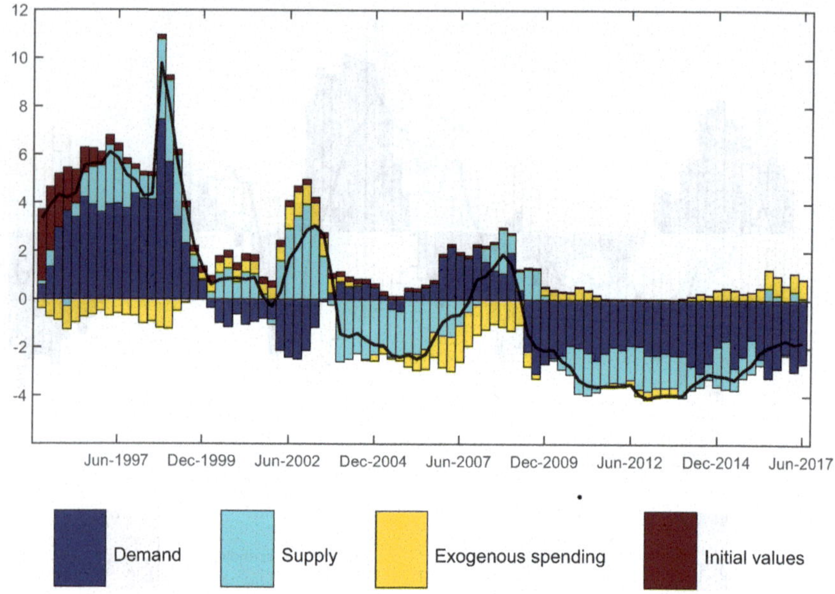

Fig. 17 Historical decomposition of the interest rate (annualized). Period: 1995Q1–2017Q2

great recession of 2008Q3–2009Q3 clearly identify demand-side factors; in fact, we find credit demand-side factors to be the predominant source of the 2008–2009 recession, but not the 2001 recession.[42] This narrative fits well with the influence of the 2008 global financial crisis, in that domestic financial factors have become increasingly pervasive since the mid-2000s. The most recent episodes of weak economic growth that began in 2014 are again both supply-side and demand-side in origin. The first and last downward phases both occurred outside the global economic boom period from 2002Q1 to 2007Q4. Persistent supply-side factors facilitated the early days of the boom. From 2006Q1, demand-side factors fuelled an over-heating economy (see output gap in Fig. 15) which led to the deep recession in 2008–2009. More recently, the persistence of output below its potential since 2014Q1 can be characterized unequivocally as one of weak domestic demand. Monetary policy was strongly accommodative from 2008 through to 2015 in attempting to close the output gap (not shown here), but was offset by large and persistent shocks to the risk premium and inflation.

The historical decomposition of headline inflation reveals that this variable is primarily driven by cost-push shocks (Fig. 16). The risk premium shock dominates the cyclical component of demand-side inflationary pressures in recent times, with monetary policy shocks playing some role during and after the financial crisis

[42] Historical decomposition figures for the *FF-NK* model, as well as detailed shock breakdowns for the other models, are available upon request.

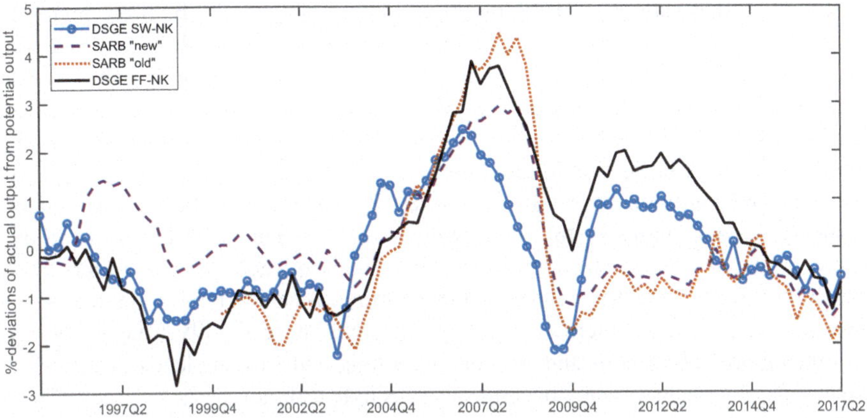

Fig. 18 DSGE model output gap comparisons with SARB output gap estimates. Period: 1995Q1–2017Q2

to counteract weak domestic demand. Similarly, interest rate movements also receive input from both demand and supply-side innovations, with demand-side components (the risk premium in particular) playing a much greater role in recent years (Fig. 16).

Finally, Fig. 18 compares the implied output gap estimates of the *DSGE-NK* and *DSGE-FF* models to that of the SARB's official finance-neutral output gap estimate. We include both the "old" estimate and the "new" estimate (Anvari et al. 2014; Botha et al. 2018). The SARB's new output gap estimate allows for potential output growth to respond to transitory supply-side shocks, such as droughts and strikes. The idea is to isolate demand-side pressures in the output gap to better inform monetary policy analysis. The SARB follows a semi-structural filtering approach as opposed to the fully structural model developed in this chapter. Notably, the SARB generates a potential output growth series based directly on a smoothed trend component of observable output, whereas the DSGE model estimates potential output from the implied flexible price equilibrium.

Figure 18 indicates that the implied theoretical output gap tracks the cyclical fluctuations of the SARB estimates fairly well. One notable exception is the period 2010Q3 to 2013Q3, where the DSGE model predicts a larger fall in potential output that results in a positive output gap. It is unclear how best to interpret this episode which corresponds with the end of the global commodity super-cycle and the beginning of South Africa's stagnating economy. The inclusion of financial factors (*FF-NK*) clearly materializes in the boom period before the 2009 recession, which is consistent with filtering approach of Kemp (2015). But including a financial factor does not explain the clear divergence of the two approaches in the aforementioned period. Furthermore, accounting for temporary supply-side factors (SARB "new" vs "old") does not appear to be a source of this discrepancy either. The SARB's new potential output estimate does, however, appear to be at a more-neutral level during the 1990s.

It is clear that estimates of the output gap are influenced by both the methodological approach and the specification of the model. These discrepancies can have a sizeable influence on monetary policy analysis—especially when using real-time data (see, e.g., Orphanides 2003; Kemp 2015). It may therefore also have a non-negligible influence in the formulation of policy—especially if the SARB's Quarterly Projection Model is used as an "integral role" in monetary policy decisions and communication (Botha et al. 2017). The reason to be cautious relates to the systematic biases of the underlying model: systematic errors from model inference and model forecasts can lead to severe consequences when it matters most (the 2008 GFC being a clear example). Furthermore, as central bank communication improves and markets internalize policy decisions more rapidly (that is, policy becomes more endogenous and operates with long and variable leads), estimating the effects of monetary policy becomes increasingly difficult.

The communication and interpretation of model results should therefore emphasize the expected path of policy given the available information fed into the model. Quantitative results should provide a range of confidence intervals to provide an informative counterfactual density path of the economy. It is also important to emphasize that the path of policy decisions are conditional on a certain monetary policy reaction function or decision making process. This may involve following a systematic rule (Calomiris 2018; Dorn 2018; Orphanides 2018) or a process of "guided discretion" whereby the central bank sets its instrument (e.g., the policy rate) to target the forecasts of its target variables (e.g., inflation and the output gap) to show how policy should be made to hit the central bank's objective over the medium- to long-run (Svensson 2003; Woodford 2007). Whether adopting a strict rule or guided discretion, it is crucial for both policymakers and the public to not be lulled into false expectations of the central banks ability to "fine-tune" the economy, and certainly not on any short-term horizon.

7 Concluding Remarks

The primary purpose of this paper is to contribute to the understanding of business cycle dynamics in the South African economy through the comparison of several dynamic general equilibrium models. We believe that the theoretical restrictions imposed, through the development of these microfounded models, creates a useful link between observed and model variables. In other words, these models help to bring theory to the data in a coherent fashion. We introduce nested models that cater to the needs of the South African macroeconomy, but also speak to the direction that the economics discipline is taking after the financial crisis. We acknowledge that these models will likely fail to predict possibly catastrophic market failures. However, this is a result of the complexities and opacity of real-world interaction that models will never be able to fully accommodate.

We interpret our main results from the benchmark New-Keynesian framework as described by Smets and Wouters (2003, 2007). Model dynamics reveal that inflation is sensitive to interest rate movements, which is observed across the different models used in this paper and in the face of different shocks imposed. Although interpreting the influence or effectiveness of the implied monetary policy transmission mechanism warrants caution. Output, consumption, investment, and labour showcase some persistence with respect to most shocks. The surprising result is the rigidity in the labour market that appears to be robust in the face of different innovations, especially once incorporating financial sector features.

When considering the variance decomposition one observes that output variability, in the long-run, is driven primarily by technology shocks. However, in the short- to medium-run the risk premium and exogenous spending play a greater part, with the risk premium having a more persistent impact. Inflation variance in the long-run is explained mostly by cost-push shocks, with price mark-up shocks contributing a significant amount. Monetary policy innovations contribute relatively little to output and inflation variance, but make up almost a half of the first quarter short-term nominal interest rate movements. Interestingly, the large and persistent role for cost-push shocks on the output gap suggests a non-negligible inflation-output trade-off for monetary authorities. The relevant contribution of these traditional shocks changes substantially once financial factors are included. Equity price shocks account for the largest share of output, inflation, and nominal interest rate variance at medium- to long-term horizons (2–5 years). Credit supply factors are more important for inflation and interest rate variance, and credit demand factors are more important for output.

Going forward, it is clear that a significant amount of thought should go into the specification of model dynamics and the identification and selection of exogenous shocks. Pertinent research questions usually require specific model assumptions and augmented features. We acknowledge that the inclusion of assumptions with respect to the financial system or open economy could distort model results, taking us further away from the correctly identified model framework. There is, therefore, an apparent trade-off to incorporating new and/or alternative features of the real world with a consistent and coherent interpretation of non-trivial theoretical interpretations. This trade-off, together with the atheoretical–theoretical trade-off at large in macroeconometric modelling, cannot be over-looked by policymakers, academics, and private sector practitioners alike.

Appendix 1: Ireland's Three-Equation New-Keynesian Model

IS Curve

$$\lambda_t = i_t + \lambda_{t+1} - \pi_{t+1} \tag{35}$$

New Keynesian Phillips Curve

$$\pi = \frac{\gamma_p}{(1+\gamma_p\beta)}\pi_{t-1} + \frac{\beta}{(1+\gamma_p\beta)}E_t[\pi_{t+1}] - \kappa_h(\lambda_t + \xi_t^b) + \xi_t^p\ , \tag{36}$$

where $\kappa_h = \frac{(1-\theta_p)(1-\theta_p\beta)}{\theta_p(1+\beta\gamma_p)}$.

Monetary Policy Rule

$$i_t = \rho_i i_{t-1} + \kappa_\pi \pi_t + \kappa_y \Delta y_t + \epsilon_t^i\ , \tag{37}$$

where the growth rate of output is $\Delta y_t = y_t - y_{t-1} + \xi_t^a$. The marginal utility of consumption with *internal* habit formation and log preferences (i.e., $\sigma_c = 1$):

$$(1-\beta\phi)(1-\phi)\lambda_t = \phi y_{t-1} - (1+\beta\phi^2)y_t + \beta\phi y_{t+1} + (1-\beta\phi\rho_b)(1-\phi)\xi_t^b - \phi\xi_t^a\ , \tag{38}$$

where ξ_t^b is the preference shock. We do not include this shock in the other models. Instead, the dynamics and relative contribution are compared to two similar shocks in the *SW-NK* framework, namely the risk premium shock and the exogenous spending shock. All three of these shocks are variant aggregate demand shocks.[43] A quick comparison with the three-equation model of the foreign economy in *HGW19* shows how similar these two linearized frameworks are (see Appendix 2 and Sect. 4). Another key difference is that ξ_t^a is a shock to the growth rate of output. A number of variables therefore need to be renormalized to remove the inherited unit root. Setting $\beta = 0$ in Eq. 38 gives the marginal utility of consumption with external habit:

$$\lambda_t = \frac{\phi}{(1-\phi)}y_{t-1} - \frac{1}{(1-\phi)}y_t + \xi_t^b - \phi\xi_t^a\ . \tag{39}$$

The efficient level of output is

$$0 = \phi q_{t-1} - (1+\beta\phi^2)q_t + \beta\phi q_{t+1} + \beta\phi(1-\phi)(1-\rho^b)\xi_t^b - \phi\xi_t^a\ ,$$

where the output gap is: $y_t^{gap} = y_t - q_t$. The laws of motion for the preference shock, the (renormalized) cost-push shock, and the technology shock are: $\xi_t^b = \rho^b\xi_{t-1}^b + \epsilon_t^b$; $\xi_t^p = \rho^p\xi_{t-1}^p + \epsilon_t^p$; $\xi_t^a = \epsilon_t^a$.

[43] Ireland's preference shock explains a significant portion of the models fluctuations over the estimated great recession period.

Appendix 2: The Open Economy

The open economy system of equilibrium conditions shown here is a direct extension of the "benchmark" closed economy New-Keynesian model presented in Sect. 3. The corresponding *SW-NK* model has some slight differences particularly related to the investment-specific efficiency shock. Specifically, the shock in *SW-NK* directly affects the accumulation of investment and its efficiency (via an adjustment cost) in physical capital accumulation, whereas the shock in *SOE-NK* affects the adjustment cost only (i.e., the relative price of capital, or, as described in *SW-NK*, the arbitrage equation for the value of capital). Also, we shut off the capital utilization channel in *SW-NK*. The flexible price (efficient) equilibrium follows by setting all price and wage rigidities to zero.

Aggregate Demand

$$\hat{c}_t^h = \gamma_c\eta_c(\hat{rer}_t - \hat{\psi}_t^f) - (\gamma_c\eta_c)\hat{pr}_t^h + \hat{c}_t \tag{40}$$

$$\hat{c}_t^f = (1-\gamma_c)(\eta_c)\hat{pr}_t^h + (\gamma_c - \eta_c)(\hat{rer}_t - \hat{\psi}_t^f) + \hat{c}_t \tag{41}$$

$$\hat{c}_t = \frac{1}{(1+\phi)}\hat{c}_{t+1} + \frac{\phi}{(1+\phi)}\hat{c}_{t-1} - \frac{(1-\phi)}{\sigma_c(1+\phi)}(\hat{i}_t^b - \hat{\pi}_{t+1} + \hat{\mu}_t^b) \tag{42}$$

$$\hat{rer}_t = \frac{\sigma_c}{1-\phi}(\hat{c}_t - \phi\hat{c}_{t-1}) - \frac{\sigma_c^*}{1-\phi^*}(\hat{c}_t^* - \phi^*\hat{c}_{t-1}^*)\,. \tag{43}$$

Equation 40 domestic consumption of home goods; Eq. 41 domestic consumption of foreign goods; Eq. 42 Euler equation; Eq. 43 is the international risk sharing condition (where $\hat{c}_t^* = \hat{y}_t^*$).[44]

Investment Schedule

$$\hat{v}_t - \hat{k}_t = \beta E_t(\hat{v}_{t+1} - \hat{k}_{t+1}) + \frac{\beta R^k}{\kappa_v}E_t(\hat{r}_{t+1}^k) + \frac{\sigma_c}{\kappa_v}(\hat{c}_t - \hat{c}_{t+1}) + \frac{1}{\kappa_v}(\hat{\xi}_t^v - \beta E_t\hat{\xi}_{t+1}^v)\,, \tag{44}$$

where $R^k = (1/\beta - (1-\delta))$ and $\hat{\xi}_t^v$ is the investment-specific shock, and $q_t^k = \kappa_v(v_t - k_t) - \tilde{\xi}_t^v$.

[44] The UIP condition holds from the Euler equations of the domestic and foreign sectors: $\hat{i}_t^b = \hat{i}_t^{b*} + E_t[\Delta\hat{\varepsilon}_{t+1}] + \hat{\Phi}_t$, which implies that the real exchange rate equates the marginal utilities of consumption between the domestic and foreign households.

Aggregate Supply and Inflation

(Real) Wage-Setting Equation

$$\hat{w}_t = \Omega\beta E_t\hat{w}_{t+1} + \Omega\hat{w}_{t-1} + \Omega\Omega^*(\hat{mrs}_t - \hat{w}_t)$$
$$+\Omega\beta E_t\hat{\pi}_{t+1} - \Omega\hat{\pi}_t - \Omega\theta_w\beta\gamma_w\hat{\pi}_t + \Omega\gamma_w\hat{\pi}_{t-1}\,.$$

The real wage ($\hat{w}_t = w_t - p_t$) setting equation can be re-written in nominal wage inflation form as:

$$\hat{\pi}_t^w - \gamma_w\hat{\pi}_{t-1} = \beta E_t\hat{\pi}_{t+1}^w - \theta_w\beta\gamma_w\hat{\pi}_t + \Omega^*(\hat{mrs}_t - \hat{w}_t), \tag{45}$$

where $\Omega^* = \frac{(1-\theta_w)(1-\theta_w\beta)}{\theta_w(1+\xi^w\sigma_n)}$, $\Omega = \frac{1}{(1+\beta)}$, and $\hat{mrs}_t = \frac{\sigma_c}{1-\phi}(\hat{c}_t - \phi\hat{c}_{t-1}) + \sigma_n\hat{n}_t$.

Domestic Production and Inflation (for Consumption Goods)

$$\hat{\pi}_t^h = \frac{\gamma_p}{(1+\gamma_p\beta)}\hat{\pi}_{t-1}^h + \frac{\beta}{(1+\gamma_p\beta)}E_t\hat{\pi}_{t+1}^h + \kappa_h(\hat{mc}_t^h + \hat{\xi}_t^p), \tag{46}$$

where $\hat{mc}_t^h = \hat{\lambda}_t$ is the real marginal cost of production, and $\kappa_h = \frac{(1-\theta_p)(1-\theta_p\beta)}{\theta_p(1+\gamma_p\beta)}$.

$$\hat{\lambda}_t = (\hat{w}_t - \hat{pr}_t^h) - (\hat{y}_t^h - \hat{n}_t) \tag{47}$$
$$\hat{\lambda}_t = \hat{r}_t^k - (\hat{y}_t^h - \hat{k}_t) \tag{48}$$
$$\hat{y}_t^h = \hat{\xi}_t^a + \alpha\hat{k}_t + (1-\alpha)\hat{n}_t\,. \tag{49}$$

Imported Inflation (for Foreign Consumption Goods)

$$\hat{\pi}_t^f = \beta E_t[\hat{\pi}_{t+1}^f] + \kappa_f\hat{\psi}_t^f, \tag{50}$$

where $\kappa_f = \frac{(1-\theta_f)(1-\theta_f\beta)}{\theta_f}$, and $\hat{\psi}_t^f$ measures the l.o.p gap[45]:

$$\hat{\psi}_t^f = \hat{\varepsilon}_t + \hat{p}_t^{f*} - \hat{p}_t^f,$$
$$= \hat{rer}_t - \hat{pr}_t^f\,. \tag{51}$$

[45] $\hat{rer}_t = \hat{\varepsilon}_t + \hat{p}_t^{f*} - \hat{p}_t$ and $\hat{pr}_t^f = \hat{p}_t^f - \hat{p}_t$.

Inflation Aggregation Equations

From the inflation aggregation equations we have

$$\hat{\pi}_t = (1 - \gamma_c)\hat{\pi}_t^h + \gamma_c \hat{\pi}_t^f .$$

Equation 52 can be re-written as

$$0 = (1 - \gamma_c)\hat{pr}_t^h + \gamma_c(\hat{pr}_t^f) . \tag{52}$$

Evolution of Relative Prices

$$\hat{pr}_t^h = \hat{pr}_{t-1}^h + \hat{\pi}_t^h - \hat{\pi}_t \tag{53}$$

$$\hat{pr}_t^f = \hat{pr}_{t-1}^f + \hat{\pi}_t^f - \hat{\pi}_t \tag{54}$$

$$r\hat{e}r_t = r\hat{e}r_{t-1} + \Delta\hat{\varepsilon}_t + \hat{\pi}_t^{f*} - \hat{\pi}_t \tag{55}$$

$$\hat{s}_t = \hat{pr}^f - \hat{pr}^h \tag{56}$$

$$\hat{w}_t = \hat{w}_{t-1} + \hat{\pi}_t^w - \hat{\pi}_t , \tag{57}$$

where Eq. 55 is the equation of motion for the relative purchasing power parity condition.[46] Here, we can think of nominal exchange rate changes ($\Delta\hat{\varepsilon}_t$) as the price adjustment mechanism that maintains equilibrium between foreign and domestic goods markets.

Evolution of Capital

$$\hat{k}_{t+1} = (1 - \delta)\hat{k}_t + \delta\hat{v}_t . \tag{58}$$

Policy Rule

The central bank conducts monetary policy according to a Taylor (1993) rule:

$$\hat{i}_t^b = \rho_i \hat{i}_{t-1}^b + (1 - \rho_i)\kappa_\pi \hat{\pi}_t + (1 - \rho_i)\kappa_y(\hat{y}_t - \hat{y}_{t-1}) + \epsilon_t^i . \tag{59}$$

[46]Derived from $r\hat{e}r_{t+1} = r\hat{e}r_t + (\hat{i}_t^b - \hat{\pi}_{t+1}) - (\hat{i}_t^{b*} - \hat{\pi}_{t+1}^{f*} + \hat{\Phi}_t)$, where $(\hat{i}_t^b - \hat{\pi}_{t+1})$ and $(\hat{i}_t^{b*} - \hat{\pi}_{t+1}^{f*})$ are the domestic and foreign real interest rates on bonds, i.e., the Fisher equations; $\hat{\Phi}_t = \hat{\mu}_t^{b*} - \hat{\mu}_t^b$.

The short-term nominal interest rate rises (falls) whenever inflation and output growth rise above (fall below) their average, or steady-state.

Foreign Economy

We assume a large open economy for the foreign market. This allows us to specify the foreign rate $\hat{i}_t^{b*}$, foreign inflation $\hat{\pi}_{t+1}^* = \hat{\pi}_{t+1}^{f*}$, and foreign consumption $\hat{y}_t^* = \hat{c}_t^*$ according to the standard three-equation New-Keynesian model, namely an IS curve, a Phillips curve, and a Taylor-type policy rate rule.

$$\hat{y}_t^* = \frac{1}{(1+\phi^*)}\hat{y}_{t+1}^* + \frac{\phi^*}{(1+\phi^*)}\hat{y}_{t-1}^* - \frac{(1-\phi^*)}{\sigma_c^*(1+\phi^*)}(\hat{i}_t^{b*} - E_t[\hat{\pi}_{t+1}^*] + \hat{\mu}_t^{b*}) \tag{60}$$

$$\hat{\pi}_t^* = \frac{\gamma^*}{(1+\gamma^*\beta)}\hat{\pi}_{t-1}^* + \frac{\beta}{(1+\gamma^*\beta)}E_t[\hat{\pi}_{t+1}^*] + \kappa_* \hat{mc}_t^*, \tag{61}$$

where $\hat{mc}_t^*$ is the real marginal cost of production, and $\kappa_* = \frac{(1-\theta_*)(1-\theta_*\beta)}{\theta_*(1+\gamma^*\beta)}$.

$$\hat{mc}_t^* = \left(\frac{\sigma_c^*}{1-\phi^*} + \sigma_n^*\right)\hat{y}_t^* - \left(\frac{\sigma_c^*\phi^*}{1-\phi^*}\right)\hat{y}_{t-1}^* - (1+\sigma_n^*)\hat{a}_t^*, \tag{62}$$

$$\hat{i}_t^{b*} = \rho_{i*}\hat{i}_{t-1}^{b*} + (1-\rho_{i*})\kappa_\pi^*\hat{\pi}_t^* + (1-\rho_{i*})\kappa_y^*(\hat{y}_t^* - \hat{y}_{t-1}^*) + \epsilon_t^{i*}. \tag{63}$$

Aggregate Equilibrium

$$\begin{aligned}\hat{y}_t^h &= \frac{C^h}{Y^h}\hat{c}_t^h + \frac{C^{h*}}{Y^h}\hat{c}_t^{h*} \\ &= \frac{C^h}{Y^h}\hat{c}_t^h + \frac{(1-C^h)}{Y^h}(\hat{y}_t^* - \xi^{f*}(\hat{pr}_t^h - \hat{rer}_t)),\end{aligned} \tag{64}$$

where ξ^{f*} is the foreign price elasticity of demand for domestic goods (i.e., the change in foreign demand for domestic goods given the foreign price of domestic goods relative to the foreign price of foreign goods).

$$\hat{y}_t = \frac{C}{Y}\hat{c}_t + \frac{V}{Y}\hat{v}_t + \frac{X}{Y}\hat{x}_t - \frac{M}{Y}\hat{m}_t \tag{65}$$

$$\hat{x}_t = \hat{c}_t^{h*} = \hat{y}_t^* - \xi^{f*}(\hat{pr}_t^h - \hat{rer}_t) \tag{66}$$

$$\hat{m}_t = \frac{C^f}{M}\hat{c}_t^f. \tag{67}$$

Exogenous Shocks

We include 10 shocks in the model. For the domestic economy, the monetary policy shock (ϵ_t^i), as given in Eq. 59, is i.i.d., whereas the domestic technology shock, the domestic price mark-up shock, the wage mark-up shock and the investment-specific shock follow AR(1) processes: $\hat{a}_t = \rho_a \hat{a}_{t-1} + \epsilon_t^a$; $\hat{\xi}_t^p = \rho_p \hat{\xi}_{t-1}^p + \epsilon_t^p$; $\hat{\xi}_t^w = \rho_w \hat{\xi}_{t-1}^w + \epsilon_t^w$; $\hat{\xi}_t^v = \rho_v \hat{\xi}_{t-1}^v + \epsilon_t^v$. Following Smets and Wouters (2007), we include the exogenous spending shock in the aggregate resource constraint: $\hat{\xi}_t^g = \rho_g \hat{\xi}_{t-1}^g + \epsilon_t^g + \rho_{g,y} \epsilon_t^a$.[47] Notably, $\rho_{g,y}$ captures spillover effects from domestic technology shocks.[48] The foreign economy follows with an i.i.d. monetary policy shock (ϵ_t^{i*}) and the following supply shock: $\hat{a}_t^* = \rho_{a*} \hat{a}_{t-1}^* + \epsilon_t^{a*}$. In addition, the risk premium shocks on domestic-currency assets relative to the policy rate and for foreign-currency borrowing abroad (equivalent to negative demand shocks) are described as follows: $\hat{\mu}_t^{b*} = \rho_b \hat{\mu}_{t-1}^{b*} + \epsilon_t^{b*}$ and $\hat{\mu}_t^b = \rho_b \hat{\mu}_{t-1}^b + \epsilon_t^b$.

Appendix 3: The Financial Frictions Model

Households

Households' Euler equation

$$\left(\frac{1}{R^h} - \beta_h\right) \hat{\lambda}_t^h = \beta_h \left(\frac{\gamma}{1-\phi}(\hat{c}_{t+1} - \phi \hat{c}_t) + \hat{\pi}_{t+1}\right) - \frac{1}{R^h}\left(\frac{\gamma}{1-\phi}(\hat{c}_t - \phi \hat{c}_{t-1}) + \hat{i}_t^h\right). \tag{68}$$

Safe-assets demand

$$\hat{b}_t = \frac{\gamma}{(1-\phi)(1-\beta_h R)}(\hat{c}_t - \phi \hat{c}_{t-1}) + \frac{\beta_h R}{1-\beta_h R}\left(\hat{i}_t - \hat{\pi}_{t+1} - \frac{\gamma}{1-\phi}(\hat{c}_{t+1} - \phi \hat{c}_t)\right) - \hat{\xi}_{b,t}, \tag{69}$$

where $1/(1-\beta_h R)$ is the asset-consumption ratio of households and is calibrated from the data as 0.856.

[47] Primarily, this is to avoid stochastic singularity in the closed economy model. In this context, we can think of this exogenous component as being exogenous government spending shocks plus shocks to the trade balance not implied by the structural model.

[48] Following Steinbach et al. (2014, p. 24), we fix ρ_g but estimate the cross-correlation coefficient.

Equity price

$$\hat{q}_t^{\psi} = E_t\left[\hat{q}_{t+1}^{\psi} - \frac{\gamma}{1-\phi}(\hat{c}_{t+1} - \phi\hat{c}_t)\right] + \frac{\gamma}{(1-\Gamma_\psi)(1-\phi)}(\hat{c}_t - \phi\hat{c}_{t-1})$$
$$+ \frac{\Gamma_\psi}{1-\Gamma_\psi}(\hat{\lambda}_t + \hat{\upsilon}_{h,t}) - \hat{\xi}_{\psi,t}, \tag{70}$$

where $\Gamma_\psi = ((1/R^h) - \beta_h)\nu_h(1-\phi_w)$.

Borrowing constraint

$$\hat{l}_t^h = \frac{\phi_w}{R^h}(\hat{w}_t + \hat{n}_t) + \frac{(1-\phi_w)}{R^h}\hat{q}_t^{\psi} - \hat{i}_t^h + \frac{1}{R^h}\hat{\upsilon}_{h,t}. \tag{71}$$

The household flow of funds constraint

$$\frac{C^h}{Y}\hat{c}_t^h = \frac{(1-\alpha)}{X}(\hat{y}_t - \hat{x}_t) + \frac{B}{Y}R(\hat{i}_{t-1} + \hat{b}_{t-1} - \hat{\pi}_t) - \frac{B}{Y}b_t$$
$$+\frac{L^h}{Y}(\hat{l}_t^h - R^h\hat{i}_{t-1}^h - R^h\hat{l}_{t-1}^e + R^h\hat{\pi}_t) + \frac{Q^\psi\Psi}{Y}(\zeta_\psi\hat{q}_t^{\psi} - \hat{\xi}_{\psi,t}) \tag{72}$$

Note that the household's optimality condition for labour supply enters in the union wage-setting equation (see Eq. 84). Specifically, in the flexible price (efficient) equilibrium the marginal rate of substitution will equal the real wage. To therefore accommodate the efficient equilibrium in our setup, we must use Eq. 72 to close the model.

Entrepreneurs in Firm Production

Labour demand

$$\hat{n}_t = \hat{y}_t - \hat{x}_t - \hat{w}_t. \tag{73}$$

Entrepreneurs' Euler equation

$$\left(\frac{1}{R^e} - \beta_e\right)\hat{\lambda}_t^e = \beta_e(\gamma^e(\hat{c}_{t+1}^e) + \hat{\pi}_{t+1}) - \frac{1}{R^e}(\gamma^e(\hat{c}_t^e) + \hat{i}_t^e). \tag{74}$$

Investment schedule

$$\hat{\upsilon}_t - \hat{k}_t = \frac{\beta_e}{(1-\Upsilon_k)}E_t[\hat{\upsilon}_{t+1} - \hat{k}_{t+1}] + \frac{(1-\beta_e(1-\delta_e)-\Upsilon_k)}{(1-\Upsilon_k)\kappa_\upsilon}(\hat{y}_{t+1} - \hat{x}_{t+1} - \hat{k}_{t+1})$$
$$+\frac{\Upsilon_k}{(1-\Upsilon_k)\kappa_\upsilon}(\hat{\lambda}_t^e + \hat{\upsilon}_{e,t}) + \frac{\beta_e(1-\delta_e)\gamma^e}{(1-\Upsilon_k)\kappa_\upsilon}(\hat{c}_t^e - \hat{c}_{t+1}^e) + \hat{\xi}_t^{\upsilon}, \tag{75}$$

where $\Upsilon_k = ((1/R^e) - \beta_e)\nu_e\phi_k$ and the shadow price of capital is

$$\hat{q}_t^k = \kappa_\upsilon(\hat{\upsilon}_t - \hat{k}_t) - \gamma^e \hat{c}_t^e, \tag{76}$$

where $\Upsilon_k = 0$ is the same as Iacoviello (2005, p. 760 (A3)).

Production function

$$\hat{y}_t = \alpha\hat{k}_t + (1-\alpha)\hat{h}_t + \hat{\xi}_t^a\,. \tag{77}$$

Borrowing constraint

$$\hat{l}_t^e = \frac{\phi_k}{R^e}(\hat{q}_t^k + \hat{k}_t) + \frac{(1-\phi_k)}{R^e}\hat{q}_t^\psi - \hat{i}_t^e + \frac{1}{R^e}\hat{\nu}_{e,t}. \tag{78}$$

Capital accumulation

$$\hat{k}_{t+1} = (1-\delta_e)\hat{k}_t + \delta_e\hat{\upsilon}_t. \tag{79}$$

The entrepreneur flow of funds constraint

$$\frac{C^e}{Y}\hat{c}_t^e = \frac{(1-\alpha)}{X}(\hat{y}_t - \hat{x}_t) + \frac{L^e}{Y}(\hat{l}_t^e - R^e\hat{i}_{t-1}^e - R^e\hat{l}_{t-1}^e + R^e\hat{\pi}_t) - \frac{\delta_e K}{Y}\hat{\upsilon}_t - \frac{Q^\psi\Psi^e}{Y}\zeta_\psi\hat{q}_t^\psi\,. \tag{80}$$

Retailers and Labour Unions

The forward-looking Phillips curve with price indexation

$$\pi_t = \frac{\beta_R}{(1+\beta_R\gamma_p)}E_t\pi_{t+1} + \frac{\gamma_p}{(1+\beta_R\gamma_p)}\pi_{t-1} - \frac{(1-\theta_p)(1-\theta_p\beta_R)}{(1+\beta_R\gamma_p)\theta_p}x_t + \varepsilon_t^p\,. \tag{81}$$

The forward-looking sticky (real) wage equation with price indexation (where $\hat{w}_t = w_t - p_t$)

$$\begin{aligned}\hat{w}_t &= \Phi\beta E_t\hat{w}_{t+1} + \Phi\hat{w}_{t-1} + \Phi\Phi^*(mrs_t - \hat{w}_t)\\ &\quad + \Phi\beta E_t\pi_{t+1} - \Phi\pi_t - \Phi\theta_w\beta\gamma_w\pi_t + \Phi\gamma_w\pi_{t-1}\,,\end{aligned} \tag{82}$$

where $\Phi^* = \frac{(1-\theta_w)(1-\theta_w\beta)}{\theta_w(1+\xi^w\sigma_n)}$, $\Phi = \frac{1}{(1+\beta)}$. The marginal rate of substitution (mrs_t) follows from the households optimality condition for labour supply:

$$m\hat{r}s_t = aa\frac{\gamma}{1-\phi}(\hat{c}_t - \phi\hat{c}_{t-1}) + \eta\hat{n}_t - aa\left(\frac{1}{R^h} - \beta_h\right)\nu_h\phi_w(\hat{\lambda}_t^h + \hat{\nu}_{h,t}), \tag{83}$$

where aa is $1/(1 + (\frac{1}{R^h} - \beta_h)\nu_h\phi_w)$, and $\hat{w}_t$ is the real wage. Under no borrowing constraints, $mrs_t = \frac{\gamma}{1-\phi}(c_t - \phi c_{t-1}) + \eta h_t$.

The real wage ($\hat{w}_t = w_t - p_t$) setting equation can be re-written in nominal wage inflation form as:

$$\hat{\pi}_t^w - \gamma_w \hat{\pi}_{t-1} = \beta E_t \hat{\pi}_{t+1}^w - \theta_w \beta \gamma_w \hat{\pi}_t + \Phi^*(\hat{mrs}_t - \hat{w}_t)\,. \tag{84}$$

Banking Sector

Interbank rate

$$\hat{i}_t^c = \hat{i}_t - \frac{\kappa_k}{r}\tau^3(\hat{k}_t^B - \hat{l}_t - \xi_{\tau,t}). \tag{85}$$

Bank capital accumulation

$$\hat{k}_t^B = (1-\delta_B)\hat{k}_{t-1}^B + \delta_B \hat{\omega}_{B,t-1} + \phi_\psi(\hat{q}_t^\psi - \hat{q}_{t-1}^\psi) - (1-\phi_\psi)\hat{\pi}_t. \tag{86}$$

Profit function

$$\frac{\omega_B}{L}\hat{\omega}_{B,t} = r^h\frac{L^h}{L}(\hat{i}_t^h + \hat{l}_t^h) + r^e\frac{L^e}{L}(\hat{i}_t^e + \hat{l}_t^e) - r\frac{B}{L}(\hat{i}_t + \hat{b}_t) - \frac{Q^\psi \Psi_B}{L}\zeta_\psi(\hat{q}_t^\psi). \tag{87}$$

Retail loan rate setting to households

$$\begin{aligned}\hat{i}_t^h = & \frac{\kappa_h}{(1-\nu_B)(\varepsilon^h-1)+(1+\beta_B)\kappa_h}\hat{i}_{t-1}^h \\ & + \frac{\beta_B\kappa_h}{(1-\nu_B)(\varepsilon^h-1)+(1+\beta_B)\kappa_h}E_t\hat{i}_{t+1}^h \\ & + \frac{2(\varepsilon^h-1)}{(1-\nu_B)(\varepsilon^h-1)+(1+\beta_B)\kappa_h}\hat{i}_t^c \\ & + \frac{(1-\nu_B)(\varepsilon^h-1)}{(1-\nu_B)(\varepsilon^h-1)+(1+\beta_B)\kappa_h}\mu_{h,t},\end{aligned} \tag{88}$$

where $\mu_{h,t} = \varepsilon_t^h/(\varepsilon_t^h - 1)$ is the stochastic markup shock.

Retail loan rate setting to entrepreneurs

$$\begin{aligned}\hat{i}_t^e = & \frac{\kappa_e}{(1-\nu_B)(\varepsilon^e-1)+(1+\beta_B)\kappa_e}\hat{i}_{t-1}^e \\ & + \frac{\beta_B\kappa_e}{(1-\nu_B)(\varepsilon^e-1)+(1+\beta_B)\kappa_e}E_t\hat{i}_{t+1}^e\end{aligned}$$

$$+\frac{2(\varepsilon^e-1)}{(1-\nu_B)(\varepsilon^e-1)+(1+\beta_B)\kappa_e}\hat{i}_t^c$$
$$+\frac{(1-\nu_B)(\varepsilon^e-1)}{(1-\nu_B)(\varepsilon^e-1)+(1+\beta_B)\kappa_e}\mu_{e,t}, \tag{89}$$

where $\mu_{e,t}=\varepsilon_t^e/(\varepsilon_t^e-1)$ is the stochastic markup shock.

Interbank spread and retail spread definitions (indexed by $z=h,e$)

$$\hat{s}_t=\hat{i}_t^c-\hat{i}_t, \tag{90}$$
$$\hat{s}_t^z=\hat{i}_t^z-\hat{i}_t^c. \tag{91}$$

Monetary Policy and Market Clearing Conditions

$$\hat{i}_t=\kappa_i\hat{i}_{t-1}+\kappa_\pi(1-\kappa_i)\hat{\pi}_t+\kappa_y(1-\kappa_i)(\hat{y}_t-\hat{y}_{t-1})+\xi_{i,t}, \tag{92}$$
$$\hat{y}_t=\frac{C}{Y}\hat{c}_t+\frac{C^e}{Y}\hat{c}_t^e+\delta_e\frac{K}{Y}\hat{\upsilon}_t+\frac{K^B}{Y}\delta_B\hat{k}_{t-1}^B, \tag{93}$$
$$\hat{l}_t=\frac{L^h}{L}\hat{l}_t^h+\frac{L^e}{L}\hat{l}_t^e. \tag{94}$$

Appendix 4: Tables and Figures

See Table 6 and Figs. 19, 20, 21, 22, 23, and 24.

Table 6 Calibrated parameters

Parameter	Description	Value
Households and firms		
β_h	Discount factor	0.99
δ	Rate of depreciation	0.03
α	Share of capital in firm production	0.30
Price setting		
ξ^p	Price elasticity of demand for goods	11
ξ^w	Wage elasticity of demand for labour	5
Shocks		
ρ_g	Exogenous spending persistence	0.82

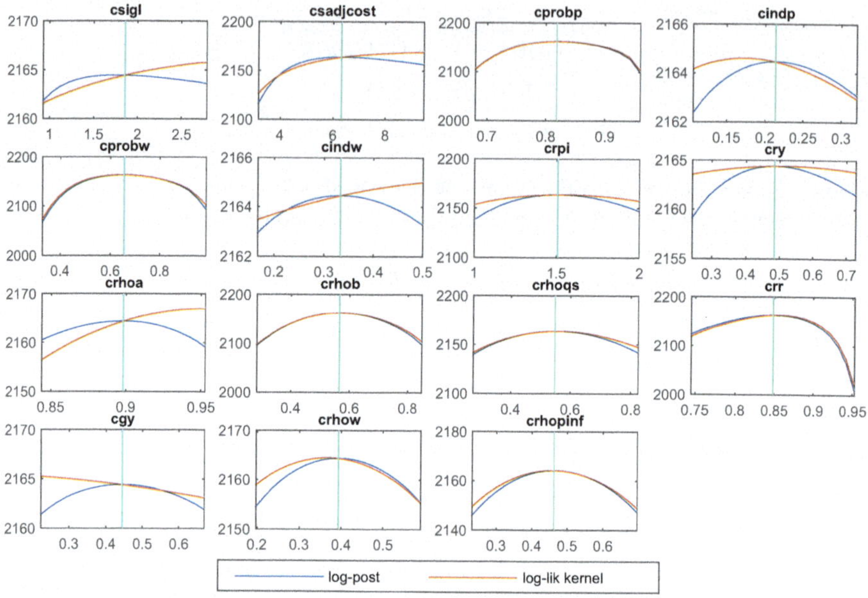

Fig. 19 Log-posterior likelihood functions and log-likelihood kernels

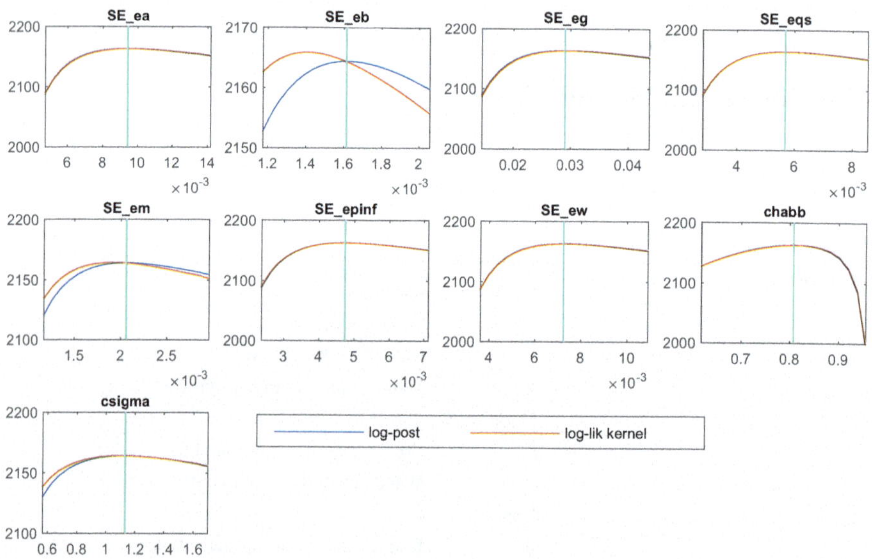

Fig. 20 Log-posterior likelihood functions and log-likelihood kernels. If the estimated mode is the local mode, it should be at the maximum of the posterior likelihood

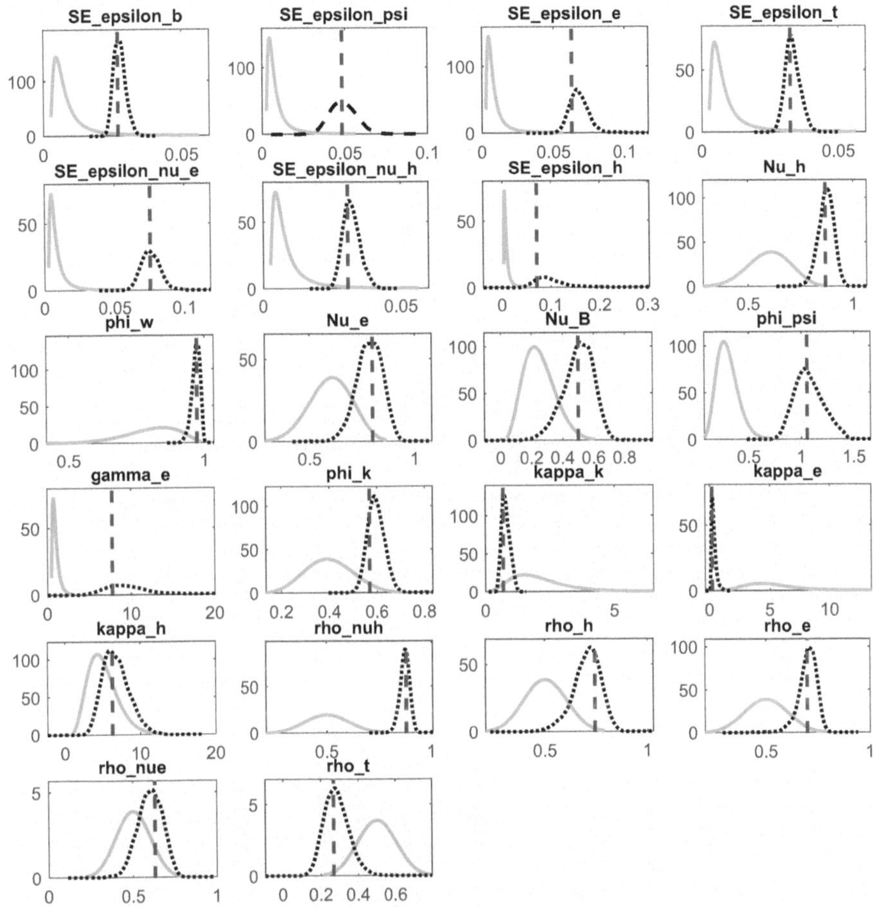

Fig. 21 Additional posterior distribution statistics for *FF-NK*

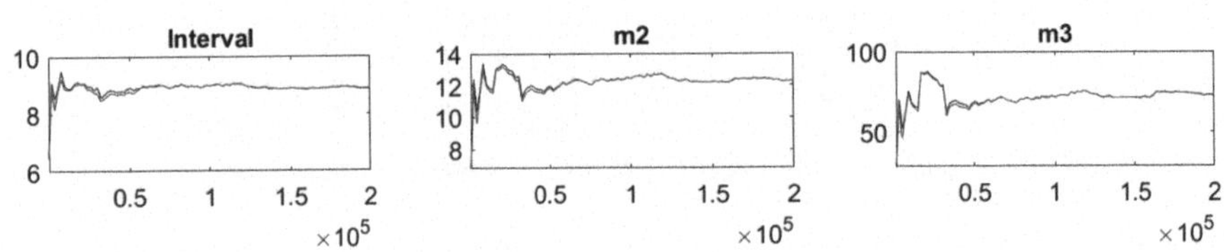

Fig. 22 Multivariate convergence diagnostic for *SW-NK*

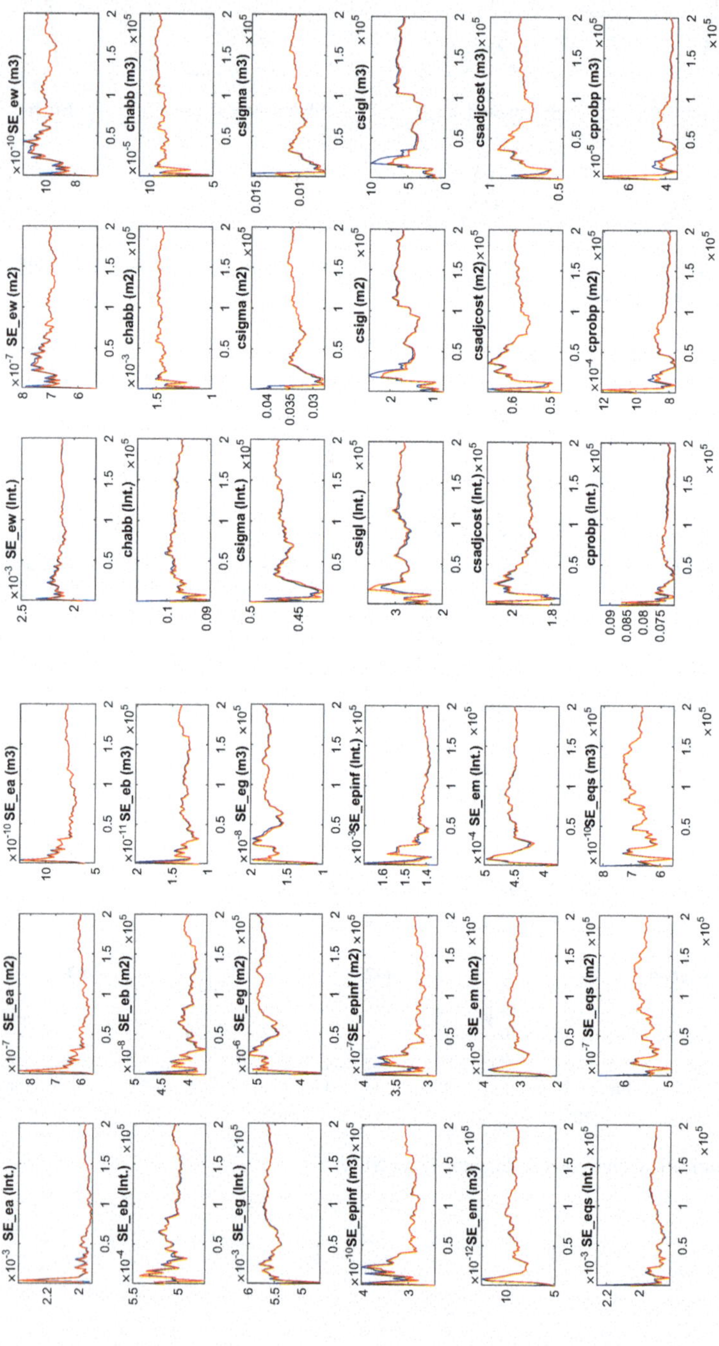

Fig. 23 Univariate convergence diagnostics for *SW-NK*

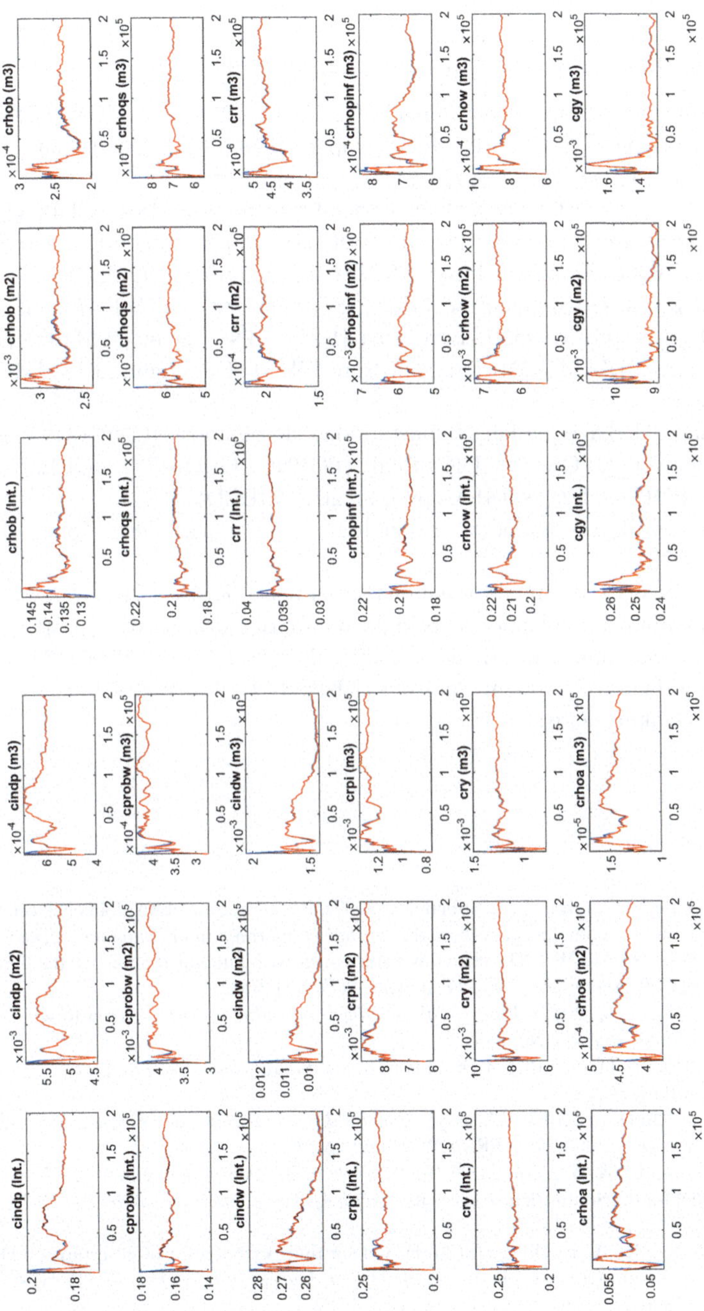

Fig. 24 Univariate convergence diagnostics for *SW-NK* (Fig. 23 continued)

Appendix 5: Data and Sources

Data sources retrieved from the Federal Reserve Bank of St. Louis (FRED), the South African Reserve Bank (SARB), Eurostat, and OECD.stat:

1. Consumer Price Index of All Items in the USA [CPIAUCSL], UK [GBRCPIALL], Euro area [EZCCM086NEST], Japan [JPNCPIALL], and South Africa [ZAFCPIALL] retrieved from FRED (Copyright, 2018, OECD)
2. Real Gross Domestic Product by Expenditure for the USA [GDPC1], UK [GBQ661S], Euro area [EURSCAB1GQEA19], Japan [JPQ661S], and South Africa [ZAQ661S] retrieved from FRED (Copyright, 2018, OECD)
3. Interest Rates, Government Securities, 3-Month Treasury Bills for the USA [Gs3M], UK [GBM193N], Euro area [EZQ193N], Japan [JPM193N], and South Africa [ZAM193N] retrieved from FRED (Copyright, 2018, IMF and Eurostat)
4. Population: USA (Civilian Noninstitutional Population) [CNP16OV], Japan (15 and over) [JPQ647S], UK (Total) [POPNC; GBQ647S], and Euro area (Total) [POPNC; EZQ647S] (Copyright, 2018, OECD)
5. SARB, Final consumption expenditure by households: Total (PCE) [KBP6007L]
6. SARB, Gross fixed capital formation (Investment) [KBP6009L]
7. SARB, Nominal unit labour costs in the non-agricultural sectors [KBP7015L]
8. SARB, Total employment in the non-agricultural sectors [KBP7009L]
9. SARB, Balance of payments statistics [KBP5000L - KBP5010L]
10. SARB, Banking statistics

References

Adolfson, M., Laséen, S., Lindé, J., & Villani, M. (2007). Bayesian estimation of an open economy DSGE model with incomplete pass-through. *Journal of International Economics, 72*, 481–511.

Adrian, T., & Shin, H. S. (2010). The changing nature of financial intermediation and the financial crisis of 2007–09. *Annual Review of Economics, 2*(1), 603–618.

Adrian, T., & Shin, H. S. (2013). *Procyclical Leverage and Value-at-Risk*. Federal Reserve Bank of New York Staff Reports, No. 338.

Ahn, K., & Tsomocos, D. P. (2013). *A Dynamic General Equilibrium Model to Analyse Financial Stability*. Working Paper.

Akinsola, F., & Ikhide, S. (2017, February). *Can Bank Capital Adequacy Changes Amplify the Business Cycle in South Africa?* ERSA Working Paper 668.

Alpanda, S., Kotzé, K., & Woglom, G. (2010). The role of the exchange rate in a New Keynesian DSGE model for the South African economy. *South African Journal of Economics, 78*(2), 170–191.

Alpanda, S., Kotzé, K., & Woglom, G. (2011). Forecasting performance of an estimated DSGE model for the South African economy. *South African Journal of Economics, 79*(1), 50–67.

An, S., & Schorfheide, F. (2007). Bayesian analysis of DSGE models. *Econometric Reviews, 26*(2–4), 113–172.

Andrle, M. (2010, August). *A Note on Identification Patterns in DSGE Models*. ECB Working Paper 1235. http://ssrn.com/abstract=1656963

Anvari, V., Ehlers, N., & Steinbach, R. (2014). *A Semi-structural Approach to Estimate South Africa's Potential Output*. South African Reserve Bank Working Paper WP/14/08.

Balcilar, M., Gupta, R., & Kotzé, K. (2015). Forecasting macroeconomic data for an emerging market with a nonlinear dsge model. *Economic Modelling, 44*(C), 215–228.

Balcilar, M., Gupta, R., & Kotzé, K. (2017). Forecasting South African macroeconomic variables with a Markov-switching small open-economy dynamic stochastic general equilibrium model. *Empirical Economics, 53*(1), 117–135.

Bernanke, B., Gertler, M., & Gilchrist, S. (1999). The financial accelerator in a quantitative business cycle framework. In J. B. Taylor & M. Woodford (Eds.), *Handbook of macroeconomics* (1st ed., Vol. 1, Ch. 21, pp. 1341–1393). Amsterdam: Elsevier Science B.V.

Bernanke, B. S. (2012). The effects of the great recession on central bank doctrine and practice. *The B.E. Journal of Macroeconomics, 12*(3), 1935–1690.

Blanchard, O. (2018). On the future of macroeconomic models. *Oxford Review of Economic Policy, 34*(1–2), 43–54. http://academic.oup.com/oxrep/article/34/1-2/43/4781808

Bosch, A., & Ruch, F. (2013). An alternative business cycle dating procedure for South Africa. *South African Journal of Economics, 81*(4), 491–516.

Botha, B., de Jager, S., Ruch, F., & Steinbach, R. (2017). *The Quarterly Projection Model of the SARB*. South African Reserve Bank Working Paper Series WP/17/01.

Botha, B., Ruch, F., & Steinbach, R. (2018). *Short-Lived Supply Shocks to Potential Growth*. South African Reserve Bank Working Paper Series WP/18/02.

Burger, P. (2008). The changing volatility of the South African economy. *South African Journal of Economics, 13*(1), 26–49.

Burger, P. (2010). The South African business cycle: What has changed? *South African Journal of Economics and Management Sciences, 76*(3), 335–355.

Burstein, A., & Gopinath, G. (2014). International prices and exchange rates. In G. Gopinath, E. Helpman, & K. Rogoff (Eds.), *Handbook of international economics* (Vol. 4, Ch. 7). Amsterdam: Elsevier B.V.

Caballero, R. J. (2010). Macroeconomics after the crisis: Time to deal with the pretense-of-knowledge syndrome. *Journal of Economic Perspectives, 24*(4), 85–102.

Calomiris, C. (2018). Reforming the rules that govern the fed. *Cato Journal, 38*(1), 109–138.

Calvo, G. (1983). Staggered prices in a utility-maximizing framework. *Journal of Monetary Economy, 12*(3), 383–398.

Canova, F. (2007). Bayesian analysis of dsge models by S. An and F. Schorfheide. *Econometric Reviews, 26*(2–4), 187–192. https://doi.org/10.1080/07474930701220162

Canova, F., & Ravn, M. O. (1996, August). International consumption risk sharing. *International Economic Review, 37*(3), 573–601.

Christiano, L. J., Eichenbaum, M., & Evans, C. L. (2005). Nominal rigidities and the dynamic effects of a shock to monetary policy. *Journal of Political Economy, 113*(1), 1–45.

Cochrane, J. H. (2008). Financial markets and the real economy. In R. Mehra (Ed.), *Handbook of the equity risk premium* (Ch. 7, pp. 237–325). Amsterdam: Elsevier B.V.

De Walque, G., Pierrard, O., & Rouabah, A. (2010). Financial (in) stability, supervision and liquidity injections: A dynamic general equilibrium approach. *The Economic Journal, 120*, 1234–1261. http://onlinelibrary.wiley.com/doi/10.1111/j.1468-0297.2010.02383.x/full

DeLong, J. B. (2011). Economics in crisis. *The Economists Voice, 2*(2), 1–2. http://www.bepress.com/cgi/viewcontent.cgi?article=1854&context=ev

Dorn, J. A. (2018). Monetary policy in an uncertain world: The case for rules. *Cato Journal, 38*(1), 81–108.

du Plessis, S., & Kotzé, K. (2010). The great moderation of the South African business cycle. *Economic History of Developing Regions, 25*(1), 105–125.

du Plessis, S., Smit, B., & Sturzeneggerb, F. (2008). Identifying aggregate supply and demand shocks in South Africa. *Journal of African Economies, 17*(5), 765–793.

du Plessis, S. A. (2004). Stretching the South African business cycle. *Economic Modelling, 21*, 685–701.

du Plessis, S. A. (2006). Reconsidering the business cycle and stabilisation policies in South Africa. *Economic Modelling, 23*(5), 761–774.

Eaton, J., Kortum, S., & Neiman, B. (2016a). Obstfeld and Rogoff's international macro puzzles: A quantitative assessment. *Journal of Economic Dynamics and Control, 72*, 5–23. Trade and macroeconomics: New approaches to enduring puzzles. http://www.sciencedirect.com/science/article/pii/S0165188916301014

Eaton, J., Kortum, S., Neiman, B., & Romalis, J. (2016b). Trade and the global recession. *American Economic Review, 106*(11), 3401–3438.

Fuhrer, J. C. (2000). Habit formation in consumption and its implications for monetary-policy models. *American Economic Review, 90*(3), 367–390.

Funke, M., Paetz, M., & Pytlarczyk, E. (2011). Stock market wealth effects in an estimated DSGE model for Hong Kong. *Economic Modelling, 28*(1–2), 316–334.

Gali, J., & Monacelli, T. (2005, July). Monetary policy and exchange rate volatility in a small open economy. *Review of Economic Studies, 72*(3), 707–734.

Gerali, A., Neri, S., Sessa, L., & Signoretti, F. M. (2010). Credit and banking in a DSGE model of the Euro area. *Journal of Money, Credit, and Banking, 42*(6), 107–141.

Gupta, R., & Steinbach, R. (2013). A DSGE-VAR model for forecasting key South African macroeconomic variables. *Economic Modelling, 33*, 19–33.

Hansen, L. P. (2014, October). Nobel lecture: Uncertainty outside and inside economic models. *Journal of Political Economy, 122*(5), 945–987.

Hansen, L. P. (2017). Uncertainty in economic analysis and the economic analysis of uncertainty. *KNOW: A Journal on the Formation of Knowledge, 1*(1), 171–197. https://doi.org/10.1086/692519

Hollander, H. (2017). Macroprudential policy with convertible debt. *Journal of Macroeconomics, 54*, 285–305.

Hollander, H., & Christensen, L. (2018, December 5). *Monetary Regimes, Money Supply, and the US Business Cycle Since 1959: Implications for Monetary Policy Today*. Mercatus Working Paper, Mercatus Center at George Mason University, Arlington, VA. https://www.mercatus.org/publications/monetary-policy/monetary-regimes-money-supply-and-us-business-cycle-1959

Hollander, H., Gupta, R., & Wohar, M. E. (2019). The impact of oil shocks in a small open economy New-Keynesian dynamic stochastic general equilibrium model for an oil-importing country: The case of South Africa. *Emerging Markets Finance and Trade, 55*, 1593–1618. https://doi.org/10.1080/1540496X.2018.1474346

Hollander, H., & Liu, G. (2016a). Credit spread variability in the U.S. business cycle: The great moderation versus the Great Recession. *Journal of Banking & Finance, 67*, 37–52.

Hollander, H., & Liu, G. (2016b). The equity price channel in a New-Keynesian DSGE model with financial frictions and banking. *Economic Modelling*, 375–389.

Iacoviello, M. (2005). House prices, borrowing constraints, and monetary policy in the business cycle. *American Economic Review, 95*(3), 739–764.

Ireland, P. N. (2004). Technology shocks in the New Keynesian model. *Review of Economics and Statistics, 86*, 923–936.

Ireland, P. N. (2007). Changes in the Federal Reserve's inflation target: Causes and consequences. *Journal of Money, Credit, and Banking, 39*, 1851–1882.

Ireland, P. N. (2011). A New Keynesian perspective on the Great Recession. *Journal of Money, Credit and Banking, 43*(1), 31–54.

Iskrev, N. (2010). Local identification in DSGE models. *Journal of Monetary Economics, 57*, 189–202.

Jooste, C., Liu, G., & Naraidoo, R. (2013). Analysing the effects of fiscal policy shocks in the South African economy. *Economic Modelling, 32*, 215–224.

Kay, J. (2012). The map is not the territory: An essay on the state of economics. *Critical Review, 5*(1), 87–99. http://ideas.repec.org/a/nos/voprec/2012-05-1.html

Kemp, J. H. (2015). Measuring potential output for the South African economy: Embedding information about the financial cycle. *South African Journal of Economics, 83*(4), 549–568.

Kirman, A. (2010). The economic crisis is a crisis for economic theory. *CESifo Economic Studies, 56*, 498–535.

Kiyotaki, N., & Moore, J. (1997). Credit cycles. *Journal of Political Economy, 105*(2), 211–248.

Korinek, A. (2017). *Thoughts on DSGE Macroeconomics: Matching the Moment, But Missing the Point?* https://doi.org/10.2139/ssrn.3022009

Kotzé, K. (2017). *Fiscal Policy Uncertainty and Economic Activity in South Africa*. School of Economics Macroeconomic Discussion Paper Series 2017-02, University of Cape Town.

Kotzé, K. L. (2014). *The South African Business Cycle and the Application of Dynamic Stochastic General Equilibrium Models*. PhD thesis. http://hdl.handle.net/10019.1/96055

Krugman, P. (2018). Good enough for government work? Macroeconomics since the crisis. *Oxford Review of Economic Policy, 34*(1–2), 156–168. http://academic.oup.com/oxrep/article/34/1-2/156/4781811

Krugman, P. R. (2011). The profession and the crisis. *Eastern Economic Journal, 37*(3), 307–312. http://www.palgrave-journals.com/doifinder/10.1057/eej.2011.8

Kuhn, T. (1996). *The Structure of Scientific Revolutions*. Foundations of the Unity of Science. University of Chicago Press. https://books.google.co.za/books?id=xnjS401VuFMC

Leeper, E. M., & Sims, C. A. (1994). Toward a modern macroeconomic model usable for policy analysis. *NBER Macroeconomics Annual, 9*, 81–140. http://www.nber.org/chapters/c11008.pdf

Leith, C., & Liu, D. (2016). The inflation bias under Calvo and Rotemberg pricing. *Journal of Economic Dynamics and Control, 73*, 283–297. http://www.sciencedirect.com/science/article/pii/S0165188916301476

Lindé, J., Smets, F., & Wouters, R. (2016, May). Challenges for central banks' macro models. In J. B. Taylor & Harald Uhlig (eds.), *Handbook of macroeconomics* (Vol. 2, Ch. 28, pp. 2185–2262). Amsterdam: Elsevier.

Liu, G. (2013). Will the SARB always succeed in fighting inflation with contractionary policy? *South African Journal of Economics, 81*(3), 330–345.

Liu, G., & Gupta, R. (2007). A small-scale dsge model for forecasting the South African economy. *South African Journal of Economics, 75*(2), 179–193.

Liu, G., Gupta, R., & Schaling, E. (2009). A New-Keynesian DSGE model for forecasting the South African economy. *Journal of Forecasting, 28*, 387–404.

Maredza, A. (2015). *Do Capital Requirements Affect Cost of Intermediation? Evidence from a Panel of South African Banks*. ERSA Working Paper 541.

Moolman, E. (2004). A Markov switching regime model of the South African business cycle. *Economic Modelling, 21*, 631–646.

Nakamura, E., & Steinsson, J. (2018, August). Identification in macroeconomics. *Journal of Economic Perspectives, 32*(3), 59–86.

Obstfeld, M., & Rogoff, K. (2000). The six major puzzles in international macroeconomics: Is there a common cause? *NBER Macroeconomics Annual, 15*, 339–390.

Ohanian, L. E., Prescott, E. C., & Stokey, N. L. (2009). Introduction to dynamic general equilibrium. *Journal of Economic Theory, 144*, 2235–2246.

Orphanides, A. (2003, June). Historical monetary policy analysis and the Taylor rule. *Journal of Monetary Economics*. http://www.sciencedirect.com/science/article/pii/S0304393203000655

Orphanides, A. (2018). Improving monetary policy by adopting a simple rule. *Cato Journal, 38*(1), 139–146.

Ortiz, A., & Sturzenegger, F. (2007). Estimating SARB's policy reaction rule. *South African Journal of Economics, 75*(4), 659–680.

Paetz, M., & Gupta, R. (2016). Stock price dynamics and the business cycle in an estimated DSGE model for South Africa. *Journal of International Financial Markets, Institutions & Money, 44*, 166–182.

Pfeifer, J. (2018). *A Guide to Specifying Observation Equations for the Estimation of DSGE Models*. Mimeo. https://sites.google.com/site/pfeiferecon/dynare

Ratto, M. (2008). Analysing DSGE models with global sensitivity analysis. *Computational Economics, 31*, 115–139.

Ratto, M., & Iskrev, N. (2011). Identification analysis of DSGE models with DYNARE. Mimeo. https://www.ifk-cfs.de/fileadmin/downloads/events/conferences/monfispol2011/RATTO_IdentifFinal.pdf

Roger, S., & Vlcek, J. (2012). *Macrofinancial Modeling at Central Banks: Recent Developments and Future Directions*. IMF Working Paper 12/21 (pp. 1–39).

Romer, P. (2016). The trouble with macroeconomics. The American Economist, forthcoming.

Schorfheide, F. (2000). Loss function-based evaluation of DSGE models. *Journal of Applied Econometrics, 15*(6), 645–670. http://ideas.repec.org/a/jae/japmet/v15y2000i6p645-670.html

Sims, C. A., & Zha, T. (2006). Were there regime switches in US monetary policy. *American Economic Review, 96*(1), 54–81. https://www.jstor.org/stable/30034354

Smets, F., & Wouters, R. (2002). Openness, imperfect exchange rate pass-through and monetary policy. *Journal of Monetary Economics, 49*(5), 913–940.

Smets, F., & Wouters, R. (2003). An estimated dynamic stochastic general equilibrium model of the euro area. *Journal of the European Economic Association, 1*(5), 1123–1175. http://doi.wiley.com/10.1162/154247603770383415

Smets, F., & Wouters, R. (2007). Shocks and frictions in US business cycles: A Bayesian DSGE approach. *American Economic Review, 97*(3), 586–606.

Steinbach, M., du Plessis, S., & Smit, B. (2014). *A Medium-Sized Open Economy DSGE Model of South Africa*. South African Reserve Bank Working Paper Series WP/14/04.

Steinbach, M., Mathuloe, P., & Smit, B. (2009). An open economy New Keynesian DSGE model of the South African economy. *South African Journal of Economics, 77*(2), 207–227.

Stiglitz, J. E. (2011, August). Rethinking macroeconomics: What failed, and how to repair it. *Journal of the European Economic Association, 9*, 591–645.

Stiglitz, J. E. (2017). *Where Modern Macroeconomics Went Wrong*. NBER Working Paper 23795 (pp. 1–43). http://www.nber.org/papers/w23795

Stock, J. H., & Watson, M. W. (2003). *Has the business cycle changed and why?* Paper presented at the Monetary Policy and Uncertainty Symposium. Federal Reserve Bank of Kansas City. Jackson Hole, WY.

Svensson, L. E. O. (2003). Escaping from a liquidity trap and deflation: The foolproof way and others. *Journal of Economic Perspectives, 17*(4), 145–166. http://ideas.repec.org/a/aea/jecper/v17y2003i4p145-166.html

Taylor, J. B. (1993). Discretion versus rules in practice. *Carnegie-Rochester Conference Series on Public Policy, 39*, 195–214.

Tovar, C. E. (2009). DSGE models and central banks. *Economics: The Open-Access, Open-Assessment E-Journal, 3*(16), 1–31. Kiel Institute for the World Economy.

Venter, J. C. (2017). Obtaining clear and timely business cycle turning point signals with a composite leading business cycle indicator. *Studies in Economics and Econometrics, 41*(3), 39–59.

Vermeulen, C., Joubert, F., Bosch, A., & Rossouw, J. (2017). From the business cycle to the output cycle: Predicting South African economic activity. *Studies in Economics and Econometrics, 41*(2), 111–133.

Vines, D., & Wills, S. (2018). The rebuilding macroeconomic theory project: An analytical assessment. *Oxford Review of Economic Policy, 34*(1–2), 1–42. http://academic.oup.com/oxrep/article/34/1-2/1/4781821

Woodford, M. (2003). *Interest and prices: Foundations of a theory of monetary policy*. Princeton University Press. http://down.cenet.org.cn/upfile/8/20095311716591108.pdf

Woodford, M. (2007). The case for forecast targeting as a monetary policy strategy. *The Journal of Economic Perspectives, 21*(4), 3–24.

Wren-Lewis, S. (2018). Ending the microfoundations hegemony. *Oxford Review of Economic Policy, 34*(1–2), 55–69. http://academic.oup.com/oxrep/article/34/1-2/55/4781813

Wright, R. (2018). On the future of macroeconomics: A New Monetarist perspective. *Oxford Review of Economic Policy, 34*(1–2), 107–131. http://academic.oup.com/oxrep/article/34/1-2/107/4781807

Part IV
Predicting the South African Business Cycle

Business Confidence and the Business Cycle in South Africa

L. H. Binge

1 Introduction

Business confidence indicators, such as the European Commission's Economic Sentiment Index, are popular and useful leading indicators of economic activity in many countries (United Nations 2015). This is also the case in South Africa, where the Bureau for Economic Research's Business Confidence Index (BER BCI) is often quoted in the media and is included by the SARB as a leading indicator to identify official business cycle turning points (Bosch 2015). Given that business confidence indicators are popular and potentially useful, it is important to measure them as accurately as possible.

Only two business confidence indicators are regularly published for South Africa: the BER BCI and the South African Chamber of Commerce and Industry Business Confidence Index (SACCI BCI). The SACCI BCI is a composite measure of economic activity, rather than a measure of confidence in the way it is defined in the literature. The BER BCI is a measure of confidence derived from the BER's business tendency surveys.

This chapter estimates new proxies for business confidence in South Africa using microdata from the BER business tendency surveys, with the aim of refining the existing measures. The BER BCIs are calculated from the responses to a single question included in all of the surveys. The surveys contain a lot of additional information which can be incorporated to create more refined composite indicators. The weights assigned to these survey responses can also be applied in a more standardised and consistent manner, which may improve the accuracy of the indicators.

L. H. Binge (✉)
Department of Economics, Stellenbosch University, Stellenbosch, South Africa

W. H. Boshoff (ed.), *Business Cycles and Structural Change in South Africa*,
Advances in African Economic, Social and Political Development,
https://doi.org/10.1007/978-3-030-35754-2_8

The new and existing confidence indicators are then used to investigate the relationship between the business confidence indicators and real economic activity in South Africa. The idea that weak business confidence and heightened uncertainty contributed to a large extent to the Great Recession and to the lacklustre subsequent recovery has inspired a substantial international literature examining the impact of changes in sentiment on output and investment decisions. The International Monetary Fund (2017) cited elevated political uncertainty and weak consumer and business confidence when it marked down South Africa's growth forecast for 2018. However, to date there has been little research on business confidence in South Africa (e.g. Pellissier 2002), in part due to the difficulty of measurement.

The aim is to assess whether the confidence indicators are useful as leading indicators for the business cycle and whether they contain useful information about current and future economic developments. This chapter evaluates whether there is a significant positive relationship between the indicators and real GDP growth, the timing of this relationship, and whether it remains significant after taking other economic variables into account.

2 Confidence

One definition of business confidence concerns firms' perceptions of, or degree of optimism regarding, current business conditions and the expected future business climate (Mendicino and Punzi 2013). In this chapter, firms' perceptions of current and future business conditions are measured using the BER business tendency surveys. Two sets of composite confidence indicators are calculated, as the weighted cross-sectional mean of responses to questions on current and future business conditions.

This section provides a brief review of the literature on confidence. It begins with a review of the theoretical links between confidence and macroeconomic outcomes. The empirical literature is then discussed, focusing on the approaches to operationalising the definition of confidence, and the evidence on the impact of confidence on economic outcomes.

2.1 Theory on Confidence and Economic Outcomes

While confidence indicators are popular measures of economic activity with the media and business players, a review of the academic literature suggests three alternative views (Barsky and Sims 2012). These range from the view that confidence measures have an important causal role in the business cycle, to the view that they contain useful predictive information but play a limited causal role, to the view that they have no value, even in forecasting.

According to the so-called animal spirits view, psychological factors have a causal impact on economic fluctuations distinct from fundamentals (Carroll et al. 1994). This view is most closely associated with Keynes (1936), who argued that: 'Our decisions to do something positive, the full consequence of which will be drawn out over many days to come, can only be taken as a result of animal spirits - of a spontaneous urge to action rather than inaction, and not as the outcome of a weighted average of quantitative benefits multiplied by quantitative probabilities'. The original Keynesian view finds resonance in the more recent literature, with Akerlof and Shiller (2015) arguing that in the face of uncertainty, decisions about the future are based on animal spirits, rather than a weighted average of quantitative benefits and probabilities, as rational theory would dictate. According to the animal spirits view, therefore, confidence has a potentially important causal impact on economic outcomes.

In contrast, the so-called news view argues that confidence indicators contain useful predictive information for economic output, but play a limited causal role. According to the news view, any relationship between confidence indicators and subsequent real activity means that confidence indicators contain information about current and future economic fundamentals (Barsky and Sims 2012). Confidence can proxy for news that agents receive about future productivity, which is not yet reflected in econometricians' information sets, by aggregating information from various sources (Cochrane 1994; Barsky and Sims 2012). Confidence indicators reflect agents' expectations about future fundamentals and economic conditions, which are not summarised in other macroeconomic variables. When agents are optimistic, they give positive responses to surveys. These are confirmed, on average, and real activity eventually increases as predicted by the confidence indicator (Carroll et al. 1994).

From the rational expectations point of view, confidence should reflect the expected values of economic fundamentals and should not offer any additional predictive information (Beaudry and Portier 2004). However, a number of studies (e.g. Beaudry and Portier 2004; Van Aarle and Kappler 2012) analyse models where agents receive imperfect signals about future productivity growth and use these signals to make investment decisions. In this context, confidence refers to a state where agents receive an above-average signal, which may generate a wave of optimism. Rational agents then learn gradually about the true state of the economy and adjust their expectations. Other factors, such as frictions in capital markets, may also explain predictive information contained in confidence indicators (European Central Bank 2013).

The literature therefore sets out theoretical links between confidence and economic activity. However, it is not clear whether confidence indicators repackage information already contained in other economic variables, or whether they contain useful independent predictive information about the economy. If they contain predictive information, it is not clear whether they reflect animal spirits or aggregated information on agents' expectations of future outcomes not captured by the macroeconomic data (Mendicino and Punzi 2013; Akerlof and Shiller 2015).

2.2 Empirical Findings

Although the findings in the empirical literature have not been conclusive, the majority of studies seems to find that confidence indicators are at least positively related to real economic activity (Taylor and McNabb 2007). The inconclusive findings may be due to two main challenges: constructing proxies for confidence and establishing whether it has a separate causal impact on real economic activity.

Measuring Confidence

As confidence cannot be observed or measured directly (Santero and Westerlund 1996), analysts typically aggregate responses from business and consumer surveys. Survey-based indicators can be helpful in discovering key economic agents' opinions on current and future economic developments (Girardi and Reuter 2017). Survey-based confidence indicators have the advantage that they are published long before the official statistics become available and are not subject to revision (European Central Bank 2013).

These surveys usually contain a small number of qualitative questions, which can be answered quickly by respondents. Indicators are derived from the subjective answers to questions on past, current, and future developments. The assumption is that agents form opinions about economic conditions before a specific business activity is implemented (e.g. new production plans, employment, or purchases). These opinions may be called 'confidence'.

The most common and widely used method to aggregate survey responses is to calculate balance statistics. In the context of business tendency surveys, balances are averages of survey responses. For most survey questions, there are three reply options, e.g. 'up', 'the same', or 'down'. Balances are calculated as the difference between the percentage of positive answers and negative answers. Balances are simple to calculate and understand and are considered both practical and entirely adequate for cyclical analysis (Organisation for Economic Co-operation and Development 2003).

Although balances are by far the most common method used by statistical agencies and analysts to aggregate survey responses, a few more sophisticated methods have been discussed in the literature, including a probabilistic approach, a regression approach, and a latent factor approach (Nardo 2003). However, these approaches usually require actual quantitative reference series for the relevant variables, which is restrictive in the case of business confidence. Moreover, these methods can become unreliable when exceptional events have a large impact on the correlation between the survey data and the quantitative reference data (United Nations 2015). Nevertheless, the evidence suggests that balance statistics tend to produce indicators that are very similar to those produced by more sophisticated methods (Organisation for Economic Co-operation and Development 2003; Driver and Urga 2004). Weighted balance statistics are therefore used in this chapter to calculate summary statistics of the responses to each survey question.

Two indicators of confidence are published in South Africa: the BER BCI and the SACCI BCI. The SACCI BCI is a composite index of 13 quantitative sub-indices thought to have the greatest influence on the business mood. These include the exchange rate, inflation, the prime rate, retail sales volumes, credit extension, commodity prices, import and export volumes, new vehicle sales, utility services, manufacturing production, building plans passed, and the stock market index. The SACCI BCI is an ex post measure of actual activity, which is dependent on external macroeconomic variables. The rationale is that recent business activity is indicative of the degree of business confidence (SACCI 2011). In this sense, the SACCI BCI is a composite measure of economic activity, or synthetic GDP tracker, rather than a confidence indicator in the way it is defined in the literature.

The BER BCI is constructed from the BER's quarterly business tendency surveys, which are similar to the business tendency surveys conducted all over the world, including the European Commission Business Tendency Surveys and the German Ifo Business Climate Survey (Organisation for Economic Co-operation and Development 2003). The BER BCI has proved useful as a leading indicator of the business cycle in South Africa. It is used by the SARB as one of the twelve leading indicator series to date official business cycle turning points (Venter 2005). In a later chapter in this volume, Venter (2020) provides a comprehensive discussion of the SARB's composite leading business cycle indicator.

In calculating survey-based business confidence indicators, the most important issues are which survey questions to use and the weights applied to the responses. The BER BCI is constructed from a specific question (Q1) that appears in all of the surveys: 'Are prevailing business conditions: satisfactory or unsatisfactory?' The BCI is the weighted percentage of respondents who rated prevailing business conditions as 'satisfactory' and is therefore based on the perceptions of firms (Kershoff 2002).

According to Kershoff (2000) there are two reasons for the use of this single question to construct the confidence indicator. Firstly, it is reasonable to assume that respondents who are satisfied with business conditions will have more confidence than those experiencing unsatisfactory conditions. Secondly, respondents take a variety of factors into account when rating prevailing business conditions, which solves the problem of weighting different factors (Kershoff 2000).

In line with international best practice, all survey responses are weighted (except for the building survey). Each response is multiplied by a factor, which is calculated as the product of a firm size weight and a subsector size weight (except for the motor trade, where there are no subsectors). Each firm receives a weighting in relation to turnover, or the size of workforce in the case of manufacturing. The subsector size weights are based on the composition of production or sales in each subsector, as calculated by StatsSA. Balances are calculated to obtain five indices for the most cyclically sensitive sectors: manufacturing, building contractors, retailers, wholesalers, and new vehicle dealers.[1] The BER BCI is calculated as the unweighted mean of these five indices.

The BER BCI is therefore a measure of current conditions based on a specific question, similar to the one calculated by the Confederation of British Industries for the UK. It has a somewhat inconsistent weighting procedure, in that it weights all sectors except for building and uses the unweighted mean of the five sectoral indices. This is done to keep the calculation of the index simple and easily understandable for the public. Previous research has suggested that the costs in terms of added complexity do not necessarily outweigh the benefits in terms of a more reliable index (Organisation for Economic Co-operation and Development 2003; Kershoff 2015). In contrast to some other international cases, the BER BCI is not designed specifically to be a leading indicator of the business cycle or a GDP growth tracker.

Internationally, the balances from multiple questions are often used to calculate composite confidence indicators. A prominent example is the German Ifo Business Climate Index, which is computed as a geometric mean of the balances referring to the current business situation and the business outlook in the next 6 months (United Nations 2015). The results for the manufacturing, construction, wholesale, and retail sectors are weighted according to the importance of the industry. The European Commission builds composite indicators by aggregating the survey responses from five sectors, using multiple questions on current and expected conditions (Organisation for Economic Co-operation and Development 2003). The aggregate Economic Sentiment Index is a weighted average of confidence in the manufacturing, construction, retail, and services sectors, as well as for consumers (European Central Bank 2013). It is designed to have good leading indicator properties.

As no single cause explains all cyclical fluctuations over the long term, it is useful to have information from many possible sources of change, i.e. to use all potentially important information (Van Aarle and Kappler 2012). Composite indicators have the capacity to react to various sources of economic fluctuations, while being resilient to fluctuations affecting single components. They often have fewer false alarms and fewer missed turning points than individual components and tend to have more stable lead times (European Central Bank 2013).

The BER surveys contain a number of questions on current and expected future developments, including questions about sales, inventories, orders, prices, employment, and business constraints. All of these potentially have an impact on business confidence. As the surveys contain questions on expectations, forward-looking responses may also provide valuable information. In this chapter, composite confidence indicators are calculated by incorporating the responses to a number of questions. The new indicators are also calculated with a more consistent and standard weighting procedure. These indicators are then used to investigate the

[1] For this reason, the BER includes only main building contractors, and not sub-contractors. It also excludes the other services sectors, until more information on their cyclical behaviour becomes available.

relationship between confidence and economic activity. The following section provides a review of the evidence on the impact of confidence on economic outcomes.

The Impact of Confidence

The majority of studies seems to find that confidence indicators are at least positively related to real economic activity, although this does not necessarily imply a causal relationship (European Central Bank 2013). Confidence indicators have been found to be useful in some cases as leading indicators, as well as for forecasting, even after controlling for other economic variables.

The empirical literature has often investigated the extent to which confidence indicators contain predictive information over and above economic fundamentals (United Nations 2015). A number of studies have shown that both consumer and business confidence indicators provided valuable information for forecasting real activity, which was not contained in other economic variables (e.g. Santero and Westerlund 1996; Ludvigson 2004; Kabundi 2004; Parigi and Golinelli 2004; Taylor and McNabb 2007; Leduc and Sill 2013; Mendicino and Punzi 2013; Kilic and Cankaya 2016). In an influential study, Barsky and Sims (2012) found that positive shocks to consumer confidence led to significant, slow-building, and permanent responses in consumption and income. If confidence contained no news about future fundamentals, and reflected only 'animal spirits', one would expect transitory responses. They concluded that their results supported the 'news' view of confidence.

The European Central Bank (2013) found that confidence indicators can play a significant role in predicting recessions. They included the European Consumer Sentiment Index, along with the OECD leading indicator for the euro area in a probit model. The model captured business cycle phases relatively well, with probabilities increasing when recessions occurred. The drawback was that probabilities also increased in some periods without recessions, i.e. there were some false positives.

Even in cases where confidence indicators are just a synthesis of economic variables and the unique information content is limited, the timeliness of survey indicators may make them useful for monitoring economic developments and for real-time forecasting (Gayer et al. 2014). In the euro area, for instance, official statistics are released at least 45 days after the reference month, while business surveys are usually available before the end of the reference month. The BER BCI is published between 2 and 4 weeks before the end of the reference quarter. Confidence indicators can provide valuable information on the evolution of the economy over this period, which is one of the reasons why they are popular (Parigi and Golinelli 2004). In this sense, even if confidence indicators have a contemporaneous relationship with real activity, that they are available earlier means that they are quasi-leading indicators.

A number of studies have demonstrated that confidence indicators are useful for nowcasting economic activity. Giannone et al. (2008), Matheson (2010), and Gayer et al. (2014) evaluated the impact of new releases of financial, real, and survey data on nowcasting GDP throughout each quarter. They found that business survey indicators improved real-time forecasting accuracy. Confidence indicators contained predictive content even after controlling for timeliness, due to their broad sectoral coverage and forward-looking nature.

In South Africa the relationship between business confidence and the real economy has been established in the past (Smit 1984; Pellissier and Smit 1994). Smit (1983) was the first to investigate the relationship between the BER opinion surveys and the business cycle. He found that series derived from the surveys had significant relationships with the expenditure components of the business cycle, and that it was possible to make reasonably accurate short-term forecasts using the survey data.

Relatively few recent studies have analysed business confidence in South Africa. Pellissier (2002) argued that the BER BCI and SACCI BCI seemed to exhibit a coincident rather than a leading relationship with the business cycle, and that the BER BCI seemed to display stable turning point attributes. More recently, Laubscher (2014) found that the BER BCI was one of the closest predictors of the official reference business cycle turning points and could improve estimates of cyclical turning points. This is particularly useful in view of the early availability of the index. The BER index results for a particular quarter are available approximately 2 months before the official GDP estimates (Kershoff 2000). Kabundi et al. (2016) included the BER Consumer Confidence Index and the SACCI BCI in a large dataset to forecast real GDP growth in South Africa in real time. They argued that the timeliness of the indicators was especially important.

This chapter attempts to establish whether there is a significant positive relationship between the confidence indicators and real GDP growth, the timing of this relationship, and whether it remains significant after taking other economic variables into account.

3 Data: The BER Business Tendency Surveys

The BER, a research institute attached to Stellenbosch University, has been conducting quarterly business tendency surveys in South Africa since March 1954. During the second month of each quarter, questionnaires are sent to firms in each of the manufacturing, construction, trade (i.e. retail, wholesale, and motor vehicles), and other services sectors. The questionnaires are completed by senior executives of the firms. The questions have remained largely unchanged since inception, and include those on current and expected future developments regarding, among others, sales, orders, inventories, prices, employment, and constraints. For the most part, the survey answers fall into three categories: ‘up’, ‘the same’, or ‘down’.

Stratified deliberate sampling is used to design the BER’s survey panels, which is the international norm. Participants are selected to be representative of particular sectors, regions, and firm sizes. The respondents are reviewed periodically to ensure reasonable representation of the population universe. The exact number of firms in the universe is unknown to the BER, as censuses of the business sector are not conducted regularly and the BER does not have access to the National Business Register (Kershoff 2002). Practical experience has shown that non-random samples can give acceptable results in conducting these types of surveys (Organisation for Economic Co-operation and Development 2003).

The BER makes no provision for firms that were not selected or did not respond during sampling, implicitly assuming that the non-participating or non-responding firms have the same distribution as the responding firms for the period. This corresponds with the 'missing at random' assumption suggested by the European Commission (2006). Kershoff (2015) argued that this is a reasonable assumption, given that the responses cannot vary infinitely, and the same factors influence firms in the same sector.

The sample of firms remains relatively stable from one survey to the next, effectively creating a panel. The panel is partly fixed and partly rotating. The fixed part reflects the opinions of the same firms over time, which ensures that the results remain comparable between surveys. The results are more likely to reflect changes in the variables under consideration than changes in the sample from one survey to the next (Kershoff 2002). Every 2–3 years the BER removes slightly more than 25% of all respondents from the panel, because they became inactive. The BER tries to ensure that the new recruits are representative of the population, but this does mean that few firms are present throughout the sample period. While the sample of firms remains relatively stable for consecutive surveys, over longer periods the firms respond sporadically and enter and exit the sample often.

Table 1 reports the details of the survey responses, which have been collated into a single micro-database. The sample runs from 1992Q1 to 2016Q3.[2] In 2005Q2 the BER also started to survey 'other services', which covers business services, catering and accommodation, transport and storage, real estate, and community and personal services.[3] The results from these surveys are not currently published, as the BER has not validated them.[4] As the microdata from these survey are available, they are included in the new composite indicators. Around 1000 completed questionnaires are received every quarter, leading to an overall sample size of 119,438. All of the surveys have a few missing quarters, when the microeconomic data was lost. The overall panel sizes have remained relatively stable over time.

In order to be representative, panels have to include a minimum number of participants, which depends on the level of aggregation and the size of the

[2]The microdata for architects, quantity surveyors, and civil engineers are only available from 2001Q1.

[3]It excludes financial, telecommunication, postal, government, and other cultural services. Its coverage is therefore narrower than the quarterly GDP numbers for the services sector.

[4]The 'other services' survey results are preliminary and have been provided to the authors to complete their research. According to the BER, of the various 'other services' subsectors, so far the cycle of only land freight transport services appears to co-move with the other typical cyclical sectors at the peaks.

Table 1 Sample characteristics

Sector	Sample	Total Obs	Obs/Quarter	Missing quarters
Manufacturing	1992Q1–2016Q3	36,915	384.53	1997Q4, 2000Q1, 2005Q4
Construction	1993Q2–2016Q3	28,139	312.66	1993Q4, 1998Q3, 2000Q2, 2005Q4
Trade	1992Q2–2016Q3	40,480	426.11	1992Q4, 1993Q3, 2005Q4
Other services	2005Q2–2016Q3	13,904	308.98	2005Q4
Total	1992Q1–2016Q3	119,438	1218.76	2005Q4

population universe. The results often remain valid even if the sample size is small and the response rate relatively low. According to the Organisation for Economic Co-operation and Development (2003), even as few as 30 respondents might be sufficient to obtain an acceptable level of precision for each stratum. This is because the variance of responses for ordinal-scaled data based on a stable panel is lower than for quantitative data derived from independent surveys. Moreover, certain activities are dominated by a few large firms. Representativeness therefore has a smaller impact on qualitative survey results than on quantitative survey results. A panel that is not fully representative will probably produce similar results to a fully representative one (Kershoff 2002).

Kershoff (2002) found that the degree of representation of the BER's construction and trade panels adequately reflects the universes, taking response rates into account and comparing the composition of the survey panels with census and other official data.

In order to test whether the entry and exit patterns of firms drive the results, a number of robustness tests are carried out. The indicators are calculated by including only firms that form part of smaller, more 'stable', samples. The smaller samples include firms that only responded to consecutive surveys, firms that responded to more than half of all the surveys, and firms that responded to more than 75% of all surveys, respectively. The indicators based on these smaller samples are similar to those for the full sample. This implies that these firms are driving the results, rather than the entry and exit patterns of firms.

4 Methodology

This section provides the methodology for calculating the confidence indicators based on the microdata from the BER business tendency surveys. As the indicators are based on subjective survey responses, they are prone to bias. Tversky and Kahneman (1974) showed that agents rely on a number of heuristics, which reduce the complex tasks of assessing probabilities and predicting values to simpler judgmental operations. In general these heuristics are useful, but sometimes lead to severe and systematic biases.

Anchoring and adjusting is one such heuristic, which entails anchoring with what is well-known, or easily recalled from memory, and then adjusting from that anchor (Tversky and Kahneman 1974). With anchoring, a respondent's view of the future is anchored in how they feel at present. Moreover, Gehlbach and Barge (2012) showed that survey respondents use anchoring and adjusting, where their response to an initial survey item provides an anchor from which they (insufficiently) adjust in answering the subsequent item, especially when adjacent items on the survey are similar. Thus, over the course of a survey, responses to adjacent item-pairs are likely to be more similar than responses to the same item-pairs in non-adjacent positions. Because the questions in the BER surveys are similar, and the questions on current conditions and those on expected conditions are adjacent, this bias may well be present. The subjective survey responses and the resulting subjective confidence and uncertainty indicators will consequently reflect this bias.

Arguably, there are three types of information contained in these survey responses (Fuhrer 1988). The first reflects current developments or economic news, not yet reflected in currently available standard macroeconomic time series (e.g. changes in firms' inventory levels). The second type reflects forward-looking information, such as agents' probabilistic assessments of uncertain future policy changes (e.g. impending tax legislation). The third type reflects 'animal spirits', where agents feel optimistic or pessimistic about future prospects for reasons not tied to fundamentals.

The significant correlations between the subjective survey-based indicators and real output in the literature (as well as in this chapter) suggest that the indicators capture at least one of these types of information. The first type of information anticipates data which will be released later. The second type may provide information about events that are either difficult to quantify or predict from the past (Fuhrer 1988). Thus, they summarise changes in agents' beliefs, i.e. their private information (Acemoglu and Scott 1994). If agents act on animal spirits, which are reflected in survey data, the third type of information will explain subsequent economic outcomes due to self-fulfilling behaviour (Fuhrer 1988).

When the agents respond to the questionnaires, they are most likely making an estimate that is partly based on the fundamentals (the first two types of information) and partly based on psychological factors or animal spirits, all of which probably contain biases. To the extent that the indicators reflect psychological factors, the biases capture the psychological phenomenon of confidence, i.e. agents' perceptions or degree of optimism about the future. If animal spirits influence behaviour, over and above fundamentals, these biased measures will determine agents' decisions to some extent and thereby might influence the business cycle. Thus, biased measures are still of interest if they reflect possibly biased psychological factors.

To the extent that the indicators summarise fundamental information, possibly in a biased way, the indicators still provide timely information on current developments, or information on expectations about events that are difficult to quantify. The proof of the usefulness of these potentially biased measures of fundamentals will be in their comovement with output. Even if the indicators are subject to biases and measurement error, they still seem to contain useful additional information on agents' expectations that is not contained in standard macroeconomic variables (Fuhrer 1988).

4.1 Measuring Confidence

Formally, one can define a k-period-ahead expectations measure of confidence (C_t^k) at time t as: $C_t^k = E_t f(\Delta^h Y_{t+k})$, where Y_{t+k} is a measure of real activity (usually output) at time $t+k$ and $\Delta^h Y_{t+k} = Y_{t+k} - Y_{t+k-h}$. A common definition of $f(\Delta^h Y_{t+k})$ relies on an up, unchanged, or down classification (e.g. Q2A in the BER survey):

$$f(\Delta^h Y_{t+k}) = \begin{cases} -1, & \text{if} \Delta^h Y_{t+k} < 0 \\ 0, & \text{if} \Delta^h Y_{t+k} = 0 \\ 1, & \text{if} \Delta^h Y_{t+k} > 0 \end{cases}$$

An alternative would be to use a binary classification in levels (e.g. Q1 in the BER survey):

$$f(Y_{t+k}) = \begin{cases} -1, & \text{if} Y_{t+k} < a \\ 1, & \text{if} Y_{t+k} \geq a \end{cases}$$

where a is determined by the preferences of the agent. In this case a is the subjective benchmark or threshold that determines when conditions are 'satisfactory', and the measure of confidence simplifies to: $C_t^k = E_t f(Y_{t+k})$.

Similar to the Ifo Business Climate and University of Michigan surveys (Ludvigson 2004), this chapter calculates two sets of composite confidence indicators: those relating to current conditions C_t^k when $k = 0$, which reflect confidence about the current quarter (in the second month of the quarter); and those relating to expected conditions C_t^k when $k = 1$, which reflect confidence about the following quarter.

The BER business tendency surveys make this distinction possible by asking for separate responses relating to current and expected future conditions. The questions on current conditions (e.g. Q2A) all have the following format: '(Estimated development in current quarter) Compared with the same quarter of a year ago, are general business conditions: better, the same, or poorer?' In other words, these questions ask whether the factor under consideration in time t is better, the same, or poorer, compared with $t - 4$.

The forward-looking questions (e.g. Q2P) all have the following format: '(Expected development in next quarter) Compared with the same quarter of a year ago, will general business conditions be: better, the same, or poorer?' As with the questions on current conditions, these questions ask whether the factor under consideration in time $t + 1$ is expected to be better, the same, or poorer, compared with $t-3$. Responses are relative to the same quarter of the previous year, which corresponds with year-on-year growth rates.

Although the survey questions imply that seasonal adjustment is not required, a common challenge is that respondents may not use the correct reference period when answering the question (Organisation for Economic Co-operation and Development 2003). For example, answers to the forward-looking questions may compare expected outcomes in the next quarter $t+1$ with period t, instead of with period $t-3$. In many cases, the time series of balances show some residual seasonality. The indicators are therefore adjusted for seasonality (United Nations 2015).

As discussed above, confidence indicators are almost always based on balance statistics, which present a single figure summarising the responses of all participants to a particular question (Santero and Westerlund 1996). It is the cross-sectional mean of survey responses if the standard quantification system is used: 'better' is quantified by +1, 'the same' by 0, and 'poorer' by -1. Confidence in period t relating to current conditions C_t^0 and confidence in period t relating to expected conditions C_t^1 may be defined as:

$$C_t^0 = \frac{1}{W_t}\sum_{i=1}^{N} w_{it} E_t f(\Delta^4 Y_{i,t})$$

$$C_t^1 = \frac{1}{W_t}\sum_{i=1}^{N} w_{it} E_t f(\Delta^4 Y_{i,t+1}),$$

where $Y_{i,t+k}$ is again a measure of real activity at time $t+k$ for firm $i = 1, \ldots, N$; $\Delta^h Y_{i,t+k} = Y_{i,t+k} - Y_{i,t+k-h}$ for firm i; w_{it} is the weight that each firm i receives at time t; and $W_t = \sum_{i=1}^{N} w_i$ is the sum of the weights.

The weights are calculated as: $w_{it} = f_{it}s_{jt}/F_{jt}$, where f_{it} is the firm size weight (i.e. the inner weight reflecting turnover) for firm i at time t; s_{jt} is the subsector weight (i.e. the outer weight reflecting the share of total value added) for subsector j at time t; and $F_{jt} = \sum_{i=1}^{N} f_{it}$ is the total firm weight for subsector j at time t. These weights are equivalent to an explicit two-step weighting procedure, whereby weighted means are calculated for each subsector separately (using firm size weights), and then aggregated with the subsector weights (United Nations 2015). The BER uses similar weights, except that they equal the product of firm and subsector weights $w_{it} = f_{it}s_{jt}$, without dividing by the total firm weight for the subsector F_{jt}.

Firm size weights are recorded by the BER for all respondents. The firm size weights are divided into nine categories. These firm size weights are applied to all the responses in all of the subsectors. The subsector weights for the manufacturing, retail, and wholesale subsectors are updated periodically by the BER, based on the composition of production or sales in each subsector, as calculated by StatsSA. Subsector weights are not recorded for the construction, motor vehicle, and other services sectors. In this chapter, the relative subsector weights for these three sectors are set equal to the average number of respondents for each subsector over the period. The results are similar when using an equal weighting procedure.

Experience has shown that the balances are not very sensitive to the choice of weighting procedure (Organisation for Economic Co-operation and Development 2003). In this case the specific weighting procedure adopted does not significantly alter the results. Indeed, the unweighted versions of the indicators, calculated by stacking all of the available responses from the surveys are similar to the weighted versions. This confirms the findings by Kershoff (2015), who showed that the balance statistics were not very sensitive to the use of the following alternative weighting procedures: a different allocation of firm size weights; the introduction of dynamic individual weights to provide for changes in response patterns; the application of a two-step weighting procedure; the inclusion of latecomers to increase the number of responses; and the use of different sector size weights for export variables.

The weighted means are calculated for each question separately. The BER surveys contain a number of questions that may be useful in gauging business sentiment in South Africa. These include questions on general business conditions, production, orders placed, employment, and profitability. Many international institutions calculate composite confidence indicators by combining the responses to a number of questions (European Central Bank 2013).

This chapter therefore combines the responses to a number of questions in the BER surveys to calculate composite indicators. For consistency, the composite indicators are derived from questions that are present in most of the sectoral surveys. Table 2 reports the questions included in each of the sectoral surveys. These questions cover five types of variables, namely business conditions, activity (production or sales), orders placed, employment, and profitability. The measure of confidence about current conditions also includes the question (Q1) on business satisfaction used to calculate the BER BCI. The composite sectoral indicators are calculated as the average of the weighted balances for the questions in each sector, as reported in Table 2. The results are similar if the different questions are combined using principal components rather than averages. The four indicators for the four main sectors are then weighted by GDP share to form the overall aggregate composite indicators (United Nations 2015).[5]

4.2 *The Impact of Confidence*

As many economic variables move together over time, without an obvious causal direction, it can be challenging to identify the directions of relationships. Timing has often been relied on for identification in the literature. In this chapter, the

[5]The trade and 'other services' indicators are slightly over-weighted, in the sense that the survey coverage is narrower than the quarterly GDP numbers for these sectors.

Table 2 Survey questions used by sector

Survey question	Manufacturing	Construction	Trade	Other services
Business conditions	X	X	X	X
Activity	X	X	X	X
Employment	X	X	X	X
Profitability		X	X	X
Orders Placed	X		X	

literature (e.g. Taylor and McNabb 2007; Barsky and Sims 2012) is followed in using standard recursive VARs to trace out the dynamic responses of economic activity to surprise shocks in confidence. The aim is to investigate whether the indicators have a significant dynamic relationship with real output, whether they contain predictive content for output growth, and whether shocks to confidence generate responses that are in line with the findings in the literature, even after controlling for other economic variables.

The relationship is investigated for the aggregate variables, as well as separately for each sector, using bivariate recursive VARs featuring a measure of confidence and real GDP growth. In the bivariate VAR, both variables are treated as endogenous:

$$y_t = \beta_{10} - \beta_{12} z_t + \gamma_{11} y_{t-1} + \gamma_{12} z_{t-1} + \epsilon_{yt}$$

$$z_t = \beta_{20} - \beta_{21} y_t + \gamma_{21} y_{t-1} + \gamma_{22} z_{t-1} + \epsilon_{zt}$$

where y is the output, z is the confidence indicator, and ϵ is the residual of each equation.

A range of VARs are estimated for the quarterly data running from 1992Q1 to 2016Q3. The indicators enter in levels, while the real GDP series enter as annual quarter-on-quarter growth rates, e.g. 2015Q1 over 2014Q1, which corresponds with the survey reference period. Unit root tests indicate that virtually all of the aggregate and sectoral indicators and the real GDP growth rates are stationary. The exception is real GDP growth in the services sector, which may be due to the shorter sample period. The appropriate number of lags is selected by means of the Akaike information criterion (AIC), the Schwarz criterion (SC), and the Hannan–Quinn criterion (HQ). The most parsimonious model is selected, provided that the diagnostic tests are satisfied (i.e. no serial correlation, homoscedasticity, and normality). In the majority of cases, the information criteria point to two lags. The model fit is best when a constant term is included.

The confidence indicators are ordered first in a recursive identification strategy, with the Cholesky decomposition used to identify structural shocks. With this ordering, shocks to confidence are allowed to have a contemporaneous impact on output, but shocks to output have no contemporaneous impact on confidence ($\beta_{21} = 0$). In other words, innovations to the confidence indicators influence economic output on impact, but not vice versa. This is the identification strategy and ordering used in the literature (e.g. Leduc and Sill 2013; Girardi and Reuter 2017; Baker et al. 2016). It can be motivated by the timing of the surveys before the release of most macroeconomic data (Leduc and Liu 2016). When the survey is completed in time t, the respondents do not know the realisations of output growth in time t, as the response deadline is generally the second month of the quarter.

5 Results

This section presents the composite sectoral and aggregate business confidence indicators for South Africa. Simple linear interpolation is used for the few missing quarters. The indicators are evaluated according to their comovement with real GDP (value added) growth, as well as their concordance with the official SARB reference cycle, to assess their usefulness as leading indicators of the business cycle.

5.1 Confidence Indicators

Figure 1 illustrates the weighted composite confidence indicators on current and expected conditions for the four sectors. The new indicators are compared with each sector's BER indicator[6] and sectoral real GDP growth.[7] Real GDP growth is calculated as year-on-year growth rates, which corresponds to the reference period in the BER surveys. Given that all the BER's questions that refer to change refer to the same period of a year ago, the year-on-year growth rate is the appropriate reference series. The BER surveys of the manufacturing and construction sectors agree with their corresponding GDP sector classification. For the other two sectors, there is the caveat that the survey coverage is narrower than the corresponding quarterly GDP numbers. For instance, the trade indicator excludes accommodation and retail fuel, while the other services indicator excludes financial, telecommunication, postal, government, and other cultural services.

[6]The new confidence indicators differ from the BER BCIs in a number of ways. First, the new confidence indicators are composite indicators that combine the responses to five types of variables. Second, the new indicators include all of the construction subsectors and the survey of 'other services'. Third, the new indicators use weights that are equivalent to an explicit two-step weighting procedure, whereby weighted means are calculated for each subsector separately, and then aggregated with the subsector weightings. Fourth, the new indicators use simple linear firm weights, as opposed to exponential firm weights, based on the size categories. Fifth, the new indicators weigh all of the sectors in the same way. Sixth, the new sectoral series are aggregated with weights based on GDP value added shares to create the overall confidence indicators.

[7]The corresponding reference series for the BER's surveys are manufacturing production, buildings completed, and sales volumes. This differs from the GDP value added series, which exclude intermediate demand.

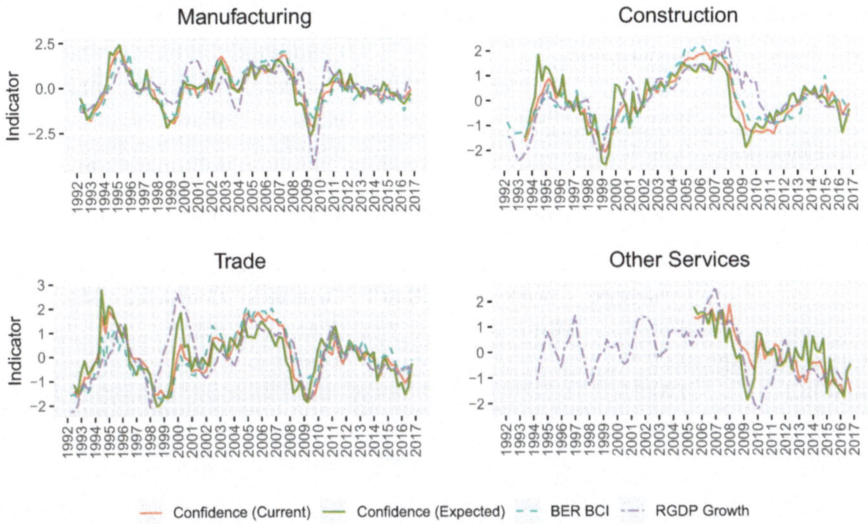

Fig. 1 Sectoral confidence indicators compared to real sectoral GDP growth

The indicators appear to capture cyclical movements in the sectors. In general, they display an increase in the early 1990s until just after the first Democratic Elections in 1994Q2. They show a sustained decrease from 1995 into the downswing of 1997–1998, associated with the East Asian and Russian crises. After troughs around the start of 1999, the indicators increase up to the global financial crisis at the end of 2007. During this extended upswing phase, the manufacturing and trade sectors reflect the two ambiguous periods in 2001 and 2003, when contractions in the SARB leading and coincident indicators obliged an evaluation of possible reference turning points (Venter 2005). The construction sector exhibited a particularly strong and sustained increase in confidence during this upswing phase, possibly due to the construction projects associated with hosting the FIFA World Cup in 2010.

The global financial crisis was followed by a large decline in the indicators for all of the sectors, which continued into the subsequent Great Recession. There was a relatively quick recovery in confidence in the manufacturing and trade sectors. Confidence in the construction sector showed a more gradual recovery, especially in confidence on current conditions. For 'other services', confidence on current conditions showed a slight recovery and then continued to decline, whereas confidence on expected conditions was quite erratic. The indicators for the other sectors exhibit a gradual decrease from around 2012, continuing into the downswing phase at the end of the sample period.

Table 3 reports the contemporaneous correlations of the sectoral indicators and their respective sectoral real GDP growth rates. All the indicators are highly positively correlated with real sectoral GDP growth rates. This is the case even though the survey coverage does not perfectly match GDP sector classification.

Table 3 Correlations between sectoral confidence and real sectoral GDP growth

	Manufacturing			Construction		
	Confidence (Cur)	Confidence (Exp)	BER BCI	Confidence (Cur)	Confidence (Exp)	BER BCI
Confidence (Exp)	0.94***			0.89***		
BER BCI	0.92***	0.85***		0.94***	0.75***	
RGDP Growth	0.68***	0.68***	0.61***	0.74***	0.56***	0.76***
	Trade			**Other services**		
	Confidence (Cur)	Confidence (Exp)	BER BCI	Confidence (Cur)	Confidence (Exp)	BER BCI
Confidence (Exp)	0.87***			0.76***		
BER BCI	0.90***	0.72***				
RGDP Growth	0.61***	0.59***	0.56***	0.76***	0.57***	

***$p < 0.01$

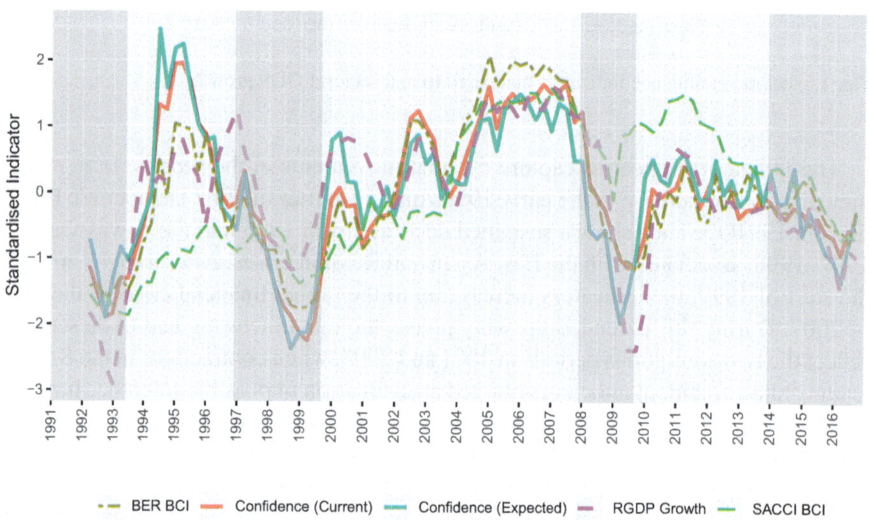

Fig. 2 Aggregate confidence indicators compared to real GDP growth

For the most part, the current conditions confidence indicators exhibit the highest correlation with the reference series.

Figure 2 illustrates the new aggregate confidence indicators, the BER and SACCI BCIs, as well as real GDP growth. The indicators appear to be strongly pro-cyclical, and follow real GDP growth closely. The shaded areas denote the cyclical downturns according to the official turning points of the SARB. The indicators appear to match the different phases of the business cycle relatively well, as is discussed in more detail below.

The indicators exhibit an increase following the downswing of the early 1990s, with peaks around 1995. There is a prolonged decrease into the downswing of 1997–

Table 4 Correlations between confidence indicators and real GDP growth

	Confidence (current)	Confidence (expected)	BER BCI	SACCI growth
Confidence (current)				
Confidence (expected)	0.92***			
BER BCI	0.93***	0.82***		
SACCI BCI growth	0.35***	0.48***	0.30***	
Real GDP growth	0.78***	0.70***	0.75***	0.24**

**$p < 0.05$; ***$p < 0.01$

1998, and a strong recovery just before the official trough in 1999. Both ambiguous periods are reflected in moderate decreases in the indicators in 2001 and 2003. Both indicators exhibit a significant decrease following the global financial crisis in 2007, and a relatively mild recovery just before the official trough in 2009. The indicators are relatively flat during the previous upswing phase (2010–2013) and decrease gradually during the downswing phase at the end of the sample period. The survey-based confidence indicators therefore appear to be plausible and potentially useful indicators of business confidence in South Africa.

Table 4 reports the contemporaneous correlations of the indicators and real GDP growth. The SACCI BCI is converted to growth rates, calculated as year-on-year growth rates, in order to remove unit roots. All the indicators exhibit a significant positive correlation with one another and with real GDP growth. The current conditions confidence indicator has a marginally higher contemporaneous correlation with real GDP growth than the existing indicators. The correlation between the expected conditions confidence indicator and real GDP growth in the following quarter is marginally higher than its correlation with contemporaneous growth. The results suggest that the indicators are all potentially useful leading or quasi-leading indicators of real activity.

Turning Points

An accurate leading indicator should show general conformity to economic activity (i.e. a high correlation), as well as a consistent matching of turning points with the reference cycle. In an earlier chapter in this volume, Boshoff and Du Plessis (2020) provided a comprehensive discussion of the properties of leading indicators and their relation to the reference cycle. Although there are too few cycles over the sample period to analyse cyclical turning points in full detail, it is still of interest to assess whether the indicators behave in a systematic way around cyclical turning points. In other words, do they systematically lead, coincide with, or lag the peaks and troughs of the business cycle.

The turning points in the indicators are determined where they breach the zero threshold, i.e. they indicate an upswing when they are positive and a downswing when they are negative. The two new indicators and the BER BCI are standardised, as their means are below zero over the sample period, and the SACCI BCI enters

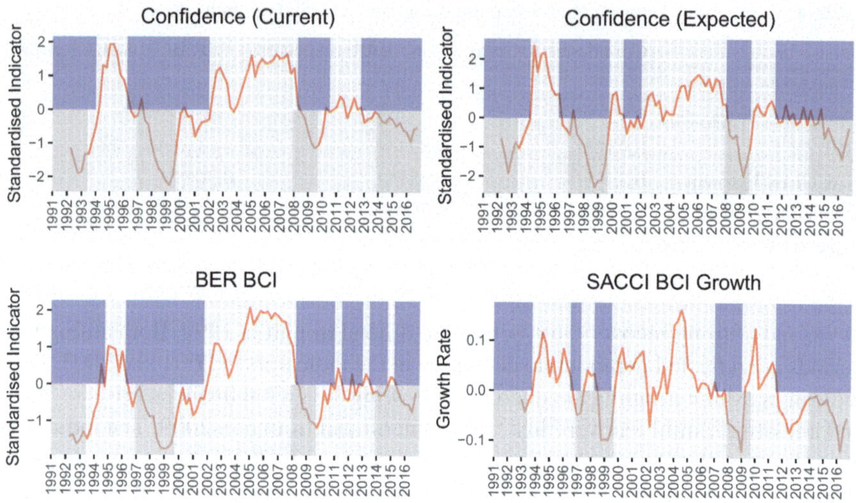

Fig. 3 Confidence indicator turning points compared to the official SARB turning points

in growth rates. Censoring rules are used to ensure that phases and cycles have a minimum duration, similar to those used in the so-called Bry–Boschan method (Bry and Boschan 1971). Following the suggestion of Harding and Pagan (2002), who developed a variant of this method for dealing with quarterly data (the BBQ method), a censoring rule based on a minimum of two quarters for each phase and five quarters for a full cycle is applied.

The resulting phases are illustrated in Fig. 3, with the downswing phases shaded. The top panel of each graph illustrates the turning points of the confidence indices, while the bottom panel of each graph shows the official SARB reference turning points.[8] The sample period includes three upswing phases and four downswing phases. In addition, in 2001 and 2003 the SARB indicators pointed to possible reference turning points. Although the SARB decided at the time that neither of these periods qualified, subsequent data revisions have shown that in hindsight there could have been official peaks, especially in 2003, if the dating procedure had been followed mechanically (Venter 2005).

The algorithm identifies four downswing phases in the current conditions confidence indicator and five in the expected conditions confidence indicator. These correspond to the official downswing phases, with the additional downswing phase

[8]The SARB's monthly business cycle dates were converted to their corresponding quarters, to agree with the BER's survey frequency. This involves an inevitable loss of detail and some potential inaccuracies. For example, if the SARB dates a turning point in April (Q2), while the confidence indicator indicates a turning point in the first quarter, it appears as if the BER data leads the cyclical indicator by one quarter, whereas the actual lead would only be 1 month.

during the semi-downturn in 2001. The turning points in the BER and SACCI BCIs are similar to those for the new confidence indicators. There is some ambiguity towards the latter part of the sample period, as the expected conditions confidence indicator and the BER BCI hover around the zero threshold. On the whole the phases identified with the indicators are longer in duration than the official phases. The indicators mostly exhibit peaks before the official peak dates, by as many as 10 quarters before the official peak. The indicators exhibit troughs concurrent with or after the three official trough dates. The indicators therefore seem to reflect the official business cycle turning points relatively well.

As discussed in Boshoff and Du Plessis (2020) in an earlier chapter in this volume, the comovement between these cycle phases can be measured with the concordance statistic suggested by Harding and Pagan (2002). The concordance statistic measures the comovement of two series, by considering the proportion of time the two series are simultaneously in the same phase. This entails testing whether $I = Pr(S_{xt} = S_{yt})$ is close to 1, where $S_{xt} = 1$ identifies an expansion in indicator x_t, and $S_{yt} = 1$ identifies a business cycle upswing phase at time t. The statistic is calculated as follows: $I = 1/T\big[\sum_{t=1}^{T} S_{xt}S_{yt} + \sum_{t=1}^{T}(1-S_{xt})(1-S_{yt})\big]$. Following Harding and Pagan (2006), statistical significance is calculated with heteroskedasticity and autocorrelation consistent standard errors.

Table 5 reports the concordance statistics for the phases of the indicator variables, compared with the official SARB reference turning points. The indicators all exhibit significant concordance with the official SARB business cycle. The concordance statistics of the three survey-based indicators are at their maximum when they are lagged by one or two quarters, but the contemporaneous concordance statistics are all significant.

The indicators therefore seem to reflect the official business cycle turning points relatively well, and provided advance warning especially of the official peaks. The results suggest that the confidence indicators are potentially useful leading indicators of the business cycle. However, the false positives and ambiguous periods imply that the indicators should be used in conjunction with other series when identifying turning points, as in Laubscher (2014). As more microdata from the BER's business tendency surveys become available, the analysis could be expanded

Table 5 Concordance statistics with the SARB business cycle

	Confidence (current)	Confidence (expected)	BER BCI	ACCI BCI growth
Lead = 3	0.60	0.62*	0.47	0.72**
Lead = 2	0.65*	0.67**	0.54	0.75***
Lead = 1	0.68**	0.70***	0.59*	0.76***
Lead/lag = 0	0.71***	0.73***	0.62**	0.75***
Lag = 1	0.72***	0.74***	0.63***	0.70***
Lag = 2	0.73***	0.69***	0.64***	0.65***
Lag = 3	0.72***	0.64***	0.63***	0.6**

$^*p < 0.1$; $^{**}p < 0.05$; $^{***}p < 0.01$

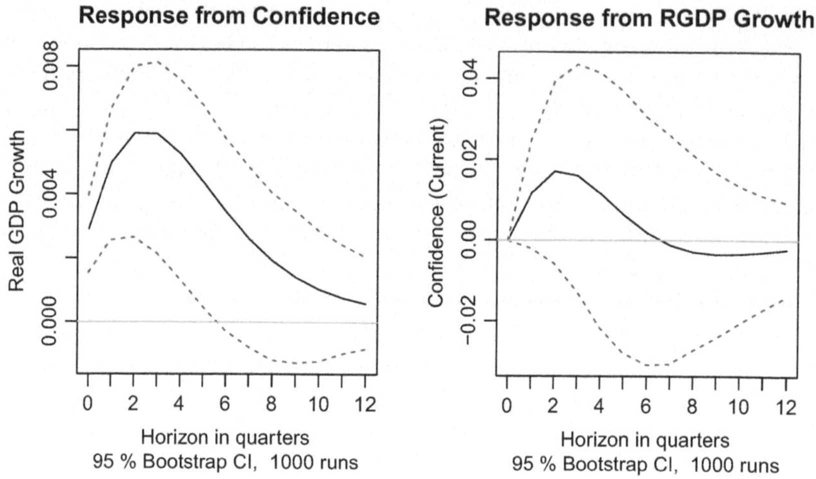

Fig. 4 IRFs of confidence (current conditions) and real GDP growth

by analysing the cyclical properties of the indicators in terms of duration, amplitude, and steepness.

5.2 *The Impact of Confidence*

In this section, a simple bivariate VAR is estimated to investigate the dynamic effects of confidence shocks on the economy. An extended VAR is then estimated to examine whether the results hold after the inclusion of additional variables.

Bivariate VAR Analysis

Impulse response functions (IRFs) can be generated to illustrate the dynamic impact on the system of a shock to confidence, which is an innovation of one standard deviation to the residual in the equation. Figure 4 illustrates the IRFs of a bivariate VAR for the confidence indicator on current conditions and real GDP growth. The left panel plots the responses of real GDP growth to an orthogonal shock in the indicator, with 95% bootstrap confidence intervals.

Following an increase in confidence of one standard deviation, real GDP growth increases by around 0.3% on impact, with a peak at two quarters. The impact on the growth rate is transitory, dying out after approximately seven quarters. This is equivalent to a permanent increase in the level of output, which confirms the findings in the literature (e.g. Barsky and Sims 2012). The right panel plots the response of confidence to an orthogonal shock in real GDP growth. Following an increase in

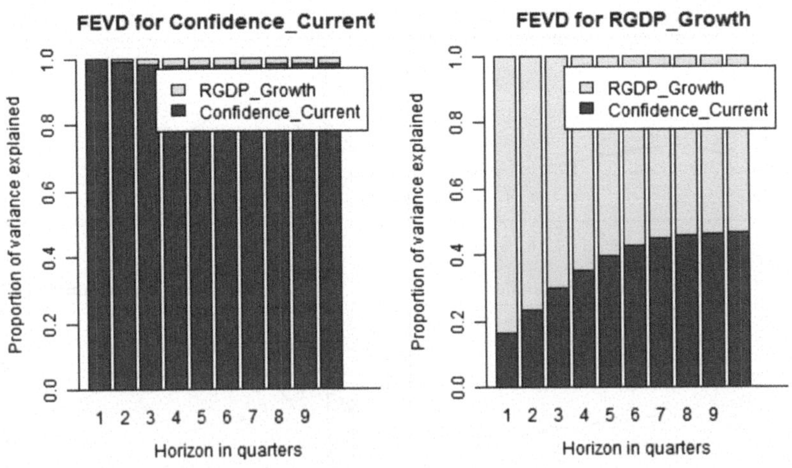

Fig. 5 FEVDs of confidence (current conditions) and real GDP growth

real GDP growth, there is an insignificant increase in confidence of around 2% after two quarters. The results are similar for alternative orderings.

The importance of innovations can also be examined with variance decompositions. The forecast error variance decomposition (FEVD) shows the proportion of the movements in a sequence due to its own shocks and shocks to the other variable. Figure 5 illustrates the FEVDs for the current conditions confidence indicator and real GDP growth. Up to around half (46%) of the movements in real GDP growth are explained by the confidence indicator over the longer term, while real GDP explains up to 2% of the variance in the confidence indicator.

The results are very similar when using the expected conditions confidence indicator and the BER BCI, whereas the SACCI growth rate exhibits a smaller significant relationship with real GDP growth after two quarters. The results for the sectoral indicators are also similar to the aggregate results, with the exception of the construction sector, where the impact of a shock to confidence on GDP growth does not die out within the forecast horizon of 12 quarters.

Expanded VAR

Though instructive, the results from a bivariate system are prone to misspecification (Girardi and Reuter 2017). A larger VAR system is estimated to test the robustness of the relationships. The extended VAR includes the variables suggested by Redl (2015) for South Africa: confidence, the JSE All Share Index, the yield spread (i.e. the Government Bond Yield minus the 3-month T-Bill rate), an employment index, and growth in real GDP, manufacturing production, and investment (gross fixed capital formation). These variables are typically included in the literature (e.g. Leduc and Liu 2016; Bachmann et al. 2013; Baker et al. 2016).

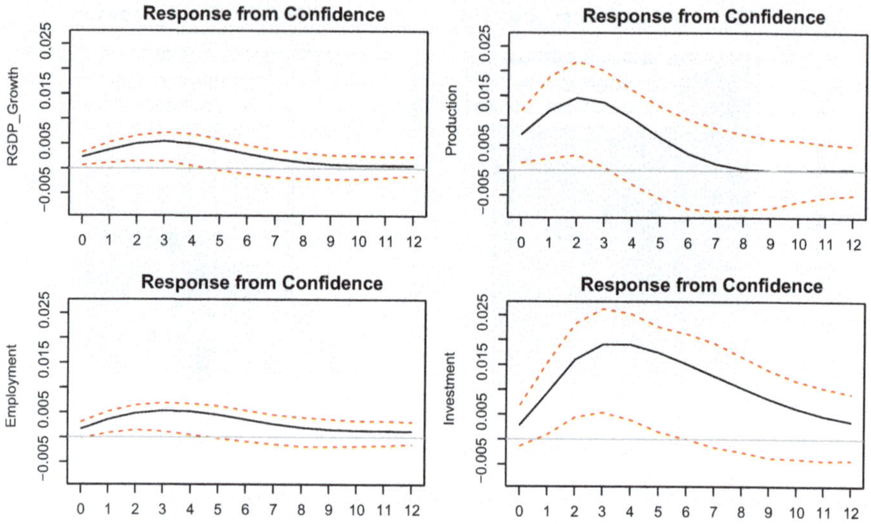

Fig. 6 IRFs of real GDP, production, employment, and investment growth to confidence shocks

The confidence indicator is ordered first, the financial variables next, and the real variables last. The financial variables are expected to move faster than the real variables (Redl 2015). An alternative ordering of placing the confidence indicator last provides qualitatively similar results. As was the case with the previous VAR, the variables enter as real annual quarter-on-quarter growth rates, except for confidence and the yield spread.

The IRFs for the impact of confidence on real GDP, real manufacturing production, employment, and real fixed investment growth are illustrated in Fig. 6. In this larger system, a shock to confidence leads to significant impulse responses in all four variables. The larger system provides similar results to the bivariate VAR in terms of the responses of real GDP growth. The responses of real employment growth are similar in magnitude to real GDP growth, while the responses of real manufacturing production and real fixed investment growth are larger. According to the FEVD (not shown), confidence explains around 35%, 25%, 30%, and 40% of the variance in the growth rates in real GDP, production, employment, and investment, respectively.

6 Conclusion

This chapter has estimated new proxies for business confidence in South Africa, using microdata from the BER business tendency surveys. The microdata from the BER surveys were collated and cleaned and can now be used for further research. The BER BCIs were refined in terms of incorporating more information from the surveys and weighing the responses in a more consistent manner. Two sets of composite confidence indicators were calculated, as the weighted cross-sectional mean of responses to questions on current and expected future business conditions.

Overall, the results provided evidence at least of significant comovement between the sectoral and aggregate confidence indicators and real economic activity. The indicators had a positive and significant impact on real GDP growth in the VAR models. Shocks to the indicators accounted for a sizeable fraction of variation in economic activity. This was the case even after controlling for other economic variables in a larger VAR system. This implies that the confidence indicators contain useful predictive content for current and future economic developments. The indicators may therefore be useful for monitoring developments in real time and for forecasting future economic activity.

References

Acemoglu, D., & Scott, A. (1994). Consumer confidence and rational expectations: Are agents' beliefs consistent with the theory? *The Economic Journal, 104*, 1–19.

Akerlof, G., & Shiller, R. J. (2015). *Animal spirits: How human psychology drives the economy, and why it matters for global capitalism*. Princeton: Princeton University Press.

Bachmann, R., Elstner, S., & Sims, E. R. (2013). Uncertainty and economic activity: Evidence from business survey data. *American Economic Journal: Macroeconomics, 5*(2), 217–249.

Baker, S. R., Bloom, N., & Davis, S. J. (2016). Measuring economic policy uncertainty. *The Quarterly Journal of Economics, 131*(4), 1593–1636. https://doi.org/10.1093/qje/qjw024. Advance

Barsky, R. B., & Sims, E. R. (2012). Information, animal spirits, and the meaning of innovations in consumer confidence. *American Economic Review, 102*(4), 1343–1377. https://doi.org/10.1257/aer.102.4.1343

Beaudry, P., & Portier, F. (2004). An exploration into Pigou's theory of cycles. *Journal of Monetary Economics, 51*(6), 1183–1216. https://doi.org/10.1016/j.jmoneco.2003.10.003

Bosch, A. (2015, March 24). *Composite Business Cycle Indicators for South Africa*. South African Reserve Bank.

Boshoff, W. H. & Du Plessis, S. A. (2020). Chapter 2: What do we know about the South African Business Cycle. In W. H. Boshoff (Ed.), *Business Cycles and Structural Change in South Africa*. Switzerland: Springer.

Bry, G., & Boschan, C. (1971). Cyclical analysis of economic time series: selected procedures and computer programs. *NBER Technical Working Paper*, No. 20.

Carroll, C. D., Fuhrer, J. C., & Wilcox, D. W. (1994). Does consumer sentiment forecast household spending? If so, why? *American Economic Review, 84*(5), 1397–1408.

Cochrane, J. H. (1994). Shocks. In *Carnegie-Rochester Conference Series on Public Policy*, December 1994 (Vol. 41, pp. 295–364).

Driver, C., & Urga, G. (2004) Transforming qualitative survey data: Performance comparisons for the UK. *Oxford Bulletin of Economics and Statistics, 66*(1), 71–89. https://doi.org/10.1111/j.1440-1754.2007.01273.x

European Central Bank. (2013, January). Confidence indicators and economic developments. *ECB Monthly Bulletin*, 45–58.

European Commission. (2006). *European Economies: The Joint Harmonised EU Programme of Business and Consumer Surveys*. Directorate-General for Economic; Financial Affairs (Special Report No. 5).

Fuhrer, J. C. (1988). On the information content of consumer survey expectations. *The Review of Economics and Statistics, 70*, 140–144.

Gayer, C., Girardi, A., & Reuter, A. (2014, December). *The Role of Survey Data in Nowcasting Euro Area GDP Growth*. European Commission Economic Papers, 538. https://doi.org/10.2765/71951

Gehlbach, H., & Barge, S. (2012). Anchoring and adjusting in questionnaire responses. *Basic and Applied Social Psychology, 34*(5), 417–433. https://doi.org/10.1080/01973533.2012.711691

Giannone, D., Reichlin, L., & Small, D. (2008). Nowcasting: The real-time informational content of macroeconomic data. *Journal of Monetary Economics, 55*, 665–676. https://doi.org/10.1016/j.jmoneco.2008.05.010

Girardi, A., & Reuter, A. (2017). New uncertainty measures for the euro area using survey data. *Oxford Economic Papers, 69*(1), 278–300. https://doi.org/10.1093/oep/gpw058

Harding, D., & Pagan, A. (2002). Dissecting the cycle: A methodological investigation. *Journal of Monetary Economics, 49*(2), 365–381. https://doi.org/10.1016/S0304-3932(01)00108-8

Harding, D., & Pagan, A. (2006). Synchronization of cycles. *Journal of Econometrics, 132*, 59–79. https://doi.org/10.1016/j.jeconom.2005.01.023

International Monetary Fund. (2017, July 23). *World Economic Outlook Update*. IMF Publications.

Kabundi, A. (2004). *Estimation of Economic Growth in France Using Business Survey Data*. IMF Working Paper, WP/04/69.

Kabundi, A., Nel, E., & Ruch, F. (2016). *Nowcasting Real GDP Growth in South Africa*. ERSA Working Paper, 581.

Kershoff, G. (2000, December). *Measuring Business and Consumer Confidence in South Africa*. Bureau for Economic Research.

Kershoff, G. (2002). An analysis of the BER's trade and building survey panels. *Journal for Studies in Economics and Econometrics, 26*(1), 1–17.

Kershoff, G. (2015). *South Africa: The BER's Business Tendency Surveys*. Bureau for Economic Research (pp. 1–19).

Keynes, J. M. (1936). *General theory of employment, interest and money*. London: Macmillan. https://doi.org/10.2307/2143949

Kilic, E., & Cankaya, S. (2016). Consumer confidence and economic activity: A factor augmented VAR approach. *Applied Economics, 48*(32), 3062–3080. https://doi.org/10.1080/00036846.2015.1133902

Laubscher, P. (2014). *A New Recession-Dating Algorithm for South Africa*. Stellenbosch Economic Working Papers, 06/14.

Leduc, S., & Liu, Z. (2016). Uncertainty shocks are aggregate demand shocks. *Journal of Monetary Economics, 82*, 20–35. https://doi.org/10.1016/j.jmoneco.2016.07.002

Leduc, S., & Sill, K. (2013). Expectations and economic fluctuations: An analysis using survey data. *Review of Economics and Statistics, 95*, 1352–1367.

Ludvigson, S. C. (2004). Consumer confidence and consumer spending. *Journal of Economic Perspectives, 18*(2), 29–50

Matheson, T. D. (2010). An analysis of the informational content of New Zealand data releases: The importance of business opinion surveys. *Economic Modelling, 27*(1), 304–314. https://doi.org/10.1016/j.econmod.2009.09.010

Mendicino, C., & Punzi, M. T. (2013, Winter). Confidence and economic activity: The case of Portugal. *Banco de Portugal*, 39–49

Nardo, M. (2003). The quantification of qualitative survey data: A critical assessment. *Journal of Economic Surveys, 17*(5), 645–668.

Organisation for Economic Co-operation and Development. (2003). In E. Giovannini & E. Burgeat (Eds.), *Business tendency surveys: A handbook*. Paris, France: OECD Publications.

Parigi, G., & Golinelli, R. (2004). Consumer sentiment and economic activity. *Journal of Business Cycle Measurement and Analysis, 2004*(2), 147–170. https://doi.org/10.1787/jbcma-v2004-art10-en

Pellissier, M. (2002). Business confidence and the South African business cycle. *Journal for Studies in Economics and Econometrics, 26*(2), 51–67.

Pellissier, M., & Smit, E. vd M. (1994) Constructing sectoral leading indicators using data reduction techniques. In *Business cycle surveys: Forecasting issues and methodological aspects* (pp. 271–290). Aldershot: Avebury.

Redl, C. (2015). *Macroeconomic Uncertainty in South Africa*. ERSA Working Paper, 509.

SACCI. (2011). *Updated and Revised SACCI Business Confidence Index*. South African Chamber of Commerce and Industry.

Santero, T., & Westerlund, N. (1996). *Confidence Indicators and Their Relationship to Changes in Economic Activity*. OECD Economics Department Working Papers, 170. https://doi.org/10.1787/537052766455

Smit, E. vd M. (1983). 'n Ekonomiese bestedingsmodel vir die Suid-Afrikaanse ekonomie gebaseer op kwalitatiewe data-insette. *Journal for Studies in Economics and Econometrics, 15*, 5–36.

Smit, E. vd M. (1984) A systematic comparison of expenditure models of the South African economy excluding and including opinion survey variables. *CIRET Studies, 34*, 219–234.

Taylor, K., & McNabb, R. (2007). Business cycles and the role of confidence: Evidence for Europe. *Oxford Bulletin of Economics and Statistics, 69*(2), 185–208. https://doi.org/10.1111/j.1468-0084.2007.00472.x

Tversky, A., & Kahneman, D. (1974). Judgment under uncertainty: Heuristics and biases. *Science, 185*(4157), 1124–1131.

United Nations. (2015). *Handbook on economic tendency surveys*. New York: United Nations Publications.

Van Aarle, B., & Kappler, M. (2012). Economic sentiment shocks and fluctuations in economic activity in the Euro Area and the USA. *Intereconomics, 47*(1), 44–51. https://doi.org/10.1007/s10272-012-0405-z

Venter, J. C. (2005, September) Reference turning points in the South African business cycle: Recent developments. *SARB Quarterly Bulletin*, 61–70.

Venter, J. C. (2020). Chapter 9: Assessing the 2013 and 2017 business cycle turning points signalled by the SARB's composite leading business cycle indicator. In W. H. Boshoff (Ed.), *Business Cycles and Structural Change in South Africa*. Switzerland: Springer.

Assessing the 2013 and 2017 Business Cycle Turning Points Signalled by the SARB's Composite Leading Business Cycle Indicator

J. C. Venter

1 Introduction

Following the global financial crisis, the South African business cycle[1] officially entered an expansion phase in September 2009, characterised by volatile output growth and during which various structural supply-side constraints became increasingly binding (Venter 2011: 66). The domestic economy was hampered by electricity-supply disruptions throughout this expansion phase and subject to protracted, and highly disruptive, labour strikes between 2011 and 2014 (Venter 2016: 107–108). Furthermore, the global economic recovery was weak over this period, offering little assistance to the domestic economy. The expansion gradually lost momentum from 2012 onwards, with a peak in the business cycle being reached in November 2013. Up to August 2019, i.e. 69 months since the preceding peak, no lower turning point in the downward phase of the cycle has officially been identified.

When considering consensus forecasts of annual output growth, South African economists, in general, did not anticipate the gradual loss of momentum in output growth from 2012 or even the downward phase of the business cycle that started at the end of 2013. Yet the South African Reserve Bank's (SARB) composite leading business cycle indicator reached a peak in February 2011 before trending gradually lower, while exhibiting some volatility. The continued decline in the

[1]The chronology of turning points determined by the South African Reserve Bank refers to growth cycles. See the earlier chapter by Boshoff and Du Plessis (2020) for an overview of cyclical concepts and subsequent discussion in the next section.

J. C. Venter (✉)
South African Reserve Bank, Pretoria, South Africa
e-mail: Iaan.Venter@resbank.co.za

W. H. Boshoff (ed.), *Business Cycles and Structural Change in South Africa*,
Advances in African Economic, Social and Political Development,
https://doi.org/10.1007/978-3-030-35754-2_9

leading indicator suggested a further deterioration in output growth over the short term. It is therefore important to assess the SARB's approach to forecasting South African business cycle turning points.

An assessment of the SARB's approach is particularly important, given more recent signals from the composite leading indicator of an end to the growth recession, which has not yet materialized. The SARB's composite leading business cycle indicator reached a trough in April 2016 and subsequently increased fairly strongly up to February 2017, suggesting the end of the downward phase to be imminent, consistent with consensus forecasts. From mid-2017, the leading indicator continued its strong upward trend until February 2019 before receding again up to March 2019. However, South African real GDP growth slowed to only 0.4% in 2016 and contracted in the first quarter of 2017. Real output growth then accelerated somewhat, with real GDP expanding by 1.4% for 2017 as a whole, before slowing again to 0.8% in 2018. Therefore, it is also important to assess whether the strong increase in the leading indicator during the second half of 2016 and in 2017, and the implied end of the growth recession, was a false signal.

Given this background, this chapter offers an exposition of the indicator approach to business cycle forecasting, with a focus on the SARB's composite leading business cycle indicator. As discussed, the emphasis is on two research questions. Firstly, this chapter studies whether the current downward phase in the South African business cycle could reasonably have been predicted. Secondly, it also examines whether the recent strong increase in the composite leading business cycle indicator provided a reliable signal that the current contraction phase might have ended. To this end, the next section discusses the business cycle definition employed by the SARB, followed by an explanation of the methodology employed in applying the indicator approach to business cycle analysis, including forecasting turning points in the business cycle. The SARB's composite leading business cycle indicator and its component time series are then analysed in relation to previous business cycle peaks and troughs.

The results show that the leading indicator and its subcomponents revealed a broad slowdown in the South African economy from 2012, contrary to consensus forecasts of improving economic growth. Furthermore, the results show that the recent upward trend in the leading indicator did initially signal the end of the current downward phase of the business cycle; the turning point signal from the leading indicator meets with the requirements for pronounced, pervasive and persistent signals, as explained later. The strength of this signal became much weaker again in the second half of 2017. The chapter concludes by suggesting that the anticipated business cycle recovery appears uncertain at the time of writing, due to idiosyncratic exogenous factors.

2 Defining the Business Cycle

Following decades of empirical study, the first comprehensive and frequently quoted definition of the business cycle was formulated by Mitchell in 1927 and later slightly revised by Burns and Mitchell (1946: 3):

> Business cycles are a type of fluctuation found in the aggregate economic activity of nations that organize their work mainly in business enterprises: a cycle consists of expansions occurring at about the same time in many economic activities, followed by similar general recessions, contractions, and revivals which merge into the expansion phase of the next cycle; this sequence of change is recurrent but not periodic; in duration business cycles vary from more than one year to ten or twelve years; they are not divisible into shorter cycles of similar character with amplitudes approximating their own.

The Burns and Mitchell definition was initially formulated to define classical business cycles, i.e. cycles in the level of aggregate economic activity, but the definition also applies to growth cycles, which refer to fluctuations around the long-term growth trend of aggregate economic activity. The SARB has identified reference turning points (peaks and troughs) in the South African growth cycle since 1945.[2]

While the different conceptualisations of the South African business cycle are fairly well documented, forecasting emerging stages of the cycle is challenging. Indeed, economic forecasters have failed to predict economic recessions across a range of countries (Ahir and Loungani 2014), leading Loungani (2000: 1) to quip that 'the record of failure to predict recessions is virtually unblemished'.

In South Africa, the gradual loss of momentum in domestic output growth after 2011, and indeed the onset of the current downward phase of the business cycle, appears not to have been widely recognised by economists, considering consensus forecasts of annual GDP growth. Figure 1 shows annual average growth in South Africa's real GDP since 2011, together with the Reuters consensus forecast of annual average GDP growth for the current year as well as the following 2 years, as at the beginning of each year.[3] Since 2012, consensus forecasts consistently predicted an acceleration of annual growth in South Africa's GDP over a 3-year horizon, depicted by the dotted lines. Participants appeared, on average, not to recognise that a broad slowdown in output growth was underway and that the South African economy had entered a downward phase of the business cycle.

One of the explanations for poor forecasting performance relates to the inadequate structure of econometric forecasting models (see Boshoff and Du Plessis (2020) for a review of South African literature). An alternative, non-econometric

---

[2] The chronology of business cycle turning points regularly published on the last page of the SARB's *Quarterly Bulletin* represents growth cycle turning points, i.e. trend-adjusted business cycle turning points.

[3] For 2015, the consensus forecast for April was used instead of January, since that was the first month in that year for which annual average forecasts for the current year (2015) and the subsequent 2 years were available.

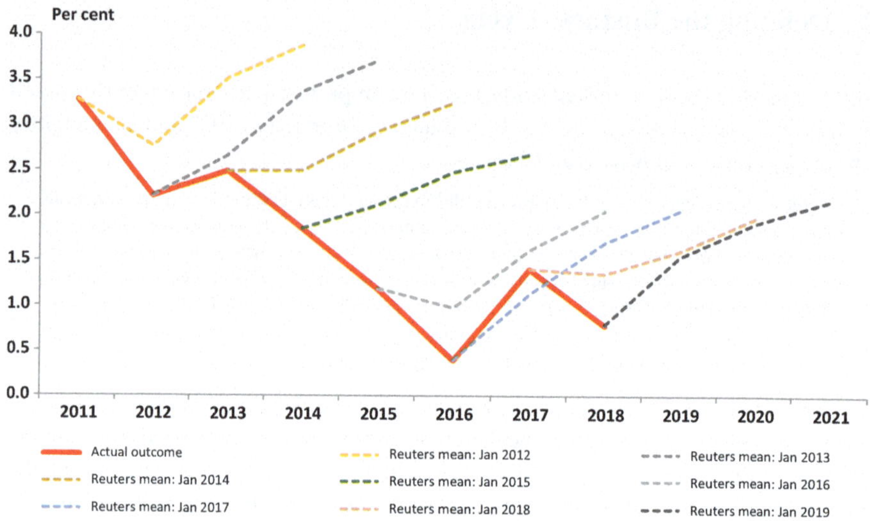

Fig. 1 Annual average growth in South Africa's real GDP and Reuters consensus forecasts (Source: Statistics South Africa and Reuters)

forecasting strategy might involve a sequential signalling system, aimed at analysing turning points in a number of individual and composite leading, coincident and lagging indicators, and which covers a range of economic sectors and processes (Achutan and Banerji 2004). This is the approach adopted by the Economic Cycle Research Institute (ECRI) and builds on decades of an empirical study of business cycles at the National Bureau of Economic Research (NBER) and later at the Center for International Business Cycle Research (CIBCR). Based on the work of Geoffrey Moore, an exponent of the Burns and Mitchell approach, the sequential signalling system is directly related to the original definition of the cycle offered by Burns and Mitchell. The method sees the Burns and Mitchell definition as offering a working definition for business cycle analysis and forecasting, highlighting three key properties of business cycle phases, including contractions (Fabricant 1972). These properties are, firstly, the *duration* of a contraction in aggregate economic activity, secondly, the amplitude of a contraction was analysed (that is, the *depth* of the decline in aggregate economic activity), and, thirdly, the extent to which the contraction is *diffused* among different economic activities was analysed (Banerji 1999b). These characteristics provide the basis for a set of criteria to analyse the business cycle. As discussed in the following section, three composite business cycle indicators are used to set up a sequential signalling system that can be employed to predict possible business cycle turning points. In addition, a composite leading business cycle indicator and its subcomponents can then be analysed in terms of the duration, depth and diffusion of their movements, which could greatly improve the reliability of turning point signals obtained from the sequential signalling system.

3 Methodology

3.1 Composite Business Cycle Indicators

One of the most important contributions made to business cycle analysis by Burns and Mitchell, and later Moore (1950), was their classification of economic time series according to their timing relation to the business cycle, i.e. as leading, coincident and lagging indicators. Coincident indicators report the current stance of the economy. They include indicators, such as GDP, industrial production, retail sales and employment, and are used to measure aggregate economic activity.

The leading indicators anticipate movements in the coincident indicators. They usually represent intentions of future activity (such as job advertisements, new building plans or new manufacturing orders) or anticipations (such as business or consumer confidence). Since no individual leading indicator is completely infallible—many of them occasionally fail to lead at certain business cycle turning points—they are usually combined into a composite leading index, with a better track record than the individual leading indicators. As noted by Van der Walt (1983: 57), the timing of changes in a composite index will usually show a more stable relationship with that of the general business cycle than any individual series. Furthermore, measurement errors and other random deviations in individual series could possibly cancel out when individual indicators are combined into a composite indicator.[4]

The lagging indicators confirm the movement first observed in the leading indicators and later in the coincident indicators. They often reflect excesses or imbalances in the economy. If the lagging indicators start rising rapidly it could signal an overheating economy. In addition, there are feedback relationships that run from the lagging indicators to the leading indicators (Moore 1983: 361–367). As such, a movement in a lagging indicator often triggers an opposite movement in a related leading indicator, e.g. a steep rise in unit labour cost (a lagging indicator) will often lead to a decline in company profits (a leading indicator). Inverting a composite index of lagging indicators thus results in a long-leading indicator—reaching turning points in advance of those in the composite leading index. Similarly, since lagging indicators measure excesses or imbalances in the economy, expressing the composite lagging index as a ratio of the composite coincident index, yields an additional leading indicator. This ratio measures the pace at which excesses or imbalances are building up in the economy relative to the pace at which aggregate economic activity is expanding. The relationship between the lagging and leading indicators assists in explaining why one business cycle tends to generate the next one.

---

[4]See also Boshoff (2005), showing that no individual financial variable can act as a consistent leading indicator for the South African business cycle.

3.2 A Sequential Signalling System

While each business cycle has unique features, all business cycles share the property of a durable sequence of turning points, whereby economic developments around turning points—as captured by various cyclical indicators—unfold in a predictable order. In particular, this durable sequence runs from inverted lagging indicators, the leading indicators, the coincident indicators and finally the lagging indicators (Achutan and Banerji 2004: 112). Table 1 shows the length of leads or lags in the SARB's inverted composite lagging indicator, the composite leading indicator, the ratio of the coincident to lagging indicator, the composite coincident indicator and the composite lagging indicator with respect to reference turning points in the business cycle, starting at the August 1974 reference peak. The median leads or lags of all of these indicators with respect to the reference turning points in the business cycle illustrate that the sequence of turning points described above also holds for the South African economy.

3.3 Evaluating Indicator Turning Point Signals

It is not easy to evaluate the accuracy of composite business cycle indicators in forecasting cyclical turning points. Granger and Newbold, taken from Banerji (1999a: 2), note:

> The index of leading indicators has become a widely quoted and generally trusted forecasting tool. However, it has been rather misinterpreted. The index is intended only to forecast the timing of turning points and not the size of the forthcoming downswing or upswing nor to be a general indicator of the economy at times other than near turning points. Because of this, evaluation of the (LEI) by standard statistical techniques is not easy.

One approach to evaluating the accuracy of turning point signals is to analyse whether the overall signal from the various indicators meets the criteria of pronounced, pervasive and persistent movements (Banerji 1999b). These three criteria are derived from the three key properties of cycles related to duration, depth and diffusion, mentioned earlier (Banerji and Hiris 2001: 335).

Cyclical changes in economic indicators tend to be *pronounced*, consistent with the final part of the Burns and Mitchell definition cited earlier, i.e. '... they are not divisible into shorter cycles of similar character with amplitudes approximating their own'. The year-on-year percentage change is often used to measure the magnitude of change in a cyclical time series, i.e. how pronounced the movement is. However, Moore (1982) introduced an alternative measure, namely the *6-month smoothed annualised growth rate* (6MSAR). The 6MSAR (S_t) of a time series (X_t) is defined as follows:

$$S_t = 100\left[\frac{X_t}{\left(\left(\sum_{i=1}^{12} X_{t-i}\right)\right)/12}\right]^{(12/6.5)} - 100$$

Table 1 Timing relationship between the composite business cycle indicators and reference turning points in the South African business cycle

Reference turning points		Timing relationship in months				
Peaks	Troughs	Lagging indicator (inverted)	Leading indicator	Ratio of coincident to lagging indicator	Coincident indicator	Lagging indicator
August 1974		−26	−12	−10	−1	+14
	December 1977	−26	−9	−11	−1	+14
August 1981		−30	−11	−3	+4	+9
	March 1983	−10	−8	−4	−1	+14
June 1984		−1	−1	−1	−1	+10
	March 1986	−11	−13	−11	0	+16
February 1989		−19	−9	−6	+4	+12
	May 1993	−39	−9	−9	−1	+6
November 1996		−36	−23	−21	−1	+23
	August 1999	−10	−10	−10	−2	+6
November 2007		−43	−16	−9	+5	+12
	August 2009	−9	−7	−7	0	+12
November 2013		−13	−32	−12	0	0
Average:		−21.0	−12.3	−8.8	+0.4	+11.4
Median:		−19.0	−10.0	−9.0	−1.0	+12.0

A *minus* (*plus*) sign indicates that the indicator leads (lags) the reference turning point

The 6MSAR has an advantage in that the denominator is smoothed over 12 months, making it less susceptible to unusual base effects in any particular month. Furthermore, because the change is measured roughly over a 6-month period as opposed to a 12-month span, it reflects a cyclical upswing or downswing more promptly than the 12-month percentage change, with lower volatility than the 12-month change.

The Burns and Mitchell definition states that 'a cycle consists of expansions occurring at about the same time in many economic activities', referring to one of the fundamental characteristics of business cycles, namely the cyclical diffusion of economic movements; from one firm to another, from one industry to another and from one region to another (Banerji and Hiris 2001: 335). A diffusion index shows the extent of the spread of a cyclical movement, i.e. how pervasive the cyclical movement is. Similar to the 6MSAR, a *twelve-month smoothed diffusion index* (12MSDI) can be constructed. The 12SMSDI shows the percentage of time series considered that are at a higher level than their respective average levels over the preceding 12 months.

A third important characteristic of a cyclical upswing or downswing is its persistence. A movement in a cyclical indicator that is pronounced and pervasive, but lasts only a few months does not qualify as a cyclical movement. The Burns and Mitchell definition states that 'in duration business cycles vary from more than one year to ten or twelve years'. Technically, a cyclical upswing or downswing has to persist for at least 5 months (Bry and Boschan 1971: 21), but most last much longer. One way to measure the persistence of a cyclical movement in an indicator is to measure the number of consecutive months that the indicator has moved in the same direction. The duration of the unbroken runs in a number of time series, averaged over the time series, provides a good measure of the degree of persistence of a cyclical movement. Similar to the 6MSAR and the 12MSDI, a *smoothed average duration of run* (SADR) can be calculated as the average of the durations over which the indicators have been higher than their respective average levels over the preceding 12 months.

4 Results

This section presents the results when applying the indicator approach methodology described in Sect. 3 to the South African economy. First, the historical evolution of the three tools (the three Ps) employed to analyse how pronounced, pervasive and persistent movements in the SARB's composite leading business cycle indicator have been are presented and discussed. This is followed by a comparison of the movements in these three tools around the November 2013 business cycle peak with their average movement around previous business cycle peaks. This provides an indication of the reliability of the turning point signal provided by the composite leading business cycle indicator prior to the November 2013 peak. Finally, the likelihood that a possible trough in the business cycle might have already been reached is investigated.

4.1 *Historical Performance of the SARB's Composite Leading Indicator*

When a composite leading indicator forecasts a directional change in the business cycle in a pronounced, pervasive and persistent manner (the three Ps), the likelihood of a cyclical turning point rises significantly. In this section, the historical performance of the SARB's composite leading business cycle indicator and its component time series are analysed in terms of the three Ps described above.

Figure 2 shows the 6MSAR in the composite leading business cycle indicator from January 1972 to March 2019—a period covering seven reference peaks and six reference troughs in the South African business cycle. This indicator provides a measure of how *pronounced* the increase/decrease in the composite leading business cycle indicator is. On only two occasions—2001 and 2002/03—did the 6MSAR dip below zero for a period of more than 5 months, without a reference peak in the business cycle being identified. Although the domestic economy did experience a slowdown during both of those periods, they were not recognised as downward phases of the business cycle for a number of reasons (Venter 2005: 69).

Figure 3 shows the 12MSDI in the composite leading business cycle indicator from January 1972 to March 2019. This indicator provides a measure of how *pervasive* the increase/decrease in the composite leading business cycle indicator is. As was the case with the 6MSAR, the 12MSDI dipped below 50 for a sustained

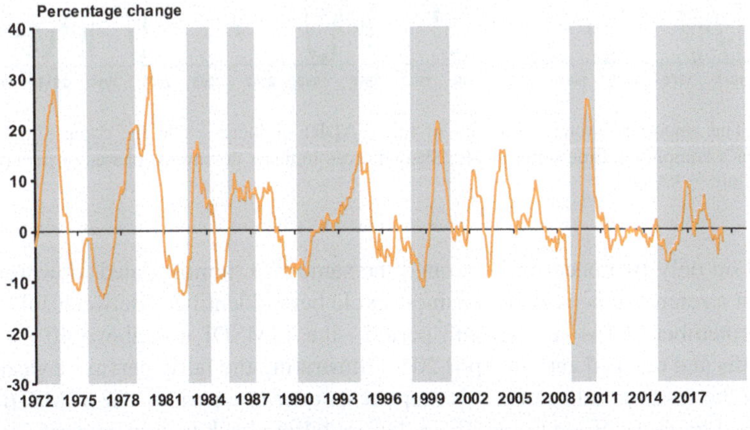

Fig. 2 The 6-month smoothed annualised growth rate (6MSAR) of the composite leading business cycle indicator (Note: Shaded areas indicate downward phases of the business cycle. Source: SARB)

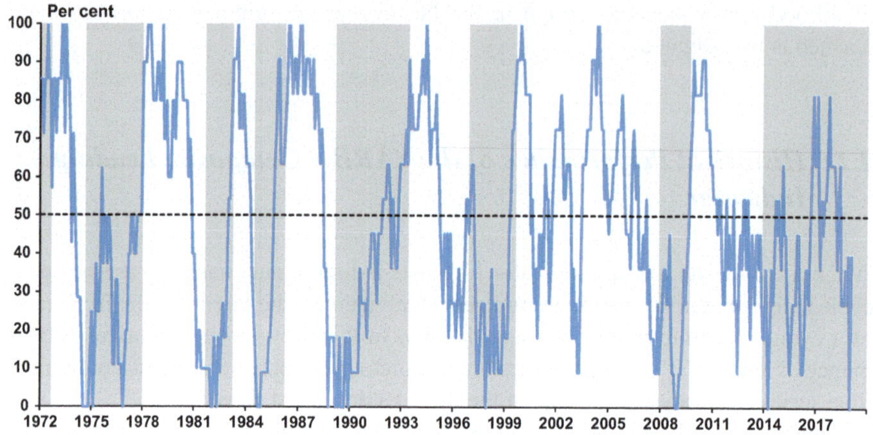

Fig. 3 The 12-month smoothed diffusion index (12MSDI) of the composite leading indicator's component time series (Note: Shaded areas indicate downward phases of the business cycle. Source: SARB)

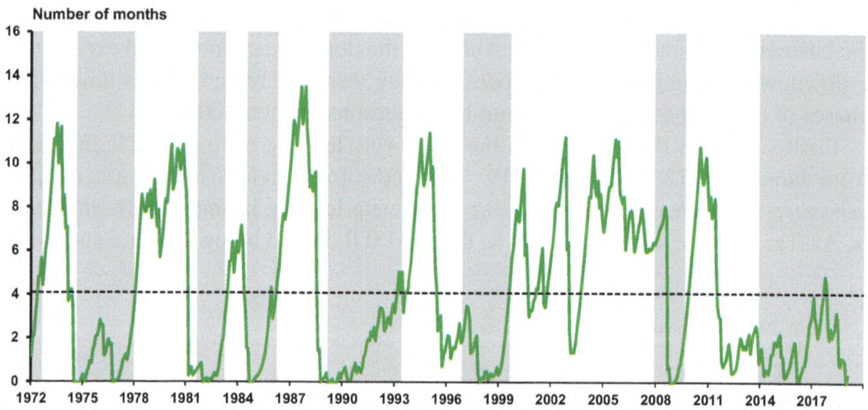

Fig. 4 The smoothed average duration of run (SADR) of increases in the composite leading indicator's component time series (Note: Shaded areas indicate downward phases of the business cycle. Source: SARB)

period on only two occasions—around the same two 'almost-dated' downturns—without a reference peak in the business cycle being identified. Between July 2011 and September 2016—a 63-month period—the 12MSDI was above 50 for only 8 months and reached zero in April 2014, illustrating the fairly pervasive weakness among the leading indicator's subcomponents over this period. The 12MSDI then increased to above 50 up to mid-2018, before falling back to zero again in January 2019.

Figure 4 displays the SADR in the composite leading business cycle indicator from January 1972 to March 2019. The solid horizontal line shows the average

SADR of 4.08 months over this period. The SADR provides a measure of how *persistent* the increase/decrease in the composite leading indicator is. During each of the past six downward phases of the business cycle, the SADR has fallen to zero at some stage. On two other occasions—the two 'almost-dated' downturns—the SADR dipped below its long-term average but did not come close to zero. The SADR dipped below its long-term average in July 2011 and has remained very weak ever since, only surpassing the long-term average for a period of 3 months in the second half of 2017.

An analysis of the 6MSAR, the 12MSDI and the SADR in the SARB's composite leading business cycle indicator shows that the indicator generally signalled the onset of peaks and troughs in the South African business cycle in advance, and in a pronounced, pervasive and persistent manner.

4.2 *Predicting the November 2013 Reference Peak*

In this section, we analyse the movement in the SARB's composite leading business cycle indicator during the period prior to, and around the November 2013 reference peak in the business cycle, in order to determine whether the indicator signalled the likelihood of a business cycle peak with a reasonable degree of certainty. First, the movement in the leading indicator and its vintage data are analysed, followed by an analysis of the three Ps to ascertain whether they confirmed the likelihood that a peak in the business cycle may have been reached.

Figure 5 shows that the SARB's composite leading business cycle indicator reached a peak in February 2011 before trending gradually lower. Initially, the moderate downward trend was accompanied by a fairly large degree of volatility in the leading indicator, indicative of heightened uncertainty at the time. From March 2013, however, the downward trend in the composite leading business cycle

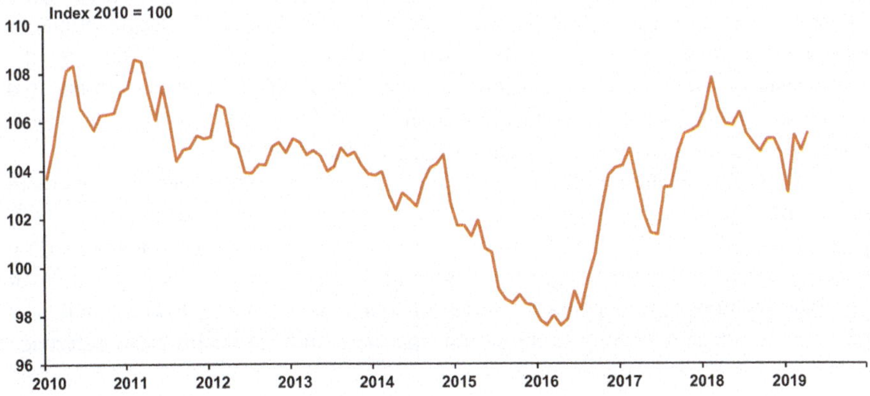

Fig. 5 Composite leading business cycle indicator for South Africa (Source: SARB)

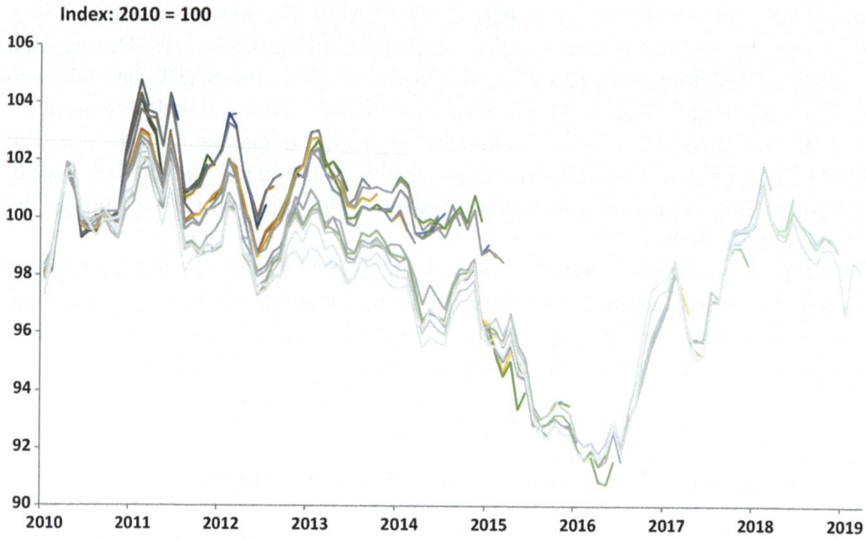

Fig. 6 Monthly vintages of the SARB's composite leading business cycle indicator for South Africa (Source: SARB)

indicator became more pronounced. The continued decrease in the leading indicator suggested a further deterioration in output growth over the short term and not an acceleration as predicted by consensus forecasts.

Figure 6 depicts vintage data of the SARB's composite leading business cycle indicator from the January 2011 release onwards. In all of the vintages, the peak remained February 2011, followed by a gradual downward trend (amid increased volatility) until early 2013, after which the downward trend became more pronounced. Of note, the vintages up to March 2015 are all on a higher level and displayed a slightly less pronounced downward trend than the subsequent vintages. This is because the constituent time series of the composite leading business cycle indicator were changed by the SARB in 2015 (SARB 2015). The earlier vintages included the index representing the prices of all classes of shares trade on the Johannesburg Stock Exchange Limited. Over time, this indicator disconnected somewhat from domestic economic developments and was removed as a component series of the composite leading business cycle indicator in 2015.

In order to gauge how pronounced, pervasive and persistent a specific movement in a composite business cycle indicator is, it is useful to compare the movement to past cycles. Figures 7, 8 and 9 compare the movement in the composite leading business cycle indicator around the November 2013 peak to its movement at previous business cycle peaks in order to gauge whether the leading indicator provided as clear a turning point signal than as it did before previous reference peaks.

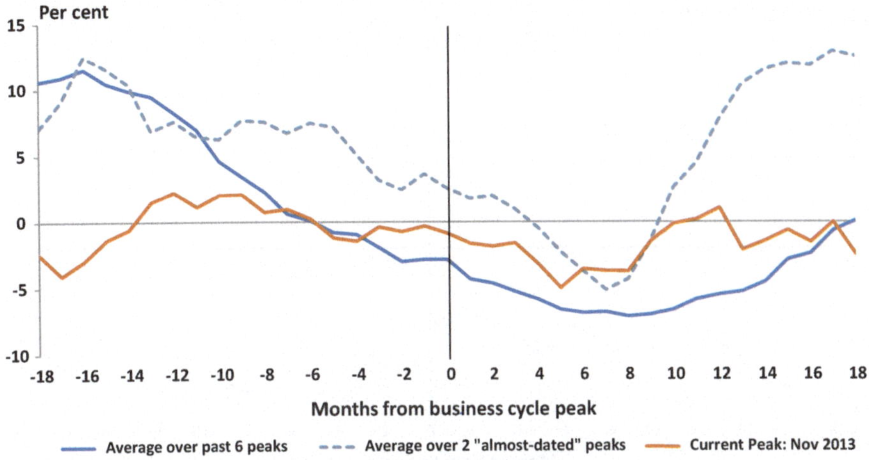

Fig. 7 The 6MSAR in the composite leading business cycle indicator around different business cycle peaks

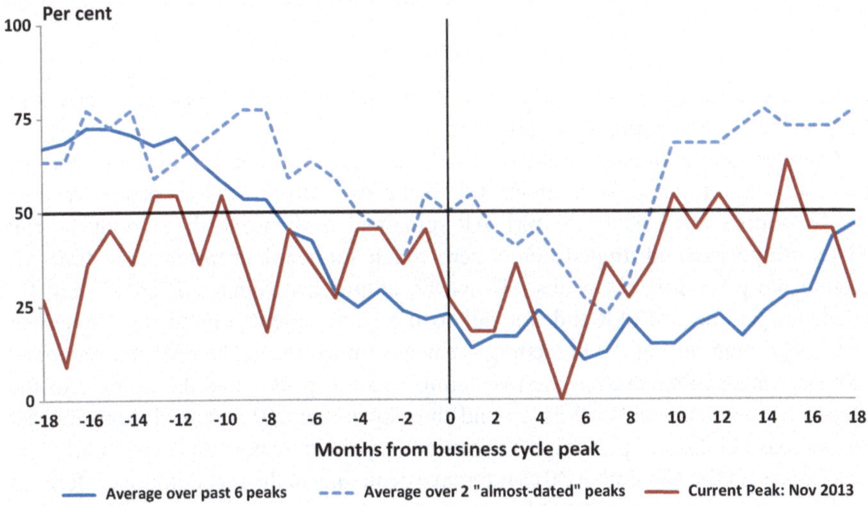

Fig. 8 The 12MSDI of the composite leading business cycle indicator around different business cycle peaks

Figure 7 depicts the 6MSAR in the composite leading business cycle indicator around different business cycle peaks, from 18 months before the peaks to 18 months after the peaks. The movement in the 6MSAR around the November 2013 reference peak is compared to the average movement in the 6MSAR at the preceding six reference peaks in the business cycle, as well as to its average movement at the two 'almost-dated' peaks in the early 2000s. Based on the analysis done at the time,

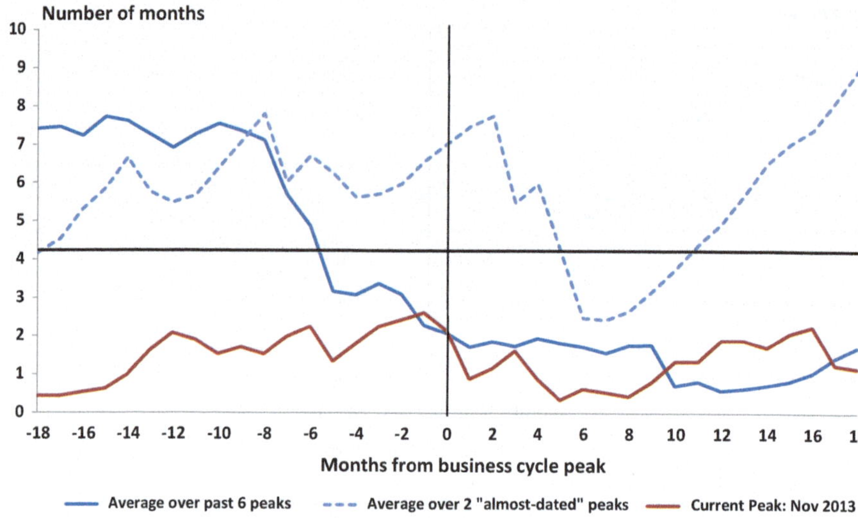

Fig. 9 The SADR in the composite leading business cycle indicator around different business cycle peaks

and for the purpose of this study, these two 'almost-dated' peaks were chosen as February 2001 and September 2002.

On average, the decline in the 6MSAR was much more pronounced around the previous six reference peaks than around the two 'almost-dated' peaks. Around the November 2013 peak, the 6MSAR remained fairly weak throughout the full 37-month period and dipped below zero much sooner than the average 6MSAR around the preceding six peaks.[5] However, although it remained fairly weak for much longer the 6MSAR did not fall to the same extent around the November 2013 peak than during the preceding six peaks on average. The 6MSAR remained more elevated, in general, at the two 'almost-dated' peaks than the average of the preceding six peaks as well as around the November 2013 peak. It appears that the decrease in the composite leading business cycle indicator has been slightly less pronounced at the November 2013 reference peak than at the preceding six reference peaks, on average, but the 6MSAR remained weak for much longer, considering that it fell below zero in July 2011 already (not shown in Fig. 7).

Figure 8 depicts the 12MSDI in the composite leading business cycle indicator around the November 2013 reference peak, the 12MSDI's average movement around the preceding six reference peaks in the business cycle, as well as its average movement at the two 'almost-dated' peaks in the early 2000s.

On average, the 12MSDI dropped much quicker and to a much lower level (below 20) around the preceding six reference peaks than around the two 'almost-

[5]The 6MSAR in the leading indicator dipped below zero in July 2011 already, and remained below zero in all but 2 months up to September 2012.

dated' peaks. Around the November 2013 peak, the 12MSDI remained relatively weak throughout the full 37-month period. Similar to the 6MSAR, the 12MSDI dipped below the neutral 50 level much sooner than the average 12MSDI around the preceding six peaks. Unlike the 6MSAR, however, the 12MSDI did fall to the same extent around the November 2013 peak than during the preceding six peaks, on average, even dipping to zero in 1 month. The decrease in the composite leading business cycle indicator appears to have been as pervasive around the November 2013 reference peak than at the preceding six reference peaks, on average. In addition, the 12MSDI remained weak for much longer, generally staying below 50 since July 2011 (not shown in Fig. 8).

Figure 9 illustrates how persistent the movement in the composite leading business cycle indicator was around selected business cycle peaks. Specifically, it depicts the movement in the SADR of the composite leading business cycle indicator around the November 2013 reference peak, its average movement around the preceding six reference peaks in the business cycle, as well as its average movement at the two 'almost-dated' peaks in the early 2000s.

The SADR's movement around the November 2013 peak appears to resemble its average movement around the preceding six reference peaks fairly closely in terms of the magnitude of the decline. However, similar to the 6MSAR and the 12MSDI, the SADR has been quite weak for much longer around the November 2013 peak, falling below its long-term average in July 2011 (not shown in Fig. 9) and remaining well below the average level until well after the reference peak had been reached. The weakness in the composite leading business cycle indicator has been quite persistent around the November 2013 peak, even more so than the persistent weakness usually observed around business cycle peaks in South Africa.

4.3 Assessing the Possibility of a Subsequent Lower Business Cycle Turning Point

In this section, the likelihood that a possible trough in the business cycle might have already been reached is analysed. The SARB's composite leading business cycle indicator reached a trough in April 2016 and subsequently increased fairly strongly up to February 2017, suggesting an imminent end to the downward phase in the business cycle, in line with consensus forecasts. The leading indicator then receded for a few months, before resuming its strong upward trend up to February 2018. However, output growth slowed further and South Africa's real GDP contracted in the first quarter of 2017. This was followed by three successive quarters of GDP growth above 2% (quarter-on-quarter annualised), before two more contractions in the first two quarters of 2018. Although the leading indicator appeared to signal the end of the previous upward phase of the South African business cycle in advance, the continued slowdown in output growth suggests that the leading indicator might have falsely signalled the end of the downward phase.

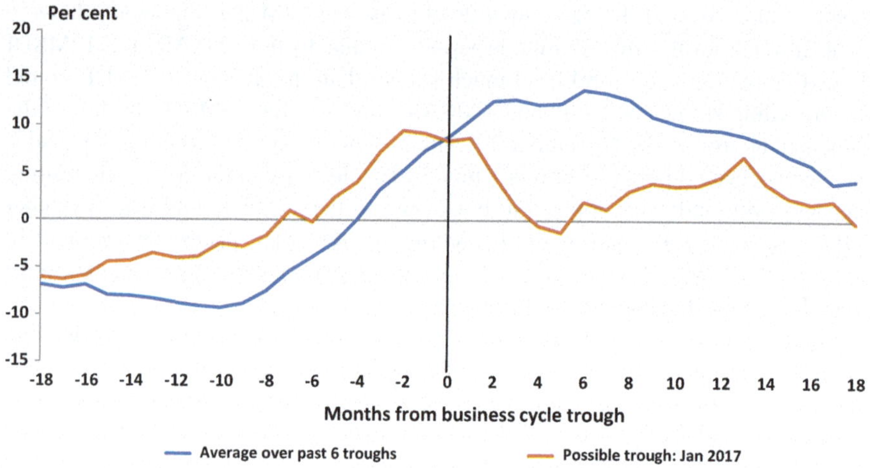

Fig. 10 The 6MSAR in the composite leading business cycle indicator around different business cycle troughs

In order to gauge the reliability of the lower turning point signal, the recent movement in the composite leading business cycle indicator is compared to its movement around the preceding six reference troughs in the business cycle. In particular, the movement is compared in terms of how pronounced, how pervasive and how persistent (the three Ps) it has been relative to its average movement around the preceding six reference troughs. Since the composite leading business cycle indicator reached a lower turning point in April 2016 and its median lead time over the previous six reference troughs was 9 months, the most recent possible reference turning point was chosen as January 2017, 9 months after the trough in the leading indicator.

Figure 10 shows the 6MSAR in the composite leading business cycle indicator around different business cycle troughs; from 18 months before the troughs to 18 months after the troughs. The movement in the 6MSAR around the possible January 2017 reference trough is compared to the average movement in the 6MSAR around the preceding six reference troughs in the business cycle.

The movement in the 6MSAR prior to the possible January 2017 trough was very similar to the 6MSAR's average movement before the previous six reference troughs, suggesting that the composite leading business cycle indicator's most recent lower turning point signal was similar to previous troughs in terms of how pronounced it was. However, unlike its average movement around previous troughs, the 6MSAR slowed to below 0% 5 months after January 2017, before accelerating gradually once more in subsequent months, but remaining fairly weak. It appears that the initial pronounced signal of a lower turning point in the business cycle was interrupted for a few months, before tentatively returning and then subsiding again.

Figure 11 depicts the 12MSDI of the composite leading business cycle indicator's component series around the possible January 2017 reference trough, together

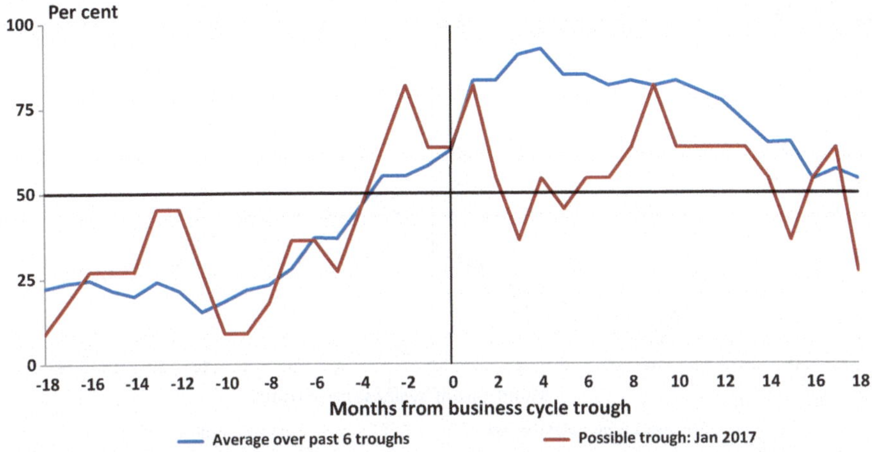

Fig. 11 The 12MSDI of the composite leading business cycle indicator around different business cycle troughs

with the 12MSDI's average movement around the previous six reference troughs in the business cycle.

As was the case for the 6MSAR, the 12MSDI behaved in much the same manner prior to the possible January 2017 trough than before the previous six reference troughs on average. The 12MSDI broke through the neutral 50 level 3 months before the possible January 2017 trough, as it did before the previous six reference troughs on average. Yet, shortly after the possible January 2017 trough, the 12MSDI fell back below 50, unlike the average for the previous six reference troughs, before breaking through the 50 level anew 6 months after January 2017. However, in subsequent months, the 12MSDI gradually receded to the 50 level again. The increase in the composite leading business cycle indicator appears to have initially been as pervasive around the possible January 2017 reference trough as at the previous six reference troughs on average. However, the initial pervasive signal of a possible reference turning point in January 2017 became much weaker shortly after the prospective January 2017 lower turning point, before it recovered in subsequent months and then became weaker again.

Figure 12 illustrates how persistent (measured by the SADR) the movement in the composite leading business cycle indicator was around the possible January 2017 business cycle trough and around the previous six reference troughs on average.

The SADR's movement prior to the possible January 2017 trough resembles its average movement around the preceding six reference troughs fairly closely. However, after reaching its long-term average of 4.08 months in February 2017 the SADR fell back in the subsequent 3 months. The SADR only broke through its long-term average in October 2017—much later than it did after the six previous reference troughs on average—and only for 3 months, before receding again in

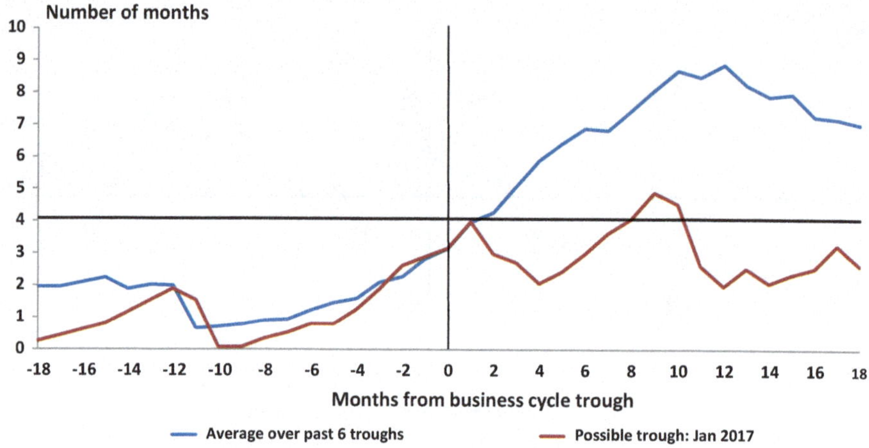

Fig. 12 The SADR in the composite leading business cycle indicator around different business cycle troughs

subsequent months. The SADR suggests that although the initial signal of a possible lower turning point in the business cycle was equally persistent to that before previous reference troughs, its persistence has not increased to the same extent that it did after previous reference troughs in the business cycle, reflecting the uncertainty surrounding the timing and strength of the general economic upturn.

5 Conclusion

The upward phase of the South African business cycle that followed the global financial crisis was characterised by a number of structural impairments and fairly volatile economic growth outcomes. As such, consensus forecasts by private-sector economists largely failed to predict the ensuing downward phase of the business cycle that commenced in December 2013. However, the SARB's composite leading business cycle indicator has trended gradually lower since March 2011, suggesting a slowdown in output growth. At the start of 2017, consensus forecasts seemed to predict the end of the downward phase of the business cycle. This was corroborated by a rising trend in the composite leading business cycle indicator after April 2016.

Cyclical analysis of the SARB's composite leading business cycle indicator suggests that the decline in the leading indicator since early 2011 has been slightly less pronounced around the November 2013 reference peak than around previous business cycle peaks. Rather, the leading indicator decreased very gradually, but the downward trend lasted for a number of years. In addition, the decline among the component time series of the composite leading business cycle indicator was more or less as equally widely diffused as around previous peaks in the business cycle.

Also, the decline in the component series of the composite leading business cycle indicator has been even more persistent than around previous business cycle peaks. These results suggest that the composite leading business cycle indicator did provide a reliable signal that the end of the upward phase of the business cycle was reached, prior to the identification of the November 2013 reference peak.

A similar analysis suggests that the composite leading business cycle indicator initially signalled that the end of the current downward phase of the business cycle may have been reached in a pronounced, pervasive and fairly persistent manner, this time consistent with consensus forecasts. However, the signal became much weaker in the second quarter of 2017. The disconnect between expectations that a lower turning point in the business cycle might have been reached and a further slowdown in real GDP growth could likely be explained by domestic idiosyncratic factors, notably political developments that led to policy uncertainty which caused a further drop in business and consumer confidence.

Although the composite leading business cycle indicator initially provided a clear signal of a cyclical recovery in the South African economy early in 2017, these exogenous developments appear to have temporarily distorted the signal. However, the composite leading business cycle indicator resumed its upward trend during the second half of 2017, followed by a marked improvement in business and consumer confidence in the first quarter of 2018 after a number of positively perceived domestic political developments. As such, the strength of the lower turning point signal—as measured by the three Ps—improved since mid-2017, with the exception of the persistence indicator. The strength of the lower turning point signal then became weaker again from the end of 2017, reflecting the continued uncertainty around the timing and strength of the business cycle upswing as political developments continued to hamper confidence and deter investment. In a previous chapter in this volume, Laubscher (2020) lists some of the factors that contributed to the increased political uncertainty, notably the weakening of governance at public institutions, widespread corruption, inconsistent policy pronouncements and prolonged regulatory concerns in key sectors of the economy. In addition, South Africa's fiscal position deteriorated, as revenue collection consistently underperformed and government debt trended higher. Political and fiscal developments are instrumental in determining a country's risk premium. It is not surprising that Hollander and Van Lill (2020), in an earlier chapter in this volume, find South Africa's risk premium to play a large and persistent role in determining output variability in the short to medium term.

By employing the indicator approach to business cycle analysis, specifically in measuring pronounced, pervasive and persistent movements in a composite leading business cycle indicator (and its subcomponents), and by comparing these movements to previous cycles, the reliability of early business cycle turning point signals can be greatly improved.

References

Achutan, L., & Banerji, A. (2004). *Beating the business cycle* (1st ed.). New York: Currency Doubleday.

Ahir, H., & Loungani, P. (2014). *There will be growth in the spring: How well do economists predict turning points?* [online]. Retrieved from http://www.voxeu.org/article/predicting-economic-turning-points

Banerji, A. (1999a, March 17–20). *The lead profile and other non-parametric tools to evaluate survey series as leading indicators*. Paper Presented at the 24th CIRET Conference, Wellington.

Banerji, A. (1999b, October). The three Ps: Simple tools for monitoring economic cycles. In *Business economics*. The Statistics Corner [online]. Retrieved from http://www.freepatentsonline.com/article/Business-Economics/56973863.html

Banerji, A., & Hiris, L. (2001). A framework for measuring international business cycles. *International Journal of Forecasting, 17*, 333–381.

Boshoff, W. H. (2005). *The properties of cycles in South African financial variables and their relation to the business cycle*. Working Paper 2/2005. Department of Economics, University of Stellenbosch.

Boshoff, W. H., & du Plessis, S. A. (2020). What do we know about the South African business cycle? In W. Boshoff (Ed.), *Business cycles and structural change in South Africa*. Heidelberg: Springer.

Bry, G., & Boschan, C. (1971). *Cyclical analysis of time series: Selected procedures and computer programs*. Technical Paper 20. New York: NBER.

Burns, A. F., & Mitchell, W. C. (1946). *Measuring business cycles* (1st ed.). New York: NBER.

Fabricant, S. (1972). The recession of 1969–70. In V. Zarnowitz (Ed.), *The business cycle today* (pp. 89–136). New York: NBER [online]. Retrieved from http://www.nber.org/chapters/c4394.pdf

Hollander, H., & van Lill, D. (2020). On the estimation and application of structural decompositions of the South African business cycle. In W. Boshoff (Ed.), *Business cycles and structural change in South Africa*. Heidelberg: Springer.

Laubscher, P. (2020). A history of South Africa's modern business cycle. In W. Boshoff (Ed.), *Business cycles and structural change in South Africa*. Heidelberg: Springer.

Loungani, P. (2000, April). *How accurate are private sector forecasts? Cross-country evidence from consensus forecasts of output growth*. IMF Working Paper No 00/77. IMF [online]. Retrieved from http://www.imf.org/en/Publications/WP/Issues/2016/12/30/How-Accurate-Are-Private-Sector-Forecasts-Cross-Country-Evidence-From-Consensus-Forecasts-of-3543

Moore, G. H. (1950). *Statistical indicators of cyclical revivals and recessions*. NBER Occasional Paper No 31. New York: NBER.

Moore, G. H. (1982, May–June). How much inflation depends on how you measure it. *Inflation Watch* (pp. 7–8).

Moore, G. H. (1983). *Business cycles, inflation and forecasting*. NBER Studies in Business Cycles No 24. Cambridge, MA: Ballinger Publishing.

SARB. (2015, June). *Quarterly Bulletin*, No 276 (pp. 14–17). Pretoria: South African Reserve Bank.

Van der Walt, B. E. (1983, March). *Indicators of business cycle change in South Africa*. Quarterly Bulletin, No 147 (pp. 53–63). Pretoria: South African Reserve Bank.

Venter, J. C. (2005, September). *Reference turning points in the South African business cycle: Recent developments*. Quarterly Bulletin, No 237 (pp. 61–69). Pretoria: South African Reserve Bank.

Venter, J. C. (2011, June). *Business cycles in South Africa during the period 2007 to 2009*. Quarterly Bulletin, No 260 (pp. 61–66). Pretoria: South African Reserve Bank.

Venter, J. C. (2016, March). *Business cycles in South Africa from 2009 to 2013*. Quarterly Bulletin, No 279 (pp. 102–112). Pretoria: South African Reserve Bank.

Conclusions

W. H. Boshoff

The aim of this volume is to advance scholarly understanding of the South African business cycle and its relation to structural change, in order to inform policymaking. It is therefore appropriate to summarize key insights. We do so in two ways. Firstly, we focus on how the volume helps us to understand business cycle developments in South Africa in the post-financial crisis era, including the role of structural evolution. In that summary, we seek to connect our insights more directly to popular narratives that pervade South African policy debates. Secondly, we present a summary that accords with the taxonomy of the business cycle literature suggested by Boshoff and Du Plessis (2020). In that summary, we group the insights into those related to business cycle measurement, business cycle forecasting, and business cycle stabilization policy.

1 The Global Financial Crisis, Structural Change, and the South African Business Cycle

The findings in this book provide deeper insights into powerful narratives that frequently feature in South African policy discourse. These include arguments related to irrationally negative business sentiment, the resilience of the economy, the impact of international shocks, and the role of finance.

W. H. Boshoff (✉)
Department of Economics, Stellenbosch University, Stellenbosch, South Africa
e-mail: wimpie2@sun.ac.za

W. H. Boshoff (ed.), *Business Cycles and Structural Change in South Africa*,
Advances in African Economic, Social and Political Development,
https://doi.org/10.1007/978-3-030-35754-2_10

1.1 *The Cyclical Impact of Business Sentiment*

Post-crisis policy discourse in South Africa includes arguments concerning the role of persistent weakness in business sentiment as an explanation for weak expansions. Indeed, some have persistently argued that South African firms are unduly negative and, consequently, "on an investment strike" (Daily Maverick 2018; Mail and Guardian 2017).

Binge's (2020) chapter is the first attempt at providing a micro-based measurement of sentiment and the most recent attempt at studying the association between sentiment and investment. The micro-measurement approach in this chapter complements recent efforts at measuring economic uncertainty and confidence in South Africa using aggregate or financial data. Binge also offers separate sentiment indicators for key sectors of the South African economy, which are useful in light of the changes in the economy's structural composition. A key finding is that the constructed business confidence measures have unique predictive ability.

Even if the predictive ability is possibly a necessary condition for a causal mechanism, the analysis cannot confirm or disprove that sentiment changes can engender business fluctuations, including via an impact on investment decisions. For example, the predictive ability of Binge's business confidence measures is restricted to a horizon of maximum length of one year. Confidence shocks, in themselves, do not have "permanent" output effects: the output effect of a shock to sentiment is transitory if it is not reinforced by other real economic developments. The converse is also true—and consistent with mainstream macroeconomics: improvement in South African economic growth due to improved business optimism has been historically short-lived and have had to be supported by other positive developments to generate sustained growth. Consequently, while the findings suggest that lower business confidence in the post-crisis era could have suggested lower future growth, the subsequent evolution of growth has been driven by various adverse economic developments, which in turn fed back into lower confidence levels.

1.2 *The Resilience of the South African Cycle*

Business sentiment is also accorded a role in another narrative of South African economic performance, the so-called "resilience" of the South African economy, as detailed in Laubscher (2020). Business cycle resilience can be defined as a muted response in the business cycle to adverse economic and political shocks and is often understood to be a benign cyclical feature, shielding the economy from deeper recessions. Yet the same forces may give rise to lackluster expansions (see, for example, the findings by Boshoff and Du Plessis (2020) and Laubscher (2020) on the amplitude of expansions and contractions). Understanding the sources of resilience is therefore important.

Freytag (2020) helps us to understand how the entire institutional structure of the South African economy mediated the impact of the global financial crisis, reducing the real effects on the economy. There is a South African literature studying financial and trade channels for the transmission of international crises to the South African economy. As discussed in Boshoff and Du Plessis (2020), there is also a literature—at least pre-2008—studying the role of policy in stabilizing the cycle. Yet there is not much written on the role of, and interaction between, structural problems and institutional features in mediating the transmission of international shocks to the South African business cycle. Freytag's analysis—which aligns with the insights from the narrative analysis by Laubscher (2020)—explains how competitiveness, financial infrastructure, and rent-seeking (via corruption and special-interest groups) shaped policy and, more generally, macroeconomic responses in South Africa to the global financial crisis.

It follows that the weakening of the institutional structure in the Zuma years may well result in reduced cyclical resilience in the wake of international economic shocks. Put differently, policymakers and businesspeople would be mistaken to believe that the South African economy will necessarily weather future international shocks as well as it has in recent times. More important, it would appear policymakers should not separate policies that—at face value—appear focused on short-run fluctuations from long-run structural policies. Structural policy is key to managing the business cycle and, vice versa, business cycle policies are key to long-run growth.

1.3 The Impact of Financialisation on South African Growth

Beyond the "negative business" and "resilient economy" narratives, a third popular narrative associated with the financial crisis is that of "financialization", according to which an increased role for the financial sector is associated with adverse real economic outcomes. Hollander and Van Lill (2020) provide some insights into the relationship between finance and the South African business cycle in the post-crisis era. Their DSGE model evidence is consistent with the hypothesis that financial markets convey information about the underlying soundness of the South African economy by pricing those risks. Indeed, alternative DSGE model specifications suggest that what could be interpreted as financial drivers of the cycle in one model (credit demand or equity shocks), represent risk premium in another specification. The results suggest that the post-crisis cycle in South Africa, including the most recent recession, is strongly related to a "risk off" position—the opposite of the "risk on" view of the 2002–2007 boom. Arguably, this risk assessment reflects deeper structural problems.

Some of the DSGE specifications in Van Lill and Hollander permit consideration of the role of structural features specifically related to the financial sector in driving the South African business cycle. In particular, some results show that monopolistic competition in retail banking, which reflect in persistent tightening of credit following an adverse shock, may well prolong South African recessions. Even so, while financialization may well contribute to cyclical features, untangling these from the normal market-pricing functions of markets remains challenging. Furthermore, the DSGE models provide much stronger and more consistent evidence concerning other structural problems in the South African economy, including the remarkable rigidity in the South African labor market over the business cycle.

1.4 Exports as a Driver of South African Cycles

Lacklustre expansions since 2008 suggest an urgent need to understand drivers of the South African business cycle and the role of structural constraints. Indeed, a fourth and last narrative, that is worth exploring in light of the findings in this volume, relates to the role of international demand. It continues to be argued that the South African economy is primarily dependent on international demand and financial conditions.

One of the insights from Laubscher's (2020) chapter concerns what he describes as the durable relationship between South African exports and G7 industrial production. Indeed, Laubscher finds this correlation to be large and significant across all cycles from the mid-1970s, arguing that exports are key to the cyclical evolution of the South African economy. More importantly, the closer the association, the stronger the expansion. It is interesting that periods during which exports are less strongly correlated with the G7 business cycle (the 1980s and the recent post-crisis experience)—in other words, periods during which exports do not respond to increasing international demand—are periods of significant political uncertainty. This finding is consistent with the well-documented role of the current account in mediating the cycle in the 1980s, during which the impact of sanctions amplified the importance of current account surpluses.

Exports, then, appear to remain a key driver of the South African cycle, even in an economy now dominated by the tertiary sector. However, the findings in this volume suggest that fixed investment is the other key driver of expansions in South Africa. Both Boshoff and Becker (2020) and Laubscher (2020) show that consumption-driven expansions do not last in South Africa—and the most recent weak expansion is no exception. Indeed, the investment appears to have shaped South African expansions in a specific way: Boshoff and Becker (2020) show that upswings in investment have generally arrived later during expansions, certainly well after the initial boost from exports and subsequent improvement in consumption and general business confidence.

The combination of investment and export behavior suggests key differences between the South African cycle and those of other commodity-export economies. The South African business cycle is similar to cycles in a range of developed economies as far as immediate post-recession behavior is concerned. While the US business cycle has an identifiable recovery phase following recessions (with growth rates significantly higher compared to those for the rest of an expansion), business cycle in other developed countries as well as the South African business cycle do not exhibit such a recovery phase: growth rates are not substantially higher in the early stages of an expansion. The South African experience differs from those in a range of commodity-exporting economies in South America and elsewhere, which do experience discernible "bounce-back" recovery phases. Therefore, while exports are a key driver of South African cycles, the response of the rest of the economy—including consumption, but notably investment—is slower than those in other export-oriented economies. This reflects structural constraints, including rigid labor markets. On the other hand, it also reflects resilience. In other words, the cyclical differences once again reflect enduring rigidities in the South African economy.

In sum, the work suggests a need for a better understanding of the investment function in a small open economy such as South Africa's. In particular, the roles of international financial and domestic factors in shaping the required rates of return for fixed investment—a feature picked up by the "risk premium" variable in the DSGE models of Van Lill and Hollander—deserve further attention.

2 What Do We Now Know About the South African Business Cycle?

An alternative approach to assessing the contributions in this volume is to return to the taxonomy suggested by Boshoff and Du Plessis (2020). That chapter classified the state of knowledge into three broad groups: (1) literature dealing with the identification and properties of the South African cycle, (2) literature on forecasting of the cycle, and (3) literature on the role of macroeconomic policy in stabilizing the South African cycle.

2.1 Measuring the Cycle

In terms of measurement, this volume has made three important contributions. Firstly, Boshoff and Becker (2020) develop new approaches to identifying and studying business cycle recoveries, which (based on the US literature) refers to the start of an expansion phase. These authors suggest a definition of recoveries that is neither duration- nor trend-dependent. Such a definition is attractive, given that trend growth cannot be uniquely identified and is the subject of much debate.

Secondly, Boshoff and Fourie (2020) introduce new macroeconomic data for the entire twentieth century, which allows the authors to study the structural transformation of the South African economy—and the accompanying changes in the business cycle—since unification in 1910. This moves well beyond the data available from the Reserve Bank (selectively starting in 1948) and beyond most research (which commonly starts around 1960).

Thirdly, Binge (2020) develops new measures of South African business confidence, based on micro-data, which are often relied upon as cyclical leading indicators.

2.2 *Forecasting the Cycle*

Binge confirms the ability of business sentiment—including at the sectoral level—to improve predictions of South African growth. The results in the Binge chapter suggest, in particular, that sentiment-related variables contain independent predictive information for output growth in South Africa. This provides scholarly support for the use of confidence surveys as predictive tools, while Binge's findings also open the way for building newer composite leading indicators.

Venter argues that the accuracy of South African business cycle predictions in the post-crisis period turns on how prediction models filter signals from multiple economic variables. The Reserve Bank's strategy involves using filtering criteria related to intensity, diffusion, and persistence of turning point signals across a variety of economic indicators. Venter argues that these filtering criteria bring the differences between the post-crisis and pre-crisis expansions into stark relief. An emphasis on persistence and diffusion highlights the slowdown in economic activity across a range of economic indicators in the run-up to the 2013 peak; contrary to previous peaks, downward trends in multiple indicators were less intense, but nevertheless diffused and persistent. In contrast, Venter effectively argues that private-sector economists overemphasized intensity as a filtering criterion, leading them to discount the probability of recession. Venter's findings concerning the unique post-crisis expansion accord with those of Boshoff and Becker (2020) as well as Laubscher (2020) in earlier chapters.

Venter also argues that understanding structural constraints contributes to business cycle prediction. Institutional decay derailed the initially positive signals from a variety of economic indicators, which suggested a trough in 2017. Again, Venter argues that the filtering approach adopted by the Bank was superior in identifying the 2017 turning point as false. At the time of writing, in mid-2018, the efforts to reverse such decay under President Ramaphosa seemed to be resulting in stronger signals of a turning point.

2.3 *Stabilizing the Cycle*

The book advances our understanding of the role of South African stabilization policy in two important ways. Firstly, Laubscher (2020) provides the first extensive narrative evaluation of successive cycles and the role of policy (including policy errors) in driving cycles.

While informative, Laubscher's narrative and a-theoretic quantitative approaches do not allow a more precise counterfactual analysis of macroeconomic stabilization policies in South Africa. Hollander and Van Lill (2020) takes an important first step in studying the role of monetary policy in various DSGE model specifications of the South African economy.

The question concerning the effectiveness of South African monetary (or indeed fiscal) policy in the post-crisis era does not allow for an easy investigation. The more successful or credible monetary policy becomes, the more difficult to identify the effects of an exogenous policy shock. One reason is that the effect of stabilization policy may be difficult to measure because it is largely endogenous to the system, especially when more credible or successful. Indeed, exogenous monetary policy innovations appear to contribute relatively little to output and inflation variance in South Africa but make up almost a half of the first quarter short-term nominal interest rate movements. Notably, this is on average for the whole sample period and does not capture important recessionary episodes where MP "steps-in" effectively. This finding provides at least negative evidence that monetary policy has not contributed to output instability in South Africa.

Even so, IRFs for various DSGE specifications in Hollander and Van Lill (2020) suggest that an 80-basis point monetary policy shock could have a short-run impact on total (headline) inflation of between 0 and 150 basis points and on the output of between −0.1 and −0.4%. This impact would be more observable if not crowded out by other shocks.

Hollander and Van Lill also suggest that the choice of DSGE specification matters when studying monetary policy transmission, as the relevant specification for model dynamics and, hence, the estimated size of structural shocks, including monetary policy shocks, vary by model. Even so, one specification allowing for a nontrivial financial sector provides preliminary evidence on how competitive features—specifically the extent of market power in retail banking—mediates the pass-through of monetary policy. This assumes that the interest rate channel is the primary mechanism for the transmission of monetary policy in a small open economy such as South Africa.

References

Binge, L. H. (2020). Business confidence and the business cycle in South Africa. In W. Boshoff (Ed.), *Business cycles and structural change in South Africa*. Heidelberg: Springer.

Boshoff, W. H., & Becker, L. H. (2020). Business cycle recoveries: A comparative view. In W. Boshoff (Ed.), *Business cycles and structural change in South Africa*. Heidelberg: Springer.

Boshoff, W. H., & du Plessis, S. A. (2020). What do we know about the South African business cycle? In W. Boshoff (Ed.), *Business cycles and structural change in South Africa*. Heidelberg: Springer.

Boshoff, W. H., & Fourie, J. (2020). The South African economy in the twentieth century. In W. Boshoff (Ed.), *Business cycles and structural change in South Africa*. Heidelberg: Springer.

Daily Maverick. (2018). *Investment strike: Unpatriotic corporate citizens are taxing South Africa*. 1 October, 2015.

Freytag, A. (2020). The role of institutional structure in mediating the impact of the financial crisis on the South African business cycle. In W. Boshoff (Ed.), *Business cycles and structural change in South Africa*. Heidelberg: Springer.

Hollander, H., & van Lill, D. (2020). On the estimation and application of structural decompositions of the South African business cycle. In W. Boshoff (Ed.), *Business cycles and structural change in South Africa*. Heidelberg: Springer.

Laubscher, P. (2020). A history of South Africa's modern business cycle. In W. Boshoff (Ed.), *Business cycles and structural change in South Africa*. Heidelberg: Springer.

Mail and Guardian. (2017, September 22). *SA's 'investment strike' is a myth*.

The manufacturer's authorised representative in the EU is Springer Nature Customer Service Centre GmbH, Europaplatz 3, 69115 Heidelberg, Germany. If you have any concerns regarding our products, please contact ProductSafety@springernature.com

Printed and bound by CPI Group (UK) Ltd, Croydon, CR0 4YY
22/09/2026
02221057-0011